Studying Religion

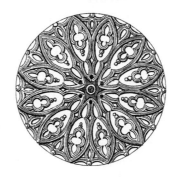

Studying Religion

An Introduction Through Cases

Third Edition

Gary E. Kessler

Professor Emeritus at California State University, Bakersfield

 **McGraw-Hill**
Higher Education

Boston   Burr Ridge, IL   Dubuque, IA   New York   San Francisco   St. Louis
Bangkok   Bogotá   Caracas   Kuala Lumpur   Lisbon   London   Madrid   Mexico City
Milan   Montreal   New Delhi   Santiago   Seoul   Singapore   Sydney   Taipei   Toronto

McGraw-Hill
Higher Education

Published by McGraw-Hill, an imprint of The McGraw-Hill Companies, Inc.,
1221 Avenue of the Americas, New York, NY 10020. Copyright © 2008, 2006, 2003.
All rights reserved. No part of this publication may be reproduced or distributed in
any form or by any means, or stored in a database or retrieval system, without the prior
written consent of The McGraw-Hill Companies, Inc., including, but not limited to, in
any network or other electronic storage or transmission, or broadcast for distance learning.

This book is printed on acid-free paper.

10 11 12 13 14 15 QVS/QVS 21 20 19 18 17

ISBN: 978-0-07-338659-1
MHID: 0-07-338659-6

Editor in Chief: *Michael Ryan*
Publisher: *Lisa Moore*
Sponsoring Editor: *Mark Georgien*
Marketing Manager: *Pamela Cooper*
Developmental Editor: *Marley Magaziner*
Production Editor: *Holly Paulsen*
Manuscript Editor: *Jennifer Gordon*
Design Coordinator: *Margarite Reynolds*
Text Designer: *Susan Breitbard*
Cover Designer: *Asylum Studios*
Illustrator: *Joan Carol*
Photo Research Coordinator: *Natalia Peschiera*
Production Supervisor: *Randy Hurst*
Composition: *10.5/13 Weiss by Laserwords Private Limited*
Printing: *45# New Era Matte, Quad/Graphics*
Cover: *Rob Melnychuk/Getty Images*

Credits: The credits section for this book begins on page C-1 and is considered an
extension of the copyright page.

Library of Congress Cataloging-in-Publication Data
Kessler, Gary E.
    Studying religion : an introduction through cases / Gary E. Kessler.—3rd ed.
        p. cm.
    Includes bibliographical references and index.
    ISBN-13: 978-0-07-338659-1 (pbk. : alk. paper)
    ISBN-10: 0-07-338659-6 (pbk. : alk. paper) 1. Religion—Case studies. I. Title.
BL48.K453 2008
200.71—dc22   2007036489

The Internet addresses listed in the text were accurate at the time of publication. The inclusion of a Web site does not indicate an endorsement by the authors or McGraw-Hill, and
McGraw-Hill does not guarantee the accuracy of the information presented at these sites.

www.mhhe.com

To all who practice compassion

Contents

Chapter 8 Explaining Evil   159

Chapter 9 Religion and Morality   186

Preface

Islam means "submission" to the will of Allah, and comes from an Arabic word meaning "peace." This peace refers to individual contentment and to social harmony, both gained by submitting to the will of God. When I explain the meaning of *Islam* to my students, the shock of September 11, 2001, shatters historical consciousness. What is going on here? How could people commit such an act of barbaric terrorism in the name of a religion that teaches peace?

Such horrific events challenge students of religion to find explanations. The events of September 11 must somehow be interpreted so that they make sense, and their strangeness must be made familiar. The process of making the strange familiar in order to understand also involves the parallel process of making the familiar strange. Students raised in Christian traditions can search for possible parallels in the horrors of Christian crusades and the immense popularity of stories about Christian martyrs eager to die for their faith. Students raised in other religious traditions can begin to explore their own traditions for possible parallels. If, as some have claimed, one of the primary goals of religious studies is to make the strange familiar and the familiar strange, then this book can provide students with some of the tools that will help them achieve that goal.

Studying Religion: An Introduction Through Cases initiates readers into the academic study of religion and leads them on a journey through some of the history, beliefs, and practices of various religious traditions from around the world. It can serve as a textbook in introductory religious studies courses, and may also be appropriate for methods or other courses. The general reader will find this book a convenient way to learn about the academic study of religion as it is currently practiced in most public and many private colleges and universities.

I wrote this book for three primary reasons. First, the study of different religious traditions can be both fascinating and exciting, and it is important for the generally educated person to understand the significance of religion in shaping people's lives and behaviors. Second, it is important to teach students how to engage in the academic study of religion, and the case study approach facilitates this process. Third, no book that I know of presently on the market uses extended cases to teach students how to approach religious studies from an academic viewpoint. Most books explain what other scholars have learned about the religious traditions of the world, but do not take the next step of inviting students to participate in the academic activity of studying religions and showing them the basics of how to undertake such a study.

COVERAGE

A glance at the contents will reveal the topics I discuss. Students will learn about many of the major ideas of the field of religious studies, some of the problems associated with defining religion, and some of the methods employed by scholars. They will also learn about diverse religious beliefs and practices. Topics covered include (among others) sacred power, myths and rituals, religion and art, religious experience, the problem of evil, religion and politics, and the relationship between religion and morality. Each topic is illustrated by case studies drawn from several historical periods and religions. I have selected the cases from religious traditions that have influenced (and are still influencing) large populations by shaping and reshaping their identities, communities, and values.

Studying Religion includes discussions of religious diversity and of questions regarding religious claims to truth that arise from the existence of a wide variety of religious viewpoints. In addition, this book pays attention to issues of gender and religious institutionalization. Many of my students claim to be spiritual, but do not belong to a specific religious organization. Religion for them is a private affair, having to do with their inner thoughts and feelings. The text invites students to reflect on the ways in which the processes of secularization, so characteristic of the modern and postmodern periods, have contributed to the privatization of religion or, as some might call it, the spiritualizing of religion.

Religious violence and cultic activity make headline news, and the very real and deadly conflicts that are often associated with religion need to be addressed when introducing students to the study of religion. Accordingly, one of the cases I analyze is Jonestown, and I also discuss the many meanings of Islamic jihad, going well beyond the oversimplified newspaper accounts.

PEDAGOGICAL FEATURES

I have designed this book to address some of the typical problems instructors encounter when introducing students to the academic study of religion. One central problem is teaching students how to recognize, acknowledge, and control their religious biases. Because bias cannot be escaped, the question is how to effectively deal with it when striving for academic objectivity in the study of religion. Another problem mentioned at the beginning of this preface is in helping students recognize that something seemingly strange can be more familiar than they at first realize, and conversely that what is familiar can be something others find strange. To help solve these problems, I address in the first chapter how we can cultivate qualities that help us become better students of religion.

The following list highlights some of the pedagogical features included in *Studying Religion: An Introduction Through Cases* that aid beginning students to develop an understanding of religion from an academic perspective. This book

- Invites readers to analyze and compare cases through specific questions and examples
- Provides examples drawn from various religious traditions and different times and places
- Emphasizes the development of descriptive, comparative, interpretative, and explanatory skills
- Includes suggestions for further readings
- Provides information on Internet resources
- Contains a glossary with definitions of key terms and concepts
- Provides review questions to aid in understanding key ideas

ORGANIZATION

Chapters 1 and 2 deal with preliminary matters including a discussion of the insider and outsider perspectives on the study of religion and problems associated with defining religion. Each of these chapters ends with review questions and what I call "explorations" that invite students to delve more deeply into some of the issues. Chapters 3 through 12 each begin with two cases relating to the topics discussed in the chapters and a comparative study of these cases designed to teach students comparative skills and start them thinking about religion in a comparative way. They also include review questions before the final research case. Some instructors have indicated they prefer to assign these questions ahead of time to guide students through the material. They can be used as review questions or as reading guides depending on the preference of instructors. A research case closes each chapter, with questions designed to help students develop their research skills. The final chapter raises questions of how religions relate to one another along with issues of how to determine the truth of religious claims. I provide students with numerous examples from the world religions as they explore these topics.

CHANGES

I have made a number of changes based on the many good suggestions of both students and instructors. My only regret is that I could not include all of them given the confines of space. In the second chapter, I have added a case on whether secular humanism is a religion because the Christian right in the United States has identified it as a religious enemy worth fighting. An expanded discussion of René Girard's theory of the link between sacrifice and violence in Chapter 5 seemed warranted because religious violence appears to be on the increase today, and Girard's insights can illuminate the violence that lurks in the sacrificial heart of religion. I have also added a new chapter on religion and politics that includes three new cases, which focus on the religious terrorism of Osama bin Laden, conflicts over separation of church and state, and the Truth and Reconciliation Commission headed by Anglican Archbishop Desmond Tutu that helped heal deep divides in South African society.

These additions have, regrettably, necessitated curtailing the discussion of other important topics. In particular, I have had to delete the discussion of the paths to salvation and modify the examination of some topics in other chapters. However, I trust the new material enriches the book and engages student interest in topics of current concern.

The overall structure of the book remains basically the same as the previous edition, although I have eliminated explicit reference to the three-part structure of preliminaries, liminaries, and postliminaries because some instructors reported students found it confusing. While some instructors suggested a different order to the chapters, I decided to leave the order largely the same because the suggestions were often conflicting. I encourage instructors to reorder the chapters in their assignments to best meet their needs.

ACKNOWLEDGMENTS

Many people have contributed to this new edition. The staff at McGraw-Hill have been most helpful. I owe my partner Katy a big thank you for supporting and helping me through the writing process. I learned many things from my students and thank them for their honest criticisms. I appreciate the comments and suggestions of my colleagues who carefully reviewed the third edition. They are:

June-Ann Greeley, Sacred Heart University
Julie Ingersoll, University of North Florida
Mary Beth O'Halloran, Century College
Rebecca Raphael, Texas State University-San Marcos
C. Hannah Schell, Monmouth College
Tim Vivian, California State University, Bakersfield

I am impressed with their concern for good instruction and finding the very best material for their students.

I trust that this third edition will stimulate people's thinking about religion and the human condition in these turbulent times.

Gary E. Kessler
Professor Emeritus
California State University—Bakersfield

CHAPTER 1

Thinking about Being a Student of Religion[1]

I T IS TEN O'CLOCK ON A Sunday morning in Toronto. A girl is beginning her Sunday school lesson. On Saturday, some Jewish boys in Florence were debating the meaning of commentaries on Genesis at a synagogue. In Philadelphia, Islamic students gathered at a mosque on Friday to pray and to recite the Quran. In Bangkok, a thirteen-year-old boy is memorizing some Buddhist scriptures in preparation for taking monastic vows.

1.1 INSIDER'S AND OUTSIDER'S PERSPECTIVES

Like the people I have just described, those of us who have read the Bible in Sunday school or synagogue school, or have recited the Quran in a mosque or Buddhist scriptures in a temple, have encountered religion from an insider's point of view. The **insider's viewpoint** is that of the participant in a religious tradition. The insider's approach presupposes religious commitment and promotes an understanding that will lead to greater commitment. It promotes the interests and furthers the causes of a specific religious organization.

There are numerous religious traditions, including Hinduism, Buddhism, Daoism (Taoism), Confucianism, Judaism, Christianity, Islam, Jainism, Sikhism, Parsi, Chinese popular religion, and many more. All of these constitute the subject matter of religious studies, or religion studies, as some prefer to call it.

The academic study of religion is different from the insider's approach. It is study done from the **outsider's viewpoint.** The student stands outside all religious traditions and studies religions using the methods and standards associated with the academic disciplines of the public university. The outsider's viewpoint does not presuppose any kind of religious commitment, although it does presuppose a commitment to the standards associated with the secular academy. Its goal is neither to increase nor to decrease an individual's religious faith, although it may have profound effects on that faith.

For the insider, the study of religion is itself a religious activity. For the outsider it is not, at least not in a sectarian sense. The difference between the two perspectives is like the difference between speaking a language and studying how a language is spoken. Studying is a **second-order activity** because it stands outside the actual **first-order activity** (speaking) that it seeks to understand. The academic study of religion is a second-order activity; it will not call on you to worship, but to observe those who do worship.

The controversial ruling of the U.S. Supreme Court (*Abington v. Schempp*, 1963) on prayer in public schools noted the difference between the insider's and outsider's perspectives by making a distinction between the **teaching of** versus the **teaching about religion.** The teaching of religion involves sectarian indoctrination, while teaching about it provides information without supporting any particular sect. Nothing, according to the Court, in the ruling prohibiting prayer in public schools, should be understood to forbid teaching *about* religion in public schools. What the public schools must avoid is the promotion of the viewpoint of a particular religious sect or group. If students in public schools come from a variety of religious backgrounds and if the United States is serious about the doctrine of religious freedom as stated in the First Amendment to the Constitution, then the public schools cannot promote one religious group over another.

If I were to ask you to list the advantages and disadvantages of the viewpoints of the insider and outsider, it would not take you long to create a list. On the one hand, the outsider's viewpoint provides a greater hope for achieving objectivity, which is particularly valuable when studying many different religions. On the other hand, the insider's viewpoint offers a greater hope for sympathetic understanding of one particular religious tradition. The insider can appreciate nuances and feelings that the observer can easily miss.

The situation is like the relationship between you and a psychological counselor. You know yourself from the inside, as it were, and hence have an advantage like no one else when it comes to self-knowledge. However, your very intimacy can lead to self-deception, distortions, and blind spots that an outside, trained observer like a counselor can detect almost immediately. For example, it may take me a while to realize that I tend to be a defensive person, but a good counselor can probably detect my defensiveness within ten minutes of an initial interview.

There can be considerable conflict between the insider's view and the outsider's view. The values that each holds appear to be opposed. The outsider appeals to such values as critical reason, disinterested and unemotional judgment, impersonal observation, and detached analysis. The insider's approach certainly involves the use of reason, but it is tempered by a personal, sometimes passionate, religious commitment. At its worst the outsider's approach can lead to a radical depersonalization of the subject matter, taking the vitality out of religions by reducing them to factors far removed from living reality. For example, some scholars claim that religion originates in fear of unseen powers—that religious faith is just another form of fear. This hardly seems plausible given the richness and diversity of religions, even if fear does play a role in religions.

At its worst the insider's approach can become so defensive and so prejudicial that it ceases to be honest, distorting facts and ignoring or suppressing evidence. For example, some insiders regard all religions other than their own as the "work of Satan." This kind of attitude reduces the study of religion to a combination of **apologetics** (a defense of an individual's own religion) and polemics (an attack on the religion of others). It is, of course, quite appropriate to defend your religious viewpoint. But this is not the task of the academic study of religion. Its goal is not to defend religion or to attack it, but to understand it.

I have identified the academic study of religion with the outsider's viewpoint in contrast to the insider's viewpoint. However, the picture I have painted is distorted. None of us is completely inside or outside in our viewpoints. Even if we practice no religion, religious traditions and values have so permeated our cultures and societies that, like fish, we live in a sea already containing religious currents. There is no view totally outside everything and no view totally inside. These extremes are "ideal types." They characterize the ends of a continuum. The real situation is more complex. The outsider can be as prejudiced as the insider, although in a different direction.

The academic study of religion requires a scrupulous self-consciousness about how fairly we are treating others, others who may have very different values and beliefs from our own. To some extent the "other" is always threatening, and the "religious other" can be extremely threatening, because he or she is often a good person who believes in his or her way of life as sincerely as we believe in our own. It is difficult in such a situation to sustain the belief that other people are totally wrong religiously.

1.2 QUALITIES WORTH HAVING

The academic study of religion challenges the student of religion to develop certain qualities—qualities that aid in promoting fairness and sympathetic understanding of other people's faiths. In cultivating an outsider's perspective that treats religions fairly, we need to develop, among other things, the qualities of openness; honesty; critical intelligence; careful observing, reading, and listening; and critical tolerance. These qualities or virtues have cognitive value, leading to better knowledge. We will examine each of these qualities in turn.

> It is conventional to use the generic singular *religion* instead of *religions* in such phrases as "the academic study of religion" and "the student of religion," and I will follow that convention. However, the use of the singular runs the danger of being misleading in two senses. First, it suggests there is some sort of *essence* to all the different religions, when there may not be such an essence, and second, it obscures the fact that the student must be the student of religions because comparative studies are such an important part of the academic study of religion(s).

Openness

To be open in the academic study of religion is to be prepared for surprises. Openness is a willingness to regard as tentative our views about religion. Openness is not a refusal to draw conclusions. To be open is to recognize that however helpful explanations and theories can be, they may be wrong and in need of revision as additional evidence comes to light. As students of religion we should welcome, as do students of physical science, evidence that we might be wrong, because if we are wrong, we have learned something new and thereby come that much closer to understanding.

Open-minded people recognize the fallibility of their beliefs. They realize that they might be wrong. Contrast this with closed-minded people, who fail to recognize their fallibility. They tend to be dogmatic and assume an air of infallibility.

Honesty

Honesty involves responsibility to others, to the subject matter, and to ourself. By *responsibility* I mean the ability to respond in a nonprejudicial way to what we learn. To be prejudiced is different from having a perspective. *Prejudice* means prejudgment. *Perspective* means a particular slant, outlook, or point of view. Even the honest person has a perspective because human beings existing in time and space see, of necessity, what they take to be real from a certain viewpoint. There cannot be a view from nowhere, just as there cannot be a view from everywhere. However, the honest person understands his or her viewpoint, thereby attempting to overcome whatever limitations it might impose.

Honesty requires eliminating prejudices and taking responsibility for them. It also requires a willingness to understand the sources of prejudices. How do we acquire them? Why do we find them useful? How do they protect us? How do they influence what we do and believe?

Acknowledging a prejudice and its influence on us can be painful. It is frequently easier to hide behind the veil of objectivity. However, we cannot progress very far down the road of the academic study of religion until we confront as honestly as we can our prejudices. The openness described earlier and the critical intelligence examined next can aid in the process of becoming academically honest.

Critical Intelligence

Some may associate the word *critical* with a negative approach or an unfavorable judgment. However, I do not mean to indicate something negative by that term. To criticize is to evaluate by exercising careful judgment. Critical intelligence implies an effort to see things clearly so judgment can be rendered fairly. Evaluations may be positive or negative, but in an important sense the goal of all fair criticism is positive. We benefit by knowing when our judgments are right and when they are wrong.

Critical intelligence involves a number of different intellectual skills, including both analysis and synthesis. In analysis we seek to take things apart, to break wholes into more basic elements. Just as we might take a clock apart in order to see what makes it tick, engaging in the academic study of religion challenges us to take apart religious practices and beliefs to see what makes them work.

When analyzing a belief or practice, we seek to identify key elements that make up the whole. These elements depend on underlying assumptions. Finding the elements and their underlying assumptions is no easy task. For example, we might seek to identify the religious roles people play and uncover the assumptions of power on which those roles are based. This requires careful analysis of such matters as gender relations, privilege, and power.

There is more to critical intelligence than analysis. Synthesis—putting things back together again—is also required. This means being alert for the discovery of previously unseen relationships and for the sudden insight that what we took to be contradictions are reconciled in a greater harmony. Our tasks as academic students of religion are not only to analyze religion, but also to synthesize its various parts so that underlying and often unexpected relationships come to light. The elements of a belief or practice always stand in relationship to other elements. Understanding how the elements work together is as important as understanding what the elements are. For example, if we know the priestly role in a certain rite is to mediate divine grace, then how that element functions in conjunction with other elements such as gestures of blessing and sprinkling holy water helps us grasp the meaning of the rite as a whole.

At the heart of critical intelligence is the pursuit of truth. Although we live in an age of relativism, when phrases like "the pursuit of truth" sound outdated, such a pursuit cannot be given up, even when we are uncertain there is any truth to be found. Criticism, be it positive or negative, is essential to any scholarly program of study.

To look for truth in the study of religion necessitates criteria regarding what is going to count as truth. The task of articulating such criteria is by no means easy. However, there are generally accepted critical standards available (for example, consistency, use of good evidence, valid arguments) for what is to count as true; and the student of religion, as the student of biology, ought to employ these standards.

Arguments supporting a particular conclusion must be carefully examined to see if the premises are true and the conclusion actually follows from the premises. If someone claims that near-death experiences *prove* there is a life after death, we must ask if that is so. What do such experiences actually prove? How much can we safely infer from a near-death experience about an afterlife? What is the difference between *prove* and *provide evidence for?*

Consistency in theory and its application is a hallmark of the pursuit of truth. Evidence must be carefully examined for reliability. If I claim that fear is the essence of religion and explains the desire to be blessed by a priest, then I must also check for possible counterevidence and counterexamples, such as the incredible sense of joy and release experienced by those who feel forgiven. Claims need to be appropriately qualified and modified in light of evidence. Rigorous experiments such as the kind found in the physical sciences are seldom possible in the academic study of religion, but that does not mean that all checking procedures are impossible.

We also need to check the precision of our terms. What do we mean by *religion,* and by *fear?* Can these terms be defined precisely enough to be useful? We do not know whether the admonition of some religions to "fear God" counts as evidence for the claim that fear is the essence of religion unless we know that the fear we are talking about and the fear they are talking about mean the same thing. We do not know whether the joy of forgiveness that people experience is a good counterexample to claims about fear residing at the heart of religion until we know how joy and fear might be related. Does the joy of forgiveness require the fear of damnation?

Crucial to the search for truth is the ability to question. Most of us are too easily satisfied with superficial answers and stop questioning too soon. The

Boy studying the Quran

willingness to continue to raise questions even when we think we understand and to pursue alternative answers is an indispensable tool in the quest for truth.

Careful Observing, Reading, and Listening

Developing the qualities of careful observing, reading, and listening sounds simple enough. However, actions, comments, questions, and textual materials are often deceptive. The actions or words say one thing, but the person behind the actions or words may be saying something else. Learning to see, to read, and to listen for the hidden meanings is especially important when dealing with religious art and religious texts. **Sacred** writings and art of all varieties contain many different levels of meaning. We can train our eyes and ears to become sensitive to as many different levels of meaning as possible.

There is great joy in studying religions when a new level of meaning in some familiar saying or ritual action surprises us. Religious rituals and experiences contain a symbolic richness that will unfold for the student who observes, reads, and listens carefully.

Careful observing, reading, and listening require sympathetic imagination. Imagination is one of our greatest assets. As children it was through imagination that we began to chart that vast unknown world of the experiences of adults. Playing teacher or astronaut is a way of trying to see what the world is like from the perspective of someone who is different from us. Through imagination we can project ourselves, at least partially, into the worldview of a **shaman** doing magical healing, a yogi in meditation, a prophet proclaiming a judgment, and a Christian or a Muslim at prayer.

The ability to imagine—to play, to make believe—is invaluable as we struggle to comprehend cultures, beliefs, practices, and experiences that seem different and strange. Sympathetic imagination requires projecting ourselves into the viewpoint of others and trying to see the world from their perspective. Insofar as we all share in a common humanity and a common world, such a projection is possible and valuable.

At the same time, beware of the limits of imagination. Projection can easily lead to distortion. For example, some early scholars, following missionary leads, equated the Lakota Sioux notion of Wakan Tanka, which they translated as "Great Spirit," with the idea of a monotheistic god as understood in the Jewish, Christian, and Islamic traditions. Wakan Tanka is better translated as "Great Mysteriousness." It is a collective name for a number of different "*wakan* (powerful and sacred) beings." To identify Wakan Tanka with the monotheistic god of nonnative religious traditions obscures important and instructive differences.

Critical Tolerance

Many who study and teach about religions hope to promote religious tolerance. Religious tolerance is a culturally approved, public virtue that allows all of us to get along in greater harmony than does religious intolerance. Religious tolerance not only permits, but also encourages the free expression and practice of diverse religious traditions. In a diverse society in which a vast variety of religious traditions exist side by side, the alternative to religious tolerance appears to be bigotry and strife.

We are so accustomed, however, to thinking of religious tolerance as a public good that we often fail to address difficult underlying issues. We tend to think of religious tolerance superficially as a kind of happy acceptance, if not approval, of religious differences.

A superficial view of toleration ignores two underlying problems. First, there are religious traditions of which people disapprove whether we think they ought to or not. Second, there are religious beliefs and practices of which we think people ought to disapprove. Few of us would advocate neglecting the medical needs of a child, even if religious reasons are given. Few of us would approve of physical mutilation, even if it is a long-standing practice in one or another sacred tradition.

Students of religion cannot be content advocating an uncritical religious and moral tolerance. Rather, they must seek to develop a **critical tolerance** that endorses freedom of religion but does not automatically approve of any and all religious beliefs and practices.

Sympathetic imagination and keeping an open mind are indispensable in studying religion, but they need to be balanced by critical intelligence. Sympathetic imagination and openness promote tolerance for those who are different, and critical intelligence promotes a tolerance tempered by evaluation. We can and should come to understand religious tragedies such as Jonestown, where people committed mass suicide, or Waco, Texas, where David Koresh and his followers were plunged into a fiery and deadly encounter with the U.S. government, but we cannot condone mass suicide and violence.

Sometimes it is easy to know where to draw the line between understanding and tolerance. At other times it is more difficult. We can understand why some religions sacrificed humans and thought it was right to do so, and we have no difficulty condemning such a practice should it occur today. However, what should we say about the sacrifice of animals, which still takes place in religious settings? Should it be tolerated or condemned? Should we tolerate sects that advocate the use of physical punishment in order to discipline children? When does physical punishment become physical abuse "in the name of God"?

As these questions indicate, there is no simple way to balance sympathetic understanding and critical intelligence in all situations. Although this is no easy task, it is a challenge worth meeting. Studying religion challenges us to examine the limits of toleration. Openness demands a willingness to suspend what might be our immediate moral and religious disapproval in order to understand more deeply.

We cannot, however, suspend our disapproval forever and in all cases. Sometimes, as our understanding deepens, our disapproval will lessen. Eventually it may seem to us just plain silly to condemn certain religious beliefs and practices. Do we really want to fight religious wars over how someone is baptized? Sometimes, however, even after we have understood as deeply as we can, we find ourselves unable to condone, let alone support, certain religious beliefs and practices. Do we really want to support the denial of equal religious rights to women? Perhaps we can do little more than advocate the right of those who are oppressed by a religious group to leave that group if they should so desire. Forcing people to accept ideas and practices they find oppressive is incompatible with human dignity and worth. However, respect for difference and the right to be different requires that we be careful in religious matters. Critical tolerance is necessary, but not easy.

> **Qualities Worth Having**
>
> 1. Openness
> 2. Honesty
> 3. Critical intelligence
> 4. Careful observing, reading, and listening
> 5. Critical tolerance

1.3 WHY STUDY RELIGION?

Many of you are taking an introductory course in the study of religion because it fulfills some sort of *general education* requirement. You are reading this book in conjunction with that course and, perhaps, wondering what this course has to do with getting a job and making money after graduation. Many people believe that if it "bakes no bread" it's useless.

Some of you may not be thinking along those lines. You may be thinking that college education is more than vocational training, and it is worthwhile to study subjects that may have no immediate or obvious practical application. You may be thinking that the *study of religion helps us understand a force that influences, for good or for ill, the lives of practically everyone who is alive.*

So much of human history and culture remains a mystery if we cannot comprehend the role religion has played and continues to play in the development of human institutions, values, and behavior. American culture, for example, cannot be fully understood without knowing something about the role that Christianity played in shaping its political, judicial, and educational institutions, not to mention its role in establishing such values as individual freedom and human rights. In America, religious ideas were used both to promote the destruction of indigenous peoples and to end it, to promote slavery and to stop it.

In addition to helping understand the role religion has played and continues to play in human history, studying religion, especially the religions of others, helps us overcome our all-too-comfortable ethnocentric attitudes and achieve a more global and multicultural perspective. *Developing a global perspective* is particularly important at a time when advanced technologies make it possible to travel to places and communicate with peoples about which past generations could only read. National borders are increasingly porous as people immigrate from one country to another. As multinational corporations rapidly create a global economy, we cannot avoid beginning to see ourselves as citizens of the world, or *cosmopolitans* (as the Greeks would say), in addition to members of different cultures and ethnic groups. It is as likely that someday some of us may be living and doing business in China or the Middle East as living and working in the United States, Mexico, or Canada. Mosques spring up down the street from Christian churches, and Hindu temples find their place in communities that once knew only synagogues and churches.

The idea of developing a global perspective is closely tied to yet another reason for studying religion: *the development of a comparative perspective.* Comparison is an indispensable tool for the student of religion. It is, however, more than just an academic tool that increases our knowledge. It also develops understanding, not just of others but of ourselves as well. Just as we learn more about our own languages and cultures by studying the languages and cultures of others, so we learn more about our own religion and values by understanding them in contrast to the religions and values of others. F. Max Müller (1823–1900), an influential linguist and historian of religions, liked to apply to the study of religion what Johann von Goethe applied to the study of language, "he who knows one . . . knows none."[2] Comparative understanding enriches our lives and aids in the search for a more humane way to live together on an increasingly overcrowded, violent, and polluted planet.

As a young student of religion, having been schooled in the Lutheran tradition of Christianity, I recall thinking, when I began the study of the Buddhist concept of "letting go of attachments," that I now understand more deeply what Martin Luther, one of the sixteenth-century founders of the Protestant Reformation, meant when he claimed that the heart of the Christian gospel is justification by faith, not by works. Luther counseled that we should give up trying to work our way into heaven. We cannot make it on our "own power." Buddhists would say we need to "let go" of that attachment.

In addition to expanding our understanding of the significant role religion plays in shaping human history and aiding us in developing a global and comparative perspective, the study of religion opens up a space in our busy lives where we can pause and *reflect on the meaning and purpose of our lives.* It provides an occasion for us to think, in a comparative setting, about what constitutes the good life. By comparing and evaluating what others have said about how humans should conduct themselves, we are in a better position to develop a reflective philosophy of life. Most of us are too busy living our lives to give much thought to how we *should* live. Although the academic study of religion cannot provide answers to the "big questions" about the purpose of human existence, it can help us understand the answers different religions have given to where we came from, how we should live, and where we are going. Studying religion provides a space in which to compare what we have been taught by our own religious traditions with what other traditions say.

Finally, I would add that it is not entirely true that the study of religion "bakes no bread." Most of you will not go into vocations that directly involve the use of expertise about religion, but some of you will. The academic study of *religion does prepare you for a career* if you become professionally interested in the field. It also aids in preparation for other kinds of careers. A wide variety of employers are looking for people who are tolerant of diversity, are able to learn from others, are adaptable to new situations, and have knowledge of history and international affairs. Studying religion can help cultivate the qualities many employers find attractive.

Why Study Religion?

1. To satisfy a requirement for general or liberal education
2. To discover the important role religion plays in the development of history and culture
3. To develop a global perspective
4. To develop a comparative perspective
5. To have an occasion to reflect on the meaning of the good life
6. To prepare for a career in the field of religious studies and other fields

REVIEW QUESTIONS

1. What are the basic differences between the insider's and the outsider's perspective?
2. What is the relationship between openness and honesty?
3. How do analysis and synthesis differ, and how are they related? Give an example of each.
4. What role does sympathetic imagination play in careful observing, reading, and listening?
5. What is critical tolerance? Give an example.
6. Why do you want to study religion, and how do your motives relate to the reasons given for studying religion discussed in this chapter?

EXPLORATIONS

Near the close of the first two chapters I will pose questions to ponder. These "explorations," as I call them, invite you to think more deeply about key issues. Jot down your answers. Compare your answers with those of your classmates, and make a sincere effort to think beyond what I have said.

1. Alasdair MacIntyre, a philosopher, wrote an essay entitled "Is Understanding Religion Compatible with Believing?" Imagine that you have been asked to write an essay with the same title. What would you say, and what reasons would you provide to support what you say?
2. Wilfred Cantwell Smith, a historian of religion and Islamic scholar, once said that no statement made by a scholar of religion is valid unless a religious believer could accept it as correct. Do you agree? Why or why not?

3. Is it morally right to tolerate and hence permit what you sincerely believe to be morally wrong? Why or why not?
4. If you belong to a religion, how did you learn it?

SUGGESTIONS FOR FURTHER READING

In addition to the material found in the notes, the reader may wish to consult the following for more information.

Braun, Willi, and Russell T. McCutcheon. *Guide to the Study of Religion.* London: Cassell, 2000. This book is a collection of essays dealing with a variety of topics (ritual, ethnicity, gender, etc.) often encountered by the student of religion.

Carman, J., and S. Hopkins, eds. *Tracing Common Themes: Comparative Courses in the Study of Religion.* Atlanta: Scholars Press, 1991. This book includes essays on the value and importance of the academic study of religion.

McCutcheon, Russell T. *Critics Not Caretakers: Redescribing the Public Study of Religion.* Albany: State University of New York Press, 2001. McCutcheon argues that the scholar of religion must be a critic of cultural practices rather than a caretaker of religious tradition.

——— ed. *The Insider/Outsider Problem in the Study of Religion: A Reader.* London: Cassell, 1999. This book contains a useful collection of writings on issues relating to the academic study of religion.

Reynolds, F., and S. Burkhalter, eds. *Beyond the Classics? Essays on Religious Studies and Liberal Education.* Atlanta: Scholars Press, 1990. The essays in this volume will take you deeper into the issues of how the study of religion relates to liberal education.

INTERNET RESOURCES

Always remember that information on the World Wide Web must be used with caution, as does information from other sources. Don't believe everything you see or read on the Web. One thing to check for is whether the information is from an insider's or outsider's perspective. You can learn from both perspectives, but be critical of both. Check for bias.

www.aarweb.org   Here is the site for the American Academy of Religion, the primary professional organization for scholars and instructors in religious studies. Once there, try the links for more information.

www.ccsr.ca   This will take you to the homepage for the Canadian Corporation for Studies in Religion, a "virtual community for the academic study of religion in Canada." Links to Canadian academic societies for the study of religion can be found here plus much more.

www.adherents.com   At this site you will find statistical and geographical information on the religions of the world. It is packed with interesting information.

CHAPTER 2

On Defining
and Studying Religion

THE QUESTION "WHAT is religion?" is deceptively simple. Most people think they know what religion is. You can look it up in a dictionary and find what is called a lexical definition. If I asked you to write a one-sentence definition, you could do so after a little thought. So, what is the problem with defining religion?

2.1 MARKS OF A GOOD DEFINITION

For the student of religion, not just any sort of definition will do. In order to engage in the academic study of religion, we need a definition that is analytically useful. That means it should be

- Useful for the purposes at hand
- As precise as possible without being too narrow in scope
- As free from bias as possible

Usefulness

Definitions are not necessarily true or false, but more or less useful. They tell us how to use words effectively depending on the situation and what we are trying to communicate. For example, historians who wish to study religious beliefs and practices (such as rites, moral behavior, aesthetic or artistic creations) that characterized people in China two thousand years ago may find one kind of definition useful for their purposes. A sociologist who wishes to describe social influences on religious practices in contemporary England may find another kind of definition useful.

Suppose sociologists or psychologists were interested in measuring religiosity, that is, the degree to which someone is religious. They would need a definition of religion that could be empirically tested (operationalized) by asking specific questions whose answers could be statistically measured. If they defined religion as "belief in God," they could operationalize this definition by creating questions about what people believe, such as "Do you believe in God?" This would be a *unidimensional* measure because only one dimension, the belief dimension, is central to the definition.

A questionnaire based on this single dimension would be of limited use because there is more than one way to be religious. Someone might believe in God, but never pray to God, offer devotion to God, strive to live a godly life, or participate in any way in organizations that promote such beliefs. Would the researchers want to call such a person "religious"? Then again, some people might be uncertain about whether they genuinely believe in God, but they might pray, read religious literature, and strive to live a moral life as they think God requires. Would such people be called "irreligious" because they did not score very high on the belief dimension?

It is clear that the definition of religion as "belief in God" is not very useful when it comes to measuring religiosity. What is needed is a *multidimensional* approach that measures, in addition to belief, religious practice, experience, devotion, knowledge, and more. Hence a more complex definition of religion is required if it is going to be useful to social scientists interested in creating measures of religiosity.

For scholarly purposes, definitions should stimulate further investigation and thought. Different academic disciplines—history, sociology, psychology, anthropology, literature, philosophy—will find different definitions more or less useful, depending on their perspective. Given these circumstances, the quest for one universal definition of religion that can be useful for all academic disciplines appears misguided.

You might be thinking that what I have just said does not sound quite right. What if the definition the historian uses and the definition the sociologist uses are totally different? How could we be sure that they were both studying religion rather than two very different things? That is a good question and leads directly to a discussion of precision.

Precision

The purpose of definitions is to draw boundaries and thereby limit a field of study. If everything fell under the category of religion, the study of religion would become quite impossible to manage. Definitions can be too precise, however, and boundaries drawn so narrowly that they exclude some things that ought to be included. For example, the above definition of religion as "belief in God" leaves out too much of importance, such as religious practices. Religions are more than belief systems; they involve **ritual** practices, moral codes, various types of social organizations, and more. In addition, religions that deny that ultimate reality is divine (some types of Buddhism), or those that center on beliefs in spirits, would be unjustifiably excluded.

The other side of the coin is drawing boundaries too broadly. Some scholars have favored definitions that involve the use of terms like *ultimate concern* or *sacred*. Unless carefully specified, these terms are so vague that practically anything can fit within their boundaries. Are capitalists, who devote their lives to the pursuit of wealth, religious because money and the power it brings have become their ultimate concern? Are socialists, who devote their lives to the equal distribution of wealth, religious because economic justice is a sacred cause for the socialist?

The questions and problems associated with precision are closely tied to two very different theories of the nature of definition. Some scholars hold to a theory of essentialism. For them, the purpose of definitions is to state the essence of something. The **essence** is a universal quality or set of qualities that makes something what it is and not something else. For example, the essence of a table is whatever characteristic(s) it must have in order to be a table and not a chair. The essence of a human being is whatever qualities or characteristics humans must have in order to be human and not a tree or a rock.

Those who pursue essential definitions of religion usually favor either a **substantive definition** that states what religion *is* or a **functional definition** that states what religion *does*. For example, if we defined religion as "belief in the supernatural," we would be stating what we think it is, or what its nature is. This substantive definition distinguishes religious belief from other sorts of belief in terms of objects. According to this definition, religious belief differs from other types of belief because its object is the supernatural. That is its essence, or substance. If we defined religion as a "set of beliefs that give meaning and purpose to human life," we would be stating what religion does, or how it functions. Its function is to provide meaning and purpose to human life. According to this definition, the essence of religion is in what it accomplishes. This example of a functional definition differentiates religious beliefs from other beliefs by stating what they do (provide meaning and purpose to human life), which is, presumably, different from what other sorts of beliefs do.

There are problems with both substantive and functional definitions. Substantive types often turn out to be too narrow because of the vast diversity of religious beliefs and practices, and functional types often turn out to be too broad because different things can often function in the same way. For example, political beliefs as well as religious beliefs can give meaning and purpose to human life.

A very different theory of definition rejects the idea of essences. According to this theory, we should look for a cluster of characteristics that makes something part of a certain family. **Cluster definitions** are based on an analogy with families. Families are made up of many members who have many different traits or qualities. Some are blue-eyed, and some brown-eyed. Some are tall, and some are short. Yet, in spite of these differences, they are all members of the same family. There may be no set of traits that are essential, but there are traits that allow us to group them into the same family. There are, to borrow Ludwig Wittgenstein's term, "family resemblances."

Perhaps religion is like a family. There are many members with many different characteristics but no set of characteristics that captures some essence. Those who favor cluster definitions of religion readily acknowledge that the boundaries between religion and other things, such as politics, are fuzzy. There is no sharp line of demarcation, but a kind of fading away of qualities until there are not enough to fit into the "family" of religion.

William P. Alston, a contemporary philosopher of religion, offers a cluster definition consisting of nine "religion-making" characteristics. No single characteristic, including belief in supernatural beings, constitutes an essence. In other words, there can be religions that do not posit a supernatural reality. Here are Alston's nine characteristics:

1. Belief in supernatural beings (gods).
2. A distinction between sacred and profane objects.
3. Ritual acts focused on sacred objects.
4. A moral code believed to be sanctioned by the gods.
5. Characteristically religious feelings (awe, sense of mystery, sense of guilt, adoration), which tend to be aroused in the presence of sacred objects and during the practice of ritual, and which are connected in idea with the gods.
6. Prayer and other forms of communication with gods.
7. A worldview, or a general picture of the world as a whole and the place of the individual therein. This picture contains some specification of an overall purpose or point of the world and an indication of how the individual fits into it.
8. A more or less total organization of one's life based on the worldview.
9. A social group bound together by the above.[1]

Alston calls these characteristics religion-making because they contribute to making something a religion. Precision, he admits, is not possible. For example, we cannot say that for x to be a religion, the first two plus three other characteristics must be present. Nor can we say that before x qualifies as a religion, it must exhibit five of these nine traits. The most we can say is that when enough of these characteristics are present, we have a religion.

What is enough? That must be an informed judgment made by scholars who are familiar with a wide range of religions. Cluster definitions avoid the problems of being too narrow or too broad that plague essential definitions. However, they do so at the price of precision. Still, they are not so imprecise that they cease to be useful for scholarly purposes.

Freedom from Bias

Useful definitions of religion should be as free from bias as possible. None of us can totally escape our biases because we must necessarily study the subject matter from some perspective. However, we can become aware of our biases. This awareness allows us to correct for bias when we formulate definitions.

Western Bias   One common bias can be called the Western bias. It is very subtle (as many biases are), and to unmask it will take careful analysis. The English word *religion* comes from the Latin word **religio**. Latin scholars are not certain about the etymology of *religio*. Some believe it stems from the root *leig*, meaning "to bind," while others think it comes from roots meaning "to reread" or "to be careful." In early Roman Latin usage, *religio* was a cultic term referring primarily to the careful performance of ritual obligations. This sense survives in the English adverbial use of *religiously* in such sentences as, "She walks her dog every morning religiously."

Early Latin Christians used the word *religio* to distinguish true worship from false. For them, *religio* did not refer to the world religions as it does today, but to genuine and sincere worship. In the Middle Ages, *religio* was not widely used, but when it was, it often referred to "the religious," that is, those who chose the monastic life. Hence *religio* distinguished the monastic life from the life of the laity.

With the dawn of the modern age, when knowledge of and encounters with religions different from Christianity increased, the word *religion* began to be used to refer to the various religious traditions of the world. So, for example, we often speak of the world's religions, meaning such traditions as Judaism, Christianity, Islam, Hinduism, Buddhism, and Daoism—to mention only a few.

The word *religion* is also used in many other ways in English, but we are not concerned with all of them here. Given the close association the word *religion* has with the development of Western culture, it is not surprising that some scholars have proposed dropping the use of the word altogether for scholarly purposes. It is tied, they argue, too deeply to Western biases and has such a wide variety of meanings in common speech that precision is impossible. Benson Saler, an anthropologist, summarizes this view when he writes, "the practitioners of a mostly Western profession (anthropology) employ a Western category (religion), conceptualized as a component of a larger

Western category (culture), to achieve their professional goal of coming to understand what is meaningful and important for non-Western peoples."[2]

Correcting for the ethnicity of the idea of religion is not easy. If we do not use the word *religion*, what word should we use? Are *faith* or *tradition* any more free from a Western bias? Probably the best we can do is recognize that ethnocentric ideas are starting points (we have to start from our own culture, whatever it may be), but ethnocentrism should not be a stopping point. If it is, it shows we have not learned anything about our biases.

Value Bias   Complicating this ethnocentric bias is a value bias. Definitions reflect how the people creating them value religion. If their attitude is positive, the definition will be positive. If their attitude is negative, the definition will be negative, and if their attitude is mixed or uncertain, their definition will reflect that too. For example, if I defined religion as an illusory hope for eternal life, you would immediately detect a negative attitude in my definition.

We can correct our value biases by adding qualifying words like *allegedly, presumably,* or *maybe.* Thus I might revise my definition of religion to "the hope for eternal life, a hope that may or may not prove to be an illusion." Once you become sensitive to value biases, rewording with appropriate qualifications often does the trick.

Theory Bias   Every definition of religion is part of a more general theory of religion. A definition is "theory-laden," to use the technical term. Behind every definition is some theory about what religion is and how it functions. This is not a bad thing, and indeed it is unavoidable. However, we need to be aware of the ways (some obvious and some not so obvious) that theory influences definition. For example, some theories hold that there is something irreducibly "religious" about religion. Religion is unique and can be understood only on its own ground. Other theories claim that religions are like any other human phenomena and can be understood in cultural, historical, sociological, or psychological terms. According to these theories, there is nothing uniquely religious about what humans believe or do. General psychological theories of human behavior, for example, can explain quite well why people act in religious ways. These two divergent theories of religion generate very different definitions.

Gender Bias   Still another subtle bias that slips into both theory and definition is gender bias. Historically, males have dominated religions, and when people think about religion they often take as the implicit model traditional patriarchal religions. Theories and definitions are then constructed under the influence of these models, and gender bias is the result. Even the word *God* implies for many a male figure. Gender bias inclines people to think of religions as having to do with belief in God or gods, rather than belief in goddesses. One unfortunate social and cultural effect of this is to encourage people to think of males as rulers and leaders. As the feminist theologian Mary Daly says, "if God is male, then the male is God."[3]

Confusion of Religion and Spirituality   Another bias that slips into definitions is the confusion between spirituality and religion. Consider these two statements:

1. A person can belong to a religion and not be religious.
2. A person can be religious and not belong to a religion.

The key term is "belong to." If "belong to" means being an official member of some organization, then statement 1 seems obviously true. The second statement is more problematic because a case could be made that the truly spiritual person will seek membership in some religious community because religious communities try to foster spirituality and provide an opportunity for spiritual fellowship. It is undoubtedly true that religious organizations present themselves as a path, or way, that fosters growth in spirituality, but there seems to be no good reason why someone could not foster spiritual growth in ways other than belonging to some religious group.

Crucial to this debate about **spirituality versus religion**, is a clear distinction between the two. If defining religion is difficult, defining spirituality is even more difficult. The situation is complicated by the fact that the adjective *religious* is used interchangeably with *spiritual.* To be spiritual is to be deeply and genuinely religious. But how can someone be religious without religion?

There have been various attempts to define spirituality. The psychologist of religion William James (1842–1910) suggested that it is a quest for a transformation from a state of perceived wrongness to a state of perceived rightness by making contact with some higher power or powers. The contemporary philosopher John Hick thinks of spirituality as a transformation from a selfish and egocentric state to an unselfish and caring state. However, all of these terms are vague and notoriously difficult to make precise. Nevertheless, I think it is important not to confuse religion and spirituality as if they amounted to the same thing. When we do, we are tempted to transfer whatever negative qualities we may associate with religious organizations to people who sincerely seek to make a better life for themselves and others.

The two statements I asked you to consider earlier (a person can belong to a religion and not be religious; a person can be religious and not belong to a religion) presuppose that spirituality or religiousness is best thought of as a personal quality—a characteristic or set of characteristics that some people have. They also presuppose that religion refers to an organized group of people. This organized group presents itself as an effective way to nurture the personal quality of spirituality, but it is always possible that it fails to do so or, at least, fails to satisfy the spiritual desires of those who join. The problem of how religion and spirituality are related is, to some extent, a product of how we conceptualize them.

Something close to our distinction between spirituality and religion is the ancient Roman distinction (derived from the Greeks) between *cultus* and *pietas*. *Cultus* refers to religion as a cultural system consisting of things like creeds, moral codes, rites, and an organized group. *Pietas* refers to religion as a personal quality of devotion. However, in the ancient world, the modern notion that someone could be spiritual (*pietas*) and not belong to an organized group (*cultus*) would be unthinkable. In the modern world religion is becoming less public and more privatized due to a number of factors that I will talk about in more detail in the last chapter.

Some Possible Biases

1. Western ethnocentric bias
2. Value bias
3. Theory bias
4. Gender bias
5. Confusion of spirituality and religion

2.2 TWO DEFINITIONS

In our discussion about defining religion, we have discovered there are some typical problems with different types of definitions. We can put our discoveries to work by critically analyzing two important and influential definitions. I want you to assume the role of analyst and critic. We learn to do religious studies by engaging in its practice, and part of that practice is the critical analysis of definitions. I will prompt you, but you need to do the work.

Paul Tillich (1886–1965), a Christian theologian and philosopher, defined religion as "the state of being grasped by an ultimate concern, a concern which qualifies all other concerns as preliminary and which itself contains the answer to the question of the meaning of life."[4]

Questions on Tillich's Definition

Please answer the following questions. In all cases support your answer by stating your reasoning.

1. What kind of definition is this—essential or cluster?
2. Is Tillich concerned with the substance or the function of religion?
3. Is Tillich's definition too broad or too narrow?
4. Do you detect any bias in Tillich's definition? If so, what?

5. Suppose someone is ultra patriotic, as people often are in time of war. Does this mean, if we used Tillich's definition, that we should count nationalism and patriotism as religions?

We turn now to an influential definition by the contemporary anthropologist Melford E. Spiro. According to Spiro, religion is "an institution consisting of culturally patterned interaction with culturally postulated superhuman beings."[5]

Questions on Spiro's Definition

Please answer the following questions. In all cases support your answer by stating your reasoning.

1. Is Spiro's definition functional or substantive?
2. Is Spiro's definition too broad or too narrow?
3. Compare Spiro's reference to "superhuman beings" to Tillich's use of "ultimate concern"? Are they the same or different?
4. Substitute the word *politics* for *religion* and reread Spiro's definition. Does it make sense as a definition of politics?
5. Do you detect any bias in Spiro's definition? If so, what?
6. Which definition, Tillich's or Spiro's, do you find most useful?

2.3 IS SECULAR HUMANISM A RELIGION?

Developing skills in analyzing and evaluating definitions is not an abstract and irrelevant activity because definitions make a difference. There can be important political, legal, and social implications. For example, the U.S. Supreme Court decision against government-mandated prayer and Bible reading in public schools in 1963 set off a firestorm (see section 1.1). It is instructive to take a closer look at this case.

Many conservative Protestant Christians protested the decision and became alarmed that government was abridging their religious freedom and further secularizing what they believed was the Founders' intention of establishing a "Christian nation."* Knowing full well that religion is something one learns and having enjoyed a public education system that nominally reinforced a generally Protestant Christian viewpoint, conservative Protestants thought they saw in this decision one more step in the drift away from God in American society. They named this drift "secular humanism" and argued that by rejecting state-mandated Bible reading and prayer in public schools the Supreme Court was not upholding the First Amendment but was violating it. The Court's ruling, they argued, amounted to supporting and legally mandating an "anti-Christian religion" they called secular humanism. The First

---

* See Chapter 10 for more information on the controversies surrounding the First Amendment.

Amendment to the Constitution forbids the "establishment" of religion, and the 1963 decision on prayer and Bible reading is, they claimed, inconsistent with that amendment. The First Amendment reads, in part, "Congress shall make no law respecting an establishment of religion, or prohibiting the free exercise thereof . . ."[6]

The argument mounted by conservative Protestants asserted that the decision to prohibit prayer and Bible reading in public schools not only violated their right to "the free exercise" of religion, but also established the anti-Christian religion of secular humanism.

Bill Bright (1920–2003), founder of the Campus Crusade for Christ, expressed the fear of conservative Christians when he wrote

> Have you ever wondered why our society is becoming more secular, why prayer and Bible reading are no longer welcome at our public schools? The religion of humanism is largely responsible. Have you wondered why Americans are much more tolerant today of sexual freedom, homosexuality, incest and abortion? The religion of humanism is largely responsible.[7]

Tim LaHaye, best known as co-author of the best-selling *Left Behind* series of novels that describe the torments of those not raptured at the Second Coming of Christ, echoes Bright's fear in his book *The Battle for the Family*. LaHaye portrays secular humanism as an octopus whose tentacles engulf the family, schools, universities, liberal churches, government, and television. He lays the "evils" of feminism, materialism, pornography, drug abuse, rock music, homosexuality, and, in general, the decay of the moral fiber of Americans at the doorstep of secular humanism. He defines secular humanism as "a man-centered [sic] religion that mistakenly thinks it can solve the problems of man [sic], independent of God."[8] LaHaye adds that it is "the most fraudulently evil religion in our country today" and is regarded with "awe" in colleges and universities. War metaphors abound as the title suggests. Secular humanism is an evil "enemy" that must be "battled" by pious Christians in a "war" to recover and reestablish the "biblical base" of America.

LaHaye is echoing a comment made by Justice Stewart, the one dissenter in an eight to one majority Court opinion who said, ". . . a refusal to permit religious exercises thus is seen, not as the realization of state neutrality, but rather as the establishment of a religion of secularism, or, at least, as governmental support of the beliefs of those who think that religious exercises should be conducted only in private."[9]

Those who supported the Supreme Court decision argued that the practice of prayer and Bible reading unfairly established the Christian religion as the official religion taught to students in public education. American students are religiously diverse. While the vast majority might be Christian, many are not. Some are Jews, Muslims, Hindus, Buddhists, and Native American. Some are atheists. Given the religious pluralism of American culture, imposing by law mandatory prayer and Bible reading violated the rights on non-Christian students.[10] They furthered argued that so-called secular humanism is not a religion, as conservative opponents of the Court's ruling claimed. It has no creed, no ritual, and no organization—in short, none of the usual characteristics associated with religion. It is merely an abstract idea created by conservatives in order to support their arguments. Supporters of the decision also reject the conservative contention that the Founders of the United States intended it to be a Christian country. They obviously recognized the religious diversity of the nation, or they would not have added the First Amendment to the Constitution.

Arguments about the role of religion in public school are still with us and surface from time to time, as indicated by the case of former Alabama Chief Justice Roy Hall, who recently displayed the Ten Commandments in the Alabama State judicial building.[11] Clearly the question of whether secular humanism exists in any concrete sense and whether it constitutes a religion is a central issue in this debate. This controversy indicates that definitions of religion do have practical and important implications.

We have discussed the marks of a good definition, some of the biases that can creep into definitions, and examined two examples. It will be helpful to apply what we have learned to the claim that secular humanism is a religion.

Questions on Secular Humanism

Please answer the following questions. In all cases support your answer by stating your reasoning.

1. Is LaHaye's definition of secular humanism a good definition?
2. What understanding of religion does LaHaye's definition presuppose?
3. If we adopted Tillich's definition of religion, could secular humanism be classified as a religion?
4. If we adopted Spiro's definition of religion, could secular humanism be classified as a religion?
5. What do you think? Is secular humanism a religion?

2.4 A SIMPLE MAP OF THE FIELD

Before discussing methods of studying religion directly, let's look at a brief outline of the field of religious studies as it is presently practiced in many colleges and universities in the United States and elsewhere:

I. History of religion
    A. Developmental studies
    B. Comparative studies

II. Social scientific study of religion
    A. Anthropology of religion
    B. Sociology of religion
    C. Psychology of religion
III. Philosophy of religion
    A. Analytical
    B. Critical

This outline does not include areas that cut across these divisions, such as feminist studies, literary studies, and scriptural studies, but it will do as a starting point.

Developmental historical studies (**history of religions**) employ the theories and methods of history to study how a religion, religions, or part of a religion have developed through time. Religions that are living traditions have changed and are changing, because nothing that survives can do so without adapting to its changing environment. Those that have ceased to change are dead religions of the past, although parts may have survived in other religious forms. An example is the spring fertility rituals using painted eggs that have been incorporated into Christian Easter celebrations of the resurrection of Christ. Developmental historians are interested in how religions have changed and what factors are at work that cause change. They are also interested in continuities, because not everything changes completely. A basic assumption of the developmental approach is that religions are complex and dynamic historical processes exhibiting both change and continuity.

Comparative studies focus primarily on comparing different religious traditions. The concern is less with the changes that religions undergo and more with structures or types (although there is no reason why a comparative study of changes could not be done). The comparativist arrests time by taking snapshots of different religious phenomena and comparing them. The comparativist may select one of the many dimensions of religion, such as ritual, and do a comparative study of certain types of ritual activities in, say, Islam and Judaism. One basic assumption of comparative studies is that there are certain analytical categories (belief, ritual, morality, and so on) that are useful for cross-cultural comparison. Ideally, the comparativist should balance the description of similarities and differences, but often, differences are submerged or overlooked in the rush to find similarities.

Social scientists use the current methods and theories of their fields to understand and explain religion within a larger setting. A basic assumption for social scientists is that insofar as religion is a human activity, it can be explained by cultural, social, or psychological factors, just as any human phenomenon can be explained by such factors. The anthropologist (**anthropology of religion**) is particularly concerned with religion in relation to culture. Although the concept of culture is vague and can have a variety of meanings, here, it refers to the sum total of the symbols humans produce in order to convey information, make sense of experience, and order relations within human groups. Cultures need symbol systems to convey information. Language, art, religion, philosophy, science, technology, manners, and morality are examples of significant cultural symbol systems that convey information and create the meaning necessary for human groups to cope successfully with their environments.

Anthropologists interested in the study of religion pay particular attention to the nature and function of religious symbol systems. One of the most influential definitions of religion derives from the work of cultural anthropologist Clifford Geertz. According to Geertz, religion is "(1) a system of symbols which act to (2) establish powerful, persuasive, and long-lasting moods and motivations in men by (3) formulating conceptions of a general order of existence and (4) clothing these conceptions with such an aura of factuality that (5) the moods and motivations seem uniquely realistic."[12]

Geertz's definition indicates one way to approach the study of religion. Following his lead, the student of religion would seek to uncover some of the ways in which religion functions to motivate humans and order social life by means of symbols. For example, some religions have symbol systems that deal with life after death in terms of heaven and hell. Symbols of heaven and hell can powerfully affect human behavior. In some cases they can motivate extreme behavior, such as suicide bombings, inquisitions, and holy wars. These kinds of symbol systems create a this-worldly/otherworldly framework for thinking about life. Life in this world is preliminary to an afterlife in another world. Symbols of the afterlife can be powerful enough to convince people that what they cannot see is real. Indeed, these symbol systems can convince people that they have genuine information about the future. People who live in a culture filled with symbols of the afterlife live in anticipation of a future yet to be. The best (or the worst) is yet to come.

For sociologists (**sociology of religion**), the operative category is society. As used here, society is a narrower category than culture. It encompasses the particular ways groups within cultures organize themselves. Sociologists are particularly interested in the social functions of religion. Many sociologists see religion as a kind of "social glue" that binds groups together. It helps to provide group identity and thereby differentiate one human group from another. Religion can also split groups apart and rearrange an old grouping into a new social order. The sociologist seeks, among other things, to discover how religions promote social solidarity and contribute to social change.

For example, a sociologist might be interested in studying how belonging to a religious group provides people with a sense of identity. Having an identity is fundamentally important to human existence. If asked who they are, people might include in their response, "I am a Muslim," or "I am a Hindu."

Establishing such identities not only tells people who they are, it also tells them who they are not: "I am Hindu, and they are not." Identities imply complex sets of beliefs, values, and behaviors. So they might think, "Hindus practice this ritual and Muslims practice that ritual, and since I am a Hindu I too must practice as Hindus do and not as Muslims do."

Psychologists (**psychology of religion**) are usually more individually oriented than sociologists and anthropologists. Rather than focusing on religion as a cultural symbol system or on its social functions, psychologists often focus on how religion expresses repressed feelings or universal psychic tendencies. Psychologists might ask how religion shapes character development. Or they may be concerned with the relationships among religious commitment, deviant behavior, mental illness, and moral development. There is little doubt that religious experiences play important roles in people's lives, and psychologists are particularly interested in the experiential aspect of religion. They seek to find out what kind of religious experiences occur and how to best understand such experiences.

I divide **philosophy of religion** into two categories: analytic and critical. This is somewhat artificial, however, because in practice they are often combined. Elsewhere I have defined philosophy of religion as "the rational attempt to formulate, understand, and answer fundamental questions about religious matters."[13] The philosophical quest for formulating, understanding, and answering fundamental questions demands both careful analysis of religious beliefs and actions and a critical response (negative or positive) whose goal is a deeper rational understanding of religious matters. Exactly what is rational and what are fundamental questions are subjects of intense debate. A basic assumption of this discipline is that if there is such a thing as religious truth, careful philosophical criticism and analysis should be able to uncover it. So philosophy of religion is typically concerned with arguments for God's existence, the reasonableness of notions about life after death, whether religious experiences provide evidence of some religious reality, whether the existence of evil in the world is incompatible with the existence of God, or other questions arising out of religious belief and practice. Historians and social scientists usually refrain from offering judgments about the truth or falsity of the religious beliefs and actions they study, but philosophers are often concerned with questions of truth. Philosophers want to know if religions are bearers of truth.

I have not listed theology as part of the field of religious studies, and some may find that odd. **Theology,** according to St. Thomas Aquinas (1225–1274), is the study of the divine, and its goal is knowledge of God. For St. Thomas, a Roman Catholic Christian, God is at the apex of a triangle that includes humans and nature; hence theology is the queen of the academic sciences, while humanities (the study of humans) and natural science (the study of nature) assume subordinate positions. Historically, religious studies evolved out of theology, and, while theology is no longer considered the queen of the sciences, both religious studies and theology find a place among the numerous academic pursuits found in modern universities.

If we think of religious studies as an activity of the outsider, then theology, as traditionally understood, is an insider activity. It is true that theologians interpret their faith traditions using critical tools, which are often the same critical tools used by the outsider. But theology is not just an act of critical interpretation, it is a confession of faith. Doing theology usually presupposes a commitment to religious truth, whereas religious studies do not. For example, some Buddhists affirm that the Buddhist experience of "enlightenment provides the ultimate criterion of interpretation."[14] Likewise many Christian theologians claim that theology must be rooted in faith. The widely accepted formula of "faith seeking understanding" often characterizes the Christian theological approach.

If religion has to do with a reality that transcends the world of ordinary experience, then theology can be characterized as an attempt to directly study transcendence; to give us, following St. Thomas, "knowledge of God." The focus of religious studies, however, is not on transcendence per se, but on believers and how they experience and interpret what they take to be transcendent. Theology, understood as the interpretive practice of the insider, is one more aspect of the subject matter with which religious studies concerns itself. Theology is the scholarly language *of* religion, and religious studies are the scholarly language *about* religion. Although some may see theology and religious studies as opposed (if not antagonistic) and others as complementary, one thing is clear: they are different, and the student of religion can learn much by reflecting on how they are different.

2.5 GOALS AND METHODS

The goals of religious studies—whether historical, social scientific, or philosophical—are very much like the general goals of all academic disciplines—namely, to describe, interpret, explain, and evaluate phenomena. We need to examine these goals in turn.

Description

There is no such thing as pure description because every description is already an interpretation; but for the moment I will artificially isolate it and characterize it as gathering and stating the facts of the case. Just as in a court of law a case cannot proceed without knowing the facts, so the study of religion cannot proceed without knowing the data. In the field of religious studies, there is an enormous amount of information in a variety of different languages and cultures, ranging from archeological artifacts, pictures, coins, statues, and the like, to sacred scriptures, commentaries on sacred scriptures, and many other kinds of writings. The range is great, and I have not yet mentioned rituals, oral traditions, and extraordinary experiences of transformation and revelation.

Gathering this information requires mastering a variety of technical skills such as learning different languages. Presenting the information fairly and accurately is not easy. Mistakes can easily creep in, especially when dealing with gestures, customs, games, and rites from vastly different cultures.

In order to facilitate the collection and presentation of data, students of religion use classification schemes. These schemes can be very general, referring to religious traditions as a whole (for example, Buddhism, Islam, Christianity), or they can be more specific, referring to aspects of different religious traditions (for example, beliefs, myths, symbols, scriptures, experiences, morality, rituals, and organization). Whatever classification scheme is used, scholars create it by reflecting on information at hand and then use it to gather and organize additional information. Generally this sort of **description** involves classifying x under a category according to some property (p) of x. Suppose x is the Islamic belief that asserts Allah is the one and only God (p). As students of religion, we might categorize such a belief as monotheistic because **monotheism** is a category that includes all beliefs that share the property of claiming there is only one God. We now know a fact about Islam that allows us to describe it as a monotheistic religion. This also allows us to compare this monotheistic belief with beliefs about the divine found among other religions.

Developing classification systems requires that we identify prototypes. A **prototype** is an ideal exemplar of the type or category in question. Other things are matched to this prototype. The closer the match, the more likely we are to describe something (bowing the head and folding the hands) as a member of the class in question (praying). If the match is not very close, we are unlikely to describe some action (slashing oneself with a knife in grief) as praying.

Typologies are schemes of classification. They organize data into different types. For example, after studying the data, we might conclude that there are two primary types of praying: supplication and thanksgiving. This typology can then be used to organize new data. The advantage of typologies rests primarily in their ability to organize vast amounts of data, but there are disadvantages as well. Typologies are often incomplete—prayers exist that do not neatly fit in one category or another—or they obscure other important features of the data. Why not create a typology of praying by classifying prayers as formal and informal, or as silent and spoken, or as communal and solitary? Lurking within every typology is a degree of arbitrariness. Sometimes typologies reveal more about the creator's biases than they do about the data.

How do we select prototypes, identify the relevant properties, and create useful typologies? We learn how to do it based on study, experience, reasoning, comparison, and intuition.

Interpretation

What does the described data mean? That is the central problem for **interpretation**. The first question is "mean to whom?" To the insider, meaning is part of the descriptive data. To the outsider, meaning reflects the best understanding an outside observer can arrive at given the data, the methods of interpretation, and the theories available.

Methods of interpretation are often called hermeneutical. **Hermeneutics** is the science of interpretation, although the word *science* is used here in a very broad sense. To interpret is to see *x* as a *sign* of *y*. We interpret when we assign a particular referent (the signified) to a sign (the signifier). Signs can be letters, words, pictures, sounds, musical notes, physical gestures—the list is almost endless because practically anything can be taken as a sign, from trees and cloud formations to flags and buildings. Hence hermeneutics is part of a more general study called **semiotics**—the study of signs.

Hermeneutical studies can focus on any aspect of religion (beliefs, rituals, experiences), but I will describe it briefly by focusing on the interpretation of written texts. The first rule of hermeneutics is that meaning is *context dependent*, that is, what a text means depends on a variety of contexts both immediate and remote. Just as words have different meanings in different contexts, so texts have different meanings in different contexts. If I said, "I am going to the bank," you would not know the exact meaning of the word *bank* until I went on to specify, "in order to fish." The context of fishing rather than the context of cashing a check lets you know what I mean—that is, what the sign *bank* signifies (edge of a body of water).

One way to uncover context is to discover the **Sitz im Leben** (situation in life) of a text. Where and when was it written? By whom and to whom was it written? What is its purpose or function? Knowing the situation in life reveals much about the meaning of a text (or any other sort of sign for that matter).

There are also certain formal features of a text that provide information about its meaning. What type of writing is it? Is it a letter, poem, narrative, scripture, or commentary? What is its surface structure, that is, its organization, style, and themes?

In addition to surface structure, there is also a "deep" structure that is more difficult to discern. Deep structures are the hidden rules governing what is said, much like the structure of language is determined by the hidden rules of grammar. In order to get at this hidden structure, scholars distinguish between the text (what the author writes) and the subtext (either explicit asides by the author about what he or she writes or indirect meanings such as irony). Scholars look at what is *included* in a text, but they must also be aware of what is *excluded*. Social rules about inclusion and exclusion determine, in part, what is said. For example, I have excluded certain words from my account of hermeneutics because I deem them inappropriate in textbook writing or I have judged them to be misleading.

Comparison is implicit in the activities of determining the type of text and in determining structure and function. The remote context of religious phenomena can be uncovered by comparing different examples and discerning the similarities and differences. A story of a saint in Christianity can be illuminated by comparison with a story of a saint in Buddhism, even if the stories are very different and unrelated culturally and historically.

Comparison involves selecting significant examples and then looking for similarities and differences among them. No attempt should be made to determine whether one example is "better" than another in the sense of truer or morally superior. (Avoid judgments such as the Christian saint is really a saint, and the Buddhist saint is a fraud.) One example might be judged more typical or less typical of the type under discussion (stories about saints), but even that judgment is tricky. As you can see, there is much room for prejudice and unconscious bias to enter the selection process. Why is one story rather than another selected as "typical"?

Developing a comparative perspective is essential to learning about others. Religion is one of the most enduring and vital traits of human societies. We learn much of value about being and becoming human from studying the similarities and differences among religions as fairly and sympathetically as possible.

Explanation

The student of religion seeks not only to collect and describe information and to interpret it by employing hermeneutical and comparative methods, but also to explain what is going on.

The word **explanation** can mean several different things. To some, it means an understanding gained by discovering the meaning of religious phenomena. In other words, interpretation is one type of explanation. To others, it means finding and describing the cause or causes of some religious phenomenon. This requires a direct and explicit appeal to some theory.

Description and interpretation are influenced by theory, but explanation is the most clearly theory-laden activity. This can be explained most easily by an example. In physics the event of a falling apple is explained by subsuming it (along with many other examples of falling things) under the theory of gravity. So a religious event like a sacrifice might be explained by subsuming it under a general theory about the causes of violence.

Historical and social scientific explanations, however, are not always causal in the sense of the occurrence of one set of events necessarily resulting in another set of events. Sometimes explanations are functional, such as Karl Marx's (1818–1883) explanation of religion functioning as an opiate. This explanation of religion is in terms of its effects (what it does), not its causes (what produced it). Other explanations are structural in nature. For example, Marx also explains religious behavior in terms of class differences between rich and poor. Social structures like a class system are not events, and if causes must be events, then social structures cannot be causes.

An important question to ask when studying any human behavior is, who benefits (*cui bono*)? In whose interest is it that certain rites are performed in certain ways? Who benefits from the way power is distributed in a religious group? Do certain worldviews benefit one social class more than another? All beliefs are not equal; some benefit certain people more than others. Although much religious morality speaks of the virtue of being altruistic or unselfish (and this is something we should not ignore), much human behavior is selfish, even when people claim otherwise. When trying to explain why humans do the things they do, the answer to the *cui bono* question reveals much.

The student of religion will encounter different kinds of explanation. Some will be causal, some functional, and still others structural. All, however, will appeal to some theory about religion, and hence the study of theory is unavoidable.

Evaluation

For an explanation to make sense, the theory that gives rise to it must be correct. How can we find that out? Physical scientists can check their theories by controlled laboratory experiments, but in religious studies such checking procedures are seldom possible. What is possible is to check the fruitfulness of a theory by measuring it against many different examples to see if it makes sense of all or most of them. Does a detailed and careful study of ten examples of religious movements selected at random from the world's religions make more sense when viewed from Marx's theory rather than some other theory? For example, Marx's theory implies that religion is primarily a conservative force working against social change. But is that always the case? Haven't religious movements also fostered social change? Religious groups and leaders have been in the forefront of promoting social change. Martin Luther King, Jr., and the civil rights movement come immediately to mind. Is Marx's opiate theory adequate to explain that movement?

Evaluation has many different levels. We might evaluate the accuracy of someone else's description by checking it against our own reading of the original data. We might question the value of someone's interpretation by checking on how rigorously the hermeneutical method was employed. We can evaluate a theory by checking its explanatory power against other possible theories. In this sense of evaluation (what I call second-order evaluation), one scholar is evaluating the work of another against such criteria as logical consistency, strength of evidence and argument, compelling counterexamples, and alternative explanations.

What about evaluating religious claims themselves? Can we engage in first-order evaluation? Indeed, should we do first-order evaluation? Many scholars acknowledge that the methods of history, the social sciences, and philosophy are limited to natural explanations. There is, they assert, no human way to evaluate supernatural claims. Was Jesus truly the Son of God, or did he and others just think so? That he made that claim or did not make it, that others made it, and what it meant—these are things that are possible to check, provided enough information survives. But the theological claim that Jesus is the Son of God—how could we check that?

Some philosophers and theologians might think we can check it just like we check other metaphysical claims—that is, is it logically consistent with everything we know about other kinds of things? Given what we know about history, about the physical universe, about human behavior, about other religions, about the effects on people's lives of believing Jesus is God's Son, is it plausible that Jesus is truly the Son of God? You can imagine the arguments on both sides, and you can imagine arguments claiming that such questions fall outside the range of questions that can be asked (let alone answered) in the academic study of religion. We shall return to this issue in the last chapter.

Goals and Methods of Religious Studies

1. Description
   a. Prototype
   b. Typology
2. Interpretation
   a. Hermeneutics
   b. Comparison
3. Explanation
   a. Causal
   b. Functional
   c. Structural
4. Evaluation
   a. First-order
   b. Second-order

2.6 FIELDWORK[15]

The study of religion requires more than the examination of texts. Fieldwork is essential. There is no substitute for talking to people who practice their religion and observing what they do. I encourage you to do this, but as a student of religions you should engage others in a way that provides the best information for describing, interpreting, explaining, and evaluating as objectively as possible what others believe and do.

Social scientists have developed fieldwork techniques that aid in the gathering of data. These techniques are called participant observation. Participant observation involves six activities. They are preparation, observation, participation, interview, documentation, and presentation of results.

In preparing for fieldwork, one should read about the history, beliefs, and practices of the target religious group. This preparation will provide a framework for interpreting what is observed. When you actually visit a group, you should be courteous, friendly, and respectful. Your presence and manner are bound to influence the sort of data you gather so try to both minimize your impact and act in a way that elicits as much candid information as possible.

What follows is a sample of the sorts of data for which one might look. It is by no means exhaustive.

1. What is the mood and atmosphere like?
2. How are people dressed, what kinds of cars do they drive, and what do these (and other factors) indicate about the social and economic status of the people?
3. What seems to be the central focus (beliefs, morality, politics, experience, money, success, etc.) of the message?
4. What are the major beliefs, rituals, moral rules, social events, festivals, etc.?
5. How does the group relate to its local community, and what is its attitude toward society?

Interviewing members, both laity and clergy, can provide important data. Prepare questions ahead of time, but be flexible enough to follow the leads the answers you get might provide.

After collecting the data, you need to interpret and explain the results to others. The customary outline in the social sciences for the presentation, interpretation, and explanation of the results is as follows:

I. Introduction—Statement of research topic, literature review, hypothesis, definition of terms, predicted results, description of procedures for gathering data.
II. Body
   A. Description of data gathered including such things as the name of the group, location, conditions under which data was gathered, general background information, what happened, in what order, characteristics of participants (age, gender, occupations, race, numbers, etc.).
   B. Discussion and interpretation of findings.
III. Conclusions—summary of hypothesis, predicted and observed results, implications of results in relationship to hypothesis (confirm, disconfirm, uncertain), limitations of research, and implications for future research.

2.7 A CONTROVERSY

Why do humans behave the way they do when it comes to matters of religion? Why do some of them believe that invisible forces from fairies to ghosts to spirits to gods control their lives and events in the world? Why do others think that belief in unseen powers amounts to little more than superstition? Questions like these brew controversy.

Part of that controversial brew centers on an issue called **reductionism.** Can the explanation of religious behavior be reduced to cultural, biological, social, historical, economic, and psychological (the list is nearly endless) factors? According to those scholars who practice the **phenomenology of religion,** the answer is no. Religion cannot be reduced to non-religious factors. At the core of religion is the apprehension of the sacred. Religions should be, indeed must be, understood as appearances (*phenomena*) of the sacred in different ways, times, and places. The world religions (Judaism, Islam, Christianity, Hinduism, Buddhism, and the rest) amount to different manifestations of the sacred.

However, according to others, religious belief and behavior is not the manifestation of an irreducible quality called the sacred. It is no more mysterious than any other human activity. We can seek and find its causes in historical, social, and biological factors.

Who are right, the phenomenologists who reject reductionism or the other scholars who think that religion can be explained without recourse to ideas like the sacred? You can decide for yourselves. Hopefully this book will help you make up your minds or, at the very least, understand how difficult it is to decide whether religion is the manifestation of something irreducibly religious or not so very different from other human attempts to understand themselves and the world in which they live.

REVIEW QUESTIONS

1. Why is the difference between a unidimensional and a multidimensional definition of religion important?
2. What is the difference between a functional and a substantive definition of religion? Give an example of each.
3. What is the difference between an essential and a cluster definition of religion? Give an example of each.
4. Write a one-sentence definition of religion and then analyze it in terms of biases. Which biases, if any, does it reveal?
5. Do you prefer Tillich's or Spiro's definition of religion? Provide reasons to support your preference.
6. How does the philosophy of religion differ from the history of religion?
7. What is a typology, and why is it important to the study of religion?

8. How does comparison relate to hermeneutics?

9. Why is it important to ask the *cui bono* question?

10. Distinguish first-order from second-order evaluation by giving an example of each.

11. Why is fieldwork important for the study of religion?

EXPLORATIONS

1. What would you identify as clear examples of religion? Why do you think they are good examples? How do your examples differ from what you would regard as not a religion?

2. Sir James G. Frazer, an early anthropologist of religion, claimed that religion is "a propitiation or conciliation of powers superior to man which are believed to direct and control the course of Nature and of human life."[16] What do you think of Frazer's definition? Is it a good definition or not? Why?

3. Do you think there is something unique about religion that historians, social scientists (anthropologists, sociologists, psychologists), and philosophers cannot understand or grasp? If so, what?

SUGGESTIONS FOR FURTHER READING

In addition to the material found in the notes, the reader may wish to consult the following for more information.

Boyer, Pascal. *Religion Explained: The Evolutionary Origins of Religious Thought.* New York: Basic Books, 2001. Boyer weaves together evolutionary anthropological and cognitive psychological theories to produce a provocative and bold explanation of why humans persist in practicing religion.

Capps, Walter H. *Ways of Understanding Religion.* New York: Macmillan, 1972. A somewhat dated but still useful collection of essays from a variety of disciplines (anthropology, history, psychology, philosophy, and more) on theories and methods.

Connolly, Peter, ed. *Approaches to the Study of Religion.* London: Cassell, 1999. A collection of essays discussing different ways of studying religions, ranging from anthropological to theological approaches.

Fieser, James, and John Powers. *Scriptures of the World Religions.* 2nd ed. New York: McGraw-Hill, 2003. This book provides a good collection of scriptures from some of the major religious traditions with brief historical introductions.

Jones, Lindsay, editor-in-chief. *Encyclopedia of Religion.* 2nd ed. Fifteen volumes. Farmington Hills, MI: Thomson Gale, 2005. This new edition provides a wealth of current and accurate information on religions around the world.

Kessler, Gary E., "The Study of Religion: One Field, Many Methods." In *Presence and Promise: Religious Studies in the University,* edited by John Hatfield and Benjamin Hubbard, 27–33. Long Beach, CA: Institute for Teaching and Learning, 1992.

Here I present an argument for recognizing the unity of the field of religious studies while acknowledging its methodological pluralism.

Penner, Hans H. "The Study of Religion." In *The HarperCollins Dictionary of Religion*, edited by Jonathan Z. Smith and William Scott Green, 909–917. New York: HarperCollins, 1995. A clear and concise account of the nature of theory, and basic approaches (sociological, phenomenological, psychological, historical, etc.) to the study of religion, along with a critical discussion of functional theories.

Smart, Ninian. *Worldviews: Crosscultural Explorations of Human Beliefs*, 2nd ed. Englewood Cliffs, NJ: Prentice Hall, 1995. Smart argues that we should subsume the category religion under the even broader category of worldviews, and we should think of and compare worldviews in terms of six dimensions: doctrinal or philosophical, mythic or narrative, ethical or legal, ritual or practical, experiential or emotional, social or institutional.

Smith, Jonathan Z. "Religion, Religions, Religious." In *Critical Terms for Religious Studies*, edited by Mark C. Taylor, 269–284. Chicago: University of Chicago Press, 1998. A useful discussion reminding us that the concept of religion is a Western anthropological notion.

INTERNET RESOURCES

http://camden.rutgers.edu/dept-pages/philosreligion/resource.html   Here you will find links to a great variety of information on different religions.

www.facetsofreligion.com   A religion Web directory with over 408 links ranging over many different categories including historical studies and belief systems.

www.religioustolerance.org   This site has many different links, and its goal is to promote religious freedom and tolerance.

CHAPTER 3

Sacred Power

Allow me to introduce you to a bewildering variety of superhuman beings. Some merely claim superiority, and others claim to be ultimate. We start with two case studies from different times, places, and religions, then survey some of the forms sacred power takes. We close with a research case, which affords an opportunity to interpret one of the many manifestations of sacred power.

3.1 TWO CASE STUDIES

Dao (Tao)

Daoism (Taoism) is a Chinese religion that today numbers over 20 million adherents. After severe persecution by the Chinese Communist government, it survives in two important schools known as the Heavenly Masters Sect and the Perfect Truth Sect. Daoism has had enormous influence on Chinese and East Asian culture, most notably in the fields of traditional medicine and science.

Once upon a time (some say as early as the sixth century B.C.E.), the western border guard of China saw an old sage approaching, riding on an ox. The Old Master named Laozi (also spelled Lao-tzu) was leaving a China whose society, in his view, had become corrupt. The border guard, so the story goes, would not let him leave until he wrote down his wisdom. The resulting book, variously known as the *Daodejing (Tao-te-ching)*, the *Laozi*, and *The Five Thousand Character Classic*, became one of the foundation texts of Daoism in particular and Chinese religion in general.

There is no firm historical evidence that Laozi ever lived, let alone authored the *Daodejing*. Historians date the book from the mid-fourth century B.C.E. Among other things, it offers political advice to rulers by praising those who gain voluntary respect and cooperation from their people by setting a virtuous example. The book claims that the good ruler sets the tone for his people by cultivating the qualities of competence, concern, and care. The people live best who follow the ways of nature and avoid the corrupting influences of society.

The book itself is a collection of individual sayings that once circulated independently. These sayings have a proverbial quality, offering bits of wisdom about how to live the good life. The sayings are organized into two parts: the first contains sayings dealing with the **Dao** (Way), and the second contains sayings focused on *de* (power). As traditionally organized, the chapter that opens the text is its most famous and one of its most obscure. In one of its many translations, it reads in part:

> The Dao that can be told of is not the eternal Dao;
> The name that can be named is not the eternal name.
> The Nameless is the origin of Heaven and Earth;
> The Named is the mother of all things.[1]

The opening lines distinguish two Ways. One is the Way that can be told or named. And the other is the Way that cannot be told or named. The named Way is the "mother of all things." The nameless Way is the "origin of Heaven and Earth." We are told that the named Way (mother of all things) of which we can speak is not the eternal Way (origin of Heaven and Earth) of which we cannot speak. To be eternal is to be without beginning or end. So the "origin of Heaven and Earth" is without beginning and end, but the "mother of all things" has a beginning and an end because it is not eternal.

The word *Dao* means "way" or "method" and, by extension, "process" or "rule of life." According to Isabelle Robinet, an authority on Daoism, the word *Dao* takes on the meaning of "ultimate truth" for the first time in the *Daodejing*.

This ultimate truth is "one and transcendent, is invisible, inaudible, imperceptible, not usable, not nameable, an unmarked trail that one must travel to know."[2] In the final analysis, there are not two different Ways, a named and an unnamed; there is only one Way, the Way of all ways.

> We look at it and do not see it;
>> Its name is the Invisible.
> We listen to it and do not hear it;
>> Its name is The Inaudible.
> We touch it and do not find it;
>> Its name is the Subtle (formless).

> These three cannot be further inquired into,
> And hence merge into one.
> Going up high, it is not bright, and coming down low it is not dark.
> Infinite and boundless, it cannot be given any name;
> It reverts to nothingness. (Chapter 14)

What can we say about the Nameless Dao? Traditionally, Daoists call it the Way of Nature and regard it as the balance or harmony between two opposite, yet complementary, cosmic powers: the active and aggressive called *yang* and the passive and yielding called *yin*. The goal of life is to live in harmony with the Dao, in part, by practicing *wu-wei* or "nonaction" (sometimes translated as "actionless action"). The power or excellence (*de*) of the Dao resides in its accomplishing things naturally, without forceful action (*wu-wei*). It acts like the emptiness of a bowl that allows it to be filled simply by being receptive. It acts like the doors and windows of a room that make it useful by doing nothing. Those who permit nature to take its course are those who live rightly.

> Dao invariably takes no action, and yet there is nothing left undone.
> If kings and barons can keep it, all things will transform spontaneously.
> If, after transformation, they should desire to be active,
> I would restrain them with simplicity, which has no name.
> Simplicity, which has no name, is free of desires.
> Being free of desires, it is tranquil.
> And the world will be at peace, of its own accord. (Chapter 37)

As the Daoist religion developed, many came to believe that living in harmony with the Dao was the key to immortality. Daoists developed elaborate rituals, diets, and meditation practices in the hope of becoming immortal. The focus here, however, must remain on the Dao itself. If the Dao is ultimate truth, why call it Nameless?

The answer, I think, can be found in the idea of linguistic transcendence. That is to say, Dao goes beyond the capacity of human language. Human language can be used to name things. But how can it be used to name something that is not a thing? The eternal Dao is not a thing among other things that can be picked out and differentiated by a name. It is not like a tree or a cat.

> There was something undifferentiated and yet complete,
> Which existed before heaven and earth.
> Soundless and formless, it depends on nothing and does not change.
> (Chapter 25)

"But," you may well ask, "Isn't the Dao a name?" In an important sense it is not. It does not, like most names, refer to something specific. In a way, we can say it refers to nothing (no-thing) because the Nameless Way transcends every-thing. We can say what it is not, but we cannot say what it is. Ultimate truth eludes mere mortal thought.

> I do not know its name; I call it Dao.
> If forced to give it a name, I shall call it Great. . . .
> Therefore Dao is great. . . . (Chapter 25)

For the Daoist, the way of nature is the ultimate mystery. It is a sacred power. The word *sacred* refers to what is extraordinary, and for the Daoist, nature is extraordinary. We humans often miss that in our attempts to domesticate nature, make it ordinary, and bend it to our will. Try as we might, we will never fully understand or fully control such an awesome force as nature. That is one of the many mysteries of ultimate truth that continually escapes us.

Anselm on God

We transition from ancient China to medieval Christian Europe, moving from a Daoist sage riding an ox, to a Christian monk in dispute. Christianity is a world religion that today numbers nearly 2 billion adherents and exists in a profusion of churches, denominations, and sects. Its major organizational forms include Orthodox, Roman Catholics, Anglicans, and Protestants. The influence of Christianity on world culture is immense due to the colonial and postcolonial impact of European and American societies.

For medieval Christian theologians of the Roman Catholic Church, the truth about nature was given by biblical revelation, not sages riding an ox. However, a major problem arose: how do we know that revelation is true? Do we know it by faith? Do we know it by reason? Monks, theologians, and philosophers took sides, and the disputes enchanted students and disturbed clergy.

Peter Damian, an eleventh-century Christian monk famous for his **ascetic** lifestyle, claimed that human reason was incapable of properly understanding divine revelation. Reason expresses itself in language, which is dependent on grammar. But human grammar is finite and hence inappropriate for the discussion of an infinite, eternal divine reality.

Lanfranc, the Italian prior* of the Benedictine Abby of Bec in Normandy, did not share Damian's pessimistic view of human reason. He argued that humans are created in God's image, and hence must have some divinely bestowed abilities to grasp something of divine reality. Of course divine revelation is authoritative for faith, but human reason can understand it, and we would be wasting God's great gift if we did not try to understand it.

A monk named Anselm (1033–1109), later to be made a saint for the miracles he allegedly performed, became Lanfranc's disciple. He entered the debate over reason and revelation, declaring that human reason and divine revelation lead to the same conclusions. Among his letters, prayers, meditations, and sermons are two books of interest here. The first is titled *Monologion*, and the second is titled *Proslogion*. In *Monologion*, Anselm claims that the "supreme nature" (one of his terms for God) is the ultimate truth.[3] It has neither beginning nor end. This supreme nature is unchangeable and unknowable. This means that the divine essence is "ineffable" (beyond speaking). Nevertheless, we can know something of God, even if we cannot know the divine essence.

In *Proslogion*, Anselm offers one of the most famous "proofs for God's existence" in the history of Western culture. He begins with a prayer asking God to help him understand Psalm 14:1, which claims that someone who declares that God does not exist is a fool. Anselm asks, why is it foolish to say God does not exist?

Anselm argues, in the so-called **ontological argument**, that God cannot be thought of as nonexistent because God is a being "than which no one greater can be thought." Anselm invites us to think about this conception of God. If the being of which we think when we think of God is indeed the greatest possible being that anyone can think of, then this being must exist in our understanding, or mind, as well as outside our mind. Anselm writes

> clearly that than which a greater thing cannot be thought cannot exist in the understanding alone. For if it is actually in the understanding alone, it can be thought of as existing also in reality, and this is greater. Therefore, if that than which a greater thing cannot be thought is in the understanding alone, this same thing than which a greater cannot be thought is that than which a greater can be thought. But obviously this is impossible. Therefore, there certainly exists, both in the understanding and in reality, something than which a greater thing cannot be thought.[4]

It might help us follow what Anselm says if we substitute "absolutely perfect being" for "that than which a greater thing cannot be thought." We can now interpret the above quotation in the following way: "If an absolutely perfect being exists in the *understanding alone*, then we can think of a more perfect being that is greater than the absolutely perfect being, namely one that exists *in* the mind and *outside* of it. But how can we think of something more perfect

---

* A *prior* is a supervisor of a religious house who is second in command to the abbot.

than an absolutely perfect being? How can we think of something greater than the greatest?" The answer Anselm wants us to come up with is, "We cannot." The conclusion he wants us to draw from this line of reasoning is that God, rightly understood, must exist both in and outside of our minds.

If this argument is so powerful, why do some people believe that God does not exist? Anselm argues that only a fool can say in his heart that God does not exist because only a fool can think an absolutely perfect being is merely a mental construct, a passing idea in the minds of mortals.

Anselm's reasoning is difficult to follow, and, while this line of dense reasoning has often been construed as a proof for God's existence, some scholars have claimed that his reasoning was not a proof in the strict sense of the term. It is an intellectual exploration into the nature of the divine. His faith in divine revelation had already convinced him that God existed. He had no doubt about that. But he wanted to understand what that meant. His faith needed to be understood by his reason, and the result is this meditation on God's nature as the greatest possible for thought and hence on God's existence.

Anselm's fellow monk and critic, Gaunilo, also firmly believed in God's existence. But he did not trust Anselm's reasoning in this matter. When Gaunilo read Anselm's *Proslogion*, he found the reasoning absurd. He counterargued that we might as well admit, using the same logic as Anselm, that an absolutely perfect lost island exists somewhere in the vast uncharted seas. If this lost island is perfect, and if we can think of no greater island than this perfect lost one, then we must have every confidence, if Anselm's reasoning about God is correct, that it exists and set sail immediately to find it.

Anselm was undeterred, responding that if his line of reasoning truly applied to perfect, lost islands, he would find that "lost island, not to be lost again." However, lost islands, no matter how perfect, are one thing, and God is quite another. Islands are conditioned, limited sorts of things, but God is not. God's existence is necessary, and the existence of islands is contingent. This is to say that God's existence is dependent on nothing other than God, but the existence of islands is dependent on all sorts of things.

3.2 COMPARISON

What are we to make of these two views—one from ancient China and the other from medieval Europe—of ultimate reality? How are they the same, and how are they different? It is obvious that different people in different times and places wrote the texts used in our case studies. They also come from different religions, which have different histories and practices, not to mention beliefs. There are many significant contextual differences that affect Laozi's and Anselm's conceptions of what is ultimate, and a complete, careful comparison would need to pay attention to these contextual differences. Here, we will briefly focus on just three factors: language, text, and social status.

In order to provide a precise linguistic comparison, we would have to know ancient Chinese and medieval Latin quite well. However, assuming the translations I have selected are good ones, we can do a linguistic comparison based on the translations with some confidence (although not complete confidence) that reasonably accurate similarities and differences will emerge.

The language Laozi uses is metaphoric, relying heavily on analogies with ordinary things and natural processes. The Dao is compared to the hollow of a bowl, the doors of a house, and, in passages I did not quote, to the lowliness of a valley and the flow of water. Most importantly, the Dao is said to be the Nameless. It is beyond human reason, definition, and thought. The Dao does not seem to be personal. It is not like a person, but most like the processes of nature.

The language of Anselm is theological, philosophical, and abstract. And while Anselm recognizes that human thought cannot completely penetrate the divine mystery, he is quite confident that human reason can not only think God, but also draw important conclusions based on that thinking. Human reason can confidently conclude that God must exist, given Anselm's conception of God as the greatest possible for human thought. God, for Anselm, is not nameless and not impersonal. He offers his thoughts to God as a kind of contemplative prayer, asking God to help him understand more deeply.

Laozi's text is not argumentative, or at least not explicitly argumentative. It is poetic, evocative, and stimulates our wonder by proverbs and cryptic aphorisms. Anselm's text is both prayerful and argumentative. He wants to understand why someone who thinks God does not exist is a fool as the Bible says, and he wants to draw reasoned judgments about God's existence based on a certain understanding of God. He draws conclusions and provides reasons to support his conclusions. It is not surprising that his text invites a counterargument from someone like Gaunilo.

Although there are important differences between Laozi's and Anselm's thinking about what is ultimate, both recognize that it functions as a notion that limits our thinking. For both, human life and thought need to be grounded in something absolute—some final, unlimited truth that humans would be well advised to acknowledge if they wish to live rightly.

Note that both Laozi and Anselm represent the educated elite of their day. Their ideas were probably not even known to the majority of people alive at the time they were writing (although the *Daodejing* became a more popular text than anything that Anselm ever wrote). Most people living in ancient China offered sacrifices in honor of their sacred ancestors and evoked a variety of deities to insure good crops and marriages that would produce sons to work the fields. Most people living in medieval Europe offered prayers to various saints, martyrs, and Mary, the mother of Jesus, for good crops and sons to plant and harvest. For most, religion was more a matter of dealing with superhuman powers that impinge on everyday existence than with thoughts about the ultimate origins of heaven and earth or the nature of the divine.

Only the educated elite of any society have the time to speculate. The peasant must earn a living. It is important to remember this because social conditions and status influence both religious thought and action. The religion of the elite is often different from the religion of the nonelite. Or to put it another way, religion on the ground is different from religion in the books.

3.3 FORMS OF SACRED POWER

Power is a basic religious category. The universe is filled with many kinds of powers that require humans to do different sorts of things in order to get along in life and prosper. According to the Romans, some of these things are to be done "outside the temple," and hence they called them *profane* (in front of the *fanum*, or temple). Other things are to be done "inside the temple," and hence they called them *sacred* (derived from the sacrifices that occurred in the temple). While the sacred and profane are often sharply contrasted and the sacred defined as that which is set apart from the profane, both have to do with power.

In many ways, profane power is easier to deal with. In our daily affairs, we can often deal with ordinary profane power in fairly straightforward ways, using the technology available to plant the corn, harvest the crops, get to work, and start the computer. Sacred power, however, is extraordinary, not ordinary. Like the Dao, it is invisible and inaudible. We are never quite sure how, where, and when it will manifest itself. Perhaps it could manifest itself as a being whose existence is unlimited, unconditioned, and necessary, thereby reminding us of our limited, conditioned, and contingent existence. Sometimes sacred power will be strong, active, and aggressive, creating and destroying whole universes. Sometimes it will be weak, passive, and yielding, yet accomplishing all that is necessary without effort. In whatever forms humans believe they have encountered sacred power, it is experienced as something beyond—to some extent—human control, and something especially important to the well-being of humans. Religions teach that human existence and welfare depend upon sacred power. It gives life and it takes life.

The *Bhagavad Gita*, one of the most important sacred books of Hinduism, provides an example of sacred power when Arjuna (a warrior chief) has a vision of Lord Krishna (one of the incarnations of the divine). Picture Arjuna's vision as you read what he says:

I see no beginning
Or middle or end to you;
only of boundless strength
in your endless arms,
the moon and sun in your eyes,
your mouths of consuming flames,
your own brilliance
scorching this universe.

You alone
Fill the space between heaven and earth
and all the directions;
seeing this awesome,
terrible form of yours,
Great Soul,
The three worlds [heaven, earth, and sky]
tremble. $(11:18-20)^5$

Sacred power takes many forms in the religions of the world. Laozi's Dao and Anselm's Perfect, Necessary Being are only two. In some ways they are the least typical because both express the sacred as ultimately unconditioned yet conditioning all else as its creator or source. Many notions of the sacred relate to powers and beings that are superior to humans in many ways but are not necessarily ultimate. Often their existence, like human existence, is conditioned and limited.

Almost anything can be sacred, from rocks to trees to people. The variety is astounding. Although whatever is deemed sacred is experienced as an awe-inspiring and extraordinary power by humans, the concept itself is a human construct. It is an idea created by people to name important aspects of their experiences. Belief that something is sacred is essential to it being taken as sacred by somebody, somewhere, at some time in human history.

Spirits, Ancestors, and Totems

Animism refers to religious practices and beliefs centering on the notion that spirits or souls inhabit and animate most, if not all, natural phenomena. A British anthropologist, E. B. Tylor (1832–1917), introduced the term in 1871 to characterize the religions of so-called primitive societies. According to Tylor, our prehistoric human ancestors, in thinking about what was going on when they dreamed, fainted, and saw others die, came up with a plausible explanation. There must be, they reasoned, an inner spirit or soul that, when it left the body during faints or in death, rendered the body immobile. This same spirit might appear in dreams, and when we wandered about in our own dreams, it was our soul wandering about. If humans have such spirits, surely other things (animals, stones, trees, etc.) do as well. Tylor located the origin of all religion in animistic belief. He argued that from this early animism more complex views, such as **polytheism** and monotheism, gradually evolved. Laozi's Dao and Anselm's God can be seen as the end product of a long evolutionary history beginning with animism.

Most scholars reject Tylor's theory. It lacks supporting evidence. Many also reject animism as a useful term for cross-cultural comparison. Nevertheless, many people, be they ancient or modern, appear to believe in some type of soul or spirit. This soul/spirit is usually represented as a quasi-material force, and not a completely separate, immaterial reality. It is often linked with the breath, shadow, image, or blood. Its primary function is to animate a body, but it is often thought to be the seat of personality and character.

Although, according to animism, trees, stones, woods, valleys, lakes, mountains, deserts, birds, bears, snakes—indeed anything and everything—can and do have spirits whose power concerns us, the vital force that animates humans and links them together even after death is of greater concern. The spirits of the deceased ancestors are particularly powerful because they can help or hinder the living. Offering prayers and sacrifices to the spirits of ancestors is commonplace in many Asian, African, and Native American religious traditions. In the Celtic Samhain—pre-Christian Halloween—the spirits of the dead were honored each autumn with food and gifts, lest they cause trouble for the living. These rites are not ancestor worship; rather, they are ways of linking the living and the dead into a single functioning community.

In Ojibwa, a Native American language, *ototeman* means "he is a relative of mine." A **totem** is another example of a superhuman force, usually (although not always) an animal that embodies the spiritual essence of a group. Often it is said to be the "first ancestor." Clan totems such as turtle, panther, and bear are typical in North America, and most tribal societies exhibit some form of totemism. Secular and profane totems survive in animal symbols for states (California is the bear state) and athletic teams (the Tigers).

Emile Durkheim (1858–1917), one of the pioneers of sociology, thought that the totemism found among Australian Aborigines held the key to the origin of religion. Noting that the totem symbolized a social group like a clan, Durkheim argued that all sacred powers (totems, ancestors, gods) are symbols for the social power of the group to control and shape the individual. Humans recognize that survival depends upon the strength of the group to which they belong. The spirit of the group is embodied in the totem or the sacred ancestor. To worship it, is to worship, in symbolic form, the social power that makes life possible.

Scholars no longer accept Durkheim's theory about the origin of religion. However, they do recognize that totems play an important role in classifying differences among social groups. Totems stand for opposing social categories and regulate such important social affairs as marriage between clans, inheritance, warfare, and ritual obligations.

Spirits, ancestors, and totems may not be thought of as ultimate in the sense that Laozi views the Dao and Anselm views the Perfect God, but they are superhuman powers thought to be of immense importance to human well-being.

Goddesses and Gods

Polytheism, the belief in many deities, is a widespread and persistent form of religion. There are thousands of gods and goddesses, and they have always been difficult to organize.

There is Thor, the Scandinavian god who loves mead (beer) and drives a chariot drawn by goats. This warrior-god crushes the powers of chaos by slaying the giant Thryn. There is also Freya, the most important Scandinavian goddess of desire, whose Greek counterpart is Aphrodite, goddess of beauty and passionate love.

We have all heard of Zeus, the greatest of Greek sky-gods, who hurls his thunderbolts to guard law, order, and justice. Hera, his long-suffering wife, is the goddess of women and matrimony. We must not forget Zeus's daughter, Athena, who springs in full armor from her father's forehead. She is goddess of wisdom and war, who is the eternal virgin defending the state against its enemies with her shield and lance. The owl is her bird.

The gods and goddesses of ancient Egypt crowd center stage, looking for attention and worship. Ra, the sun-god, crosses the heavens in his boat, spreading light over the land and defeating Apophis, the dragon, who seeks to prevent Ra's life-giving journey each dawn. Osiris, set upon by his brother Seth, is killed and dismembered. Isis, his wife, reassembles him and brings him to life, thereby assuring continuing fertility of the land and resurrection from the dead for all the faithful.

The scene shifts to Africa, where Nzambi, great god of the Bakongo, creates humans and punishes those who violate his prohibitions. The Yoruba of West Africa worship the orisha deities such as Ogun, the god of iron and of war, Oko the god of farming, and Eshu, a trickster god who must be appeased to maintain "peace in the market place."

Turning to the Native American religions of North America, we find, among the Oglala Sioux, Wakan Tanka, the Great Mysteriousness. J. R. Walker, a Sioux medicine man explains:

> Every object in the world has a spirit and that spirit is *wakan*. Thus the spirits of the tree or things of that kind, while not like the spirit of man, are also *wakan*. *Wakan* comes from the *wakan* beings. These *wakan* beings are greater than mankind in the same way that mankind is greater than animals. They are never born and never die. They can do many things that mankind cannot do. Mankind can pray to the *wakan* beings for help. . . . The word *Wakan Tanka* means all of the *wakan* beings because they are all as if one. . . . Mankind is permitted to pray to the *Wakan* beings. If their prayer is directed to all the good *Wakan* beings, they should pray to *Wakan Tanka;* but if the prayer is offered to only one of these beings, then the one addressed should be named . . . *Wakan Tanka* is like sixteen different persons; but each person is *kan*. Therefore, they are only the same as one.[6]

The deities and spirits can be organized by cosmic regions: the sky, the earth, and the underworld. There appears to be a deity for every place, if not a place for every deity. They have been related in elaborate **pantheons**—divine family trees of mothers, fathers, sons, daughters, aunts, uncles, and cousins.

They personify natural forces; so they might be organized by wind and storm, flood and rain. They are **anthropomorphic** beings, described as being like humans but with more power. But are they all one, as J. R. Walker suggests? Do they all manifest a single divine, sacred power pervading the heavens and the earth?

It is perhaps best to continue an analogy between gods and humans. Just as humans form a single human species, but are different persons, so the gods and goddesses form a single superhuman species, but are different deities. It is even possible to recognize the existence of many gods, but worship only one (**henotheism**). The first of the Ten Commandments from the Hebrew Bible hints at henotheism when it says that the "Lord God" who brought the Hebrews "out of the land of Egypt" commands, "You shall have no other gods before me" (Exodus 20:3).

The deities provide comfort, help, protection, and security. However, superhuman powers are not always good. We have yet to mention the bad **demons** (some demons are good), devils, and dangerous deities that also populate the religious landscape. Sacred power can be good, but it can also cause harm. Often the gods of the conquered become the demons of the conquerors. So the Greek god Pan, half-human and half-goat, became the model for Christian images of Satan, the fallen angel and adversary of God. In Japanese mythology, demons are fierce, ugly, and foul smelling. They prey on young children and inhabit lonely places.

Demons, in many religions, are not actually deities, but superhuman forces midway between humans and gods. Nor are they always bad. In Bali there are good demons that work for the benefit of humans. Sometimes demons are merely merry pranksters, causing trouble and playing tricks. Even superhuman powers can have fun.

Monotheism and Deism

Monotheism refers to the belief that there is only one God. It comes in several varieties. **Unitarianism** is the view that the nature of this God is an absolute unity. Unlike other beings, God has no parts. Judaism, Islam, and some forms of Christianity and Hinduism are monotheistic in the unitarian sense.

The second of the "Thirteen Principles" of Moses Ben Maimon, a medieval Jewish theologian and philosopher, states, "I believe with perfect faith that the Creator, blessed be his name, is a Unity, and that there is no unity in any manner like unto his, and that he alone is our God, who was, and is, and will be."[7] The Islamic scripture called the Quran declares, "Allah: there is no god but Him, the Living, the Eternal One . . . He is the Exalted, the Immense One. . . . Allah is One, the Eternal God. He begot none, nor was He begotten. None is equal to him" (Surahs 2 and 112).

Trinitarianism is the view that the nature of the one and only God is a tri-unity. This is the major form of monotheism found among Christians who hold that God is three persons in one divine nature. The persons are called Father, Son, and Holy Spirit. The Father creates and sustains the universe, the Son redeems humans in the person of Jesus the Christ, and the Holy Spirit sanctifies (makes holy or sacred), teaches, and inspires.

Controversies about God's nature abounded among early Christians, and the Roman Emperor Constantine, hoping to have a unified religion to support a unified empire, called bishops (leaders) of various Christian groups to gather in a council at Nicea in 325 to formulate a confession of faith (creed) to which all might agree. According to this Nicene Creed, all Christians should confess:

> I believe in one God the father almighty, maker of heaven and earth, and of all things visible and invisible. And in one lord Jesus Christ, the only begotten son of God, begotten of his father before all worlds, God of God, light of light, true God of true God, begotten, not made, being of one substance with the father, by whom all things were made. Who for us men, and for our salvation came down from heaven, and was incarnate by the Holy Spirit of the Virgin Mary, and was made man, and was crucified also for us under Pontius Pilate. He suffered and was buried, and the third day he rose again according to the scripture, and ascended into heaven, and sits on the right hand of the father. And he shall come again with glory to judge both the living and the dead; whose kingdom shall have no end. And I believe in the Holy Spirit, the lord and giver of life, who proceeds from the father (and the son), who with the father and the son together is worshipped and glorified, who spoke by the prophets. And I believe in one universal and apostolic church, I acknowledge one baptism for the remission of sins, and I look for the resurrection of the dead, and the life of the world to come. Amen.[8]

As you might guess, the Nicene Creed did not settle matters or produce the unity Constantine desired. Exactly how the three persons of the Trinity are related was, and has been ever since, a focal point of often bitter and divisive controversies among Christians.

Speculation about the nature of God is not confined to Christians. The Hindu notion of *trimurti* (three forms of the divine) is another example. Hinduism is a name for a wide variety of religions associated with India, whose devotees number well over half a billion. Among Hindus the *trimurti* is very old. In Hindu iconography, the gods Brahma, Vishnu, and Shiva are combined into one figure with three different faces. Brahma creates a universe, Vishnu sustains or preserves it, and Shiva destroys it. I say "a" universe, because within the belief structure of Hinduism, universes are infinite. We live in only one phase of an infinite number.

Brahma, the creator, is not much worshiped today in India. Also, Hindus often say another god, such as Vishnu or Shiva, creates him. Hindus recognize that all "forms of divinity" are significant, but often claim that whatever form of deity they worship, be it Vishnu or Shiva, is the one who is the creator, maintainer, and destroyer of universes. Like the Christian focus on Jesus as the incarnation of God's Son, the incarnations of Vishnu (such as Lord Krishna) play a large role in devotion.

From a sociological and historical view, two factors are important in these examples. First, as peoples become more united socially and politically, the gods of each group tend to merge into one divine power. Second, as the one divine power (or one of its aspects like the Father or Brahma) becomes more abstract and distant from the everyday concerns of people, other divine beings (and/or saints) concerned with specific areas of life become more important in devotional life. People want their gods accessible and nearby.

However, not all people want personal divine power close at hand. In the eighteenth century, both in Europe and the American colonies, **deism** became popular among the educated elite. Deism is a type of unitarian monotheism based on the belief that God created the universe but no longer has anything to do with it. The universe runs according to the physical laws discovered by Newton, and to think, as traditional monotheism does, that miracles occur or God intervenes directly in worldly affairs is to indulge in anthropomorphic fantasies.

The deists argued that without a divine First Cause, the universe remains unexplainable. Out of nothing, nothing comes. There must be a cause that is not the effect of any prior cause.

Once the universe has been created by this divine First Cause, it runs according to natural laws much like a clock keeps running after it is started. Praying to God for help, as well as most religious devotional activities, makes little sense to a deist, because it would be irrational of the deity to interrupt the chain of cause and effect started so very long ago in order to attend to your or my momentary needs. To think otherwise is selfishness on a truly cosmic scale.

Dualism Divine

Zoroastrianism, the ancient religion of Persia (Iran), was founded by Zarathustra (also called Zoroaster), perhaps as early as 1000 B.C.E. Today, there are about half a million Zoroastrians, now known as Parsi. According to tradition, Zarathustra received a revelation from Ahura Mazda (later called Ohrmazd), the supreme God and "Wise Lord of Light." Based on this revelation, Zarathustra set about reforming Persian polytheism, claiming that when Ahura Mazda created the world, he gave humans freedom to choose between two competing spirits. Spenta Mainyu is the good and holy spirit of Ahura Mazda, who is constantly challenged by Angra Mainyu, the evil and satanic spirit. According to the *Gathas* (hymns written by Zarathustra), "the two primal Spirits, who revealed themselves in visions as Twins, are the Better and the Bad in thought and word and action—between these two the wise one chose right, the foolish not so."

Zarathustra did not teach a strict dualism between good and evil divine powers because he believed that, in the fullness of time, the good spirit, Spenta Mainyu, would destroy the evil spirit, Angra Mainyu. Centuries later, however, when Ahura Mazda and his good spirit Spenta Mainyu were transformed into Ohrmazd, and the evil spirit Angra Mainyu had become Ahriman, the Evil One, people began to recognize that these forces were coequal. So in the Zoroastrian priestly text called *Vendidad* (ninth century), Ohrmazd is pictured as the creator of all that is good and Ahriman as creator of all that is evil.

In contrast to monotheism, dualistic religions like Zoroastrianism have the advantage of ascribing evil to an evil superhuman source. Given this dualistic hypothesis, the world in which we all live, a world with a mixture of good and bad, is understandable if it can be seen as the result of a moral and cosmic battle between good and evil. The disadvantage of the dualistic view centers on how secure we may feel living in a universe whose moral outcome is uncertain. If we do not know who will win the battle between good and evil, how secure can we be about our future? Then again, the uncertainty may inspire us to make every effort to secure the victory of good by doing good to our fellow creatures.

Pantheism and Monism

The word **pantheism** comes from Greek and literally means "all god." Some use this term for any belief or theory that holds that the essence of the universe is divine. Others use it to refer to views asserting that the sum total of the universe is divine. However it is understood, pantheistic ideas deny that there is a deity greater than the universe. In other words, the supernatural transcendence of the divine is denied, along with the idea that the divine has some sort of personality.

Some claim that Daoism, with which we opened this chapter, is pantheistic, or at least closer to pantheism than monotheism. I think it is misleading to think of the Dao as some kind of god. Nevertheless, it is clear that according to Daoist philosophy the "Way of Nature" is the ultimate truth.

Stoic philosophers like the Roman Emperor Marcus Aurelius (121–180) and the Roman statesman Cicero (106–143) were pantheists because they subscribed to the view that God is identical to the rational order of the universe, which the Greeks called the *logos*. This identification of God with the universe's rational order influenced the Dutch philosopher Benedict Spinoza (1632–1677). Spinoza was of Jewish origin but abandoned traditional Jewish monotheism because both science and philosophical reason convinced him that there is only one substance. Everything else is but a mode or quality of this one substance. When asked to name this substance, Spinoza said we can call it God or we can call it Nature. However, this one substance, unlike traditional Jewish monotheism, creates no universe out of nothing, hears no prayers, and does not act in the unfolding of history.

Some views of sacred power are monistic. Plotinus (204–270), a Neoplatonic philosopher, represents one kind of **monism.** He argued that there was one ultimate reality from which all other principles emanate (similar to rays emerging from the sun). He called this ultimate reality the One, as well as God. Notice that this One does not *create* the world out of nothing, but somehow *emanates* it out of itself.

In the Hindu context, monism often refers to the claim that there is no difference between the essence of consciousness (called Atman) and the essence of the universe (called Brahman). In the *Chandogya Upanishad,* an early Indian text, a father teaches his son, Shvetaketu, the relationship between his individual self and the Atman. The father says, "The finest essence here—that constitutes the self of this whole world; that is the truth; that is the self (atman). And that is how you are Śvetaketu" (6.9.4).[9]

Shankara (ca. 788–820), an important member of the Advaita (nondualistic) Vedanta school, developed this Upanishadic insight into the nature of human consciousness. Shankara preferred the term *nondualism* to *monism* because human language is limited. We can say what ultimate reality is not, but we cannot say what it is. Shankara distinguishes between a lower and a higher knowledge. According to lower knowledge, the divine appears to humans as a personal lord called Ishvara (the Sanskrit word for "lord"), but according to the higher knowledge, the divine essence is revealed as Atman/Brahman, the one true and only reality. Atman is often translated as "Self," but it is best to think of it as "Pure Consciousness," that is, consciousness purified of all individual elements. It is neither my individual consciousness nor yours, but consciousness as such.

It is difficult to translate Brahman by a single English word; perhaps "Divine Essence" or "True Reality" is the best we can do. So, when Shankara argues that Atman is Brahman, he is asserting that Pure Consciousness is True Reality. He is also asserting that everything else that appears to us to be real is just that, only an appearance. Beyond Atman/Brahman nothing genuinely real exists. It is as if we are living now in a dream, and we think there are many different things because we dream many different things. When we wake up from the dream, we will realize that all those things were just dream images. There is only Atman/Brahman, and that is how we all are.

> **Different Views of Sacred Power**
>
> 1. Animism, ancestors, and totems
> 2. Goddesses and gods
> 3. Monotheism and deism
> 4. Dualism divine
> 5. Pantheism and monism

3.4 AGNOSTICISM AND ATHEISM

Differing conceptions of sacred power—such as animism, totemism, poly-theism, monotheism, and pantheism—presuppose that humans are in a posi-tion to know something about superhuman realities. **Agnosticism** refers to the claim that humans cannot know about divine matters, in particular, whether any divine powers exist or not.

Agnostic arguments often presuppose a particular theory of knowledge called *evidentialism*. According to evidentialism, it is wrong to believe any state-ment true on the basis of inadequate evidence. William K. Clifford (1845–1879), a British mathematician, wrote a famous and influential article titled "The Ethics of Belief." Clifford argued that "it is wrong, always, everywhere and for anyone to believe anything upon insufficient evidence." He gives the example of a ship owner who, believing his ship seaworthy, sends it out to sea without checking on its safety. Whether the ship sinks or not, Clifford argues, the owner is morally responsible for holding a belief in the safety of the ship without sufficient evidence. "He had," Clifford writes, "no right to believe on such evidence as was before him."

For Clifford, nonempirical (not available to our senses), superhuman enti-ties like gods or God are beyond the reach of our minds. We simply are in no position to get the sort of evidence required to justify believing in some divine reality. Any such belief must be a leap of faith based on insufficient evidence. It is as morally wrong for humans to make such a leap as it is for the ship owner to believe his ship seaworthy without sufficient evidence.

Atheism, the claim that there is no God, is often based on a particular sort of analysis and explanation of religion. Ludwig Feuerbach (1804–1872), for example, maintained that a careful analysis of religion shows that humans project their highest and best virtues into a spiritual realm and create a being called God. God is a projection of idealized humanity. We create our gods in our own images.

Feuerbach's atheism is, odd as it may seem, religiously motivated. He saw himself as a second Martin Luther (1483–1546). Just as Luther had given birth to the Protestant Reformation in Germany, thereby creating a new form of Christianity, so Feuerbach hoped to give birth to a new form of Christianity, a form he called "realized Christianity."

Feuerbach argued that a correct analysis of religion shows that it amounts to a symbolic and mythical expression of an unconscious self-estrangement. Humans are divided selves. There is a division between our actual selves and our idealized selves (recall the cartoons with a devil on one shoulder and an angel on the other, whispering advice). Religion reflects this division between the real and the ideal. On the one hand, we project our idealized selves (what we ought to be) as a divine being (God), and on the other, we project our own existence as one of sin in comparison with this God. When this "hidden truth" of religion is made plain, then humanity will be freed from its estrangement and freed for a "realized Christianity"—a humanized religion that has at its core the love of neighbor, not the love of an illusory God.

Feuerbach's critique of religion and his atheism have a religious significance. Although he was well aware of the differences among different religions, he believed that in all the so-called higher religions there is a common core of teaching, best exemplified in Jesus' teaching about love. However, this common core of moral teaching has been obscured by supernaturalistic elements. Thus, for example, in Christianity, the teachings about a supernatural God, the Trinity, Christ's divinity, and the like have deflected human love from its true object. Feuerbach's atheistic humanism had as its goal nothing less than to remove these supernaturalistic smoke screens and redirect human love to its proper object, humanity itself:

> Religion is the dream of the human mind. But even in dreams we do not find ourselves in emptiness or in heaven, but on earth, in the realm of reality; we only see real things in the entrancing splendour of imagination and caprice, instead of in the simple daylight of reality and necessity. Hence I do nothing more to religion . . . than open its eyes, or rather to turn its gaze from the internal towards the external, i.e., I change the object as it is in the imagination into the object as it is in reality.[10]

REVIEW QUESTIONS

1. How do Laozi's and Anselm's ideas of ultimate truth differ?
2. Define in your own words animism and totemism.
3. Explain E. B. Tylor's and Emile Durkheim's theories of the origin of religion.
4. What is polytheism, and how does it differ from both henotheism and monotheism?
5. What is the difference between unitarian and trinitarian versions of monotheism?

6. Are monism and pantheism the same? Why or why not?
7. Can agnosticism and atheism be morally motivated? Briefly explain your answer.
8. Peter Berger, a sociologist of religion, remarked "religion is the audacious attempt to conceive the entire universe as being humanly significant."[11] Does the evidence presented in this chapter support Berger's claim or not? Briefly explain your answer.

RESEARCH CASE— GANESHA

In spring 1999 a 650-pound black granite statue of a human body with an elephant head arrived in Orange Park, Florida. In September of the same year, this statue was the focal point of a three-day installation ceremony, which, according to Daya J. Patel, president of the Hindu Society, will "instill cosmic energy into the idol, so that God will come into it."[12]

The "idol," or image, is Ganesha ("guh-nay'shuh"), one of the most worshiped gods in all of India. He is the lord who removes obstacles and brings success. He is worshiped by the devotees of other Hindu deities as the god who starts them either on a spiritual path or on the road to worldly success. By some he is worshiped as the supreme deity and the creator of the universe. He operates on all levels of the Hindu pantheon, from the level of subsidiary gods to that of the supreme God, and his worship crosses the boundaries of different sects. It also crosses borders. He has worshipers in Tibet, China, Japan, and elsewhere in Asia. He even crosses religions, finding a place in the Buddhist pantheon of gods.

You have probably seen pictures of him. He has the head of an elephant and the body of a short human or chubby child with a potbelly. Sometimes he is pictured sitting on a throne with a crown, and sometimes he is seated in meditation. Sometimes we see him with multiple arms, sometimes riding on an elephant, and sometimes he carries an axe, noose, sweet cakes, and a tusk. Often he has one tusk broken off. His image frequently graces the entrance to temples and shrines.

In the *Puranas*, a collection of Indian sacred stories, we encounter tales of Ganesha's birth, his beheading, his family, and his exploits. We are told he is the son of Parvati, wife of the god Shiva, destroyer of worlds. Parvati conceives Ganesha by herself because she wants a son to keep her company and guard the door to her bath, and Shiva, who is practicing asceticism and thus retaining his "seed," will not have sexual intercourse with her. When Shiva regains interest in Parvati and tries to enter her bath, Ganesha attempts to prevent him. Shiva, not knowing who Ganesha is, beheads him, much to the sorrow of Parvati. In order to comfort his wife and bring peace to his household, Shiva replaces the severed head with an elephant head, restores Ganesha to life, and adopts him as his own son.

The Hindu God Ganesha.

Robert L. Brown offers an interpretation:

In the Indian context, Ganesha is the liminal god of transitions: he is placed at the doorway of temples to keep out the unworthy, in a position analogous to his role as Parvati's doorkeeper, and he can set up, as he did for his father, obstacles to the successful completion of goals. His parents' ambivalent relationship, founded on the opposing concerns of asceticism and sexuality, places Ganesha in between. He is created by Parvati as a result of Shiva's asceticism and refusal to have children, but is annihilated due to Shiva's sexual interest in Parvati, only to be restored, transformed, as a bond between the two. He is here fulfilling his transitional role as a means to integrate opposing elements.[13]

In a frequently repeated myth, Ganesha has gorged himself on sweet cakes and begins his ride home at night on his rat vehicle. A snake frightens the rat, who shies, causing Ganesha to fall, breaking open his belly and spilling the cakes. In anger, Ganesha breaks off one of his tusks and throws it at the moon, which causes the moon to disappear. Ganesha restores the moon, but to this day it continues to wax and wane. This is also why Ganesha is often pictured with only one tusk.

The sanctification rite I mentioned at the beginning of this case also marked an overcoming of obstacles. More than 800 Hindus live on the northeast coast of Florida, and, in holding its first installation of Ganesha, this community begins the process of surmounting a problem faced by other immigrants to the United States—how to keep their religious traditions alive and well in an often hostile society. In pulling the Hindu Society of Florida together and bringing Ganesha to American shores, the immigrant Indians have become far more involved in their faith than they would have been in India. Most immigrants become "more religious" here than at home simply because there are fewer of them to keep the faith and culture alive. After traveling all over Asia, Ganesha is now alive and well in America.

QUESTIONS ON THE CASE OF GANESHA

1. What sort of additional information about Ganesha would you like? Be as specific as you can, and say why you want that information. (You may wish to review section 2.5 "Goals and Methods" to get some ideas about the kinds of questions to ask.)
2. How would you classify the worship of Ganesha? Is it polytheistic, henotheistic, monotheistic, deistic, or pantheistic? Why do you classify it as you do?
3. Do you agree with Brown's interpretation of the Ganesha birth story? Why or why not? What would you add?
4. Compare Ganesha to the Dao and to Anselm's Perfect Being. How are they the same and how different?
5. How do you think worship of Ganesha can help the Indian immigrant community in the United States overcome obstacles?

Fieldwork Option: Visit a Hindu temple and write a participant observation report (see section 2.6).

SUGGESTIONS FOR FURTHER READING

In addition to the material found in the notes, the reader may wish to consult the following for more information.

Armstrong, Karen. *A History of God: The 4000-Year Quest of Judaism, Christianity and Islam.* New York: Alfred A. Knopf, 1994. This is a highly readable account of how the idea and experience of God evolved among the monotheistic faiths of Judaism, Christianity, and Islam.

Clifford, William K. *Lectures and Essays*, vol. II. London: Macmillan, 1897. This volume contains the essay "Ethics of Belief."

Csikszentmihaliji, Mark, and Philip J. Ivanhoe, eds. *Religious and Philosophical Aspects of the Laozi*. Albany: State University of New York Press, 1999. Leading scholars carefully examine important religious and philosophical aspects of the *Daodejing*.

Fiorenza, Francis Schüssler, and Gordon D. Kaufman. "God." In *Critical Terms for Religious Studies*, edited by Mark C. Taylor, 136–159. Chicago: University of Chicago Press, 1998. This is a careful study of the many different ways the word *God* is used.

Holm, Jean, ed. *Picturing God*. London: Pinter Publishers, 1994. This collection of essays covering views about the divine in all the major religions contains much useful information.

Kessler, Gary E. *Ways of Being Religious*. Mountain View, CA: Mayfield Publishing Company, 2000. A collection of scriptures and other key texts from various religions organized historically with introductory comments.

Neville, Robert Cummings, ed. *Ultimate Realities: A Volume in the Comparative Religious Ideas Project*. Albany: State University of New York Press, 2001. This collection of essays explores notions of the ultimate in Chinese religion, Buddhism, Hinduism, Judaism, and Christianity, with essays on the difficulties of using the comparative method.

O'Flaherty, Wendy Doniger. *Hindu Myths*. Baltimore: Penguin Books, 1975. O'Flaherty presents a collection of classic stories about Hindu gods and goddesses.

INTERNET RESOURCES

www.cix.co.uk/~ganesh/ganesha.htm   This site provides a good image of Ganesha with quotations from the *Mudgala Purana* on the philosophical significance of Ganesha's form and a collection of stories about his origin. There are links to many other sites.

www.chinapage.com/laotze.html   This site provides a complete text of the *Daodejing* in both English and Chinese.

www.utm.edu/research/iep/a/anselm.htm   The material you will find here is from the *Internet Encyclopedia of Philosophy*. It provides background on Anselm's life and times, along with a clear summary of his ontological argument.

CHAPTER 4

Myth as Sacred Story

THERE ARE MANY different kinds of sacred literature in many different forms ranging from poetry and parables to proverbs. Here our focus is on one of these many forms; a form usually called myth.

The English word *myth* comes from the Greek word *mythos*, which means "story." In common usage the word has come to mean a false story. In the scholarly study of religions, **myth** has a technical meaning. It refers to a particular type of story, a story some people regard as sacred (that is, an extraordinary narrative radically different from profane stories). If a story is thought to be sacred, its truth is beyond question for those who so regard it. Believers in sacred stories may argue whether their stories are literally or symbolically true, but true they must be for the believer, because such stories reveal something of great importance about the meaning of human life and about the universe in which we live and die.

Although myths are sacred stories taken to be true in some sense by believers, other people's sacred stories—other people's myths—are often thought to be false. The sacred stories by which we live seem so obviously true, that we are shocked when others question them, yet the falsity of the myths (sacred stories) of others seems obvious to us.

In this chapter, we shall explore some sacred stories and some scholarly theories about them. After examining two case studies, we will review some of the many different types of myths and some of the many ways myths function to provide meaning for humans. A discussion of different scholarly theories about how we should best understand myths will lead directly to an examination of the relationship between myth and science. A research case brings our study to a close by focusing attention on the primal, or first, man from whom, some have claimed, this whole, vast universe is derived.

4.1 TWO CASE STUDIES

Enuma elish

Our first case comes from the ancient religion of Babylon (located in what is now Iraq). Babylonian religion did not survive the fortunes of history, but it did have significant influence on religions that have survived. Echoes of its creation myth can be heard in the scriptures of Judaism, Christianity, and Islam. Its tale of a primal combat between the forces of order (good) and the forces of disorder (evil) is a cultural universal.

Enuma elish ("ay-noo'mah ay'leesh"), "When on high," are the opening words of a very old myth honoring Marduk, the chief God of Babylon. The myth takes its title from these words, and a written copy was discovered in the ruins of King Ashurbanipal's (668–626 B.C.E.) library at Nineveh. It was probably composed in the reign of Nebuchadrezzar I (1125–1104 B.C.E.) but circulated much earlier in oral form. Some of the gods mentioned are Sumerian, who were predecessors of the Babylonians in the Mesopotamian region of the Tigris and Euphrates rivers.

The *Enuma elish* is a poem of more than a thousand lines, divided into seven parts. In the introduction (Part 1), the gods emerge from chaotic waters, and tension mounts between old and young gods. The scene opens:

> When [on high] there was no heaven,
> no earth, no height, no depth, no name,
> when Abzu was alone,
> the sweet water, the first begetter; and Tiamat
> the bitter water, . . .
>
> When sweet and bitter
> mingled together, no reed was plaited, no rushes
> muddied the water,
> the gods were nameless, natureless, futureless, then
> from Abzu and Tiamat
> in the waters gods were created, . . . [1]

The poem continues by recounting how "discord broke out among the gods although they were brothers." Mummu, the primordial mist and the "dark counselor," advises Abzu to kill his offspring. And, although Tiamat, the "Old Hag, the first mother," suggests they wait until the gods have grown up some, Abzu will not be deterred. In the ensuing conflict, Ea, the god of wisdom, kills Abzu along with his hopes to subdue the unruly divine children.

Victorious Ea, god of wisdom and son of Anu, "the empty heaven," fathers Marduk whose "body was beautiful; when he raised his eyes great lights flared; his stride was majestic; he was the leader from the first." We are told Marduk is the tallest and strongest god, and lightning played around him crying, "My son, my son, son of the sun, and heaven's sun."

Tiamat, seeking revenge for her husband's death, "mothers a new brood." This time the brood is composed of monsters, not gods, and led by the demon Kingu. Four times in the course of the poem we are told (as if the author is seeking to justify the fate that awaits Tiamat):

> She made the Worm
> the Dragon
> the Female Monster
> the Great Lion
> the Mad Dog
> the Man Scorpion
> the Howling Storm . . .

This "new brood" plots, growls, roars, and ruts, getting ready to be led by Kingu against Ea, his son Marduk, and the rest of the gods. The clouds of battle loom.

The second and third parts of the poem recount the story of Marduk's testing by the other gods, his receiving magical aids, and his final selection to champion the cause of the younger gods against the dreadful "new brood" of monsters and demons. He demands, if he wins, to be "set over the rest" and allowed to "decide the world's nature."

The long-awaited battle unfolds in Part 4 as Marduk mounts the storm, "his terrible chariot" drawn by Killer, Pitiless, Trampler, and Haste, who know the arts of "plunder" and have "skills of murder." Marduk is armed with powerful weapons and a magic word "clenched between his lips." He confronts Tiamat and shouts, "Mother of all, why did you have to mother war?" Tiamat, the bitter waters of chaos, is killed by Marduk and slit in two. The upper part of her body becomes the vault of the sky and lower part becomes the earth.

Part 5 tells how Marduk sets about creating cosmos (*cosmos* is the Greek word for "order") out of chaos using parts of Tiamat's body. Tiamat's eyes give rise to the mighty Euphrates and Tigris rivers on which Babylonian civilization depends. Marduk builds Babylon and its temples as his city and a home for all the gods. We are told, in Part 6, how Marduk creates humans from the blood of the demon captain Kingu for the purpose of serving the gods. These human servants of the gods are told they "must remember" whose creatures they are and sing the "Hymn of the Fifty Names of Marduk." The hymn continues in Part 7, lauding Marduk as "King of Kings, and Lord of Lords, Almighty God, Deliverer, and King of the Cosmos." An epilogue enjoins us mortal servants of the gods to remember the names of Marduk and to celebrate his defeat of Tiamat.

This story, sacred to the Babylonians, is a radical revision of traditional Mesopotamian belief. Prior to the rise of Marduk, the pantheon of Mesopotamian gods had a different leadership. As Babylon grew in power and influence, its city-god Marduk, once a minor deity, takes over leadership of the traditional pantheon. The myth dramatizes and celebrates the political history of Mesopotamia as it moves from warring communities, to city-states, and finally to empire. If, among gods, order emerges out of chaos by means of conflict, battle, and war, so too must order emerge out of chaos among mortals. This myth validates the history of the rise of Babylon by giving it a cosmic foundation. As the *Enuma elish* says, there is to be "a likeness on earth of what he [Marduk] did in heaven."

Some scholars have argued that the myth contains a dim memory of the overthrow of matriarchal rule by males, thus establishing patriarchy. Tiamat is a goddess, and the "Mother of All." Marduk is a male warrior-god who slays her. While we should be cautious about inferring historical events and social arrangements from mythic narratives, it is important to note the gender roles and relationships in this or any myth.

Moses

The second case comes from Judaism (although it can also be found in Christian and Islamic scriptures). Judaism today numbers over 15 million adherents, and its contemporary major organizational forms include Reform, Conservative, Orthodox, Hasidic, and Reconstructionist. The influence of Judaism on human culture, with its contributions to art, music, science, and literature, are immense.

One of the great heroes of the Jewish **Torah** (the first five books of the Hebrew Bible) is Moses (in Hebrew, *Mosheh*, in Arabic, *Musa*), who led Israel out of Egypt and transmitted divine commandments. He is celebrated as a great prophet in a Jewish hymn called "Yigdal" and in the Quran, the holy scripture of Islam. The Jewish rabbinic tradition claims that "Moses, our rabbi" (*rabbi* means "teacher") not only handed down the written Torah, but also an oral Torah that became the basis for later rabbinic commentaries.

Moses is an Egyptian name, perhaps from the root "to be born," and the biblical text links him closely to Egypt by indicating he was adopted by a daughter of the Pharaoh. The story of Moses that we find in the Torah is a composite picture. Some scholars think there may have been as many as four "Moses" figures, each associated with one of four major themes: (1) exodus from Egypt, (2) revelation at Mt. Sinai, (3) wilderness wandering, and (4) entrance into the Promised Land. Editors of the Torah used the "Moses" character we find in the text as the central figure holding these originally separate themes together. I will concentrate on the composite Moses as we find him after the editors have done their work. However, a more complete scholarly study would have to try to identify the component parts and their sources.

Man Using a Yad (Pointer) to Read from a Torah Scroll.

Some scholars argue that the story, or at least parts of it, has a firm historical base and can be dated from about 1350–1200 B.C.E. Other scholars dispute the historicity of much of the story, pointing out that Egyptian records make no reference to Moses, the Israelite slaves, or the exodus events. Whatever its historical base, there is little doubt that the story of Moses has become sacred to Jews, Christians, and Muslims alike. And, like the *Enuma elish*, it is a foundation story linking the identity and development of a unified people—a nation—with divine activity.

The Moses story opens in Egypt where the Hebrews are enslaved. We are told a woman from the priestly tribe of Levi bore a son, a "goodly child," and hid him because Pharaoh, fearful of the Hebrews' growing numbers, had decreed that "every son born to the Hebrews you shall cast into the Nile"

(Exodus 1:22). When she could no longer hide her son, she made a bulrush boat, put him in it, and cast him adrift. A daughter of Pharaoh found the boat and "took pity" on the Hebrew baby, eventually naming him Moses and raising him at the Egyptian court.

One day, when he is an adult, Moses witnesses an Egyptian beating a Hebrew slave. He kills the Egyptian and then flees to the land of Midian because Pharaoh seeks to kill him. By a well in Midian, Moses defends the daughters of Jethro, "the priest of Midian," from shepherds and eventually marries one of the daughters, named Zipporah. One day, while tending sheep, he sees a burning bush that is not consumed by the fire. Drawing close to the burning bush, he hears his name called and is told, "Do not come near: put off your shoes from your feet, for the place on which you are standing is holy ground" (Exodus 3:6). He does as instructed, and the voice from the burning bush continues by identifying itself as the Elohim (Hebrew for "gods," although usually translated "God") of Moses's ancestors. The Elohim tells Moses that he has seen the affliction of "my people," and commands Moses to return to Egypt and lead his people out of Egypt to a "land flowing with milk and honey, the land of the Canaanites" (present-day Israel and Palestine).

Moses does not want to go back to Egypt, so Elohim promises him a sign. Then Moses asks what he should say if the people ask the name of the Elohim that sent him. The voice in the burning bush replies, "I AM WHO I AM (YHWH) . . . say this to the people of Israel, I AM has sent me to you" (Exodus 3:14). YHWH was probably pronounced "Yahweh" (not "Jehovah," as some translations have it), but the name is considered so sacred that Jews do not say it. Instead, they say "Adonai" (Lord) whenever they encounter YHWH in the text.

Moses is still reluctant, complaining he cannot speak very well; so the Elohim named YHWH gives him several dramatic signs and a magic rod. Moses finally returns, and his natural brother Aaron meets him and speaks to the Israelite slaves on Moses's behalf, convincing them to follow Moses. However, Pharaoh will not let the people go because YHWH has "hardened his heart." So YHWH sends a series of plagues—frogs, gnats, flies, boils, hail, locusts, darkness—culminating in YHWH's promise to kill all the "firstborn" of Egypt. However, his "angel of death" will pass over houses of the Hebrew slaves on whose doors the blood of a sacrificial lamb has been smeared. The people are instructed to "observe this rite forever."

After the horrible death of all the firstborn of the Egyptians, the Hebrew slaves were set free and driven out. They left in such haste that the dough did not have time to rise, so they had to eat unleavened cakes. As he had done so many times in the past, Pharaoh changed his mind, pursued the escaped slaves, and Moses had to use his magic rod to part the sea, allowing the Hebrews to pass safely. When the Egyptian army pursued them into the dry seabed, the waters came rolling back, destroying "the chariots and the horsemen and all the host of Pharaoh that had followed them into the sea" (Exodus 14:28).

The liberated Hebrews wander in the Sinai dessert, led by Moses and Aaron. They are fed and protected by YHWH. They camp at Mount Sinai where Moses first encountered the burning bush. YHWH instructs Moses to climb to the top of the mountain, and the Lord descends with "thunders and lightning, and a thick cloud upon the mountain." A "very loud trumpet blast" is heard, and the people "trembled." On the mountaintop, YHWH gives Moses the Ten Commandments or Decalogue (Exodus 20:1–17). These include the commands to have no other gods before YHWH, not to make idols or "any likeness of anything that is in heaven above, or that is in the earth beneath, or that is in the water under the earth," not to take YHWH's name in vain, to remember the sabbath day "to keep it holy," and to honor one's parents. The commands continue (20:13–17):

> You shall not kill.
> You shall not commit adultery.
> You shall not steal.
> You shall not bear false witness against your neighbor.
> You shall not covet your neighbor's house; you shall not covet your neighbor's wife, or his manservant, or his maidservant, or his ox, or his ass, or anything that is your neighbor's.

The people want Aaron to make a golden calf to worship while Moses is gone on the mountaintop, and Moses, when he sees it, breaks, in his wrath, the tablets of stone on which the laws were written. Once the people have been chastised for worshiping idols, YHWH in his mercy makes another set of stone tablets on which YHWH rewrites the law.[2]

The Hebrews continue to wander in the Sinai desert, and finally YHWH permits them to enter the promised land of Canaan. But Moses is not allowed to enter. He dies after seeing it at the age of 120 years, and we are told "when he died, his eye was not dim, nor his natural force abated."

I think you can see in this sacred story that Moses is portrayed as both a "culture hero," who brings great cultural benefits to the Hebrews, and a "spiritual hero," who establishes the foundations of Israel's faith. I think you can also see some of the themes typical of hero tales: the remarkable birth of the hero, a situation that needs correcting, the hero told to go to a place where he or she receives a commission and magical aid, conflict with an adversary, and a final victory.

There is a rich variety of detail in the Moses story, but we will confine our discussion to the big events. They are the liberation from slavery, the revelation of the divine name, and the giving of the law. These three events leave an indelible mark on the Jewish faith. To a large extent they define the heart of Judaism—a religion that celebrates freedom from bondage, the revelation of the true divine but mysterious name of the one and only God, and the law by which people ought to order their lives.

4.2 COMPARISON

On the surface, these two myths seem very different. One is a story about the creation of the world out of the body of the first mother, Tiamat. The other is a story about the adventures and deeds of a culture hero. While it is true that the *Enuma elish* is often treated as a creation myth, the central character in that story is also a hero, Marduk, and it can be persuasively argued that the story is more about the hero Marduk than it is about creation. The typical themes of hero myths noted in the case of Moses can also be found in the Marduk story: a remarkable birth, a situation that needs correcting, the hero told to go to a place where he receives a commission and magical aid, conflict with an adversary, and a final victory.

Marduk is a god. Moses is a human being. This is a major difference between the two myths. Further, the *Enuma elish* contains an account of creation that the Moses story does not. Nevertheless, both stories are about beginnings. Marduk is responsible for the beginnings of cosmic order, human beings, and Babylon, including its buildings, laws, rites, religion, and political structure. Moses is responsible for the beginnings of the Hebrew nation and its laws.

However, the ways in which the two heroes are responsible differ. Marduk, once he is commissioned by the council of gods, proceeds to manifest his own power in bringing about these important events. Moses, while commissioned by YHWH to lead the Hebrews out of Egypt and through the Sinai wilderness, often manifests weakness and reluctance to follow his calling. We get the overwhelming impression that YHWH remains in control of events throughout. He is the real leader and real author of the law code given at Sinai. Moses, unlike Marduk, is a transmitter, a go-between, and a servant of a higher power. Marduk, once given authority to act by the other gods, is his "own man."

It might be more appropriate to compare Marduk to YHWH than to Moses. Both are divine beings, both engage in conflicts, both form a nation, and both give laws. Although the story of YHWH creating the universe and humans (by very different means than Marduk) is not mentioned in the Moses story, it forms the backdrop to the story. YHWH, like Marduk, is a creator-god. Marduk appears to be more a warrior-god of the storm than YHWH, yet there are hints in the Torah that YHWH is also a warrior- and storm-god, originally perhaps, a local deity of the Midianites associated primarily with Mount Sinai. Marduk's temple in Babylon was constructed like a mountain and is referred to in Genesis as the Tower of Babel. The story of Moses is, like the story of Marduk, a story of a local deity assuming a more universal role and extending his influence from Sinai to Egypt and, eventually, to the land of Canaan and well beyond.

In both stories humans are viewed as servants of the divine. In the *Enuma elish* they are explicitly created to fulfill that role. In the Moses story it is clear that the Hebrews are expected to become YHWH's servants out of gratitude for what he has done for them—delivered them from slavery, given them the law, and promised them a land in which to live. Here we see one of the oldest laws of human relationships: a gift requires a gift in return.

Humans, in the Genesis story, are created out of the dust of the ground and in the "image of God." In the Babylonian account they are created out of the blood of a demon. They do have a superhuman origin, but it is not a flattering family tree. These are very different conceptions of human origin, even if they agree that humans are created to serve the divine.

It is clear that the Hebrews are not very good at serving YHWH. They start running after other gods like the golden calf. Both stories are strongly henotheistic. There may be many gods, but service ought to be focused on one: Marduk in the case of the Babylonians and YHWH in the case of the Hebrews. Just as ancient law codes commanded people to be loyal to their own king and not the kings of others, so too they demanded loyalty to their own god and not the gods of others.

Conflict and death play a significant role in both stories. Marduk's main conflict is with Tiamat and her "new brood" of monsters and demons. Moses' conflict is first with the Egyptian who beats a slave, then with Pharaoh, and later, when the Hebrews turn to the worship of the golden calf, with the Hebrews themselves. Out of the death of Tiamat comes life. Out of the death of the firstborn of Egypt and the Passover lamb comes life for the Hebrews. A nearly universal teaching of all religions, which we will encounter again and again, is illustrated by this motif: out of death comes life. Death, seen in a religious context, is a sacrificial act. Something old is sacrificed so something new can begin.

4.3 TYPES AND FUNCTIONS

Recall from Chapter 2 that typologies are systems of classification. They organize different things into groups, classes, or types based on some feature or function they have in common. There are numerous typologies of myths because stories have so many different features. Also the line between myths, legends, and folklore is not always clear. Myths can be grouped in many of different ways. Here is one typology:

1. **Cosmogonic** and **cosmological** myths about the origin and order of the universe.

2. Myths of lesser beginnings, often called **etiological** because they explain why some rite, law, custom, feature of the landscape, and so on, came to be.
3. **Eschatological myths** about the end of the world.
4. Myths of lesser endings, such as the fall of a city or empire.
5. Myths about death and the life after death.
6. Myths about divine, semidivine, and demonic beings.
7. Myths about heroes and saviors.
8. Myths about transformations and incarnations, such as movement from animal to human, human to animal, human to divine, and divine to human.
9. Myths about kings, wise men and women, ascetics, martyrs, and saints. (Some might classify such stories as legends rather than myths.)

I think it is clear that this typology is organized according to subject matter. One limitation of this sort of typology is that there always seems to be something left out. You might already be thinking of stories you would call myths that do not fit any of these types. All typologies seem to require the category "other."

Types of Myth

1. Cosmogonic and cosmological
2. Etiological
3. Eschatological
4. Lesser endings
5. Death and the afterlife
6. Divine, semidivine, and demonic beings
7. Heroes and saviors
8. Transformations and incarnations
9. Kings, wise people, ascetics, martyrs, and saints

How do myths function? What do they do for people? Before looking at some specific functions, we need to distinguish between manifest and latent functions. **Manifest functions** are consciously intended and obvious, for example, to tell a story about something or someone. **Latent functions** are hidden and most likely unintended. For example, a myth may function to reinforce the power of a priestly elite. An important clue to the meaning of a myth can often be found by asking and answering the question, what are the main functions (manifest and latent) of this myth? Asking who benefits from this tale can often reveal latent functions.

It is appropriate to begin with some religious functions before discussing social, psychological, and expressive functions. Four important religious functions are (1) **hierophanic** (to reveal something holy or sacred); (2) **numinous** (to elicit and reinforce a sense of awe and finitude with respect to the divine); (3) **ritualistic** (to give a narrative explaining and justifying ritual actions); and (4) **cosmological** (to render a picture of the order of the universe). If you think again about the *Enuma elish* and the story of Moses, I think you can readily see how these two myths function religiously in all of these ways. The ritualistic function may not be obvious to you now, but in the next chapter we shall examine two rituals, the Akitu festival and Passover, that are closely linked to these stories.

Three important social functions also stand out in the two myths examined here: (1) integration of individuals into a group (that is, establishing a group identity and social solidarity), (2) supporting and reinforcing a current social order, and (3) criticism of a current social order by presenting a new one or recommending an old one. I think it is rather obvious how the Moses story establishes the identity of a people (1). The Jews are reminded by this story that they are those people freed from slavery, given a divine law, and expected to serve God. Marduk creates the city of Babylon, builds its temples, sets up its laws, and establishes its religious and political life. The Babylonian empire is given divine sanction by this story (2). However, these are not just conservative tales. They are also revolutionary. Marduk overthrows a previous organization of the gods and goddesses and the social organization that accompanied it. Moses and the Hebrews challenge the established social order of Egypt and its gods. To establish a new order requires the destruction of an old order.

Myths fulfill numerous psychological functions, but I will describe two: (1) the establishment of ego identity and (2), on the deep psychological level, the establishment of a self. If we call our sense of personal and individual identity the ego (I), then both the *Enuma elish* and the Moses story invite us to think of ourselves as servants of the divine. If, in addition to our ego identity, we suppose that we are, as we live, creating a wider, more inclusive identity called the self, then *Enuma elish* invites us to create peaceful order out of the chaos and conflicts of our lives. The Moses story urges us to reject all forms of bondage in the name of freedom for obedience to a divine law.

Most if not all myths that have survived in writing from the past were originally passed on orally from one generation to another before being written down. Sometimes certain people or clans were responsible for a set of stories. They were the official storytellers. Oral storytelling is a dramatic and often entertaining event. The goal of the telling is in the telling. This is the expressive function of myth. It is fun to tell and hear stories. The very expression of them is fascinating and satisfying.

Some scholars have argued that stories told for the sake of entertainment should not be classified as myths because they lack the serious intent of myth. Even if myths have more serious intent than entertainment, I think we cannot ignore the expressive function. Myths are often good stories, and we all enjoy a good story.

However, myths are more than good stories. They establish an **ideology.** An ideology is a set of doctrines or beliefs that form the basis of a political, economic, or religious system. Religious ideologies are particularly powerful because they convince people that the gods create a particular social order when in fact humans create such order.

> ## Functions of Myth
>
> 1. Religious
> 2. Social
> 3. Psychological
> 4. Expressive
> 5. Ideological

4.4 THEORIES OF MYTH

The purpose of theory is to provide a general framework that aids in interpreting and explaining. There are a variety of theories available to the student of mythology. I will discuss five such theories here. A sixth theory, called the **myth and ritual theory,** will be discussed in the next chapter after we have had an opportunity to examine religious rituals.

The first type of theory is called the **rationalistic theory.** Its basic premise is that myths are attempts to explain things. Myths are similar to scientific theories that explain, for example, the origin of human life or the cosmos. The difference is that myths are false explanations.

According to this theory, the purpose of the *Enuma elish* is to explain the origin and structure of the universe, human life, and the Babylonian empire. Likewise the purpose of the Moses story is to explain how the Jews escaped from slavery and received the law of YHWH. However, these explanations are false from both a historical and scientific view. History and science offer different explanations that, if not completely true (scientific and historical explanations are constantly being revised and updated based on new evidence), are closer to the truth than myths.

This theory makes it difficult to explain why people, indeed whole societies, often persist in believing what is false. Many Jews (not to mention

Christians and Muslims) believe that the Moses story is true, and many believe the account of creation given in Genesis is true. There are no Babylonians left, but if there were, they too might persist in their beliefs about Marduk and the origin of Babylon. Presumably, evolution would weed out false beliefs because they don't work and are not conducive to survival. We have discarded the belief that the world is flat or the earth is the center of the universe. So why have we not discarded myths that, based on present-day scientific and historical evidence, we know are literally false?

Functionalist theories of myth are common in the social scientific study of religion (anthropology, sociology, and psychology). According to this type of theory, the meaning of myth is to be found in what a myth does—that is, in its functions. Myths function to satisfy the needs of societies and individuals, such as the need for meaning, identity, and social solidarity. These functions explain why belief in myths persists, even though the stories are literally false. Although there is little agreement on exactly what the basic needs are that myths satisfy, they are often identified as biological (indirectly contributing to survival), psychological (providing meaning and purpose), sociological (creating a sense of belonging), or some combination of these three kinds of needs.

Critics have pointed out several problems with functionalist theories. They question whether the meaning of a myth is totally exhausted by its functions, and whether it is even correct to identify meaning with use or function. Also, as pointed out above, there is lack of agreement about what precisely are the needs that myths supposedly satisfy.

Symbolic theories of myth are often closely tied to functional theories and stand opposed to rationalistic theories. Myths, according to symbolic theories, do not explain anything. Rather, they contain symbolic representations; what they contain symbolic representations of, depends on the symbolist. Here is a partial list of the sorts of things different symbolists say that myths represent: repressed material from the individual unconscious, universal patterns from the collective unconscious, social organization and structure, transcendent sacred realities. For example, if I think that there are universal patterns that exist in an unconscious, then one of these might be the hero. In that case, both Moses and Marduk would be different expressions of a psychological reality buried deep in humanity's shared unconscious. (See the discussion of Carl Jung in Chapter 7.) This would explain why certain stories are universal and why some stories seem ageless—told and retold with countless permutations, from Marduk to Superman.

The basic assumption of symbolic theories is that myths have hidden meanings that must be decoded. The task of the student of mythology is to disclose this hidden meaning. So, for example, the escape of the Jews from Egypt symbolizes the desire to be free that is found in all of us.

This theory does not explain why people continue speaking in a coded language, that is, continue to tell symbolic sacred stories or myths. Add to this the fact that the people who speak this coded language are unaware of the real, hidden meaning of the myths they tell; indeed, many of these believers think the language they speak is literally true. Presumably only the scholar of mythology is in a position to know what myth-tellers and believers are "really" talking about. They are not really talking about the commandments given by YHWH when they tell the story of Moses at Mount Sinai. They are instead talking about the deep-seated human need to think that the laws humans create are more than conventional, that they are somehow rooted in the eternal or the way things were meant to be. Some argue that symbolic theories are the expression of scholarly arrogance.

Phenomenological theory claims myths are manifestations of the sacred and opposes all reductionistic interpretations such as the rationalistic and functional approaches discussed above. Myths must be interpreted by careful and nearly exhaustive comparative methods. According to phenomenologists, myths will interpret themselves once you have enough examples to reveal a common pattern. For example, Mircea Eliade (1907–1986) claims that after you study enough myths comparatively you will discover that:

> Myth narrates a sacred history; it relates an event that took place in primordial Time, the fabled time of the 'beginnings." In other words, myth tells how, through the deeds of Supernatural Beings, a reality came into existence, be it the whole of reality, the Cosmos, or only a fragment of reality—an island, a species of plant, a particular kind of human behavior, an institution. Myth, then, is always an account of a "creation"; it relates how something was produced, began to be . . . Because myth relates the [deed] of Supernatural Beings and the manifestations of their sacred powers, it becomes the exemplary model for all significant human activities.[3]

Eliade's view of myth is insightful and clearly applies to the *Enuma elish* and the Moses story, but it does not apply to all myths. Not all myths are about creations, large or small. Another problem with the phenomenological theory has to do with the claim that myths are manifestations of the sacred and provide exemplary models. While this may be true, does it reveal anything of great value about myths? Does it help us discover the meaning of myth, or just restate the obvious in scholarly language?

The final theory we will examine here is the **structuralist theory**. According to this theory, myths are cognitive structures by which people think. Just as language has a syntax that allows people to form meaningful sentences, so myths have a basic logical structure that allows people to organize their experiences and their world into a meaningful whole. This logical structure is most often described as a system of relations that form binary oppositions like off/on or up/down. Sometimes this system is simply a way of classifying things and ordering experience. Other times the oppositions are mitigated or reconciled, thereby relaxing social tensions in the group. For example, the primary binary opposition in the *Enuma elish* is between chaos and cosmos, disorder and order. Babylonian society depended upon the waters of the Tigris and Euphrates rivers. Each year they would flood, causing widespread damage and destruction. Yet the crops depended on the water. One of the first things Marduk does in establishing Babylonian society is to build a system of canals that control this yearly flooding. Thus the order he established did, in a very real sense, overcome the chaotic waters unleashed in floods.

I think you can easily see that one of the difficulties with this theory is very much like the difficulties of the symbolic theory. Myths have hidden structures, a logical base akin to the syntax of grammar that only the scholar can uncover. The speakers of the mythic language remain, for the most part, ignorant of this hidden structure. However, is this a powerful objection? After all, most of us learn how to speak a language before we learn the grammatical rules that govern our speech. Just because we do not know the rules or cannot detect them without some education does not mean they don't exist.

In spite of the problems, each of these theories of myth (rationalistic, functional, symbolic, phenomenological, and structuralist) provides different, yet important, insights into the function, meaning and structure of myth. Indeed, many scholars of myth are eclectic, drawing on elements in different theories when they find them useful to illuminate the myths with which they are dealing. These theories form part of the toolbox of the student of religions.

Theories of Myth

1. Rationalistic
2. Functional
3. Symbolic
4. Phenomenological
5. Structuralist

4.5 MYTH AND SCIENCE

According to the Bible, the Israelites, under the leadership of Moses, spent forty years in the Sinai wilderness. Finally, under the leadership of Joshua, they began the conquest of Canaan, the Promised Land, with the aid of YHWH. The Book of Joshua tells us of the bloody sacking of Jericho after YHWH made its walls fall down. The Canaanite city of Ai fell next. According to the Book of Joshua, YHWH threw the Canaanites into a panic as the Israelite army advanced. Indeed, he even "threw down great stones from heaven . . . and they died." (Joshua 10:11). Not only did YHWH personally kill with the hailstones more men than Israel "killed with the sword," he also made the sun stand still so Joshua and his army could continue the slaughter for almost a day:

> Sun, stand thou still at Gibeon,
> And thou Moon in the valley of Ai'jalon.
> And the sun stood still, and the moon stayed,
> Until the nation took vengeance on their enemies.
> Is this not written in the Book of Jashar? The sun stayed in the midst of heaven,
>   and did not hasten to go down for about a whole day. (Joshua 10:13)

Obviously, the authors of the Book of Joshua believed that the sun moved around the earth. But we now know that it does not.

In 1543, the year Nicholas Copernicus (b. 1473) died, his book on astronomy was published. This book—dedicated to Pope Paul III—revolutionized astronomy because it showed that the earth revolves around the sun. The sun stands still and the earth moves. When Galileo Galilei (1564–1642) confirmed by observation Copernicus's conclusions, and published the results, the Roman Catholic Church vigorously opposed the heliocentric (sun-centered) view. Galileo was brought to trial by the Inquisition in 1633 and forced to deny his heliocentric views. Heliocentrism contradicted not only what was said about the sun in the Book of Joshua, but also the widely accepted geocentric (earth-centered) view inherited from Greek philosophy. It was not until the late twentieth century that the Roman Catholic Church officially apologized for its condemnation of Galileo. In the long run, the heliocentric view prevailed.

In the nineteenth century another conflict between the Christian religion and science broke out. Charles Darwin (1809–1882) published *The Origin of Species* in 1859, and biology has not been the same since. His theory of evolution along with his views on the origin of human beings met with vigorous opposition, and today some conservative Protestant Christians still wage a bitter battle, arguing that the Genesis account of God creating the universe in six days is literally true and contradicts the view that life evolved slowly over millions of years.

When the sacred myths of religion conflict with the established views of science, what should we think? None of us thinks that the world came to be as the *Enuma elish* says, and no one would oppose the Big Bang theory of the origin of the universe on the grounds that there was no Big Bang, but rather a Big Cut, severing in two the Mother of All. So why do some people persist in believing in a literal interpretation of the Genesis myth and use it to oppose evolution?

The answer is complex, but part of it is to be found in the rationalistic theory discussed earlier. If people take myths as explanations of the way things came to be and if those explanations contradict the conclusions of science, then only two choices seem possible: either cling to the truth of the myth and reject scientific accounts as "only theories" or accept the scientific account and reject the mythic explanations as false.

There are other alternatives, however. The symbolic theory (also discussed earlier) is attractive to many people because it allows them to take myths seriously (in a metaphorical sense, although not a literal sense) and to accept as literally true the conclusions of modern science. This is an old strategy. Averroes (Abu-al-Walid Muhammad Ibn Ahmad Ibn Rushd, b. 1126 in Cordova, Spain), an Islamic philosopher and theologian, argued that Islamic faith in the truth of the Quran was in harmony with the scientific and philosophical knowledge of his day. Although his position is somewhat complex, in essence he argued that when the Quran appears to contradict science, the Quran must be interpreted allegorically unless there are compelling reasons to take it literally. Similar arguments have been made by Christians and Jews with respect to the Bible, both before Averroes wrote and since.

This move from a literal to a symbolic or allegorical reading, however, seems to confirm that myths have hidden meanings that many believers do not grasp and only those properly trained in the art of symbolic interpretation can grasp. As Averroes says, "The double meaning [literal and allegorical] has been given to suit people's diverse intelligence. The apparent contradictions are meant to stimulate the learned to deeper study."[4] There is an elitist attitude in the presumption that only learned scholars are capable of understanding the symbolic or allegorical dimensions of myth.

This sort of objection to symbolic theories is, it seems to me, not fatal. Many believers not trained as scholars understand their myths allegorically. Guided evolution (the theory that God uses evolution as the means to create life in the universe) has long been popular with many Jews and Christians. Religions are constantly reinterpreting their sacred stories. If they did not, history would leave them so isolated in the past that they would eventually die. If we studied the history of Jewish, Christian, and Islamic interpretations of the Bible, we would be amazed at the variety and richness among the various readings. One aspect of this variety and richness stems from the many possible ways people have thought about the relationship between religion and science in general. Michael Ruse, who wrote the introduction to Bertrand Russell's *Religion and Science* (1997), thinks there are at least four distinct ways.[5]

The first relationship, and one that most people think of because it gets so much attention, is *uncompromising opposition*. A wall divides two worldviews: the worldview of science and the worldview of religion. From the science side of this wall, those who oppose science on religious grounds appear hopelessly ignorant, confused, and misguided. When a preacher rejects any science that contradicts what the Bible seems to say on the grounds that it is godless "secular humanism" and when a scientist rejects any literal interpretation of the Bible, there seems little room for compromise. For example, if someone argues that the world was created in six days because that is what Genesis says, and rejects all scientific evidence concerning the age and evolution of the universe, he or she draws clear battle lines between science and religion.

Second, some think that science and religion *exist separately*. Science deals with the "how" questions and religion with the "why" questions. Science shows us how things work on the physical level, but religion explains why things are the way they are on the spiritual level. Science, in this view, can never tell us why there is something rather than nothing, but religion can. Science can tell us what that something is and how it works, but it cannot tell us why it is there in the first place. Religion can tell us that the universe exists to fulfill some divine purpose. Science can tell us how the existing universe works. There is no conflict here, only separate tasks and different questions.

Third, some go beyond separatism and argue that science and religion can learn from one another. They exist, or at least ought to exist, *in dialogue*. Scientists and theologians should talk with one another in mutual respect, thereby entering into a conversation from which each can learn because each has something important to contribute from their different perspectives. From the dialogic point of view, uncompromising opposition will get us nowhere, and predetermined separatism creates artificial boundaries. Both science and religion are here to stay, so why not talk, share, and try to understand their different points of view? For example, one issue that can be mutually explored is the role that authority and imagination play in both processes. Myths are the result of human thought and imagination, and so is science. However, science insists on supporting its conclusions by critically examined evidence, controlled experimentation designed to test hypotheses, and observation. Galileo looked through a telescope to verify previous claims and rejected authority as the determiner of truth about the physical universe. Nevertheless, scientists do use imagination to develop new hypotheses for testing and do accept the authority of previously tested conclusions. Clearly imagination plays a major role in the creation of sacred stories, and the authority of the source of these stories becomes important as they pass from one generation to the next. How do these processes compare? Is there a crucial difference?

While the dialogic position maintains that there may well be irresolvable differences between religion and science, a fourth position moves beyond dialogue and boldly asserts that science and religion are *integrated*. They are necessarily connected and mutually supporting. Pierre Teilhard de Chardin (1881–1955), a Jesuit priest and scientist, argued that the evolutionary change from simple life-forms to more complex forms such as humans mirrors the spiritual evolution of humans toward a more Christ-like and spiritual existence. Ghose Aurobindo (1872–1950), a leading Indian nationalist and spiritual leader, relied heavily on both the ideas of evolutionary biology and Hindu **mysticism** to craft a comprehensive philosophy that integrated science and religion. Much like de Chardin's notion that we are evolving both spiritually and physically toward becoming more Christ-like, Aurobindo argued that the whole universe was geared toward development in ways that would lead to what he called "the life-divine."

> **Relationships Between Science and Religion**
>
> 1. Opposition
> 2. Separation
> 3. Dialogue
> 4. Integration

The problem of the relationship between myth and science is part of a larger debate about the relationship of religion and science. It is an ongoing debate in scholarly circles. I have recounted a very brief part of the story, but I hope enough to stimulate you to further thought.

REVIEW QUESTIONS

1. What is the difference between the popular meaning of the word *myth* and its technical meaning in religious studies?
2. How do the *Enuma elish* and the story of Moses link the earthly social order with the divine? Be specific.
3. Describe the common elements found in hero myths.
4. Why are typologies of myths useful, and what are their limitations?
5. Describe the manifest and latent functions of the modern secular myth of Superman. Be as specific as you can.
6. What is the difference between the hierophanic and numinous functions of myth? Why do you think both are classified as religious functions rather than social?
7. What role do you think the Moses story of liberation from bondage in Egypt might have played among African American slaves in the United States?
8. Of the five different theories of myth discussed in this chapter, which do you think is most helpful in understanding the meaning of myths and why?
9. Of the different relationships between religion (myth) and science discussed in this chapter, which seems more plausible to you? Briefly explain your answer.

RESEARCH CASE—THE PRIMAL MAN

A number of Indo-European myths recount the story of creation in a similar pattern. There is a death, usually by violent means (sacrifice, murder, battle) and dismemberment of a primordial, or first, being. The physical and social universe is formed from the pieces of the victim's body.

An example of this story can be found in *Rig-Veda* 10.90, composed about 900 B.C.E. The *Rig-Veda* (a collection of poems and hymns from various time periods) constitutes some of the oldest scripture of Hinduism. In this "Hymn of Man," we hear about a cosmic giant called Purusha (person or human being) who is the first male and a victim of a Vedic sacrifice.

> When they divided the Man [Purusha], into how many parts did they apportion him? What do they call his mouth, his two arms and thighs and feet?
>
> His mouth became the Brahmin [priests]; his arms were made into the Warrior, his thighs the People, and from his feet the Servants were born.
>
> The moon was born from his mind; from his eye the sun was born. Indra [a warrior and storm god] and Agni [god of the sacrificial fire] came from his mouth, and from his vital breath the Wind was born.
>
> From his navel the middle realm of space arose; from his head the sky evolved. From his two feet came the earth and the quarters of the sky from his ear. Thus they [the gods] set the world in order. (RV 10.90, 11–14)[6]

Ancient Indian society was divided into four hierarchically ordered classes: the priestly class, the warrior class, the commoner class, and the servant class. The *Laws of Manu* (*Manu* means "the wise one" and is a mythological king described as the ancestor of the human race), another ancient Indian text, details the status, duties, and responsibilities of these classes. Here we are told that Purusha, "the radiant one," appointed teaching, study, sacrifice, generosity, and the acceptance of gifts for the priestly class. The warrior class is assigned the duties of protection of the people, generosity, the patronage of sacrifice, and study. Commerce and agriculture are the proscribed duties of the commoners, and "the Lord assigned only one activity to a servant: serving these (other) classes without resentment" (1:91).[7]

Although Manu is said to be a king and hence a member of the warrior class, *The Laws of Manu* portrays the priestly class as the superior class. Hence it seems safe to conclude that these laws were written by priests and for priests. They instructed priests on the details of law and morality, details that they should teach to all the people. It should also be noted that males who were concerned with controlling the conduct of females wrote them. Hence it is not surprising to find the rules for females to be much more restrictive than the rules for males. For example, Manu counsels that "Men must make their women dependent day and night. . . . A woman is not fit for independence."[8]

I have referred to these social groups as classes (*varnas*) rather than castes (*jatis*) because over time, hundreds, perhaps thousands, of distinct castes evolved. *Jatis* means "birth" and refers to the group into which someone is born. The four classes, or *varnas*, of priests, warriors, merchant-farmers, and servants were and are a convenient and more general way to group all the many different castes. So some castes are assigned to one class and some to another. Theoretically, all the castes, except the outcastes, could be reduced to one of these four classes.

It is important to know something about the social context in which stories like the "Hymn of Man" were created. The links between myths and societies must be understood in order to make sense of myths. Bruce Lincoln writes that Indo-European creation myths like the one about Purusha present:

> More a picture of how things ought to be than how things were, describing the social order in the best light. But an ideology—any ideology—is not just an ideal against which social reality is measured. . . . It is also, and this is more important, a screen that strategically veils, mystifies, or distorts important aspects of real social processes. Like any other ideology, myth largely serves to create false consciousness in many members of society, persuading them of the rightness of their lot in life, whatever that may be, and of the total social order.[9]

QUESTIONS ON THE CASE OF THE PRIMAL MAN

1. Draw a picture of the primal man, and indicate which of his parts gives rise to which cosmological and social features. What does this visual image help you to see? What is the significance of the fact that he is a male? What is the significance of the fact that the servant class comes from his feet?
2. Discuss some possible functions of this myth. Be specific and cite evidence.
3. How do Bruce Lincoln's comments about myth and ideology apply to the Purusha myth?
4. Compare the Purusha myth to the *Enuma elish*. How are they the same and how different? Pay particular attention to gender issues and the roles males and females play in these myths.

SUGGESTIONS FOR FURTHER READING

In addition to the material found in the notes, the reader may wish to consult the following for more information.

Barbour, Ian. *Myths, Models, and Paradigms: A Comparative Study in Science and Religion.* New York: Harper and Row, 1974. An early but classic study that has influenced much subsequent thinking on the topic.

Campbell, Joseph. *The Hero with a Thousand Faces.* Reprint. Princeton: Princeton University Press, 1972. This is a popular but much criticized account of what Campbell takes to be the "monomyth" of the hero.

Dundes, Alan, ed. *Sacred Narrative: Readings in the Theory of Myth.* Berkeley: University of California Press, 1984. This collection of essays by leading scholars deals with the problems and issues associated with the interpretation of myth.

Eliade, Mircea. *Patterns in Comparative Religion.* Translated by Willard R. Trask. New York: New American Library, 1963. This volume contains a massive amount of interesting information by one of the greatest scholars of religion in the last century.

Griffin, David Ray. *Religion and Scientific Naturalism: Overcoming the Conflict.* Albany: State University of New York Press, 2000. Griffin argues for the harmony of science and religion, criticizing traditional religion for a misguided concept of supernaturalism and traditional science for a misguided understanding of naturalism.

Kirsch, Jonathan. *Moses: A Life.* New York: Ballantine, 1998. The life of Moses is clearly retold and analyzed based on the Bible, Jewish commentary, and recent scholarship.

McCutcheon, Russell T. "Myth." In *Guide to the Study of Religion,* edited by Willi Braun and Russell T. McCutcheon, 190–207. London: Cassell, 2000. After a brief survey of different ways of interpreting myth, the author concludes that myths need to be demystified to be understood. There is also a helpful list of suggested readings.

Rosenberg, Donna. *World Mythology: An Anthology of the Great Myths and Epics.* 2nd ed. Lincolnwood, IL: NTC Publishing, 1994. Rosenberg provides a useful collection of myths from around the world.

INTERNET RESOURCES

www.sacred-texts.com/ane/enuma.htm   At this site you will find a translation of *Enuma elish.* Visit the home page of sacred-texts.com for a complete list of the books on religion and translations of scriptures available online. Because of copyright issues, many of these translations are dated.

www.jewishvirtuallibrary.org/jsource/biography/moses.html   You will find a lot of information about Moses on the Web, and you need your critical faculties on alert. This site provides an insider's viewpoint.

www.unesco.org/courier/2001_05/uk/doss24.htm   There is no single Hindu myth of creation, but here you will find a discussion of the Primal Man myth in terms of class structure and in the wider context of Hindu mythology.

CHAPTER 5

Ritual as Sacred Action

XUNZI (HSÜN TZU, pronounced "Shyun'-dz"), a Confucian scholar of the third century B.C.E. wrote:

> The meaning of ritual is deep indeed
> He who tries to enter it with the kind of perception that
> distinguishes hard and white, same and different will
> drown there.
>
> The meaning of ritual is great indeed.
> He who tries to enter it with the uncouth and inane
> Theories of the system-makers will perish there.[1]

Xunzi warns us not to reduce ritual to simple categories and not to get caught up in theories about ritual, for fear we will lose sight of the ritual process itself. While heeding his advice, it is necessary on an introductory level to simplify somewhat and acknowledge that theories can be helpful as well as misleading. I shall take Xunzi's warning to apply not only to ritual studies but also to the study of religion in general. It is a warning that all our conclusions must be tentative. They are fallible and subject to correction.

This tentativeness is evident right at the beginning because scholars do not agree on how best to define ritual. Some favor a broad definition that would include secular activities (such as sports events) as well as sacred activities (such as worship). Others prefer a narrower definition, using ritual in the sense of a sacred action that usually involves some superhuman reference. The title of this chapter indicates that I will, for the most part, be using the word *ritual* to pick out actions regarded by some people as sacred. I do not intend to exclude a broader understanding and argue that we must always regard actions as sacred if they are to count as examples of rituals. My more narrow focus is purely pragmatic. It is more useful for my purposes.

Ritual, as I am using the term here, involves stylized, symbolic bodily gestures and actions (including verbal actions) usually repeated in specified ways on occasions of significance and in special contexts frequently involving what the participants take to be sacred presences.[2] As this chapter unfolds, we will examine several examples, look at some varieties and some functions of ritual, and explore the myth and ritual theory.

In many respects, the study of ritual is fundamental to understanding religion. Religion lives and breathes through ritual. People are socialized as children into religion by ritual (learning to pray, for example), and people's religious lives center to a great extent on activities in temples, shrines, churches, mosques, and synagogues. Most people learn their religion by doing it, and as long as they do it, they remain committed to it. The proverbial person on the street may know little of the doctrine, history, or theological controversies of their religion, but they know its rites, holy days, festivals, pilgrimage sites, and rituals.

5.1 TWO CASE STUDIES

Akitu Festival

The first case study is taken, once again, from the ancient religion of Babylon. (See the *Enuma elish* discussed in Chapter 4.) We will examine a scholarly reconstruction of the Babylonian New Year (Akitu) festival involving a ritual dramatization of the creation story and Marduk's victory over Tiamat.

The Babylonian Akitu festival occurred during the first twelve days of the month of Nisan (March–April). It is a seasonal ritual intended to secure both the continuance of the seasonal cycle (summer, fall, winter, spring) and well-being of the community. According to Theodore Gaster (1906–1992), seasonal rituals follow a fairly uniform pattern:

> First come rites of MORTIFICATION, symbolizing the state of suspended animation which ensues at the end of the year, when one lease on life has drawn to a close but the next is not yet assured.
>
> Second comes rites of PURGATION, whereby the community seeks to rid itself of all noxiousness and contagion, both physical and moral, and of all evil influences which might impair the prosperity of the coming year and thereby threaten the desired renewal and vitality.
>
> Third comes rites of INVIGORATION, whereby the community attempts by its own concerted and regimented effort, to galvanize its moribund condition and to procure that new lease of life. . . .

Last comes rites of JUBILATION, which bespeak men's sense of relief when the new year has indeed begun and the continuance of their own lives . . . is thereby assured.[3]

Assuming Gaster is right about these aspects of seasonal rituals, try to identify each phase as we examine the Akitu festival of Babylon.

The first four days of the ritual were somber, expressing the powerlessness of the king and the desolation of the winter season. Marduk was asked by the priests to have pity on the city. These prayers were offered at a temple called Esagila. The king may have been symbolically slain, and Marduk was regarded as "bound." On the fourth day, the *Enuma elish* was chanted, signifying the passage from winter to spring and from chaos and death to order and new life.

On the fifth day of Nisan the priests enacted rites of atonement. The temple was sprinkled with water, fumigated with incense, and in other ways purified. They beheaded a sheep and rubbed its body against the walls of the temple, thereby absorbing any remaining pollution. This **scapegoat** was thrown into the river. The king was slapped twice by a priest and ordered to kneel in an act of penitence. He was divested of his right to rule, and his crown, scepter, and ring were removed.

During his divestiture, a carnival atmosphere prevailed in the streets. The normal social order was overturned; slaves became masters and masters slaves. A criminal was symbolically enthroned as king, along with stylized combats representing the cosmic battle between Marduk and Tiamat. When the king was reinvested with power and authority, the next phase of the ritual began.

From the sixth to the eighth day, the priests and people symbolically acted out the victory of Marduk over Tiamat. And on the ninth day a triumphant procession of the king from Esagila to the House of the New Year's Feast (the Akitu House built outside the city) took place. On the tenth day a feast was held for the king, gods, and priests. That night the return of fertility to the land is signaled by the return of the king to Esagila, where a sacred marriage is consummated between a female temple slave and the king. This elaborate ritual culminates with the couple emerging from "the chamber of the bed" to great jubilation and another feast.

> Around the shoulders of his beloved bride he has laid his arms . . .
> The king, like unto a sun, sits beside her,
> A sumptuous meal is placed before her . . .
> The king is glad,
> The people are passing the day in abundance.[4]

This ritual operates on two levels: a cosmic and a political level. Cosmically, the fertility of the new year is ensured, and politically, the king's authority is renewed. Gaster remarks that for this ancient community, life is not a progression from cradle to grave but a series of leases periodically renewed.

We can clearly see the pattern of mortification, purgation, invigoration, and jubilation to which Gaster refers. For Gaster, the details of the festival "made real" in concrete time and space this enduring, transcendent, and ahistorical pattern. This festival renews the city, the king, and the people, or so Gaster claims. But is Gaster right?

Little is known about the ancient Babylonian Akitu except that it celebrated the agricultural cycle of sowing and harvesting, and during the era of Ur III (2100–1900 B.C.E.), there was a procession to the "Akitu House" built outside the city. Most of the detailed textual information comes from a much later date (perhaps from around 709 B.C.E. when Babylon was under Persian control. Gaster assumes that later versions were nearly the same as earlier ones and creates his "seasonal pattern" based on a synthesis of rituals from diverse cultures and times. Because he was a member of the myth and ritual school (see section 5.5), Gaster argued, on almost purely theoretical grounds, that the key to the Akitu is to be found in the *Enuma elish* since, according to the theories of that school, myths and rituals are *always* connected.

Jonathan Z. Smith argues that the ritual texts describing the rite do not reflect the ancient Akitu as Gaster thought, but a much more recent version of the ritual that took place during a time when a foreign king sat on the throne of Babylon. It is this historical context that is decisive for interpreting a very puzzling feature of the ritual, the humiliation of the king. The text reads as follows:

(415) When he [the king] reaches [the presence of the god], the *urigallu*-priest shall leave [the sanctuary] and take away the scepter, the circle and the sword [from the king]. He shall bring them [before the god Bel] and place them [on] a chair. He shall leave [the sanctuary] and strike the king's cheek. (420) He shall place the . . . behind him. He shall accompany him [the king] into the presence of the god Bel . . . He shall drag (him by) the ears and make him bow down to the ground . . . The king shall speak the following words (only once): "I did [not] sin, lord of the countries. I was not neglectful (of the requirements) of your godship. [I did not] destroy Babylon. I did not command its overthrow. (425) [I did not] . . . the temple Esagila. I did not forget its rites. I did not rain blows on the cheeks of a subordinate [some translate 'protected citizen'] . . . I did not smash its walls."

(Response of the *urigallu*-priest)

"Have no fear . . . (435) The god Bel [will listen to] your prayer . . . [The god Bel] whose city is Babylon . . . whose temple is Esagila . . . whose dependents are the people of Babylon . . . (445) The god Bel will bless you . . . forever. He will destroy your enemy, fell your adversary." After (the *urigallu*-priest) says (this), the scepter, circle and sword [shall be restored] to the king. He (the priest) shall strike the king's cheek, (450) if the tears flow, (it means that) the god Bel is friendly; if no tears appear, the god Bel is angry: the enemy will rise up and bring about his downfall.[5]

According to Gaster, this humiliation and restoration of the king is a symbolic death and resurrection motif associated with the agricultural cycle. Smith argues, however, that the historical context cannot be ignored. In the context of foreign rule, a number of important questions probably arose. If the king is the divine center of the human community, just as the king-god is the center of the whole universe, then what is going to happen if the king is the wrong king, a foreign king? Do rituals of renewal really work anymore?

Interpreted in that context, Smith asserts that the ritual was not a historical repetition of some ahistorical cosmogonic pattern, as Gaster thought, but a ritual that tried to make sense of foreign rule and send a political message. Smith interprets the slapping of the king differently from Gaster. "If the king does not comport himself as a proper, native Babylonian king (first slapping), the gods will be angry and 'the enemy will rise up and bring about his downfall' (second slapping)."[6] The Akitu festival becomes, given Smith's reading, "a piece of nationalistic propaganda." It is a ritualized way of sending a strong message to a foreign king: either rule kindly, or the gods will punish you. If you rule well, the gods will bless you and protect you along with Babylon.

Does the Akitu have to do with a dying and resurrected god of vegetation and with an act of atonement involving a scapegoat? It is tempting to think so because this helps to make sense of later rituals described in a variety of texts from the Hebrew Bible to the Roman Catholic Mass (especially the pre-Vatican II liturgy). The Jews celebrated a Day of Atonement involving the use of a scapegoat, and the liturgy of the Mass begins with *mortification* (confession of sins and entreaties for forgiveness). The Mass progresses to *purgation*, which starts with a reading from the Bible. (Recall that this phase of the Akitu may have begun with a recitation of the *Enuma elish*.) Rites of *invigoration* follow as the priest consecrates the bread and the wine, transforming them into the body and blood of Christ, and worshipers join in a sacred meal. One of a number of prayers offered by the priest during this phase reads:

> Most humbly we implore Thee, Almighty God . . . that those of us who, from sharing in the heavenly sacrifice, shall receive the most sacred Body and Blood of Thy Son, may be filled with every grace and heavenly blessing.[7]

The Mass ends with rites of *jubilation*, such as prayers, hymns of thanksgiving, and a blessing (benediction) conferring grace. And finally, the central divine figure thought to be present in the Mass is a "dying and rising god" who bestows immortality instead of fertility.

The power of Gaster's theory to explain a wide range of rituals, including Christian rituals, makes it attractive. But we cannot ignore Smith's political interpretation. Smith's theory has the advantage of taking the immediate historical context seriously. Only a detailed and careful reexamination of the evidence for the Akitu festival can help us solve the controversy.

Perhaps both interpretations shed light on this ancient Babylonian ritual because the symbolic nature of ritual allows it to send multiple messages simultaneously.

A word should be said about the significance of the carnival phase in which normal social roles are inverted. These are widespread ritual events. (Think of Mardi Gras, which is still celebrated today right before Lent.) Scholars interpret them as socially useful rituals because they relieve tensions that inevitably build up in hierarchical societies in which classes with power and wealth oppress classes with little power or wealth. It is probable that this is a latent function of carnival rites. Even an outlaw can be "king for a day"! However, there is a more sinister side to carnival. Using Karl Marx's notion of religion as an opiate, we could argue that this temporary relief only serves to make the poor more willing to live in their poverty. It is a small price for the powerful to pay in order to repay the lower classes for accepting their normal state of powerlessness.

Her Alone They Sing Over (Ishna Ta Awi Cha Lowan)

The second case study comes from Native American religion; specifically, it is one of the seven main rites of the Oglala Sioux. Its name is *Ishna Ta Awi Cha Lowan*, which can be translated as in the title of this section or, literally, as "they sing over her menses." I will refer to it as *Ishna*, for short. It is a ritual intended to prepare young girls for womanhood.

The primary sacred power for the Sioux is Wakan Tanka (Great Mysteriousness). Christian missionaries associated Wakan Tanka with the Christian Creator God, which led to the claim that a "primitive monotheism" characterizes Native American religion. More accurately, Wakan Tanka refers to what is most sacred and designates the totality of spirit beings (see J. R. Walker's comments in Chapter 3). Wakan Tanka is identified as the source of the vision that inspired the initiation rite we will be studying.

Native American religion and culture were nearly wiped out by the European invaders of the Americas. However, they have survived against overwhelming odds, and today are in a period of rebirth. Native American religion shows a vitality and ability to adapt to changing circumstances, even in the face of intensive missionary efforts. Out of the bewildering variety of past forms, Native Americans are now developing a Pan-Indian culture and religion that unites the nations and people in new and creative ways.

In 1932, John G. Neihardt published *Black Elk Speaks*, a book that reinvigorated Native American religion and radically changed perceptions about that religion by nonnatives. The book gives an account of Neihardt's interviews with Black Elk (Hehaka Sapa), who was born in 1863 and died in 1950.[8]

Black Elk lived in two worlds. One world, the world of traditional Native American culture and spirituality, he saw destroyed by the European invaders. The other world, the world of the invaders, he entered as part of the cast of the Buffalo Bill Wild West Show and as a convert to Roman

Catholicism. His Christian name was Nicholas, and he learned from the missionaries that the "old ways" in which he had been born and bred were "the work of Satan." However, the old Lakota spirituality lived on in him, and eventually he came to see that his purpose in life was to transmit the old ways to a new generation.

Black Elk was an Oglala Sioux. In 1947, Joseph Epes Brown interviewed Black Elk and the result was a book, *The Sacred Pipe,* in which Black Elk describes the seven major rituals of the Oglala. In the foreword, Black Elk draws an analogy between God sending his son to earth to "restore order and bring peace" and Wakan Tanka turning an animal into a "two-legged person in order to bring the most holy pipe."[9] This animal/person's name was White Buffalo Cow Woman, and, according to Black Elk, she will appear again at the end of this world.

Black Elk introduces his account of this initiation rite as follows:

> These rites are performed after the first menstrual period . . . [and] are important because it is at this time that a young girl must understand the meaning of this change and must be instructed in the duties, which she is now to fulfill. She should realize that the change which has taken place in her is a sacred thing, for now she will be as Mother Earth and will be able to bear children, which should also be brought up in a sacred manner. She should know, further, that each month when her period arrives she bears an influence with which she must be careful, for the presence of a woman in this condition may take away the power of a holy man. Thus, she should observe carefully the rites of purification which we shall describe here, for these rites were given to us by *Wakan-Tanka* through a vision. (116)

Black Elk then recounts how Slow Buffalo had a vision of a buffalo cow cleaning her calf and interpreted this as a sign to introduce new rites to prepare young girls for womanhood. A few moons after this vision, Feather on Head brought his fourteen-year-old daughter, White Buffalo Cow Woman Appears to Slow Buffalo to undergo the new rites he had received in his vision.

Feather on Head was instructed by Slow Buffalo to make the necessary preparations by building a tipi "just outside the camping circle" with a sheltered way leading to it. Slow Buffalo entered the tipi with the young girl and her close relatives, burned sweet grass, and addressed a prayer to Grandfather and Father Wakan Tanka and to Grandmother and Mother, the Earth.

Slow Buffalo, after purifying himself with the smoke of the sweet grass, took a pinch of tobacco and offered it to Wakan Tanka, and the four cardinal directions. With each offering he called on these powers to bless, aid, and protect the young girl and all the generations that will come from her.

The next phase of the ritual was done in secret, with only the close relatives of the girl, the girl herself, and Slow Buffalo in attendance, because it was "too sacred to be seen by all." Again Slow Buffalo purified himself and then "demonstrates" that he has truly received the power to do this rite from the buffalo by singing a song they had taught him:

> *This they are coming to see!*
> *I am going to make a place which is sacred.*
> *That they are coming to see.*
> *White Buffalo Cow Woman Appears*
> *Is sitting in a* wakan *[sacred] manner.*
> *They are all coming to see her!*

Then, as Slow Buffalo bellowed like a buffalo six times, red dust came out of his mouth, "just as a buffalo cow is able to do when she has a calf." He then dug out a hollow in the shape of a buffalo wallow near the center of the tipi and piled the dirt in a mound slightly to the east of the hollow. He placed tobacco in the center of the mound, and made a line with tobacco from west to east and from north to south. Black Elk comments, "The whole universe was now within this holy place."

Slow Buffalo painted blue lines on top of this tobacco cross, and again Black Elk interprets, "Blue is the color of the heavens, by placing the blue upon the tobacco, which represents the earth, we have united heaven and earth, and all has been made one."

Slow Buffalo instructed White Buffalo Cow Woman Appears to stand, and he held a bundle of sacred objects (sweet grass, bark of the cherry tree, and hair of a live buffalo) over her head. Slow Buffalo now declared:

> You are the tree of life. You will now be pure and holy, and may your
> generations to come be fruitful! Wherever your feet touch will be a sacred place,
> for now you will always carry with you a very great influence. May the four
> Powers of the universe help to purify you, for, as I mention the name of each
> power, I shall rub this bundle down that side of you. (123–124)

After the girl sat down, Slow Buffalo recounted his vision from which this rite derives, mentioning how he saw people who turned into buffalo and purified a child/calf. The story ended with the declaration that White Buffalo Cow Woman Appears "is that little calf." Slow Buffalo placed a piece of buffalo meat in her mouth and told her:

> You will cherish those things which are most sacred in the universe; you will
> be as Mother Earth—humble and fruitful. May your steps, and those of your
> children, be firm and sacred! As *Wakan-Tanka* has been merciful to you, so you,
> too, must be merciful to others, especially to those children who are without
> parents. If such a child should ever come to your lodge, and if you should have
> but one piece of meat which you have already placed in your mouth, you should
> take it out and give it to her. You should be as generous as this! (125–126)

After a closing prayer, White Buffalo Cow Woman Appears was brought out of the tipi and presented to the people as a woman. The people rushed forward to touch her because she was full of sacred power. Then a great feast was held, along with a "give away" during which "all the poor received much." Black Elk comments once more, "It was in this manner that the rites for preparing a young girl for womanhood were first begun, and they have been the source of much holiness, not only for our women, but for the whole nation."

It is important to note that the *Ishna* is both a purification ritual and a rite of passage marking the transition from girl to woman. Arnold van Gennep, in his classic study of many different types of these sorts of rites, found that they exhibit three phases: separation, transition, and incorporation. Victor Turner used the word *liminal* to characterize the phase of transition and argued it is characterized by "**communitas.**" (See "Suggestions for Further Reading" for information on van Gennep and Turner.) In a state of liminality people are "betwixt and between" their normal social roles. They exist outside the bounds of ordinary social rules and, socially speaking, are neither fish nor fowl. During this period they experience solidarity with others undergoing the rite or who have undergone it before. A state of egalitarian comradeship exists because all prescribed social roles are momentarily suspended. People feel free and able to truly be themselves in this state of communitas—rather than a child, or an adult, or married, or a student, or any of the other many social roles their cultures expect them to play.

Bruce Lincoln argues (based on a limited number of cases) that van Gennep's phases, while fitting boys' initiation rites into manhood, do not fit girls' initiation rites into womanhood. In the cases Lincoln studied, there was no separation, but there was an enclosing. Since girls had little if any social status in these societies, Lincoln argues that there is no liminal state for women, but what he calls a metamorphosis or magnification in which they are often identified with a goddess, endowed with sacred power, and placed, metaphorically, on a pedestal. Emergence replaces van Gennep's final stage of incorporation, and Lincoln uses the image of insect metamorphosis (caterpillar to butterfly) to indicate that after the rite, the female initiate emerges from seclusion to be presented to the community as a woman.

In the case of the Sioux rite, the first stage is a stage of separation (the girl is taken outside the camping circle), although it is not complete separation because a covered path connects the village to the initiation tipi, much like an umbilical cord. However, there is also an enclosure, since once separated, the girl is enclosed in a tipi, which comes to symbolize, as the rite proceeds, the whole universe.

Since the account I have described is the first time this rite was conducted, it is hard to imagine White Buffalo Cow Woman Appears experiencing communitas with all the other women, because none of them had gone through an initiation exactly like this one. There is, however, clearly a metamorphosis and magnification. She is given new duties and responsibilities. Demands are placed on her that would never be placed on a child. She is, in addition to acting in a holy manner, to be generous, humble, and bear children. She is identified with Mother Earth, the tree of life, repeatedly called holy, and her name itself indicates identity with White Buffalo Cow Woman, the revealer of sacred rites. When she emerges, she is no longer a young girl, but a woman ready for adult roles—marriage and motherhood. While she does emerge from an enclosure, as Lincoln's structure indicates, she is also incorporated into the people by feasting and a "give away" on the part of her family. She is now ready to play new and different roles.

There is clearly a cosmic dimension to the *Ishna*. All the powers of the universe end up in that tipi, the cross connecting the four directions brings order to chaos, and the union of heaven and earth foreshadows the union of male and female from which all good "fruits" will come. The young girl becomes, if only briefly, the very creativity of the universe.

It is of great importance to note that this ritual derives from the vision of a male, is conducted by a male, and that the female plays an almost completely passive role. Women play no significant part in the ritual except to prepare the food for the feast and, if a close relative, to witness it. The father initiates the process, not the mother. Men control this rite throughout. It is conducted by men and ultimately for men, since the roles the initiated woman will eventually play are wife, mother, and domestic servant to her husband. Indeed, the very account we have of the rite is told by a man to a man. Karl Marx would see it as a prime example of a religious opiate, compensating an oppressed class for their sociopolitical deprivation. As Bruce Lincoln puts it, "The strategy is that of placing woman on a pedestal . . . speak of her as a goddess to make her a drudge."[10]

In Sioux society, as in many others, women are considered dangerous during menstruation. Note Black Elk's opening reference to this danger. The ritual that this rite replaces called for separating a woman from the tribe each month during her period and subjecting her to purification rites. Menstrual blood pollutes, or so it was thought. (Blood symbolizes the power of life, and the loss of blood the potential destruction of life.) This reinforces the idea that rituals such as these were self-consciously conducted to control perceived female danger to the community.

While this may be the "dark side" of women's rites of passage, there is also a "bright side"—specifically, the instructions to be kind to the poor and the "give away" by the family in celebration of this happy event, which benefited the poor. These initiation rituals have been and are quite often the means whereby the lives of women take on meaning and purpose. And, as Lincoln also remarks, "This is ultimately the most profound claim that any ritual or any religious system can make: that through their thoughts and actions, people can fill their existence with meaning."[11]

5.2 COMPARISON

From a comparative perspective, major differences between the Akitu and the *Ishna* appear. One is a seasonal ritual celebrated once a year, the purpose of which, among other things, is to continue the seasonal cycle. The other is a periodic ritual, celebrated whenever a girl reaches the age of her first menstruation and her family can afford to sponsor the rite of passage into womanhood. Its purpose, among other things, is to continue the community by sanctifying the passage from infertile girl to fertile woman. The Akitu celebrates the beginning of the cosmos and the coming new year, the *Ishna*, the beginning of womanhood and the coming generations.

The specific activities and events of both rituals also differ. A creation myth and hero myth is told (according to Gaster) at an important juncture of the Akitu, while a report of Slow Buffalo's vision is told in the *Ishna*. There is no sacred marriage in the *Ishna* (although the union of heaven and earth is mentioned), nor is a king involved in any way, because the Sioux had no kings. The atonement and scapegoat theme found in the Akitu is absent in the *Ishna*.

The political and social context, not to mention the historical context, were completely different. Babylon was an ancient urban society dependent on agriculture with a well-defined hierarchy of social classes. The Oglala Sioux were a tribal, nomadic hunting and gathering society with less well-defined social classes. The bison was central to the survival of the people as well as to their religion and culture. I hardly need point out, Babylonian religion and culture did not center on the bison.

In spite of these differences, there are some interesting similarities on a more abstract level. Both rituals involve a cosmic dimension and are concerned with purification and fertility. Both end in jubilation, and both have a death/resurrection motif, although it is prominent in the Akitu (if you accept Gaster's reconstruction) and more muted in the *Ishna* ("death" of the girl, "birth" of a woman). The people, in both instances, believe that the Akitu and the *Ishna* contribute to the well-being of the whole society.

The communitas of the liminal phase of the *Ishna*, if there is one at all, is less apparent than it is in the Akitu. The festive carnival on the fifth day of the Akitu exhibits a sense of communitas as social boundaries are temporarily suspended. Also note that just as an outlaw is made king for a day, so White Buffalo Cow Woman Appears is made a kind of "queen for a day." Indeed, she is made more than a queen, for she becomes Mother Earth and the "tree of life" connecting heaven and earth.

5.3 TYPES AND FUNCTIONS

There are a number of different ways to classify rituals. Typologies are not true or false, they are more or less useful. The typology I provide here derives from Anthony Wallace, an anthropologist, who argues that ritual behavior is the primary and most fundamental aspect of religion, and it can usefully be understood as purposeful or goal-directed behavior. (See "Suggestions for Further Reading.") Religious rituals aim to bring about or to prevent changes and therefore can be classified in terms of the kinds of changes or transformations they are thought to cause or prevent. As I describe Wallace's categories and give examples, see if you can extend the list of examples based on your own knowledge and experience.

1. **Technological rituals** seek to produce or prevent a change of state in nature so that humans benefit in some way. Examples include rain dances, fertility rites, hunting rituals, prayers for good weather, rituals for insuring a good harvest, and the like.

2. **Therapeutic and antitherapeutic rituals** seek to produce a change in the state of human health, either to heal the sick or bring sickness to the healthy. Examples include laying on of hands, anointing, witchcraft and so-called voodoo rites, prayers for health, and a vast variety of healing rituals using eggs, herbs, special ointments, dancing, singing, and sweating.

3. **Ideological rituals** seek social control by changing the mood, behavior, sentiments, motivations, and values of people, usually for the sake of the community as a whole. Examples include rites of passage, taboos that are ritually transmitted, teaching, preaching, studying sacred scriptures, and even "rituals of rebellion," such as carnival, Mardi Gras, and days of the dead (Halloween).

4. **Salvation rituals** seek to change a person's identity from a spiritually corrupt, polluted, sinful, or lost state to a spiritually saved state that provides freedom from sin, corruption, ignorance, and the like. Examples include baptism, communion, spirit possession, meditation, conversion, and altar calls.

5. **Revitalization rituals** seek to revitalize a culture or a religion seen as dying or in the process of being lost. They try to do for the community as a whole what salvation rituals do for the individual. These are not simple rituals, but what might be called ritual movements involving a number of complex actions. Examples include messianic movements like early Christianity, nativistic movements such as the Indian Ghost Dance, and early Mormon attempts to revitalize Christianity. New religious movements (what some people call "cults"), such as the Unification Church, also fall into this category. Political and religious movements such as the Moral Majority find their home here as well.

I think it is clear that the categories of this typology are not mutually exclusive. A single ritual might fall into one or more categories depending upon its complexity and the presence of multiple goals. For example, the Akitu festival is a technological and ideological ritual complex, while *Ishna* is primarily ideological.

Rituals, like myths, have important social functions. The two rituals we have examined in this chapter function to integrate individuals into a group and to reinforce a current social order. Note, however, that if we follow Smith's interpretation of the slapping of the king in the Akitu, we might want to add that the Akitu also contains a threat to overturn the current social order if the foreign king fails to do his duty for the Babylonians. Rituals can be both reactionary and revolutionary.

In addition to providing religious, social, and psychological meaning, rituals serve an expressive function, allowing people and societies to "act out" some of their deepest fears and hopes. In fact rituals are probably more effective than myths in producing a sense of the sacred. Rituals involve bodily movements and gestures, including vocalization through telling, singing, and chanting; whereas myths primarily recount or tell a story. Bodily memory is often deeper and longer lasting than verbal memory. Ritual is religion dancing, and the feel of the dance lasts far longer than the memory of what was said at the dance.

Typology of Rituals

1. Technological rituals
2. Therapeutic and antitherapeutic rituals
3. Ideological rituals
4. Salvation rituals
5. Revitalization rituals

5.4 SACRIFICE AND VIOLENCE

Sacrifice plays such a central role in so many different rituals and as a theme that permeates so much of religious teaching that some scholars argue that to understand sacrifice is to understand religion. The word itself comes from the Latin *sacrificare*, which means "to make sacred." And that is what many have claimed religion is all about—making something sacred.

There are many different kinds of sacrifice. Sacrifices may involve the spilling of blood (for example, the ritual slaying of an animal), or they may be bloodless when vegetable or cultural products are used.

There are numerous theories of sacrifice, and scholars often appeal to one or more of them to explain ritual sacrifice. Any useful theory must explain why humans are willing to sacrifice things of value, such as crops, cattle, oxen, sheep, and even each other, to invisible powers. One theory of sacrifice centers on the principle of "give in order to get (*do ut des*)," which explains why humans are willing to give up things of value in sacrificial rituals. Sacrifices are gifts, given with the hope of a good return on the investment. Giving and getting are basic to human relationships. Exchange establishes a situation of reciprocity. If it works between humans, then it should work to establish reciprocity between humans and gods. Humans offer food, and the gods give prosperity, or peace, or even immortality.

This same principle of giving in order to get also explains why so many sacrifices center on offering thanks. We should always say thank you when we receive a gift. It is not only polite, it may help to get more gifts in the future if we are appropriately appreciative. I do not intend to be cynical here. Undoubtedly, people feel genuine gratitude and wish to express it in some ritual fashion. People may not even be aware that they have mixed motivations when offering sacrifices of thanksgiving. However, if we are to use the theory of *do ut des* (I give in order to get) as a general theory of sacrifice, then it must also explain why people give thanks.

Other theories view the idea of substitution as the key to explaining sacrifice. The most valuable sacrifice is oneself. But mass suicide does not contribute to the survival of the species. If a reasonable substitute can be found, then a basic rule of survival, "better him or her than me," requires that the substitute be sacrificially destroyed. Hence the widespread use of the scapegoat in many religious rituals. The scapegoat is the substitute that allows the rest of the members of a society to keep what is most valuable to them: their own lives.

Frequently the sins, pollution, corruption, shame, and guilt of the group are transferred to the scapegoat before it is sacrificed. The substitution thereby becomes an act of atonement. This allows the substitution system to work. If I am the one who deserves to die because of my sins and corruption, then the substitute is only acceptable to the offended gods or goddesses if it carries my sins and guilt.

It could be the case, however, that my relationship to the scapegoat is not one of identification, but of difference. René Girard (b. 1923) has suggested that the scapegoat is made an outsider, an "other," to the members of a group precisely in order for the group to become aware of its own identity in contrast to the otherness of the scapegoat. (See "Suggestions for Further Reading.") The victim is not like me, but different. It is "not-me" or "not-we," and therefore enacting violence upon it is acceptable.

Girard argues that tensions and conflicts inevitably arise among humans when they form social groups or communities. These conflicts frequently erupt in violence, which threatens the social fabric because an act of violence against one person demands revenge by that person's relatives or the community as a whole. Violent revenge can spin out of control in an endless series of retaliatory acts as we are witnessing today in Iraq. How can these cycles of violence be stopped once they start? Additional violence by some third party does not work because that third party usually gets sucked into the cycle.

Religions developed rituals of sacrifice involving scapegoats or substitutes in an effort to bring cycles of violence to an end by selecting victims (usually animals) that are not from the community and expelling them from the community either by death or banishment. These substitutes, however, had to meet at least two requirements. They had to be acceptable to the feuding parties, and they could not have the power to retaliate violently. Sacrifice, the central act of religion, is, Girard maintains, a violent action paradoxically intended to expel violence that threatens the existence of the community. This is why, among other things, rituals have a sense of urgency about them and an obsessive attention to details that otherwise seem trivial. Everything must be done exactly the "right" way or the ritual will fail.

For Girard, the scapegoat sacrifice is a universal and continually repeated event that occurs in a wide variety of forms and circumstances and holds the key to understanding ritual and, indeed, religion itself. It not only controls, channels, and legitimates violence by ritualizing it, but also renders violence deceptively invisible by cloaking it with the respectability of a religious act done with the blessings of the gods. Religion is not all love and peace. Indeed, according to Girard, a correct understanding of why people sacrifice reveals that at the heart of "making sacred" lurks violence as well as the human attempt to expel it from social life.

Still other theories claim that sacrifices are reenactments of primal events, such as the symbolic slaying of Tiamat or the king during the Akitu festival, or the sacrifice of the Primal Man. Some theories stress that sacrifices should be understood as a means of communication between the gods and humans. As the smoke rises to the heavens, so too do our prayers.

Which of these many explanations of sacrifice should be taken as basic (if any) is difficult to say. All of them contribute something of value to our understanding of sacrifice and its importance to humans. Perhaps humans sacrifice for many reasons, some obvious and some not so obvious. In any case, sacrifice is a complex act that defies simple explanations; but given its universality and persistence, it seems to be of major significance to human survival and well-being.

> ### Explanations of Sacrifice
>
> 1. Exchanges and thanksgiving
> 2. Substitutions
> 3. Ways to channel and disguise violence
> 4. Reenactments of primal events
> 5. Communication between humans and superhumans

5.5 MYTH AND RITUAL

The myth and ritual theory derives its name from one of its major claims—
that myth and ritual *must* go together. They are necessarily connected as "the
thing said" and "the thing done." It follows that one cannot be understood
without the other. They go together like a script of a play (the myth) and the
play performed (the ritual action).

Not all of the members of this widely influential school agree on all
particulars. Some claim that, originally, myth and ritual were combined.
Ritual action requires a recited story as an essential part. Others claim that
rituals came first and myths are derivative, arising as a way of explaining why
certain things were done and to establish their verbal meaning.

Theodore Gaster's theory of the seasonal pattern, which we examined
in conjunction with the Akitu, is an example of the myth and ritual theory.
The seasonal pattern is a ritual pattern intended to renew and revitalize the
social, political, and cosmic order. It involves death (mortification and purgation) followed by resurrection (invigoration and jubilation). The *Enuma elish* is
not, for Gaster, a mere spoken correlate of what is being done, but a way of
translating the ritual, which happens periodically in real time, into an idealized and timeless model that can be told and retold, even when the rites are
not being performed. Myth is the idealization of ritual.

If there is a necessary connection between "the thing said" (myth) and
"the thing done" (ritual), then to fully understand a myth we must discover
or, if necessary, reconstruct the ritual action to which it is linked and vice
versa. The meaning of both becomes clearer when they are, as it were, "read
together."

As I mentioned, the various theories associated with the myth and ritual school have enjoyed enormous popularity. They have been applied by
classicists to Greek myths and rituals, by literary and drama critics to both
literature and drama, and by music theorists to the American blues. Their
popularity has not, however, stopped criticism. While it is true that some
myths are clearly related to rituals, it is just plain "silly," as one critic put it, to

claim that *all* are. Further, the claim that the relationship is one of necessity can never be empirically established.

While there are legitimate criticisms of the myth/ritual theory, the research case with which we close this chapter illustrates the insights of this approach. Both the ritual acts performed during the Passover meal (see below) and the sacred story of the escape from Egyptian bondage mutually illuminate each other.

REVIEW QUESTIONS

1. Describe two important differences and two important similarities between the Akitu festival and the *Ishna* rite of passage.
2. How does Smith's interpretation of the Akitu differ from Gaster's interpretation?
3. What is *communitas,* and what role does it play in rites of passage?
4. How do technological rituals differ from salvation rituals? Provide an example other than the ones mentioned in this chapter.
5. How do therapeutic rituals differ from ideological rituals? Provide an example other than the ones mentioned in this chapter.
6. What is the goal of revitalization rituals?
7. Which of the various theories of sacrifice discussed in this chapter seems most correct to you and why?
8. How would the myth and ritual school interpret the *Ishna* rite of passage?

RESEARCH CASE—SEDER

The *seder* (literally, "order" of service) is a Jewish ritual meal held in the home on the first night of the seven-day holiday of Passover. It is both a seasonal ritual celebrated once a year and a commemorative ritual recalling the exodus from slavery in Egypt. (See the Moses story in Chapter 4.)

The modern-day seder has a long and complex history. It is a combination of what were two separate holidays. One was a pastoral festival of *pesah* (passed over) associated with the new year in the southern tribes of Judah. Central to *pesah* was the sacrifice of a firstborn lamb. Eventually this came to commemorate the exodus from Egypt. The second ancient holiday was a seven-day agricultural festival of *matzah* (unleavened bread) celebrated in the spring in the more northern areas of Israel.

In 620 B.C.E. King Josiah instituted certain reforms in Jewish practice. One of these was the requirement that every male head of a household bring an animal offering to be sacrificed at the Temple in Jerusalem during Passover. This transformed the domestic Passover supper into a pilgrimage to Solomon's Temple, making it a public, cultic act supporting political

Serving Food During Seder

centralization. After the return from exile and the rebuilding of the Temple, the Passover festival continued to be celebrated at home and at the Temple. It may well be this Passover meal (although the evidence is uncertain) that Jesus was celebrating with his disciples in Jerusalem just before his crucifixion. Christians call it the Last Supper, and it forms the basis of the Christian communion ritual (also known as the Eucharist, or the Lord's Supper).

After the destruction of the Second Temple by the Romans in 70, and the forced exile of the Jews, Passover was gradually reinterpreted as a ritual focused on the home and the newly organized synagogues. The sacrifice of an animal was no longer central, and the eating of unleavened bread (*matzah*) became a more dominant symbol.

Today, the *Haggadah* (telling), which recounts the events of the exodus, is recited during the family seder. The story begins with the "humiliation" of the Israelites and ends with their "glory" as they regain the land of Israel and build the Temple. It is both interesting and unexpected that as the story is told in the seder ritual there is no mention of Moses. The myth is told as a story of the people—it is "our story"—and Adonai (the Lord) is given all the credit for the exodus events.

The manual for the seder (also called *Haggadah*) contains a collection of stories, songs, and prayers used at the seder. It prescribes that the oldest male be the "master of the seder." He opens the ritual meal by offering the first cup of wine for "the sanctification of the day," which is followed by reciting the *kiddush*. The *kiddush* tells of God's creation of the world and his selecting the Jews "from every people" and sanctifying them by giving them his commandments.

After the master of the seder removes a shank bone and egg from a platter, he says:

> This is the bread of poverty, which our forefathers ate in the land of Egypt. Let all who are hungry enter and eat; let all who are needy come to our Passover feast. This year we are here; next year may we be in the Land of Israel. This year we are slaves; next year may we be free men.[12]

The seder is an occasion to learn about the history of the Jews, to identify with those who have gone before, and to learn the meaning of certain ritual foods and actions. This process is started by the youngest male asking four questions:

> Why does this night differ from all other nights? For on all other nights we eat either leavened or unleavened bread; why on this night only unleavened bread?
>
> On all other nights we eat all kinds of herbs; why on this night only bitter herbs?
>
> On all other nights we need not dip our herbs even once; why on this night must we dip them twice?
>
> On all other nights we eat either sitting up or reclining; why on this night do we all recline?

Those present take turns recounting the story of the exodus and explaining each symbol present at the table. In the course of doing so, each of the four initial questions is answered.

> The Passover Sacrifice which our fathers used to eat at the time when the Holy Temple still stood—what was the reason for it? Because the Holy One, blessed be he, passed over the houses of our fathers in Egypt. . . .
>
> This *matzah* which we eat, what is the reason for it? Because the dough of our fathers had not yet leavened when the King over all kings, the Holy One, blessed be he, revealed himself to them and redeemed them
>
> These bitter herbs we eat, what is the reason for them? Because the Egyptians made the lives of our forefathers bitter in Egypt . . .
>
> In every generation let each man look on himself as if *he* came forth out of Egypt.

In due course the symbolic meaning of other foods is explained. The *haroset* (a paste made of nuts, fruit, and wine) represents the mortar made into bricks by the Jews while in bondage. A bowl of vinegared or salted water represents the tears of suffering. A roasted shank bone and hard-boiled egg symbolize the paschal lamb. At specific places in the ritual four cups of wine are drunk in celebration of God's deliverance. After a closing set of prayers, the seder ends with hymns, the last verse of which reads:

> Compassionate is he, forceful is he, strong is he, he will build his Temple soon.
> Speedily, speedily, in our days and soon.
> God build, God build, build your Temple soon.

You may have noticed that males do the main ritual action, and only males are mentioned in recounting the events of the exodus. Recently, as feminists have confronted the male dominance found in most religions, there have been rewrites of older patriarchal rituals. E. M. Broner and Naomi Nimrod have created a women's seder. In this seder the traditional questions asked by the youngest male child are changed:

> "Why is this Haggadah different from traditional Haggadoth?"
> "Because this Haggadah deals with the exodus of women."
> "Why have our mothers on this night been bitter?"
> "Because they did the preparation but not the ritual. They did the serving but not the conducting. They read of their fathers but not of their mothers."
> "Why on this night do we recline?"
> "We recline on this night for the unhurried telling of the legacy of Miriam."[13]

This, like other feminist rituals, focuses on the themes of bonding among women and personal empowerment. It replaces language that is today considered sexist if for no other reason than its exclusion of women. Reading the traditional *Haggadah* leaves you with the impression that only men were slaves and only men were delivered. The feminist version exposes that as an illusion. This revision also illustrates how sacred rituals and stories change over time in response to cultural and social changes.

QUESTIONS ON THE CASE OF THE SEDER

1. How does the seder link the present to the past?
2. Using Wallace's fivefold classification system, how would you classify the seder? Why?
3. How would the theories of the myth and ritual school approach the interpretation of this ritual meal?
4. Do you think the revised feminist version of the seder promotes solidarity among women and is empowering? If yes, how does it accomplish this?

Fieldwork Option: Visit a Jewish synagogue during Passover if possible and do a participant observation report.

SUGGESTIONS FOR FURTHER READING

In addition to the material found in the notes, the reader may wish to consult the following for more information.

Bell, Catherine. *Ritual Theory, Ritual Practice.* Oxford: Oxford University Press, 1992. This important work is packed full of useful information and examples.

Burkert, Walter. *The Creation of the Sacred: Tracks of Biology in Early Religions.* Cambridge: Harvard University Press, 1996. See in particular Chapters 2 and 6 for a provocative and fascinating discussion of the biological foundations of sacrifice.

Carter, Jeffrey, ed. *Understanding Religious Sacrifice: A Reader.* New York: Continuum, 2002. This reader contains essays that explore the relationship of sacrifice to topics such as magic, violence, and symbolism.

Girard, René. *Violence and the Sacred.* Translated by Patrick Gregory. Baltimore: Johns Hopkins University Press, 1972. Here Girard explains his controversial and provocative theory of the role that violence plays in religion.

Holm, Jean, and John Bowker, eds. *Rites of Passage.* London: Pinter, 1994. This collection of essays by various authors describes the rites of passage commonly found in Buddhism, Christianity, Hinduism, Islam, Judaism, and Sikhism and Chinese and Japanese religions.

Neihardt, John G. *Black Elk Speaks.* New York: Pocket Books, 1971. Black Elk tells his life story to Neihardt. Neihardt made some important changes to Black Elk's account. For an edited version of the original field notes, see *The Sixth Grandfather,* edited by Raymond J. DeMallie (Lincoln: University of Nebraska Press, 1984).

Turner, Victor. *The Ritual Process: Structure and Anti-Structure.* Ithaca, NY: Cornell University Press, 1969. Here Turner develops the important concepts of liminality and communitas.

van Gennep, Arnold. *The Rites of Passage.* Translated by Monika B. Vizedom and Gabrielle L. Caffee. London: Routledge & Kegan Paul, 1960. Van Gennep explains the structure and function of rites of passage in this groundbreaking study.

Wallace, Anthony. *Religion: An Anthropological View.* New York: Random House, 1966. Read Chapter 3 for Wallace's discussion of his fivefold typology of myths and their functions.

INTERNET RESOURCES

www.heroesofhistory.com/page89.html   At this site you will find more information about Black Elk and his life.

www.gatewaystobabylon.com/religion/sumerianakitu.htm   This site provides an account of the Sumerian Akitu festival, which centered on the moon-god Nanna.

www.rigal.freeserve.co.uk/jewish/seder/seder.htm   Go to this site for more information on the seder symbols.

CHAPTER 6

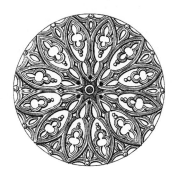

Sacred Space and Time

ONE FUNCTION OF myths and rituals is to establish sacred spaces and times. Every myth of origin, such as the *Enuma elish*, constructs both a place and a time filled with unusual and extraordinary events of power. Every ritual, such as Passover, creates a holy place where the ritual happens and a holy time when the mundane concerns of daily routines are set aside in order to enter a special time of power.

Phenomenologists argue that sacred space and sacred time are fundamental comparative categories. They highlight universal features of all religions because all religions create and express some form of sacred space and sacred time. Myths tell us about the primordial times of the beginning of the universe. Humans renew themselves by making contact with the pristine and holy times in which everything started. Rituals establish a sacred space—a place that is holy and unique. In our ritual behavior we enter this sacred space and thereby come in touch with the power of the sacred. By ritually entering sacred space, we also enter sacred time. In ritual action we temporarily suspend ordinary, profane time and leave behind profane space.

Some scholars of religion, using the comparative method, search for common features in the hope of discovering the basic characteristics of sacred space and time. Fascinated with similarities and often ignoring important differences, they attempt to articulate the essence of sacred space and time. Many claim that sacred space essentially differs from profane space insofar as sacred space is the place where people can make contact with the power of superhuman beings. It is an **axis mundi** or "axis of the world," connecting heaven, earth, and the underworld. It is a place where a road to the divine can be found.

Some scholars also claim that the essential difference between sacred and profane time consists in the direction in which time flows. Profane time is linear, moving from one age to another in succession. The past is left behind as the present arrives, and the future will eventually make the present past. The profane past inevitably disappears, leaving only ripple effects like a rock thrown into water. Sacred time is cyclical and moves in a circle. It always returns to primordial times when everything began. The past, or at least the sacred past in which superhuman power was manifested, is available in any given present.

The linear feature of profane time is not totally absent from sacred time. Indeed many religions teach that time starts with the creation and is moving toward a conclusion, often involving divine judgment. Yet this linear time is different because through myths and rituals we can connect to sacred power at any point along the time line.

The first case study in this chapter focuses on sacred mountains. There are sacred mountains all over the world. Mount Sinai, where Moses received the Torah from YHWH, comes immediately to mind. Others include Mount Everest, the five imperial peaks of Tai Shan in China, Mount Fuji in Japan, Mount Olympus in Greece, Mount Shasta in California, Harney Peak in the Black Hills, and the Andes in South America. Sacred space is always attached to a sacred place. Since prehistoric times, mountains have quite naturally suggested a link between earth and sky—they visually connect humans with their gods. Some of the earliest temples were shaped like mountains, and the grand cathedrals of Europe soar into the sky like mountain peaks. The pyramids of ancient Egypt and of the Mayans are also examples of sacred mountains artificially re-created as sacred sites of connection between heaven and earth.

The second case study has to do with sacred time as well as sacred space, although our emphasis will be on time. We look at the notion of the **Dreamtime** found among Australian Aborigines. This is a time of beginnings in which great power was present on earth. This great power not only created sacred places but also sacred ceremonies and rituals that, when celebrated today, return the Aborigines to this time of power.

The research case at the end of the chapter provides an opportunity to practice your evolving skills as students of religion. You will be invited to interpret the case of the Cathedral of St. Andrew from an outsider's viewpoint, applying methods, theories, and ideas developed in your reading so far. Remember that the outsider's viewpoint sympathetically imagines the insider's experience. This is especially important when dealing with sacred space and time because so much of what the experience means is in how it feels.

6.1 TWO CASE STUDIES

Mount Kilimanjaro

Mountain symbolism is diverse and complex. The mountain as center of the universe, as touching the heavens, as the abode of gods and demons, as the place where the dead go, and as the link between hell, earth, and heaven—all these themes surround and penetrate mountain symbolism. The mountain is awe inspiring, fascinating, and strange. What is up there? Who lives there? Have people climbed it? Majestic mountain peaks like Mount Kilimanjaro prompt us to ask questions that reflect the awe we feel when we gaze on their heights.

Mount Kilimanjaro is located in northern Tanzania on the east coast of Africa. This majestic peak rises more than nineteen thousand feet above the surrounding flat plain and is visible more than a hundred miles in every direction. The contrast between this isolated, towering mountain standing in what appears to be the middle of nowhere, and the flat plain below carries your eyes from an endless flat horizon to a vertical shaft thrust into the heavens. You know immediately that this is something special. You can actually see the earth touch the sky as the top of the mountain disappears into the clouds. If you saw it, you would certainly understand why the Masai call it "house of God."

Mount Kilimanjaro is not one peak but three separate volcanic peaks linked by an elevated plateau. The highest is Kibo, the one most people identify as Mount Kilimanjaro. Mawenzi is the second highest peak, and the oldest and lowest peak is called Shira. The mountain rises through diverse climate zones ranging from dry scrubland, damp jungles, and alpine meadows to arctic glaciers.

To the Chagga people who inhabit the slopes of Mount Kilimanjaro, the mountain is sacred. They tell a story that explains why one of the peaks, Mawenzi, appears disfigured and rough. Very, very long ago, the story goes, when the peaks were still active volcanoes, Kibo and Mawenzi were the wives of Ruwa, the creator. One day Mawenzi arrived at Kibo's home just before mealtime. According to Chagga custom, Kibo had to offer her food. When she finished eating, Mawenzi said she had come to get embers to light her own cooking fire. As she walked home, Mawenzi thought that the food Kibo cooked was very good and, being lazy, she herself did not want to cook. So she returned again just before dinner, saying that while crossing a stream she had tripped and the embers got wet. So Kibo had to feed her again. Mawenzi, realizing that she had a good thing going, came back for a third meal. However, Kibo had prepared just enough food for her husband Ruwa, and she flew into a rage. She began to beat Mawenzi with a wooden paddle, giving her the battered look she has today. People say that Mawenzi is now so ashamed of

Mount **Kilimanjaro**

her battered and ugly face that she hides herself in clouds. Kibo faces away from Mawenzi out of disgust.

This is more than just a charming etiological tale. It identifies two of the most important peaks of Kilimanjaro with the wives of the creator-god. It also reflects the domestic conflicts that must have arisen in Chagga society between wives of a chief or a wealthy man.

Living on the mountain is also a sign of superiority. The Chagga call Kilimanjaro "God's backyard" and regard others who live in the grasslands as inferior to them because they live closer to heaven. As one Chagga said, "You are not a full human being if you don't come from Kilimanjaro. In fact, the higher up the mountain you live, the more fully human and blessed you are."[1] Only men who have received the proper initiation can go to the most sacred region above the inhabited zone, which ends at about seven thousand feet.

Before European missionaries converted them to Christianity, the Chagga thought of the mountain as the embodiment of all that was divine, exalted, nourishing, and eternal. Their chiefs were given the title of Kibo, and they used the name in expressions of good luck and long life, such as "May you endure like Kibo." They regarded the side of a village oriented toward Kibo as one of honor, holding their feasts and councils there. If they met someone of higher rank on the road, they would show respect by allowing that person to pass on the side of the road closest to Kibo. They buried their dead with their heads toward Kibo, and in a year or two, they removed the skulls and reburied them in an ancestral grove facing Kibo. There, it is said, they can commune with the ancestors who dwell on Kibo. The Chagga today, even though Christianized, follow nearly the same burial customs. Most of their Christian churches have their altars on the side closest to Kibo.

Most of the time, in the Chagga language, special words are put before place names to indicate what kinds of places they are, such as "flat area so-and-so" or "point of land so-and-so." Usually the word meaning *mountain* is put before different names of mountains, but in the case of Kibo it is not. They simply say, "I go to Kibo," not "I go to Mount Kibo." Two other places are treated linguistically in the same way—home and heaven. This way of talking replicates in language an important difference between profane and sacred places. Sacred places are like the home we spend our earthly lives in and the heaven where we live eternally.

This case of a sacred mountain indicates some of the rich and complex symbolism associated with sacred places and hence sacred space. While the theme of connecting earth and heaven is less prominent than other themes, there can be little doubt that Kilimanjaro is holy ground. It is where the ancestors live, a home of the gods, and where full humanity can flower. Mount Kilimanjaro both centers and orients the space of the Chagga. It is where they live and work (hence their home), where the very peaks are divine beings, where sacred events once took place, and where they face to show honor and respect. The mountain draws a boundary between profane grasslands and sacred heights as well as a boundary between different kinds of people. It helps anchor and order the Chagga world, giving life meaning, establishing Chagga identity, and bestowing on the people a sense of belonging to a place. It simultaneously serves religious, cultural, and social functions. And its slopes provide food for the people. It is literally the source of their life.

It is difficult to generalize about African religions because they are so diverse. This diversity not only reflects the different ethnic groups and geographical regions but also different historical periods. The religions of precolonial Africa (often referred to as traditional) differ in significant ways from colonial and post-colonial religions. However, there are some common features such as myths explaining why humans die. Among Bantu-speaking peoples, which includes the Chagga, traditional stories explain the origin of death as due to the speed of different animals. The creator God desired eternal life for the people he created but sent that message along with the message of death with two different animals. The one carrying the message of eternal life was slower than the one delivering the message of death so the message of death arrived first.

The post-colonial religion of most Wa-Chagga (plural) is Christianity and the Christian explanation of death is different from the traditional precolonial story relating to the speed of different animals. The Christian story attributes the cause of death to human disobedience while the traditional story attributes it to natural differences among animals.

Diviners, healers, prophets, and the revered ancestors play important roles in many African religions. All of these figures link the divine and the human realms and can communicate important information about events. The ancestors of the Chagga, as we mentioned above, live on Kibo. They can influence the outcome of human actions and hence knowing what the ancestors want is important to the daily life of the people. Kilimanjaro, as the home of the ancestors, constitutes a vital communication link with the past, present, and future.

The Dreamtime

The first human inhabitants arrived in Australia about fifty thousand years ago. They developed without much contact with other cultural groups until Captain James Cook landed in 1788 and claimed Australia for Great Britain. The subsequent European invasion killed 95 percent of the Aboriginal population through massacres, disease, starvation, and forced resettlement. As you might imagine, many social problems of today are the result of this cultural, religious, and human devastation. Imagine 95 percent of the people you identify with dying traumatically over a short period of time.

We must be cautious when generalizing about religious practices and beliefs among Australian Aborigines. Much information has been lost over time, tribes are quite diverse, and all the variations have not been completely mapped. Many changes have occurred over a fifty thousand year history, even though early anthropologists believed these people and their religion were a pure, living example of "primitive" society.

The religion of the Australian Aborigines is usually classified as totemic. Early anthropologists, under the influence of evolutionary models, believed that totemism was one of the earliest forms of religion because it seemed only logical to them that early forms of society would manifest early forms of religion. Today we know that the religion of the Australian Aborigines is far more complex than the simple classification of totemism indicates. The word *totemism* itself comes from anthropologists and does not always accurately reflect what the Aborigines believe and do.

An illuminating example of sacred time can be found in the Australian Aboriginal conception of the Dreamtime or simply, The Dreaming. Aborigines adopted this terminology in order to refer to a primordial epoch, which begins when extraordinary, creative powers rose from the ground, descended from the sky, or appeared from over the horizon. The creative beings of this Dreamtime are called Dreamings and are the ultimate source for all things. Anthropologists called these Dreamings totems, but, as we shall soon see, they are far more than totemic ancestral beings from which a tribe or clan descended.

The English word *dream* often connotes something unreal, but this is not at all what the Aborigines mean by it. The Dream beings are not illusions, although they do often reveal themselves in dreams and trance states. For many they are more real than what we hear and see every day in a waking state.

The Dreamtime is an age of unprecedented creative power when everything we know today originated. However, it is not some Golden Age, after which there is decay over time that will result in some inevitable final destruction. The universe has no end as far as the Aborigines are concerned. If it ever had any evolutionary development, that phase ended with the completion of the creation and the withdrawal of the Dreamings.

According to some Aboriginal myths, the physical world existed as a featureless, formless plain in which spirit beings or Dreamings slept. During the Dreamtime these beings awoke and decreed the laws that govern all aspects of life as well as the penalties for breaking the laws. They established the relationship of each member of the community to the other members and created the ceremonies that must be performed if the created order is to continue. They created animals, plants, humans, natural features of the landscape, tools, rituals—in short, everything of importance that exists today—as they traveled across the land.

After the Dreamings finished their work, they withdrew. The stories of how they left vary from group to group. What is important is not how they left, but what they left behind. They left not only traces of their creative work in the landscape, but also they left themselves in a transformed state.

Jonathan Z. Smith comments:

> In the majority of the ancestral myths, the ancestors are, themselves, transformed into rocks, trees, or *tjurunga* objects as well as the "stuff" of the individual tribespeople. Each feature of the landscape, as well as, each living Tjilpa, is an objectification of these ancestors and their deeds.[2]

Sacred creative time is here fused with space. The creative ancestors are invisible. They are gone. Yet they are not gone. Their handiwork can still be seen in the geography of the land, the ceremonies and songs they left, and in the very people who are their descendants.

In one sense this sacred time of great creativity ended when the Dreamings withdrew and finished their work. But in another sense it has not ended. The creative power they left behind is still effective. This is one reason why the Aborigines say the Dreamtime is eternal, even though they tell stories about when it ended.

Even the present social order is explained by the Dreamtime. While women play major roles in many Dreamtime stories, today males dominate Aboriginal society. According to one story, this came about when two female creators momentarily left their powerful creative objects unprotected and men stole them, thus appropriating their power. As this story indicates, the power of males is derivative from females and achieved by theft. This simple story speaks volumes about gender relationships.

The rituals and ceremonies of the Aborigines recall and "re-present" today the power of the past. Participants wear designs that symbolize Dreamings, and they mime their actions. Each new generation is introduced to Dreamings in their initiation rites. For instance, the Wulamba, a group from the northern tip of Australia, hold an annual ceremony in which the women and children of the tribe wriggle under a mat while the men dance around, poking it with sacred poles. If asked why they do this, they will tell a story about a Dreamtime event in which the Djanggawul beings (a brother and two sisters) created the first humans. The brother pulled children out of the womb of his sisters, and when a girl baby came out it was placed under a mat to protect it from the sun. The mat now symbolizes the womb of the Djanggawul sisters, and the poles represent sacred objects used in the creation.

Though the sacred past is over, it is also not over. The Aborigines have a sacred obligation to make sure it is relived, reenacted, and re-presented so the cosmic order created during Dreamtime will endure. A basic assumption of Aborigine religion is that deities, spirits, humans, animals, and plants form a dynamic, interactive, and interdependent matrix. The present exists only because of the Dreamtime. The present and the future are dependent in a crucial way upon the past. If the past is forgotten—if the Dreamtime ceases to be celebrated in song, art, dance, ritual, and myth—the present and future will die. The power of creativity will cease. Hence the Aborigines are religiously and morally obligated to keep the cosmos in good working order now that the Dream beings have left.

6.2 COMPARISON

At first sight it appears that any comparison between Mount Kilimanjaro and Dreamtime must concentrate more on differences than similarities. We also need to ask whether comparison is even fruitful. What can we learn from a comparative approach that we have not already learned?

I think comparing these cases can highlight certain features that might be useful in cross-cultural analysis. It can also bring the concepts of sacred space and time into sharper focus. Certainly one thing comparison can do is remind us how social values get reflected in religious stories and how religious stories serve to legitimate social values by obscuring their human source.

One similarity is that in both of these cases the subordinate status of women is given religious legitimation. Notice that Kibo does the cooking for her husband and for any guests that might show up. Notice the supreme god Ruwa has more than one wife. There is no tale I know of told by the Chagga that speaks of a woman having more than one husband. In Australia men dominate the ritual and ceremonial affairs and hence inherit from the Dreamings the primary responsibility for keeping the universe running and preventing it from returning to formlessness. A story is even told about how they got this power from a primal theft of creative objects originally belonging to females. Males may dominate now, but only because of a past, primordial deceit.

Gender roles are not the only social arrangements reflected in these stories. The Chagga actually use the location where people live on Mount Kilimanjaro as a way of distinguishing between different social classes. The higher on the mountain people live, the higher their social status, indeed, their human status. The Australian Aborigines use the stories about the ancestors created in Dreamtime to distinguish different groups and their status. These stories of descent not only identify tribes, but also establish their social power.

In both cases space and time become sacred because the stories link them to superhuman beings and their activities. Two important peaks of Kilimanjaro are related to the supreme god by marriage. Kilimanjaro is "God's backyard," and during the Dreamtime the superhuman and creative Dreamings are active on earth. They left tracks that are visible today, and the creative power of the Dreamings can become available today by repeating the rites and singing the songs they created.

People ascribe eternity to both Kilimanjaro and the Dreamtime and yet also talk about them as if they are not eternal. The Dreamtime comes to an end when the Dreamings leave, and clearly the Chagga believe that Mount Kilimanjaro was not always as it is now. What probably motivates this sort of talk is the need of both groups to explain how things came to be and also to make the power of their sacred origins available now. Causes precede effects, so the causes of the present must be in the past. And if the causes cannot be seen now, that past must, in some sense, be over. However, if something is also eternal, people can tap into its power any place they may be or at any time. Kilimanjaro and the Dreamtime are always with the Chagga and the Aborigines no matter how far from the sacred mountain they travel or how far in the past the Dreaming took place.

A comparison of these cases shows that both sacred time and sacred place establish order and hence meaning. Humans order things by establishing connections. Kilimanjaro connects the earth with the sky and orients the living and the dead, the sides of villages, and different structures. The Dreamtime connects the present with the past and orients life around the ceremonies and rituals given in the past that sustain the tribes in the present. People can find the answers to questions about who they are and where they came from in sacred time and space. Answers to these questions not only establish identity, but also promote a sense of belonging. Most people feel more secure when they know their past and the place from where they come.

6.3 FEATURES OF SACRED SPACE AND TIME

Sacred space and time take many different forms. Some of the most obvious sacred spaces are temples, shrines, churches, mosques, synagogues, altars, cemeteries, arks, reliquaries (structures containing relics), convents, and monasteries. Humans create these sorts of sacred places for a variety of purposes such as to pray, conduct rituals, bury the dead, house the gods, store sacred objects, and much more. Within these spaces sacred time is celebrated—the creation; the hoped for time of salvation; the birth or life of a prophet, savior, or holy person; significant past events crucial to a religion's history; and special present events of marriage, baptism, initiations, and deaths.

Some sacred places are natural, such as Mount Kilimanjaro and the features of the Australian landscape. They may be rocks, mountains, lakes, springs, rivers, and valleys. These sacred locations may be places of great beauty and majesty, but they do not have to be physically impressive. Ordinary looking places that only the members of a particular religion find special can also be sacred. Entering these sacred places carries people into both sacred time and space. Frequently, people conduct ceremonies and rites in such natural settings. These places are often associated with some action of superhuman powers, such as conflicts with demons, or special events, such as the Buddha's enlightenment under the bodhi tree.

Sometimes natural settings are combined with constructed spaces. For instance, one of the most famous places of divination in the ancient world was located at Delphi. The site is awe inspiring. Located on a sacred mountain overlooking a vast valley with a grand view of the ocean, one glance tells you that this is indeed a special place. It is also special because of the stories associated with the site. According to one story, Zeus, wishing to find the center of the earth, let two eagles loose from two ends of the earth. The sacred birds met at Delphi; hence Zeus designated it the "navel" of the earth. Like human navels, which mark the center of human beings and the place where they were once attached to their mothers, Delphi marks the center of the earth around which everything is oriented and a place where earth and heaven were once connected. But in the realm of sacred time, once connected means always connected. So a temple compound was built at the site, and from time to time a medium, called the Pythia, went into a trance, was possessed by the god Apollo, and uttered oracles in answer to the questions posed by pilgrims.

Delphi was a gate, or opening, to superhuman power and knowledge. So too are many other sacred spaces. People may enter a mosque, church, or synagogue to talk with the divine through prayer. They may go to a shrine honoring a saint or spiritual hero to ask for healing, a long life, or some special blessing. Native Americans enter a sacred circle to dance, drum, sing, and pray because there they can communicate with the holy. Christians enter special places at special times to become possessed by the Holy Spirit, to offer praise, and to hear the great stories of creation, life, death, and salvation.

In addition to functioning as openings to superhuman power, sacred spaces and sacred times draw a boundary between the pure and the impure. People "enter" and "exit" these places and times. Such places are marked off, distinguished, separated from profane places and times. Those that enter must cleanse themselves with water to wash off the pollution and impurities of daily life. So Muslims symbolically bathe before entering a mosque, the devotees at Delphi washed in a sacred spring before entering the sacred compound, and Roman Catholic Christians cross themselves with holy water.

Besides the boundaries between those within and those without, sacred places draw boundaries among those who are within—between priest and laity, men and women, children and adults, preachers and hearers, healers and the healed, sinners and saints. Sacred places and sacred times can create distinctions as well as erase distinctions. Those who arrive at Mecca for pilgrimage cover themselves with white robes. This act not only symbolizes purity, but also obliterates all distinction of social class and wealth. Everyone is dressed the same. Paradoxically, what is worn in sacred places and times can both establish social and gender differences and conceal them.

Sacred space and time provide opportunities that are uniquely open to superhuman power and mark all kinds of social and religious boundaries. In addition, they provide a stable center of orientation. For example, Delphi is the center of the earth. The spatial and temporal orientation is both vertical and horizontal. Cathedral towers rise from earth to heaven, and under the cathedral the holy are buried. In Europe, cathedrals were often built in the center of town on a high hill. All roads, as they say, lead to the holy city of Rome. From Chaco Canyon, an ancient Native American holy site in New Mexico, roads radiate in all directions.

The sacred history narrated in the Bible orients us in time. Calendars mark time from events that are sacred to different religions, such as the birth of Jesus. Seasonal celebrations like the Akitu, Passover, Ramadan, and Christmas periodically reclaim the past for the present, and the rites of passage mark human development. Religions locate people in time and space, thereby ordering their lives, making time meaningful, and pointing out the way. They provide maps and time lines that help people negotiate life.

Sacred space and time are paradoxical. They are times and places that are here and yet not here. The Dreamtime is not now; yet it is now as the songs

---

Functions of Sacred Space and Time

1. Provide spatial and temporal openings to superhuman power
2. Establish spatial and temporal boundaries
3. Orient people in time and space

are sung, the rituals performed, and the tracks followed. The Dreamings are gone, but what they made remains. The superhuman wives of Ruwa are no longer wandering the high plateau of Kilimanjaro arguing and fighting, yet they are still there as Kibo and Mawenzi for all to see.

Similarly, sacred times and sacred spaces make what is strange familiar and what is familiar strange. The world of superhuman power and the feats of superhuman beings are different and strange to creatures who are limited, conditioned, and powerless in all kinds of important ways, and yet this strangeness becomes familiar and comfortable as people tell about it, sing about it, and celebrate it. And the places and times people know so well—that familiar mountain over there, that date on the calendar, this returning fall or spring—become tinged with the unfamiliar and strange power of the gods when they become holy sites and holy times.

So far I have been giving a phenomenological description of sacred space and time. To change theoretical focus for a moment, let me speculate on the possible biological origins of the human need to create special times and places. We can observe similar behavior in nonhuman animals. Animals have seasonal times for mating, ritualized mating behaviors, and special places they travel for food, shelter, and protection during the year. Elephants have burial grounds, birds annually migrate, salmon return to the stream of their birth to spawn, bears often return to the same dens to hibernate and, in the spring, to their favorite hunting and fishing grounds. The evolutionary value of such behavior is evident.

I am not suggesting that the special times and places that other animals utilize are sacred to them in the same sense as they are for humans. However, they are certainly special. They may well be regularly marked with scent, and protected, sometimes by violent fights often involving injury or death. Humans will also mark their sacred places with emblems, symbols, walls, temples, and frequently fight over them. Think of the battles waged over holy sites in Jerusalem, India, and many other places around the world. The fact that people will lay down their lives for a place or for the freedom to celebrate a holy day indicates that establishing special places and times is as important for the survival of human animals as it is for the nonhuman animals with which we share the earth.

David Chidester and Edward T. Linenthal in *American Sacred Space* show the ways that "ritualization, reinterpretation, and the contest over legitimate ownership of the sacred" establish and reestablish sacred space in America.[3] Too often we focus rather idealistically on rituals that consecrate, memorialize, and turn otherwise "ordinary" land into something holy and special. We ignore or forget the bitter battles fought over such places as the Black Hills. In many ways the fight between environmentalists over issues like global warming and those whose interests are primarily economic are secular counterparts of battles waged with Native Americans over control of what is, for them, the sacred landscape of America. The line between profane space and sacred space is not as firm as some would like to think.

6.4 GLIMPSING THE SACRED

Religion and art are two of the most important forms of cultural creativity. Think of different kinds of art like architecture, painting, dance, sculpture, music, poetry, literature, and drama. Like religion, these arts concern themselves with space, time, order, and meaning. Also like religion, they use symbols, signs, emblems, and codes to convey meaning and elicit emotional responses. It is impossible to do an analysis of sacred space and time without talking about the sorts of art that symbolize, structure, and order time and space and mark them as sacred.

Traditionally, religions have assumed an instrumental view of art: art does not exist for the sake of art, but to serve other purposes. For example, icons (images) such as paintings of saints, while artistically pleasing, primarily serve a devotional function. The consecrated statue of a god makes the god present in space and time. The worshiper who offers sacrifices and prayers to the image is not offering devotion to the actual image or idol, but to the divine *in* the image. The divine inhabits the image or statue, either temporarily or permanently. The image is the instrument or means of the divine presence and not the object of devotion.

The paradox of sacred space and time is repeated on the artistic level. The god is there in the idol and not there. The spirit of the divine dwells in a sanctuary and does not dwell there. This paradoxical and ambiguous relation between what we can call the materiality of art and the superhuman power it symbolizes accounts for the tension often found in religions between creating sacred art and destroying it.

From time to time, **iconoclastic** controversies erupt, and "purification" movements arise. The Protestant "plain style" churches of New England, with few or no images, are a reaction to the elaborately decorated cathedrals and churches of medieval Europe, with their ornate stained-glass windows and profusion of images and statues of saints, angels, Christ, and sacred scenes from the Bible filling almost every available space. The Roman Catholic, Anglican and Orthodox traditions of Christianity have emphasized what Paul Tillich called the **sacramental principle**—the drive to make the material sacred, stemming from the belief in the incarnation of the divine in human form. The Protestant tradition, in contrast, has emphasized what Tillich called the **prophetic principle**—the drive to distance the divine from the material in order to avoid idolatry and allow the world to come under the critical judgment of the transcendent divine. Thus in a traditional Catholic church the altar provides a sacred space to house the consecrated bread and wine, the very body and blood of the crucified Christ; while the pulpit dominates the Protestant church, the place from which the word of the Lord can be proclaimed, condemning human efforts to save themselves and offering hope of divine forgiveness to those who surrender their lives to God.

Some religions remain permanently iconoclastic, forbidding any and all images of either humans or the divine. Judaism and Islam come immediately to mind. Synagogues and mosques are empty of statues and sacred images. Devotion and prayer is directed to a spiritual reality, not a material representation of it. However, even in iconoclastic religions, all art does not disappear. Islamic mosques contain beautiful and intricate geometric designs and calligraphy of the highest quality. Line, shape, and artistic renderings of the Arabic language of Allah found in the Quran remind the worshiper of the revelation of Allah's will. Likewise, Hebrew letters adorn synagogues, and wonderful calligraphy highlights the sacredness of the Torah, as the scrolls containing scripture are exhibited for the devout to kiss.

The Taliban, when they were in control of Afghanistan, destroyed the statues of buddhas carved centuries ago. These were invaluable world art treasures. World culture and history is diminished by their destruction. But the Taliban believed they were on a holy crusade to wipe out idolatry by destroying these precious, priceless statues. Most iconoclastic movements destroy other people's art, just as many believers declare the sacred stories of others to be "mere myths."

Religious art, in addition to serving a devotional function, also serves a teaching function. The great Buddhist **stupa** at Borobudur, Java, visually displays the Buddhist view of reality. The path from the prison of ignorance to the freedom of enlightenment circles its sides. In churches, stained-glass windows tell stories from the Christian gospels. Even the way images or icons are painted can convey information. Many Greek Orthodox icons have elongated and nearly transparent features. The golden light comes from behind the image, telling the faithful in graphic form how they should understand the material world. The material is a veil for the spiritual light that shines through it.

Architecture

Sacred buildings are one of the most visible symbols of a religion's teachings, wealth, and power. Architecture is the most complex of the fine arts and is used effectively by many religions to express their vision of the spiritual. Geometry, building materials, verticality, orientation, enclosure, and ornamentation come together in architecture to create sacred space and time, to teach about superhuman realities, and to inspire devotion. Of the many different kinds of religious architecture, we will focus on three of the most common types—the shrine, the temple, and congregational structures.

Shrines are structures, some simple and some complex, that mark a burial place of importance, house revered relics of founders and saints, or commemorate the site of some sacred, miraculous event. Shrines need not be buildings

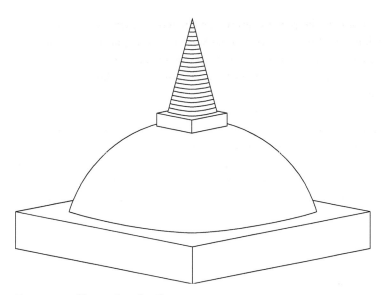

Figure 6.1 Example of a Stupa

intended to house people, but may be simple memorials such as the cross
with flowers often seen by a road. Many shrines mark places of pilgrimage,
so they are often circular or square structures with external space that allows
pilgrims to pray or circle them (circumambulate). One example of a shrine is
the Buddist stupa, a memorial structure inspired by Gautama Buddha's burial
mound. Stupas have characteristic shapes, like the one pictured in Figure 6.1.
In Japan and China the stupa form has evolved into a many-storied pagoda
tower. Pagodas and stupas are emblems of the cosmic order in miniature as
well as homes for sacred relics.

A temple is a building that houses images and statues of gods and goddesses. The temple and shrine are among the oldest types of religious structures. Just as humans require houses, so too do the gods. Temples are homes of
the gods, and the priests attend the sacred images housed there as they would
royalty in a palace. Hindu temples have a square shape because Hindus believe
that the square is the perfect form. They are elaborately decorated with figures
of all sorts, including animals and humans along with demons, gods, and goddesses. Altars are usually outside, in front of the temples, where offerings to
the divine within can be given. Frequently, the area where the gods and goddesses dwell is a darkened sanctuary suggesting mystery and holiness.

Temples are often located in temple compounds surrounded by a wall.
Gates leading into the compound, usually at the cardinal points of the com-
pass, mark the separation of sacred from profane space. There are gates within
the compound itself, marking off different areas, and frequently, in the more
elaborate temples in China, India, and Japan, there will be refreshing gardens,

ponds, meandering streams, and piles of rocks reminiscent of mountains. Often the chanting of monks can be heard, or sacred music will be playing, and it, along with the strong smell of incense, will gently and gradually separate the devotee or the visitor from the profane time of the hustle and bustle of the outside streets into the calm, sacred time of the temple compound. Walking from a busy street in a Chinese city into a Daoist temple compound is like walking into another world.

Congregational structures require a different sort of architecture. Sacred spaces to house worshipers rather than gods and goddesses need to be created so people can congregate with other believers to pray, sing, hear sermons, and read scripture. Typically, these buildings have one roof with a large space inside to hold people together in one place. Jewish synagogues, Islamic mosques, and Christian churches are typical examples of congregational structures. The architecture of these buildings creates spaces for people to congregate and engage in corporate worship.

A Jewish *synagogue* (Greek, meaning "assembly") is not a temple where priests offer sacrifices to the gods that dwell therein, but an unconsecrated house of worship and study created for and run by the laity. Jewish law requires no particular architectural design, and any place with ten males over the age of thirteen and a Torah scroll can serve as a synagogue. However, synagogues do have some features reminiscent of temple worship. This should be no surprise since the temple at Jerusalem located on Mount Zion was the primary place of Jewish worship before the Romans destroyed it in 70 C.E.

Many synagogues are rectangular, with a large room where people can gather. The visual center of the room is the holy ark (*aron kodesh*) that houses the Torah scrolls and is in the wall facing east, toward the holy city of Jerusalem. The ark represents the Ark of the Covenant that, according to tradition, contained the tablets given to Moses on Mount Sinai and on which YHWH had inscribed the Ten Commandments. The ark is covered by a curtain (*parokhet*) symbolizing the curtain that covered the holy of holies in the Jerusalem Temple. Over the ark hangs the "eternal light" reminding the faithful of the seven-branched menorah that burned in the Temple.

Another focal point, in addition to the ark, is a raised platform called the *bimah* from which the Torah scroll is read and singing is led. This platform is often in the center of a synagogue, but may be located on the west wall, where the people enter, or integrated into the front, eastern area, where the ark is located. In Orthodox synagogues, the men usually pray on the main floor, and the women are situated in a gallery above. This separation by gender reinforces traditional patriarchal views with respect to gender. In Reform and Conservative congregations, the genders mix and have no assigned spaces.

The church, like the synagogue, is a congregational structure built so people can gather for worship. However, it does retain some features of temple worship, such as an altar (although the altar is inside the building, not

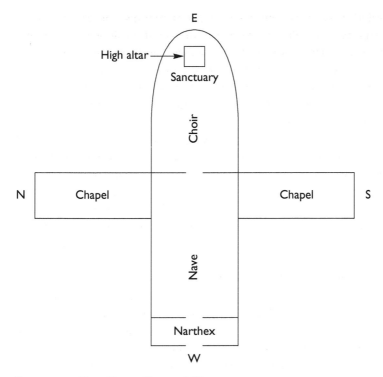

Figure 6.2 Cruciform Ground Plan

outside). The altar is located in either the center of the church or at the end facing east, toward the holy city of Jerusalem.

A popular floor plan is the Latin cross (Figure 6.2). The congregants enter at the foot of the cross (typically the west end) and occupy the nave, which is oriented to the east, where the altar is often located. There may be chapels in the cross arms of the church. Often the baptismal font is located near the west entrance. Other churches have a simple rectangular floor plan, often with a steeple area whose base serves as the entrance. A pulpit is usually located near the front. Modern church architecture takes many forms, with different kinds of floor plans, but, whatever the architecture, there must always be some sort of space in which people can gather to worship.

Major Types of Sacred Architecture

1. Shrines memorializing sacred tombs, relics, and places
2. Temples housing gods and serving as a place of sacrifice
3. Congregational structures providing assembly places

My classification of religious architecture in terms of shrines, temples, and assembly places for congregations, like all classification schemes, is too simplified. Some mosques, for example, serve as shrines, and some assembly halls serve as temples, providing places for the divine presence on the altar. Buddhist temples can be places for housing venerated images of the Buddha as well as places for assembly. The same building can serve different functions, and there are other types of structures such as monasteries and convents that I have not discussed. Whatever the type, all embody the idea of a sacred space in which people can become close to superhuman reality, and the architectural splendor or simplicity reinforces the sacredness of the place.

Music

An art form closely related to religion and even more universal than architecture is music. Myths abound about music coming from other realms or from superhuman beings. These stories indicate that many religious traditions find in music a revelation of something special and otherworldly.

Music, like religion, has the power to transform human lives and to transport people into another time and place. The tension between the here and the not-here is repeated in music. We know that music is made of patterned sound waves that can be mathematically represented. Yet it is so much more than its analyzable structure, precisely because through the music people hear a "beyond," an "other," that is in the sound but not reducible to the sound. Myths, before they became written literature, were sung, chanted, or in other ways musically performed, thereby bridging the gap between myth (what is said or sung) and ritual (what is done or performed).

Ceremonial space, whether it is in a building or in the open, is pervaded by sounds that fill the area with tangible energy and power. The music signals that something special is happening here. It frames ritual activity, often starting it and ending it. It is synchronized with ritual time by techniques such as repetition, contrast, development, and variation.

The Australian Aborigines believe the Dreamings gave their songs to them, and when they sing them now they ritually become their own ancestors. These sacred songs from the Dreamtime are not just sung, they are danced. As the singing and dancing return the participants to that creative time when the ancestors brought all things into existence, the modern-day Aborigines can participate in those creative acts, thereby ensuring health, food, and the perpetuation of the social and cosmic order.

The peoples of sub-Saharan Africa use music and dancing to get into and out of trance states. Changes in intensity and pitch affect the mood of worship. Much of the singing and dancing is repetitive. Repetition is probably the most widespread and basic way to structure time through music. Hindus chant **mantras** like *Om*, which they believe to be sacred sounds that capture the echoes of creation. The chanting of mantras often induces trance states because of the repetition, and it facilitates meditation and prayer by focusing the mind on a sound that reverberates throughout the body. *Om* sounds like "aum" when chanted. The *a* starts with an open mouth and symbolizes ordinary waking consciousness. The *u* occurs as the mouth begins to close and symbolizes dreaming consciousness. The *m* occurs with the mouth shut, is prolonged, and gradually fades into nothingness. It symbolizes sleeping consciousness, and the silence that follows as the sound fades away symbolizes the mystical consciousness where union with absolute reality occurs. *Om* is not merely the leftover echoes of creation; it is a channel, a means, for taking individual consciousness back to its origin and on to its fulfillment.

Music enhances devotion. Bach's magnificent religious chorales carry our emotions away to other times and places, even if we do not believe. Music makes present what is absent and creates moods of exaltation. The start of music marks the beginning of sacred time, and its ending marks the close of sacred time. Without the arts, our sense of the sacred would be greatly diminished.

REVIEW QUESTIONS

1. Explain how sacred space establishes an *axis mundi*. Illustrate your answer by reference to the case study on Kilimanjaro.
2. Describe the differences between sacred and profane time. Illustrate your answer by reference to the case study of the Dreamtime.
3. How do the cases of Kilimanjaro and the Dreamtime show how religions legitimate gender roles and social status. Be specific.
4. Illustrate with clear examples the functions of sacred time and space.
5. Explain how and why sacred space and time are paradoxical. Give two examples.
6. What does *iconoclastic* mean, and how does it relate to the sacramental and prophetic principles?
7. Describe the three major types of sacred architecture, and explain how each reflects the tension between the presence and the absence of superhuman powers.
8. Using the mantra *Om* as an example, discuss how music can both enhance devotion and teach "sacred truths."

RESEARCH CASE—THE CATHEDRAL OF ST. ANDREW

The Cathedral of St. Andrew is located at Wells, England. Its architectural style is Gothic. Among other things, Gothic designates a style developed in Western Europe between the twelfth and sixteenth centuries. It is characterized by the use of ribbed vaulting, pointed arches, and steep roofs. Cathedrals are Christian churches that contain the *cathedra*, or "throne," of a bishop.

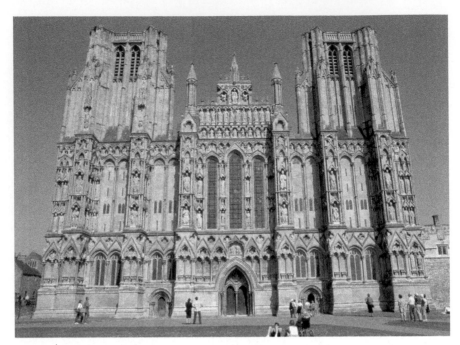

The Cathedral of St. Andrew at Wells, England

Wells is located in a lush countryside with deep springs or "wells." The abundant water supports rich and luxurious vegetation. The location is peaceful and quiet, adding to the grandeur of the church. It may well have been a Celtic sacred site prior to the Christianizing of England. The construction started before the end of the twelfth century, and, while additions and restorations have taken place since, much of the original structure survives today. It is no longer a Roman Catholic church, however, but an Anglican church. During the sixteenth century, Protestant iconoclasts plundered and desecrated the church. In 1685 it was used by Protestant troops as a stable.

The ground plan is in the form of a cross, or *cruciform* (see Figure 6.2). The main body of the church is divided into three main sections—the sanctuary, the choir, and the nave. As you approach the main entrance, which is located at the foot of the cross facing west, you see two massive towers in which there are niches containing various sculptures representing saints, angels, and biblical scenes, one of which shows the dead rising naked from their tombs. There are about three hundred figures, some as tall as eight feet and many smaller ones. At one time the west front was covered with a variety of stunning colors—silver, gold, scarlet, purple, and blue. At sunset, just looking at the front must have transported people, however briefly, into heaven. The whole cathedral, but especially the front, is a virtual "sermon in stone."

The Nave of Wells Cathedral

As you enter through large and impressive doors, you find yourself in a porch area called the *narthex*. There is a small fountain containing holy water, which has been blessed for the special purpose of defeating the devil. Worshipers dip their fingers into this water and make the sign of the cross on themselves, thereby symbolizing the baptism that first made them members of the church or "Body of Christ."

Beyond the narthex is the nave, where the lay worshipers stand facing east toward the choir and sanctuary, which contains the high altar. The baptismal font is on the extreme west wall of the nave, just beyond the narthex. Baptism is the first of seven sacraments practiced in the Roman Catholic Church. (Protestant Christians usually recognize only two of the seven, baptism and Holy Communion, as genuine sacraments.) The faithful believe that baptism washes their sins away and inducts them into the Body of Christ. The other six sacraments are holy chrism or confirmation, the mass that celebrates the Eucharist, penance or absolution, holy matrimony, holy orders (ordination), and anointing of the sick.

The pulpit is located before the sanctuary and choir at the front of the nave. Near there, you find what is called the *crossing*. It is the place where the arms of the cross intersect with the main part of the church. The two arms are usually referred to as the north transept and the south transept. In the Cathedral of St. Andrew, chapels dedicated to St. Calixtus and to St. Martin occupy the transepts. One of the rare works of Christian art showing God the Father is found on a tomb in the chapel of St. Calixtus. God the Father is shown seated in majesty upon a throne, and between his knees is a cross bearing the crucified body of Christ, the Son of God.

The stained glass windows of St. Andrew present abstract arrangements of different colored glass. They are constructed from pieces of glass taken from the windows destroyed by reforming Protestants. The present abstract forms are nonrepresentational and give an almost modern feel to this ancient cathedral.

The tombs of bishops and nobles on the sides of the nave are elaborately decorated. One on the south wall has a panel portraying the annunciation to Mary that she would be the mother of the Messiah. Mourners are also depicted along with the Holy Trinity. Wells was not a major pilgrimage site because it had no saint of its own, but one bishop who had good teeth was venerated by the laity as a saint in the late thirteenth century because people believed that a visit to his grave can cure dental troubles.

Footfalls of nearly seven centuries have worn down the eighteen-step stairway linking the north transept with the Chapter House, where the clergy of Wells deliberated. From earliest times it is said that visitors called these steps "the heavenly stairs." Inside the Chapter House, at the head of the stairs, are fifty-one stalls raised above a bench. A window ledge bears the painted arms of King James I with a Latin inscription declaring the king to be the "nurturer" of the church.

Inside the north transept stands the oldest clock in England. It dates from the fourteenth century. Every hour on the hour horsemen engage in a tournament. Also, Christ rises and ascends to heaven. Symbols of the four evangelists (Matthew, Mark, Luke, and John) adorn the four corners. The clock displays the twenty-four hours of the day along with the month and phases of the moon. The Greek goddess of the moon, Phoebe, is painted on the central disk of the circular moon window. A Latin inscription proudly declares, "This spherical globe shows the world in microcosm, its archetype."

Within this fantastic space, the main Christian rites of passage, called sacraments (baptism, confirmation, ordination, and marriage) were celebrated. In addition, the mass was celebrated every day. Catholics believe that in the mass the bread and wine become the body and blood of Christ. Participation unites worshipers with the death and resurrection of Christ and bestows the grace of God's forgiveness and assurances of eternal life. Also within this space each year the sacred seasons of the Christian calendar were and are celebrated.

The Christian year starts with the season of Advent (four weeks) when the announcement and preparation for the birth of the savior are celebrated. It is followed by Christ Mass (Christmas), or the celebration of the birth of Jesus the Christ, lasting twelve days. The season of Epiphany, celebrating the appearance of Jesus as the Christ, is celebrated for one to six weeks.

The season of Lent (forty days) follows Epiphany, during which the faithful seek forgiveness of their sins and perform penance. Lent culminates in the Easter, or Paschal, season, which celebrates the resurrection and ascension into heaven of Jesus the Christ. The Day of Pentecost, also known as Whitsunday, ushers in the long Trinity season. Pentecost celebrates the founding of the Christian church when the Holy Spirit inspired the first apostles to spread the gospel, or good news, that Christ has overcome death. Trinity ends with All Saints' Day, and then the cycle begins again with Advent. Interwoven within this cycle are Old Testament events that serve as prophecies intended to validate the ritual events and the Christian story. Alan Watts writes:

> From this point of view, history begins with Adam and begins again with Christ, so much so that what happens in between occurs within a epoch of darkness wherein God is known only through "types and shadows." That is to say, the *Old Testament*—the Law of Moses, the Prophets, and the history of Israel—is significant to the Catholic mind only because it is a symbolical foreshadowing of Christ. Thus the *Old Testament* stories enter into the Christian story in so far as they seem appropriate "types" of the various "mysteries" of the life of Christ which are celebrated throughout the course of the Christian year.[4]

At the Cathedral of St. Andrew in Wells, sacred space, time, history, art, and ritual all blend in a complex aesthetic experience of the sacred. The mysteries of the faith are revealed, yet concealed enough to elicit that sense of awe and mystery so essential to religion. Now you see it and now you don't. The sacred presence is felt in, around, and under the stone, the statues, the incense, the chanting, the stained glass, and the architecture, but it is never quite captured by it. In the end, the spirit blows where it will, no matter how inspired and brilliant humans are at bringing it into time and space.

QUESTIONS ON THE CASE OF THE CATHEDRAL OF ST. ANDREW

1. In what ways do the architecture and decoration of the Cathedral of St. Andrews at Wells announce that this is sacred space?
2. Why do you think the cathedral is oriented toward the east? What is the significance of entering the church from the west?

3. What is the significance of the cruciform ground plan? Why do you think important people like bishops and nobles are buried in the church?
4. What connections do you see between this case and the first two cases that opened this chapter? Be specific.

Fieldwork Option: Visit a Roman Catholic church or cathedral. Pay particular attention to the art and architecture. Write a report on the sacred significance of the art

SUGGESTIONS FOR FURTHER READING

In addition to the material found in the notes, the reader may wish to consult the following for more information.

Andronicos, Manolis. *Delphi.* Athens: Ekdotike Athenon S.A., 1976. This book contains a description with pictures of the history and archeology of Delphi.

"Architecture and Religion." In *The HarperCollins Dictionary of Religion,* edited by Jonathan Z. Smith, 67–71. San Francisco: HarperCollins, 1995. I am indebted to this article for basic information about temples, shrines, and congregational structures.

Bernbaum, Edwin. *Sacred Mountains of the World.* Berkeley: University of California Press, 1997. This book is filled with beautiful pictures of sacred mountains from around the world, along with insightful commentary.

Eliade, Mircea. *The Sacred and the Profane: The Nature of Religion.* Trans. Willard R. Trask. New York: Harper and Row, 1961. The first two chapters contain a classic and widely influential study of sacred space and time.

Holm, Jean, and John Bowker, eds. *Sacred Place.* London: Pinter, 1994. This collection of essays by various authors describes sacred place in different religions.

Kessel, Dmitri. *Splendors of Christendom.* Lausanne, Switzerland: Edita Lausanne, 1964. This is a truly marvelous photographic collection, with commentary, of different kinds of churches ranging from Byzantine to modern. The chapter on Wells is particularly helpful.

van der Leeuw, Gerardus. *Sacred and Profane Beauty: The Holy in Art.* Trans. David E. Green. New York: Holt, Rinehart and Winston, 1963. The author provides a classic phenomenological study of the differences between sacred and profane art.

INTERNET RESOURCES

www.everyculture.com/wc/Tajikistan-to-Zimbabwe/Chagga.html   The Chagga are the third largest ethnic group in Tanzania. For general information visit the above site.

www.newyorkcarver.com/cathedrallinks2.htm   This site gives a virtual tour of great Gothic cathedrals.

http://members.tripod.com/siekman/religion.html   At this site you will find basic information about the Australian Aboriginal religion.

CHAPTER 7

Experiencing the Sacred

In 593 B.C.E. a priest named Ezekiel had a vision of a heavenly throne with fire shining bright around it. Ezekiel took this vision as the appearance of the "likeness of the glory of the Lord." With the vision came a voice calling Ezekiel to undertake a prophetic ministry to the "rebellious people of Israel" who were in exile in Babylon (Ezekiel 1 & 2).

Somewhere around 531 B.C.E. a man named Siddhartha Gautama sat down under a tree in India to meditate. While meditating he achieved enlightenment. Wisdom, serenity, and release from suffering came with this enlightenment. The gods rejoiced and the demons ran in fear. This man arose from his meditation as a buddha, a perfectly and completely enlightened being.

Around 35 C.E. a Jew named Saul set out on the road to Damascus to investigate the Jews in the synagogues there to see if they were members of a new Jewish movement called the Way. The Jewish sect to which Saul belonged regarded the Way as a heresy because it taught that a man named Jesus was the Messiah ("Christ" in Greek) sent by YHWH to redeem the Jews. On the road to Damascus Saul was temporarily blinded by a bright light from heaven and heard a voice saying, "Saul, Saul, why do you persecute me?" Saul asked, "Who are you?" The voice replied, "I am Jesus, whom you are persecuting . . ." This experience converted Saul to the new movement, and he became Paul, the apostle (messenger) for the Way. He helped to convert others and to turn this Jewish movement into a new religion that today we call Christianity.

I am not concerned with the historical accuracy of these accounts. Rather, I wish to pose a question. If you had to classify all of these different experiences under a single title, what would you call them? Most likely you would call them all, no matter how different they are, "religious experiences." But why would you call them that? What is it about them that makes them religious?

Scholars coined the term *religious experience* some three hundred years ago as a convenient way to refer to a wide variety of different experiences. It is a collective term that gathers together many different kinds of experiences— enlightenment, prophetic calls, visions, voices, conversions, revelations, and many more. What could all of these different experiences have in common that would allow us to refer to all of them by the same term?

Ever since the term was first coined, scholars have been debating that question. Some maintain, as we shall see below, that there is a common core to these experiences; others maintain there is not. While controversies rage about exactly what is meant by religious experience, one thing is clear—we have to pay close attention to what the person having the experience says about it. Two people can experience an inexplicable bright light. One may exclaim it is the light of the Lord, and the other finds it a curious, abnormal event of no great moment. A **religious experience** can be any kind of experience, from visions and voices to intense feelings of love and devotion, that the person having the experience believes to be religiously significant.

Much of this chapter will be devoted to discussing what might make an experience religiously significant for someone. First, however, that ambiguous word *experience* needs to be clarified. This word can refer to sensations, emotions, conceptual thought, intuitions, hallucinations, dreams, ecstatic states of great joy, and moments of serene calm. Besides having a variety of meanings, there is another ambiguity that is significant in our study of religious experience. It amounts to the difference between "I *seem* to see a book" and "I *see* a book." The first refers to what immediately appears to someone's consciousness. If the person is telling the truth, then we cannot doubt that he or she "seems" to be seeing a book. But seeming to see a book and actually seeing a book are two different things. The second statement, "I see a book," can be doubted because there may in fact be no book present to be seen. The person could be dreaming or imagining. That people seem to see books is quite true, but it is not the same as actually seeing real books.

We must keep that distinction in mind when we study religious experiences. Undoubtedly, Ezekiel and Paul *seemed* to hear a voice. But that is not the same as hearing a voice. A question about the reality of the object of an experience is different from a question about what someone's immediate experience was like. What it was like is what they reported it to be like. However, critical questions can still be raised. Most religions admonish their followers to "test the spirits."

After examining two classic cases of religious experiences, one from Islam and the other from Buddhism, we will examine some attempts to organize these experiences into types. Two particular types will receive more detailed study: shamanic ecstasy and mysticism. While there are many different theories about religious experience, we will focus on the psychoanalytic theories of Sigmund Freud and Carl Jung. Our research case will return to an examination of mystical experience by looking at one of the great mystics of the Christian tradition, St. Teresa of Avila.

7.1 TWO CASE STUDIES

Muhammad

One night in 610 a forty-year-old Arab named Muhammad ibn Abdullah (ca. 570–632) was in a cave on Mount Hira near a city in Arabia called Mecca. Suddenly he heard a voice, a voice like reverberating bells. The voice said, "Recite!" Startled and frightened, Muhammad stammered that he did not know what to say. Once again the voice commanded him to recite, and once again Muhammad replied that he did not know what to recite. Finally, words came to him: "Recite in the name of your Lord who has created, Created man out of a germ-cell. Recite for your Lord is the Most Generous One Who has taught by the pen, Taught humans what they did not know" (Quran 96:1–5).

Muhammad did not know what to make of this experience, just as he did not know what to make of previous experiences that occurred when he was sleeping in the cave and dreaming. On one of these previous occasions a mysterious, personal presence had come to him and announced, "Muhammad, you are the Messenger of Allah." He was so struck by terror that he feared he might be going mad or some *jinn* (desert spirit) was playing tricks on him. Where was the voice coming from? What did these experiences mean?

Islamic tradition tells us that Muhammad consulted his wife, Khadija, who assured him he was not mad. She suggested they speak with her cousin Waraqa ibn Qusayy, who was a Christian. Khadija thought that she might know about such things because Christians had prophets to whom Allah spoke. Waraqa told Muhammad that the voice had been "sent down" by Allah through the angel Gabriel and that Muhammad had been called to be a prophet to his people.

The night when the recitations started is called, in later Islamic tradition, "The Night of Power and Excellence," because it was the beginning of a series of revelations to Muhammad lasting about twenty-two years. At first, when Muhammad shared these recitations, proclaiming them to be revelations from Allah, many of his people did not believe him. However, he was eventually accepted as a prophet and became known as the "Messenger (*Rasul*) of God."

Eventually Muhammad's revelations were written down in a book called the Quran (The Recitation). This book became the basis for a new religion called Islam (submission) whose followers are called Muslims (those who submit). In addition to the Quran, Muslims recognize both the Hebrew Bible (Old Testament) and the New Testament as containing revelations to prophets who preceded Muhammad. However, Muslims believe that the prophetic era, which started with the Jews, came to an end with Muhammad and that the Quran is the definitive and final revelation from God.

The first converts came from Arabia, where Muhammad lived and preached, but eventually Islam became a worldwide religion. Today it numbers about 1.2 billion members and is the second largest religion in the world. It is also the fastest growing religion in the United States.

The central core of Islamic teaching and practice is to be found in the **Five Pillars of Islam.***

1. Witness that there is no God but Allah and that Muhammad is his Prophet.
2. Perform mandatory prayers five times a day.
3. Give alms to the poor.
4. Fast from sunrise to sunset during the month of Ramadan.
5. At least once during life make a pilgrimage to Mecca.

While Muhammad came to believe that the voice he heard involved a movement from heaven to earth, another experience, known as the "Night Journey," involved a movement from earth to heaven. The story of this journey occurs in the Hadith (report), which is a collection of narratives about the actions and sayings of Muhammad. It is second only to the Quran as an authoritative source for Muslims.

The Kaaba, a Meccan shrine once central to pre-Islamic Arab polytheism, continued to be a sacred shrine and holy site for Islam once it was purged of its many idols. One night when Muhammad was sleeping near the Kaaba, a remarkable event took place. It is uncertain whether it was originally considered to be a dreamlike, spiritual experience or an actual physical event, but the angel Gabriel came to the sleeping Prophet and, after splitting open his chest and belly, drew out Muhammad's heart and bowels. Gabriel washed these in a golden basin "filled with faith" (another version has Zamzam water from the spring beneath the Kaaba) and replaced them in the Messenger's body, which was then closed up.

After this, a small horse, whose name was Buraq and is often depicted with the head of a woman, was brought to Muhammad and he mounted. Gabriel then led Muhammad through the sky to Jerusalem, where Muhammad prayed at the holy temple, referred to by Muslims as the "farthest mosque."[1] Gabriel then led Muhammad in an ascent through the seven heavens. At the first heaven the gatekeeper asked, "Who is it?"

---

* Different groups of Muslims have different lists of pillars, but these five make up the most common list.

Gabriel answered, "Gabriel." It was asked, "Who was accompanying you?" Gabriel replied, "Muhammad." It was asked, "Has Muhammad been called?" Gabriel replied in the affirmative. Then it was said, "He is welcomed. What an excellent visit his is!" The gate was opened, and when I went over the first heaven, I saw Adam there. Gabriel said (to me), "This is your father, Adam; pay him your greetings." So I greeted him and he returned the greeting to me and said, "You are welcomed, O pious son and pious Prophet."[2]

In the second heaven Muhammad saw Yahya (John) and his cousin Isa (Jesus). He saw Joseph in the third heaven, and eventually he met Moses in the sixth heaven. Moses wept because the followers of the Prophet Muhammad "will reach Paradise in greater numbers" than the Jews. In the seventh heaven Muhammad meets Abraham and ascends to the "farthest limit" of the heavens:

> Then Al-Bait-ul-Ma'mur (i.e., the Sacred House) was shown to me and a container full of wine and another full of milk, and a third full of honey were brought to me. I took the milk. Gabriel remarked, "This is the Islamic religion which you and your followers are following." Then the prayers were enjoined on me: They were fifty prayers a day (147).

On the descent Muhammad passed Moses, who asked what he had been ordered to do. Muhammad replied that he had been commanded to enjoin on the faithful fifty prayers a day. Moses said that people cannot bear that many prayers and told Muhammad to go back to Allah and ask for a reduction. Allah reduces them to forty, but again Moses advises that this is too much and instructs Muhammad to go back to Allah for more reductions. After repeated trips between Moses and Allah, bargaining over the number of prayers Muslims must say a day, the number five was finally agreed upon.

Later, when an Islamic mystical movement called **Sufism** developed, the mystic Sufis placed great importance on the Night Journey and traced their authority back through a long line of *shaykhs*, or masters, to Muhammad, who "had been with God." For them, this Night Journey into the heavens showed that Muhammad himself was not only a prophet, but a mystic as well.

It is clear that the main focus of these stories is not on giving precise and detailed information about the psychological features of Muhammad's experiences. They probably were embellished as they were orally passed on in the Muslim community, and when they were written down, it is clear that the editors' purpose was, in part, to establish Muhammad's authority as the Messenger of Allah. Nevertheless, they provide us with enough information to discern the kinds of experiences that stand behind the stories.

The first collection of experiences is revelational.[3] These sorts of experiences involve a human becoming an agent or spokesperson of the divine. Revelations can be personal or communal. In the personal type, the message relates primarily to the life of the individual who receives the revelation. In the communal type, the revelation relates to a wider group of people.

Muhammad's first experiences of the angel Gabriel commanding him to recite are communal. Revelations of this sort continued for some years until the entire Quran was completed. Hence Muslims believe that the Quran contains the very words of Allah transmitted by Gabriel to Muhammad in Arabic.

According to the influential German sociologist Max Weber (1864–1920), we can distinguish between emissary prophets and exemplary prophets. **Emissary prophets** believe that the divine has commissioned them to convince others to believe the messages revealed to them concerning a wide variety of topics such as how to worship, how people should conduct their lives, and what is proper to believe. **Exemplary prophets** see their task as helping others have their spiritual experiences rather than convincing others to believe what they have to say. It seems clear that Muhammad understood his experiences with Gabriel as commissions to be an emissary of Allah.

If we understand **ecstatic** experiences to involve intimate contact with gods, goddesses, spirits, or God, with the primary psychological feature of losing control of one's self, then Muhammad's Night Journey is more ecstatic than revelational (although it does include a revelation concerning how many times a day Muslims should pray). The English word *ecstasy* comes from a Greek word, which literally means "to stand outside of one's self." Two widespread and common forms of ecstatic experiences are possession by some spiritual force, which temporarily replaces the normal personality, and extraordinary out-of-body journeys to spiritual realms. The Night Journey to Jerusalem and the ascent through the seven heavens is an extraordinary, ecstatic journey.

Muhammad's hearing of voices and his ecstatic journey may be associated with dreaming, as some of the traditions indicate. This might cause the modern reader to doubt the authenticity of Muhammad's experiences. However, we must remember that one of the first theories of dreaming in the ancient world was the theory that spiritual powers communicated to humans through dreams. The fact that you dreamt something was not a strike against the authenticity or truth of what you dreamt at that time, but a strike in favor of authenticity, particularly if the dream involved revelations from spiritual agents.

These stories functioned among Muslims to confirm Muhammad's status as a prophet and the divine authority of the Quran. They also functioned, as the Night Journey clearly indicates, to affirm the superiority of Islam over both Judaism and Christianity, its monotheistic rivals. Jesus is only in the second heaven, and while the Jewish prophets Moses and Abraham are encountered in the higher heavens, none gets as far as Muhammad does. The message is clear: the Prophet Muhammad supersedes all previous prophets.

It is interesting that, at first, Muhammad himself doubts the authenticity of his experiences. He was well aware that the insane hear voices and that demons can be the source of misleading revelations. His doubts are an important clue to how people come to ascribe religious significance to their experiences. The characteristics of these experiences (hearing voices, ecstatic travel to the heavens) may be uncommon, but there is nothing about them that compels people to conclude they come from a divine source. It is the judgment that they are authentically divine that gives them their religious significance. A different judgment would result in a different conclusion, such as "it may have been just a weird dream."

This is an important point to keep in mind because, as we shall see, scholars have spent much time and energy looking for some distinctive characteristic of experiences that makes them religious. It may well be that the religious quality of certain experiences has less to do with emotional features and more to do with judgments made about them, judgments that enter into the experience itself, or are made after the fact. Once Muhammad was convinced that it was indeed an angel sent by Allah who was speaking to him, the subsequent revelations not only increased, but also were identified immediately as revelations from Allah.

Types of Religious Experiences

1. Revelational
   a. Individual or communal
   b. Exemplary or emissary prophets

2. Ecstatic
   a. Possession
   b. Out-of-body

The Buddha

A son of a king living in northern India, named Siddhartha Gautama (566–486 B.C.E. or 448–368 B.C.E.), became enlightened and thereby joined an illustrious host of enlightened beings called buddhas. However, this particular buddha, often called Shakyamuni ("shak-yu-moo'ne"), meaning "sage of the Shakya clan," became the founder of what is today the fifth largest world religion with some 370 million adherents.

The dominant religion of his own day was ancient Hinduism, sometimes called Vedic Hinduism. It contained polytheistic, henotheistic, and monotheistic elements. However, in Siddhartha's eyes, questions concerning the gods and offering sacrifices to them seemed unimportant compared to the great human task of becoming enlightened.

After his enlightenment experience, the Buddha[†] preached what has become known as the core of Buddhism, the **Four Noble Truths**:

1. There is suffering.
2. The cause of suffering is desire.
3. There is a way to overcome desire and become free from suffering.
4. The **eightfold path** leads to freedom from suffering.

This eightfold path leads to **nirvana**, or release from suffering and from the nearly endless cycle of rebirths that keep people attached to lives of suffering. The path is known as the **Middle Way** because it avoids the extremes of living a life of severe austerity and living a life of self-indulgent pleasure seeking. It consists of:

1. Right understanding
2. Right thoughts
3. Right speech
4. Right action
5. Right livelihood
6. Right effort
7. Right mindfulness
8. Right concentration

Following the first two disciplines (right understanding and thoughts) leads to wisdom about the nature of reality and about the nature of one's own self. Cultivating the morality associated with right speech, action, and livelihood leads to living an appropriately ethical life of compassion toward all living beings. The practices associated with the last three (right effort, mindfulness, and concentration) lead to developing the appropriate mental discipline for expanding awareness and stilling the mind.

According to tradition, his father secluded Prince Siddhartha in the palace to protect him from the outside world. He married, had a son, and lived a life of luxury in the palace. Then one day he ventured forth, curious about the outside world. He was immediately horrified by the misery and suffering he found among those less fortunate than himself. He vowed to find the solution to suffering and, leaving the palace and his family, ventured forth seeking a teacher who could show him how suffering can be overcome.

He began to practice extreme austerities, eating barely enough to keep alive, drinking little, and living under harsh conditions. His teachers claimed that by engaging in ever more severe ascetic practices he could learn to gain complete control of his body and detach himself from pain. Prince Siddhartha practically starved himself to death, but he found that he did not overcome

---

[†] I will capitalize Buddha whenever I am referring to the historical Buddha (also called Shakyamuni and Siddhartha Gautama). Buddha is a title, not a family name.

suffering by this means. Remembering a meditative trance state he had entered when a boy, he thought that meditation, not ascetic austerities, might be the path to overcoming suffering.

> I thought of a time when my Sákyan father was working and I was sitting in the cool shade of a rose-apple tree: quite secluded from sensual desires, secluded from unprofitable things I had entered upon and abode in the first meditation, which is accompanied by thinking and exploring with happiness and pleasure born of seclusion. I thought: Might that be the way to enlightenment? Then following up that memory there came the recognition that this was the way to enlightenment.[4]

So Shakyamuni determined to meditate until he reached enlightenment. He sat cross-legged under a *pipal* tree, a variety of fig tree considered sacred in India. This tree would later become known as the *bodhi* tree or tree of enlightenment. What happened next varies in the different accounts that exist. No firsthand account from the Buddha himself exists, and later accounts embellish the story with miracles and tempters.

I will follow the account found in *The Deeds of the Buddha (Buddhacarita)*, which dates from the first or second century. This account has become widely popular among Buddhists. The author (perhaps the poet Ashvaghosha) is less interested in the psychological features of the experience than in the moral and spiritual teachings of the Buddha.

According to *Buddhacarita*, when Shakyamuni began to meditate, Mara, the evil god of passion and ruler of the realm of desire, tempted him with his daughters—Discontent, Delight, and Thirst. Shakyamuni, now known as a **bodhisattva**, or buddha-to-be, resisted the temptations of desire. Mara then attacked him with his sons—Fury, Gaiety, and Sullen Pride. Eventually Mara assailed the bodhisattva with his whole army of tempters because he knew that if this bodhisattva succeeded in gaining enlightenment, he would lose control of his kingdom where people were kept in bondage to desire. Shakyamuni defeated this attack, and Mara, along with his army, ran away in defeat.

> The great seer, free from the dust of passion, victorious over darkness' gloom, had vanquished him. And the moon, like a maiden's gentle smile, lit up the heavens, while a rain of sweet-scented flowers, filled with moisture, fell down on the earth from above.[5]

Now the Bodhisattva Shakyamuni put himself into a meditative trance and eventually gained complete mastery over "all the degrees and kinds of trance." During the first watch of the night, he remembered all of his past lives— thousands of births and thousands of deaths. This turned his mind toward compassion for all the people trapped in the world of suffering and rebirth, called *samsara*. The Bodhisattva Shakyamuni came to see that samsara was without real substance, which was contrary to what most people thought.

In the second watch of the night, he obtained the "supreme heavenly eye" with which he looked upon the entire world, "which appeared to him as though reflected in a spotless mirror." He came to understand the law of **karma**, which controls the endless samsaric round of rebirths and deaths. That whole process depends on what sort of deeds people do. Bad deeds lead to a bad rebirth, and good deeds lead to a good rebirth. Karma is an ironclad law of cause and effect. What we sow is what we shall reap. However, once again he found nothing substantial in this samsaric world of constant change.

In the third watch of the night, entering even deeper into meditative trance, the Bodhisattva saw that karma was linked to ignorance. This great "mass of ill" involving birth, old age, death, and rebirth was fueled by ignorance.

> When the great seer had comprehended that where there is no ignorance whatever, there also the karma-formations are stopped—then he had achieved a correct knowledge of all there is to be known, and he stood out in the world as a Buddha. He passed through the eight stages of Transic insight, and quickly reached their highest point. From the summit of the world downward he could detect no self anywhere. Like the fire when its fuel is burnt up, he became tranquil. He had reached perfection, and he thought to himself: "This is the authentic Way on which in the past so many great seers, who also knew all higher and lower things, have traveled on to ultimate and real truth. And now I obtained it!"[6]

The English word *enlightenment* is a translation of the Sanskrit word *bodhi*, which means "awakening," or "understanding." The opposite of being awake is being asleep, and the opposite of understanding is ignorance. Enlightenment involves coming to know something you did not know before. It comes, according to Buddhism, in degrees—first learning about past lives, then understanding how karma works, and finally, understanding the link between ignorance and suffering along with what can be done about it. While those on the path experience various degrees of enlightenment, only a buddha experiences complete understanding of all things.

Using Weber's distinction between an emissary prophet and an exemplary prophet, it seems clear that the Buddha falls into the latter category. He has something to teach, but most importantly, he has a kind of experience, insight, and freedom from suffering that he wants others to share. Is this experience revelational? It seems to be, insofar as the Buddha comes to learn things he did not know before. But these "revelations" do not come from any god. They are more like discoveries than revelations that descend from above. In fact, images of descent are not as prevalent as images of ascent. Not only does Shakyamuni's knowledge expand in the course of the night, but also there is a brief reference to ascending the eight stages of trance until he reaches the "highest point."

The fact that Shakyamuni's enlightenment occurred while he was meditating and entering into trance states has led most scholars to classify this as a mystical experience. Mystical experiences will be discussed in more detail later in the chapter. For now I wish to focus on meditation.

In Buddhism, the word *meditation* is a general label for a wide range of consciousness-altering practices. One such practice is called the "cultivation of tranquility" and is referred to in the eightfold path as right concentration. Tranquility is cultivated by concentrating the mind in ways that reduce the range and intensity of emotions along with the uncontrolled wanderings of the mind.

Another meditation practice found in Buddhism is called the "cultivation of insight" and is referred to in the eightfold path as right mindfulness. To achieve insight the meditator must expand consciousness by the practice of mindfulness, which involves a close, careful, emotionally detached observation of every process that makes up the individual's psychological and physical life. For example, I might apply mindfulness to my breathing or to feelings of fear and anger. The idea is to pay careful attention to the causally connected chain of events that make up such physical activities as breathing or various emotional states like fear. By carefully noting how they arise and pass away, the meditator comes to understand, according to Buddhist thought, the insubstantiality and impermanence of all things.

Many of us assume that there is some sort of permanent, substantial self or soul that persists through change and is the seat of our emotions and thoughts. Some believe that this self or soul can survive even such a radical change as death. Becoming mindful of our bodily states and of our mental states teaches us that such states come and go. They do not last. They are impermanent and insubstantial. It is a short step from there to the conclusion that there is no self or soul that persists through change.

When the Buddha realized this during the third watch, he realized how ignorance keeps us bound to *samsara*. The second Noble Truth tells us that desire is the cause of suffering. More specifically, it teaches us that selfish desire is the cause of suffering because through it we become attached to things. Once attached to the things we like, we do not want them to change. We want them to remain permanent so that our permanent self can enjoy them. But nothing remains the same, and when things change we are sorrowful. In a word, we suffer. But if there is no self to begin with, if what we call a permanent self or soul is an illusion, then selfish desire and attachment make no sense. It is simply impossible to continue to enjoy pleasant things forever. It is ignorance of our true nature and the true nature of everything else that leads to the illusion of a substantial, unchanging self. Suffering is the inevitable result of this ignorance.

In order to help you understand Shakyamuni's enlightenment experience, I have had to explain some Buddhist philosophy and meditation practices. This indicates that descriptions of his enlightenment experience serve more as teaching devices than as careful descriptions of the psychological features of the experience. Just as the story of Muhammad's ascent to the highest heaven helps to establish his authority as the last prophet with a fuller revelation than the Jewish and Christian prophets that precede him, so this story of Shakya-muni becoming the Buddha establishes his authority to teach the knowledge of the true nature of things.

Two Types of Buddhist Meditation
1. Cultivation of tranquility (right concentration)
2. Cultivation of insight (right mindfulness)

7.2 COMPARISON

We begin our comparison by noting the vast difference in time, in place, and in culture that separates Muhammad from the Buddha. Over a thousand years of history and thousands of miles of geography separate them. The culture of Arabia, with its tribal society of nomads and warriors, is far removed from that of North India, an urban society dependent on agriculture. Muhammad, living where and when he did, was most interested in questions of polytheism versus monotheism, disobedience, and finding a way to learn to submit to Allah's will now in preparation for a life in paradise to come.

Given the Buddha's historical and cultural context, it is not surprising that his spiritual concerns should be very different. The problem was human suf-fering, not disobedience, and while most people went to temples and offered sacrifices to the many gods, it was clear to the young "Prince of the Shakya clan" that worshiping gods and offering sacrifices was not very effective. If it were, why did so many people still suffer? There must be another path, a path Gautama determined to discover.

Muhammad's first experiences of revelations from the angel Gabriel appear far removed from the enlightenment experience of Shakyamuni. The Bud-dha hears no voices and receives no divine command to write down the final and most perfect revelation from the divine. He does discover truths—truths important for overcoming suffering—but no god reveals them. Muhammad realizes that his prophetic task is to get others to believe that the revelations he has received are true. "Believe my message from Allah," he cries to his fel-low Arabs. The Buddha realizes that his "prophetic" (that word somehow does not even seem to fit the situation) task is to get others to follow a path that will lead them to enlightenment. Suffering is an intensely personal experi-ence, and so too is the way to overcome it.

Comparing the Night Journey of Muhammad with the enlightenment expe-rience of the Buddha may produce greater similarities than we have so far found. Both experiences are ecstatic, and ascent images prevail. Muhammad rides a horse up through seven heavens led by an angel, and the Buddha passes through various states of consciousness produced by meditation. However, in those heavens Muhammad encounters past prophets and gets a command from Allah about praying, while the Buddha encounters no other beings, except for the initial encounter before his enlightenment with the god of evil desire, Mara, nor does he get commands. Instead, he gets insights into the "true nature" of things.

It should be noted, although it is not surprising, that the insights into the "true nature" of things that the Buddha discovers are precisely the teachings of Buddhism. An interesting question is which came first, the insights or the teachings? Likewise the revelations that Muhammad receives correspond precisely to the teachings of Islam. Again, which came first, the experience or the teachings? Because these seem to be foundational experiences, we are tempted to say that in these cases experience precedes teachings. Experiences reported by the followers of the Buddha and Muhammad may be shaped by the teachings of the tradition they inherit, but surely the first experiences of the founders of these religions are not?

I think it is quite difficult to say for sure one way or another. Perhaps this should be dismissed as one of those impossible-to-answer, chicken-and-egg-type questions. More likely, the interplay between doctrines and experiences is complex and ongoing, even for foundational experiences. One thing is clear: these experiences attributed to the revered religious founders become models for subsequent experiences and the authoritative standard by which both teachings and experiences are to be judged. Perhaps it is best to think of them not so much as foundational experiences, but as standards of true teachings and practices presented *as if* they were foundational experiences.

One final point of comparison is worth bringing up. Within the Islamic religion there has been a fierce resistance to the tendency of many religions to deify their founders. Muhammad, no matter how favored by Allah or how pious he was, is a human being. There is only one God and hence only one source of ultimate truth. Muhammad remains the human agent of the divine. However, we could read the Night Journey as an expression of the tendency to make founders gods. In the Night Journey, Muhammad communes with Allah, indeed bargains with Allah, in a most intimate way. Normally humans are not allowed such access; only gods or other divine beings can enter the realm of the divine.

Various schools of Buddhism have reacted in different ways to the question of the Buddha's possible divinity. The oldest traditions retain the notion that he is a human being who became enlightened. Other human beings can become enlightened too. Shakyamuni has no monopoly on buddhahood. Other schools of Buddhism have deified the Buddha. He is worshiped, prayed to, and otherwise treated as divine. Indeed, according to one tradition he was, is, and always will be divine. His appearance as the human named Siddhartha Gautama of the Shakya clan is just that, only an appearance. He was not really human; he only seemed to be. Perfect beings cannot be human.

7.3 DEBATES ABOUT THE NATURE OF RELIGIOUS EXPERIENCES

The modern scholarly interest in the topic of religious experience begins with a Christian theologian named Friedrich Ernst Daniel Schleiermacher (1768–1834). Schleiermacher was dismayed that many of his well-educated, urbane, and cultured friends had come to despise religion. Among intellectuals in general he discovered an antireligious attitude. He believed that they could adopt such an attitude only because they misunderstood what religion is really about. They confused it with dogmas, rituals, repressive moral codes, and conservative institutions. However, the heart of religion is to be found, according to Schleiermacher, in experience, not in dogmas, rituals, or organizations.

Schleiermacher thought he knew the answer to the question posed above about which came first, the experience or the teachings. Experience came first for Schleiermacher, and this is what his cultured friends did not understand. Dogmas, doctrines, teachings—the sorts of things some people think of when they think of religion—miss the mark. Experience is primary, all else secondary and dependent.

Not only did Schleiermacher think experience was the most important part of religion, he also thought that all the different types of religious experience could be reduced to a common core. This common core, he argued, is absolutely unique and irreducible to anything else. There is, in other words, a distinct religious feeling. What is this unique and distinctive feeling at the core of all religious experience?

Schleiermacher characterized it in different ways, but in a book titled *The Christian Faith* he identified the unique and irreducible feeling at the heart of all religious experience as "the feeling of absolute dependence." It is a moment in consciousness when we become aware that our lives are conditioned and limited by all kinds of factors. We do not have complete control of what happens to us. We are dependent on an "other"—a power much greater than ourselves—and when we face the limiting situations of life (such as serious illness or death), this dependency on a greater power becomes clear to our consciousness.

While Schleiermacher believed that he had identified a universal core of all religious experience, it is quite clear that what he means by a feeling of absolute dependence is absolute dependence *on God*. He writes:

> The common element in all howsoever diverse expressions of piety, by which these are conjointly distinguished from all other feelings, or, in other words, the self-identical essence of piety, is this: the consciousness of being absolutely dependent, or which is the same thing, of being in relation with God.[7]

This formulation of the core of religious experience (what Schleiermacher here calls "piety") has proved remarkably influential. It is often stated as a sense of finitude that pervades all human life. We may not always be conscious of this feeling, but in crisis situations it emerges. We often pray out of fear for our lives. So-called foxhole conversions are common. This feeling at the heart of all religion is always "waiting in the wings" of human consciousness, ready to take center stage when conditions are right and erupt into religious experiences of one kind or another.

However insightful Schleiermacher's analysis is, there is a major problem. It is impossible to identify a feeling of absolute dependence without the concept of God. But there is no hint in many religious experiences of any feeling of absolute dependence on a divine power. Such a feeling is present in Muhammad's experience, for example, but it is not present in Buddha's enlightenment experience. Schleiermacher's understanding of religious experience betrays a theistic bias.

In his book *The Idea of the Holy,* Rudolf Otto (1896–1937) continued the examination of religious experience begun by Schleiermacher. Like Schleiermacher, he thought there was a distinctive religious feeling. However, while he thought that Schleiermacher had identified an important feature of religious experience, he had erred by making it too subjective. Schleiermacher's description made religious experience merely an awareness of a state of consciousness. Given this account, Otto thought, the divine could only be *inferred* as the cause of the feeling of absolute dependence.[8]

However, like Schleiermacher, Otto had theological motives. He wanted to show that there is an element in religious experience that cannot be explained away. To Otto, religious experience was not reducible to mere wish fulfillment, delusion, or chemical reactions in the brain. He called religious experiences "numinous experiences," and he characterized them as an experience of the Holy. He further described them as *mysterium tremendum et fascinans.*

The word *numinous* is derived from the Latin word *numen,* which means "a spirit." By the term *Holy* Otto means a pre-ethical, indeed prerational object of the numinous experience that can be characterized only as a mysterious "Wholly Other." That is, it is something utterly different from anything else we might encounter and beyond all normal moral and rational categories that we frequently use to help us understand the world.

Tremendum literally means "to be trembled at," and this trembling Otto characterizes as an experience of dread, awe, urgency, and majesty. Some have compared it to the experience we have when, in the grip of fear, the hairs on the back of our necks stand up, or the experience we might have in the presence of a great king or an important and powerful person.

This encounter with a mysterious and awe-inspiring Wholly Other also leaves us fascinated. Fear is involved, but fascination is involved as well, and this fascination draws us toward the mysterious, holy object. It is something like looking over a cliff. We are fearful of the great height and danger, yet drawn toward the precipice, sometimes so strongly that we must make an effort to pull back.

Otto provides a variety of examples, including Moses's encounter with the burning bush and the revelation of the divine name YHWH. Muhammad's first encounter with the mysterious voice of an unseen presence clearly has numinous qualities. Numinous qualities are less pronounced in the Shakyamuni's enlightenment experience. In fact, there is no sense of the presence of the Wholly Other, let alone fear, dread, awe, or wonder.

Experiences like Shakyamuni's enlightenment have led some scholars to conclude that however valuable and insightful Otto's characterization of the numinous element in religious experiences may be, it is not the whole story. Ninian Smart, in his book *Worldviews* (1995), argues that at least one additional type of experience must be added to Otto's numinous type. This additional type Smart calls the "mystical experience" and explicitly cites the Buddha's experience as an example.

In mystical experience, unity, not duality, is the central theme. Otto emphasizes difference and a sharp duality between the subject of the numinous experience and its holy object, but descriptions of mystical experiences are different. Where numinous experiences are dualistic (a subject encounters an object), mystical experiences are often nondual (subject and object become intimately related, in some cases united). Where numinous experiences are often turbulent, mystical experiences are quiet. Where numinous experiences often involve hearing voices and experiencing images, mystical experiences (at least in their more developed state) are often empty of any auditory or visual events.

We will learn more about mystical experiences later in the chapter, but for now we can conclude that there are at least two major types of extreme religious experiences: the numinous and the mystical. I use the word *extreme* because for most people religious experiences are not nearly so dramatic. Most experiences that people identify as religious are of the *confirming* type.[9] They involve a feeling or kind of intuition that their religious beliefs are true. These experiences can range from a generalized sense of sacredness associated with natural settings, such as the awe and wonder inspired by majestic mountains or immense oceans, to specific awareness of some kind of divine presence while in church or synagogue, perhaps when singing hymns, or praying.

Additional Types of Religious Experiences

1. Feelings of absolute dependence (finitude)
2. Feelings of awe or wonder (numinous)
3. Feelings of unity (mystical)
4. Feelings of confirmation

7.4 SHAMANIC ECSTASY

The shaman ("shah'men" or "shay'men") is a religious functionary found in tribal societies, who engages, with the aid of spirit guides and helpers, in healings and other activities important to the community. Shamans embody the local interests of the community they serve by addressing such every-day concerns as illness, finding game for the hunters, making rain, and guiding people through critical life transitions such as birth and death. We have already encountered a type of shaman, Slow Buffalo, who received a vision detailing a new rite of passage to guide young girls into womanhood.

The individual who becomes a shaman often inherits the job or has an experience of being called by a spirit. Sometimes an initiation ritual conducted by other shamans confirms the shamanic calling. Sometimes a person's first cure or successful entry into trance or possession states may validate shamanic powers. Frequently the ecstatic states involve journeys to the underworld or to the heavens in search of a lost soul (soul-loss is often considered the primary cause of illness), game animals, or spirits to aid the tribe in some way.

A typical account relates how an Eskimo shaman descends to the bottom of the sea in order to get the sea goddess to release seals. He makes this ecstatic journey on behalf of the whole community, which is experiencing famine because of the lack of game. He enters a trance and, with the aid of his spirits, travels to the bottom of the sea. He must successfully pass all kinds of obstacles, each putting him in grave danger. During this journey the people sing songs and hear strange voices, including breathing that sounds as if it comes from "under water." Sometimes they witness the shaman's clothes flying about the house where this séance is taking place.

At the bottom of the sea he meets the sea goddess, whose hair is tangled because the people have broken taboos (forbidden acts). She is angry and tells the shaman in "spirit language" what sins have been committed. He calms her by combing her hair (the sea goddess has no fingers), and the sea goddess releases the seals. Then the shaman returns from trance, gasping for air as if he were emerging from under water. For a long time there is silence. At last the shaman speaks, "I have something to say." The people respond, "Let us hear, let us hear." The shaman then demands a confession of sins, and one after another the people confess breaches of taboos and repent.

Shamanistic ecstasy is the oldest type of religious experience, and it continues to the present day. Shamanism is still practiced in traditional cultures, and you can learn how to be a shaman in workshops run by New Age gurus. There are elements of shamanistic experience in many other types of religious experiences as well. The Night Journey of Muhammad is a good example. The ascent into heaven has definite shamanistic elements, although the only "spirit guides" are the angel and the spirits of previous prophets. Shakyamuni's enlightenment experience involves discovering supernormal truths and gaining supernormal powers, even though it does not involve contact with spirits. The Buddha, like many shamans, utilizes trance techniques as well, although the method for entering trance and the trance states themselves appear to be quite different from shamanic trances.

7.5 MYSTICAL TECHNIQUES AND STATES

Typologies of Mystical Experiences

Scholars have offered a variety of typologies of mystical experiences. One influential typology derives from Walter T. Stace's book, *Mysticism and Philosophy* (1961). According to Stace, there are two types of mystical experiences. One he calls *extrovertive* and characterizes as a "unifying vision" in which the unity of all things is apprehended behind the multiplicity of the world. It is as if the many things that normally appear to us have a unitary or inner core that is often described in terms of Life or Consciousness. The second type he calls *introvertive* and characterizes as "the unitary consciousness" in which all sensate and conceptual content disappears, and the mystic experiences a state of pure consciousness. All sense of space and time disappear.

Stace's Typology of Mysticism

1. Introvertive
2. Extrovertive

Both of these experiences, Stace believes, are also marked by a sense of having experienced the final truth about things, and by feelings of sacredness, joy, paradoxicality, and ineffability (cannot be fully expressed in words). Stace goes beyond description, however, by asserting that the introvertive experience is "superior" to the extrovertive because the subject/object dualism and the sense of space/time are transcended in the introvertive, but not in extrovertive experience.

This value judgment caused R. C. Zaehner to revise Stace's typology in his book, *Mysticism: Sacred and Profane* (1961). According to Zaehner, Stace does not give adequate attention to theistic mysticism. Zaehner argues that we must distinguish among nature mysticism, soul or monistic mysticism, and theistic mysticism. Zaehner describes nature mysticism as the experience of the mystic's ego or self expanding to include the whole universe or dissolving into nature so that "without and within are one." It is closest to Stace's extrovertive type. Soul or monistic mysticism is, Zaehner believes, the same as what Stace calls the introvertive type. The monistic mystic experiences a total transcendence of the subject/object distinction and identifies with what she or he takes to be ultimate reality. Theistic mysticism involves an ecstasy of union, but not identity, with the divine. Theistic mystics believe their experiences are due to the grace of God, and they are overcome by intense feelings of bliss and love.

Zaehner, like Stace, makes his own value judgment about which is superior. Theistic mysticism is superior as far as Zaehner is concerned because it involves a strong moral sense, whereas nature mysticism is premoral and monistic mysticism is amoral. It should come as no surprise that Stace is attracted to the philosophy of Shankara, the Hindu mystic philosopher who taught that the true self is identical with ultimate reality, and Zaehner is a Roman Catholic Christian with a strong attraction to Christian theistic mystics.

Zaehner's Typology of Mysticism

1. Nature mysticism
2. Soul or monistic mysticism
3. Theistic mysticism

No typology is perfect because there are always excluded cases, borderline cases, and hybrid cases that do not fit neatly into the categories. Hence other attempts have been made to create more complex and less biased categories. Shakyamuni's enlightenment experience is mystical but does not quite fit any of Stace's or Zaehner's categories. It does not qualify as nature mysticism because it does not involve experiencing oneness with nature. Nor is it a type of theistic mysticism because there is no union with God. The last type, soul or monistic mysticism, seems just the opposite of what the Buddha experiences. He comes to see that there is no substantial soul or self and that believing there is constitutes the ignorance that keeps people attached to things, thereby prolonging their suffering. However, there do seem to be monistic implications associated with his experience insofar as the "soul" dissolves into the impermanence that characterizes the nature of all things.

Mystical Experience: Pure or Culturally Conditioned?

A debate rages today about whether mystical experiences are conditioned, shaped, and informed by the cultural, historical, and religious context of the mystic or transcend such contextual conditioning. Those who argue that the context is decisive point to the fact that Christians, Muslims, Jews, and members of theistic religions in general have, by and large, theistic mystical experiences; while Buddhists have experiences of the insubstantiality of the soul, monists experience identity with an impersonal ultimate reality, and Daoists find unity with the Dao. Those who argue that mystical experiences transcend culture, history, and the different religious traditions treat the differences among mystics as matters of how they interpret their experiences and not descriptions of the experience. We must, they argue, take seriously the mystic's claims to have had pure experiences, untainted by contextual factors.

This debate is important because if it could be proved that mystics from different times, different places, and different religions all have the same or nearly the same experiences, the case for religious truth would be strengthened. One reason we trust our sense experiences is because, by and large, people agree about them. If I seem to see a tree and nobody else does, that is cause for concern. If I seem to see a tree and everybody else does as well, I can have greater confidence in the trustworthiness of my senses. Likewise if mystics from around the world, from different historical periods, and from different religions all have the same or nearly the same experiences, that is cause for some confidence that their experiences may provide genuine knowledge of ultimate reality. If they all have different experiences that reflect their religious traditions, that is cause for doubting whether they are in touch with any reality outside of the workings of their own minds.

Mystical Techniques

Debates about mystical experiences become more complex when we look at the techniques employed by mystics. We can borrow the Sanskrit word **yoga** from Hinduism and use it as a general term for any discipline or path designed to promote religious experiences, many of the mystical type. There are many different types of yoga, but several have been particularly influential and widespread.[10]

Raja, or royal, yoga was first described in detail by the Indian sage Patanjali ("*puh-tuhn'juh-lih*") sometime in the third century. He defined yoga as the "cessation of the mental whirlwind." Patanjali asserts that through the practice of raja yoga one can isolate the individual eternal spirit from matter and unite it with the supreme spirit. His yogic path consists of eight hierarchical stages; hence it is sometimes called "eight-limbed yoga."

The first two limbs, or stages, involve purification and preparation for advanced stages. The first stage, called restraint, consists of ethical prohibitions against injury and dishonesty, and the second includes the practice of such virtues as cleanliness, studiousness, and serenity. The next three stages teach how to develop correct posture for prolonged meditation, breath control, and detachment from the senses. Mastering these physical techniques (often called Hatha yoga) prepares one for the mental discipline of the last three stages. These are called concentration, meditation, and absorption or *samadhi*. Mastering these three stages results in obtaining superhuman powers called *siddhis* as well as absorption into the supreme spirit. According to Patan-jali, a god may aid yogis in achieving *samadhi*.

Various meditation and concentration techniques have been developed and practiced by mystics around the world in order to promote altered states of consciousness. These states, usually called trance states, do not automatically result in mystical experiences, but sometimes they do promote intense experiences of oneness.

Another type of yoga is called *bhakti* yoga, or discipline of devotion to the divine. It promotes devotion as a way to experience a loving union with the divine. According to one version there are several stages: hearing the Lord, glorifying him in song, remembering him, attendance at his feet, worship, adoration, servanthood, friendship, and offering oneself to him. By these methods one attains love for the Lord, which intensifies into passionate attachment and even obsession. When one arrives at total love one sees the divine in everyone and everything.

You may have seen members of the Hare (Lord) Krishna sect dancing and singing in public. They are lovers of Krishna as the supreme Name and Form of the divine. Their goal is to overcome selfishness in complete devotion to Krishna. Devotion to the divine or an incarnation of the divine occurs all over the world and in most religions. From a Hindu viewpoint, Christianity, with its worship of and devotion to Jesus the Christ, is another form of *bhakti* yoga.

Still another type of yoga is called *karma* yoga, or the discipline of action. This discipline has taken many forms throughout history. In the early period of religious history in India, it was interpreted primarily as the performance of ritual actions associated with sacrifices. Today it promotes liberation from selfishness through self-sacrifice and doing one's duty. Liberation from self-interest can be gained, according to this yoga, by learning how to act without attachment to the fruits of one's action. Mohandas Gandhi (1869–1948) interpreted his nonviolent resistance to the British as a type of *karma* yoga. If we can characterize the goal of *bhakti* yoga as a loving union with the divine, then we can think of the goal of *karma* yoga as a union of human and divine wills. If one is successful at following this yoga, one's own selfish will disappears and one's will and the will of the divine become united. From this point of view, the practices of Muslims that promote submission to the will of Allah are one kind of *karma* yoga.

Jnana yoga, or the discipline of knowledge, is intended to overcome ignorance and the false views that keep us bound to a world of many things. Through the disciplined study of scripture and philosophy, the devotee eventually learns that behind the experiences of the many things that make up the world lies an ultimate oneness. In other words, the devotee comes to know that nondualism, or monism, is true. This is not just an intellectual understanding, but an intense personal experience of identity with ultimate reality.

There are other yogas besides *raja, bhakti, karma,* and *jnana,* but we can see two important ideas in these four types. First, all of these disciplines are intended to overcome selfishness, and second, the type of mystical experience that these paths promote varies according to the techniques employed. *Raja* yoga promotes a mysticism of absorption, *bhakti* yoga encourages a mystical loving union with the divine, *karma* yoga teaches how to realize a union of wills between the self and the divine, and *jnana* yoga leads to a mystical identity with and knowledge of the oneness that lies at the foundation of reality.

Types of Yoga

1. *Raja*
2. *Bhakti*
3. *Karma*
4. *Jnana*

7.6 PSYCHOANALYTIC THEORIES

It is obvious that religious insiders have their own explanations for their experiences. Indeed, it is their religious explanations that indicate to the scholar of religion that such experiences should be classified as religious experiences in the first place. However, the outside scholar has an obligation at least to suggest explanations other than the religious.

One form of the symbolic theory of religion that used to be quite popular (although its influence is waning) relies on psychoanalytic theory. There are a variety of such theories, but we shall concentrate on two versions here—the theories of Sigmund Freud (1856–1939) and Carl Jung (1875–1961).

According to Freud, religion in general and religious experience in particular is a projection of unconscious wishes and desires. Religion is just one of the ways humans sublimate or redirect psychic energy into socially acceptable forms. Our deepest psychological motivations reflect emotional relationships of childhood dependency on parents. Our adult relations with our gods symbolize childhood relations with our parents. So gods and our imagined relationships of love, guilt, security, and sacrifice with them symbolically reflect actual childhood relationships.

Freud thought that mystical experiences of oneness with the divine reflect very early feelings of security experienced as small infants. Freud characterized mystical experiences as "oceanic feelings" and thought they reflected long-repressed experiences in the womb. He explained ecstatic experiences of rapture, trance, and intense love as self-produced substitutes for unconscious and repressed sexual desires.

He also found the repetitive and obsessive nature of religious rites reminiscent of neurotic behavior. Just as neurotics may compulsively wash their hands to get rid of unconscious feelings of guilt, so those who practice religious rituals and seek religious experiences are motivated by unconscious feelings of guilt that first arose in relationship to parents. The practice of asceticism and self-mortification is a way of acting out in a socially acceptable way repression of illicit sexual desire and its accompanying guilt.

Religious doctrines like eternal life and its rewards are, according to Freud, illusions stemming from our desires to have our wishes and needs for security and approval fulfilled. In religion, we unconsciously picture reality the way we want it to be. This is, of course, unrealistic and at base irrational. Therefore, Freud concluded, the true liberation of humanity could only happen when humans outgrew their need for religious illusions and faced reality squarely.

If we imagine how Freud might apply his theory of unconscious symbolic projection to Muhammad's experiences, we would have to probe Muhammad's childhood and particularly his attempts to obey his father and the guilt he felt when he failed. By learning to submit to the will of Allah, who is a projected father figure, Muhammad relieved his unconscious guilt feelings and finally got approval for his obedience, an approval he never felt from his own father.

It is more difficult to apply Freud's theory to Shakyamuni's enlightenment experience because there is no obvious symbolic substitute father figure. The initial struggle with evil personified as Mara could be explained as Shakyamuni's struggle with his own desires to do "bad" things. Freud might say that the insight into the nature of suffering and how to overcome it is symbolic of the deep unconscious relief the Buddha felt when he finally overcame what he considered to be his "evil" tendencies.

As you can imagine, Freud's view of religion has been criticized from many different angles. One of his early critics was a former student and heir apparent to Freud himself named Carl Gustav Jung. Jung thought that Freud's view of the unconscious as filled with repressed childhood experiences of parental relationships was far too narrow. Jung saw the unconscious not just as a garbage dump, but as a collective unconscious of the human race containing far more material than Freud thought.

Jung believed that the unconscious is filled with creative energy. Among other things, it contains **archetypes**, which are recurring patterns in which the human ego (individual self) finds itself in relation to the collective unconscious. Archetypes can be thought of as the psychological version of instincts. One of these psychological instincts is the realization of what Jung called the archetype of the "self."

As the individual ego develops from child to adult it passes through (if its development is normal) three main stages: (1) dependency, (2) autonomy (freedom), and (3) integration. Each of these stages corresponds to levels of religious experience and the mythological expression of religious ideas.

The first stage (dependency) is the stage of infancy and childhood in which the unformed ego finds itself in complete dependency on its environment, in particular, the mother. This appears in religious mythology and experience as a projected trouble-free state of bliss typically symbolized in stories about some "paradise of innocence" like the Garden of Eden or some past Golden Age. In religions that emphasize goddess worship, the mother-goddess who supplies all that is necessary and nourishes her children also symbolizes this stage.

The second stage (autonomy) corresponds to adolescence and young adulthood in which the dependent ego must now assert its independence and difference from parental power that, from this perspective, now appears to have been dominating and restrictive. This struggle for independence is expressed in religious myths of heroes who, through conflict, suffering, struggle, and sacrifice, gain a reward or treasure (see the Marduk and Moses myths discussed in Chapter 4).

Obtaining the treasure signals the transition to the third stage (integration) in which the psyche must come to terms with its weakness, in particular, its own lack of wholeness. The creation of a balanced, integrated, and whole self is the challenge of "the second half of life." Here religious symbols dominate. Spiritual paths to inner peace and harmony emerge. Religious experiences of the harmony of all opposites, mystical unions, and mystical marriages, speak with ever greater intensity and appeal as we grow older and enter our final years.

If the ego is the center of consciousness, the self-archetype is the center of an integrated consciousness and unconsciousness. It has a more holistic and unselfish outlook than the ego and is the transformative and creative power that draws people toward the final stage of integration. Jung believed that this self-archetype is frequently symbolized by the "god-image." The gods, goddesses, saviors, spiritual teachers, and other spiritual beings are projections of the self-archetype. They are idealized "others" that, once projected, can now offer advice and guidance to us as we work through our anxieties about the end of our lives. This projection is necessary because many egos are in danger of being overwhelmed by the self-archetype. Gods are easier to deal with "out there" than "in here." Nevertheless, in some cases divinity is understood as a higher spiritual self within everyone.

While both Freud and Jung talk about projection, the projections are very different in each. For Freud, the father figure is projected as divine in order to relive the secure dependency experienced in childhood. For Jung, what is projected is the self-archetype that plays a positive role in helping the ego to integrate conflicting desires and finally gain a peaceful wisdom as a realized self. The gods, for Jung, help us to become better people.

Jung would analyze the experiences of Muhammad and Buddha differently from Freud. If we apply his theories to these cases, a Jungian analysis might go something like the following. Allah is the self-archetype communicating wisdom and guidance to Muhammad. He is not the domineering projected father figure that Freud finds. The prophets encountered in the Night Journey are wise old men who are offering advice and guidance to a Muhammad who is struggling to overcome his selfishness in order to reach successfully the stage of integration. His ascent into the heavens is symbolic for a descent into the collective unconscious. Muhammad, in turn, becomes an idealized self for Muslims who seek to model their lives after him in their own journeys toward integration.

The Buddha finds wisdom within himself in his enlightenment experience. Rather than relating to a projected self-archetype, he connects with the self-archetype within. His trance states are, once again, symbolic for the journey within the collective unconscious to recover a wisdom that has always been there but, before this experience, was blocked from conscious awareness.

The Buddha's awakened knowledge of past lives symbolizes a total integration of all aspects of his personality, and his discovery that ignorance is the cause of karma allows him to gain freedom from its ironclad laws. Paradoxically, the discovery that the individual self is without substance allows him to discover the larger, more inclusive self within. The discovery of the insubstantial nature of what most of us take to be real allows the Buddha to discover the truth about an ever changing world. His discovery of insubstantiality paves the way for recovering the psychological reality that is at the base of religious experiences and ideas.

Jung was much taken with number symbolism. The seven heavens correspond to the seven planets (the moon and the sun were thought to be planets) that were recognized in the ancient world. But since the planets were thought to control events on earth, their mystical correspondence to the seven-day week, the seven phases of the moon, the seven metals, the seven colors of the rainbow, the pilgrimage ritual of going seven times around the Kaaba, and so on, is psychologically significant. It was widely believed that the number seven is the number of perfection and completeness. It has also been associated with mystics and philosophers. Seven is the perfect number to symbolize the completeness of Muhammad's Night Journey, and the attainment of a fully integrated self.

Likewise the number eight has mystical significance. The eight trances of Buddhist meditation are reflected in the eightfold path as well as eight-limbed yoga. It is generally held to be the number of new beginnings as well as infinity. In some cases it symbolizes the achievement of higher consciousness. Jung would probably find this a most appropriate number for Shakyamuni's enlightenment.

It is no accident, Jung would say, that the symbolism of seven and of eight should appear in these experiences. These numbers derive from the collective unconscious and serve to underscore the significance of the foundational experiences of Muhammad and the Buddha.

I do not know if Freud or Jung would approve of the above application of their psychoanalytic theories.[11] They would probably have much more to say with far greater profundity. However, this application of their ideas gives us some idea of how we might proceed with our own psychoanalytic explanation. Whatever metaphysical realities may stand behind these experiences, psychoanalytic theories remind us of their symbolic character and the psychological realities on which they are based.

REVIEW QUESTIONS

1. Explain in your own words the difference between seeming to experience something and actually experiencing it. Why is this distinction important for understanding religious experience?
2. Compare the Five Pillars of Islam with the Four Noble Truths of Buddhism. What, in your opinion, is the most significant difference between them? Why do you think the difference is significant?
3. What is the primary difference between an exemplary prophet and emissary prophet?
4. What is the difference between cultivation of tranquility and cultivation of insight?
5. Which theory of religious experience do you prefer, Schleiermacher's or Otto's and why?
6. What is the difference between introvertive mysticism and extrovertive mysticism, and how does this distinction relate to Zaehner's threefold typology of mystical experience?
7. How might Freud and Jung analyze shamanic experiences? Be specific.
8. Of the four yogas, which appeals to you most, and why does it?

RESEARCH CASE—ST. TERESA OF AVILA

One of ten children, Teresa of Avila (1515–1582) was a Spanish Roman Catholic. Her strength of character (some called her "uppity") is partly revealed in the fact that as a child of seven she, along with her brother of eleven, ran away from home in order to journey to the "country of the Moors" (Muslims) so they could be "martyrs for Christ." An uncle encountered them outside the walls of Avila and promptly escorted them home. While this incident reveals her determination, it also reveals a pious resolve and a desire to suffer for Christ. She retained that desire throughout her life.

Teresa entered a Carmelite convent at the age of nineteen in order to become a nun. To do this she had to defy the will of her father. This experience was so traumatic that she later recalled that "it felt like every bone in her body was being sundered."[12]

She became seriously ill in 1538, lapsed into a three-day coma, and was taken for dead. Teresa managed to revive, but she was left so paralyzed that it was three years before she could walk.

At the age of thirty-nine Teresa underwent a spiritual transformation and began to have visions and raptures that carried her away in ecstatic love and joy. After a terrifying vision of hell, she vowed to reform her Carmelite order. In 1560, she founded a strict order of Carmelites called the Reformed or Discalced (sandal-less) Carmelites, and in 1568 she convinced her friend and fellow mystic, John of the Cross, to found a reformed house for men.

Her teachings were based primarily on her interpretation of her mystical experiences, not on the technical theology of her day. In one memorable vision, an angel pierced her heart with a flaming arrow, which left her burning with love for God. Her spiritual directors were suspicious of her many visions and raptures, fearing she might be mentally unbalanced or, worse yet, seduced by Satan.

Her life coincided with the time when Spain was the greatest power on earth, controlling the seas and establishing colonies in the New World. It also coincided with the Spanish Inquisition, which critically reviewed her writings for "erroneous" teachings. She was under great suspicion, in part, because she did what women were not supposed to do. She wrote books and founded convents.

One Alonso de la Puente, an energetic prosecutor for the Inquisition, found her works definitely heretical. After her death he sought to have her writings destroyed. His prosecution reflects the attitude that many in positions of power had when she was alive. His sexism and fear shows through in this statement:

> That learned men should come to learn from a woman and recognize her as a leader in matters of prayer and spiritual doctrine . . . is an argument for the novelty [heresy] of this doctrine, in which this woman was wise, and the men who subjected themselves to her were foolish; for in the ancient doctrine of the Church educated and learned men knew more than women.[13]

Alonso, amazed that a woman could even write heretical things, speculated that the writings were so diabolical she was probably not the true author because "they exceed the capacity of woman." Oddly enough, this sexism cut both ways, because on the occasion of her beatification in 1614, the Jesuit Cipriano de Aguayo argued that since no "ignorant woman" could write what she did, it must have been written by "divine inspiration."[14]

News of the conflicts among Christians spawned by the Protestant Reformation in northern Europe, the corrupt lifestyles of many priests in Rome, and the many souls yet to be saved in the New Indies (the Americas) made Teresa's heart burn even more intensely with a desire to serve God perfectly. Teresa thought that if Christ has so few friends, these few must serve "His Majesty" (Teresa's way of referring to Jesus the Christ) more passionately.

In *The Interior Castle*, which she wrote in 1577, Teresa used the metaphor of seven series of mansions containing many different rooms to represent various stages of spiritual development. The castle is the soul, which the Christian enters through prayer. In the fifth mansion, God through the "Prayer of Union" possesses the soul. Progressing through the sixth and seventh mansions, the soul experiences a spiritual betrothal and finally a spiritual marriage—the most intimate of unions with the divine.

In 1556, Teresa first experienced rapture. She heard Christ speaking to her not, as she put it, through her bodily ears but in her soul. About two years later she experienced "intellectual visions" that convinced her Jesus was at her side. These visions, which were without images, did not pass but became a part of her everyday life. She said of it, "In the prayer of union or quiet some impressions of the Divinity are bestowed; in the vision, along with the impressions, you see that also the most sacred humanity accompanies us and desires to grant us favors."[15] She did have visions of Christ involving images of him, but she regarded them as inferior in quality because they were transitory.

The last stage in her mystical journey centered on the "mystery of the Holy Trinity." In 1571 she "entered" a part of her soul in which the three persons (Father, Son, and Holy Spirit) of the Trinity dwell. Shortly afterward she experienced herself dwelling in God. She wrote that "It seemed to me there came the thought of how a sponge absorbs and is saturated with water; so, I thought, was my soul, which was overflowing with that divinity and in a certain way rejoicing with itself and possessing the three Persons. I also heard the words: 'Don't try to hold Me within yourself, but try to hold yourself within Me.'"[16]

On November 18, 1572, Teresa received the "grace of the spiritual marriage." Christ told her, she believed, that from then on she should consider as her own all that belonged to Him. She was then given the strength to engage in service to others, which constitutes the "fruits of the spiritual marriage."

Teresa used metaphors to explain the difference between the "prayer of union" and the "spiritual marriage" that takes place in the very center of the soul.

> Let us say that the union is like the joining of two wax candles to such an extent that the flame coming from them is but one, or that the wick, the flame, and the wax are all one. But afterward one candle can be easily separated from the other and there are two candles; the same holds for the wick. In the spiritual marriage the union is like what we have when rain falls from the sky into a river or fount; all is water, for the rain that fell from heaven cannot be divided or separated from the water of the river. Or it is like what we have when a little stream enters the ocean, there is no means of separating the two. Or, like the bright light entering a room through two different windows; although the streams of light are separate when entering the room, they become one."
> (*The Interior Castle*, 7.2.4)

In the following chapter of *The Interior Castle*, she spoke of the spiritual marriage like this:

> There are almost never any experiences of dryness or interior disturbance of the kind that was present at times in the other dwelling places, but the soul is almost always in quiet. There is no fear that this sublime favor can be counterfeited by the devil, but the soul is wholly sure that the favor comes from God; for . . . the faculties and senses have nothing to do with what goes on in this dwelling place [the center of the soul]. . . . Nor does the Lord in all the favors He grants the soul here, . . . receive any assistance from the soul itself, except what it has already done in surrendering itself totally to God. . . . So in this temple of God, in this His dwelling place, He alone and the soul rejoice together in the deepest silence. There is no reason for the intellect to stir or seek anything, for the Lord who created it wishes to give it repose here . . . At times . . . sight is lost and the other faculties do not allow the intellect to look, but this happens for only a very short time. In my opinion, the faculties are not lost here, they do not work, but remain as though in amazement.

Alison Weber, in her study of St. Teresa of Avila, is less interested in the psychology of Teresa's mystical experiences than in the rhetoric Teresa employs. She was struck by the profusion of self-depreciatory remarks, confessions of incompetence and of wretchedness. Looking at rhetoric like "[I am] the most wretched person on earth" forced Weber to wonder whether Teresa was really sincere in these sorts of statements, or, given the times, Weber asks, was "self-depreciation the only self-referential language available for women?"

Weber became convinced after a careful study of the rhetoric Teresa employs that

> Self-depreciation was rhetorical but that it had a very non-traditional function. It seemed possible that Teresa's "rhetoric for women" was a "rhetoric of femininity," that is, a strategy that exploited certain stereotypes about women's character and language. Rather than "writing like a woman," perhaps Teresa wrote as she believed women were perceived to speak.[17]

In a sermon given in 1627, on the occasion of Teresa's nomination as co-patron saint of Spain (the other was Santiago de Compostela, the Moor Slayer), Jesuit Rodrigo Niño found in Teresa's life a true miracle. He argued that "Sanctity in women usually consists in being quiet, obeying, staying in a corner and forgetting about oneself." But Teresa's case was different. It was "a new miracle and rare prodigy" because she obtained sanctity "not by keeping quiet, but by speaking, teaching and writing; not only by obeying, but by ordering, commanding, governing; not by observing enclosure but by traveling, disputing."[18]

"Ecstasy of St. Teresa" by Bernini, 1645–52.

Alison Weber comments:

The only way to comprehend such virtue in a woman was to reassign her
gender, to transform her into a "virile woman." Teresa was a prodigy because
of her sex and a saint in spite of it. Her rhetoric of femininity, which served
her own needs of self-assertion so successfully, also paradoxically sanctioned
the paternalistic authority of the Church over its daughters and reinforced the
ideology of women's intellectual and spiritual subordination. With her golden
pen she won a public voice for herself, if not for other women.[19]

QUESTIONS ON THE CASE OF ST. TERESA OF AVILA

1. How literally do you think we should take the metaphors of water and
   light that Teresa uses to characterize the spiritual marriage? Why?
2. Do you think Teresa has had some sort of universal mystical experience
   that transcends religions, cultures, and historical contexts? Why
   or why not?

3. Using either the theory of Freud or of Jung, write a psychoanalytic commentary on Teresa and her experiences.
4. Compare Teresa's experience of the spiritual marriage with both Muhammad's Night Journey and Buddha's enlightenment.
5. How do you react to Alison Weber's rhetorical analysis of Teresa's writings? What do you think accounts for your reaction?

Fieldwork Option: Interview several of your friends asking them to describe their religious experiences. Write a report analyzing and interpreting their experiences by applying ideas developed in this chapter.

SUGGESTIONS FOR FURTHER READING

In addition to the material found in the notes, the reader may wish to consult the following for more information.

Eliade, Mircea. *Shamanism: Archaic Techniques of Ecstasy.* Princeton, NJ: Princeton University Press, 1964. This is a famous and influential comparative study of shamanism packed full of many interesting examples.

Freud, Sigmund. *The Future of an Illusion.* Translated by James Strachey. New York: W. W. Norton & Company, 1961. Freud's writings on religion are scattered among several books and articles. In this book he articulates his view that religious beliefs, while not delusions, are illusions.

Glock, Charles Y., and Rodney Stark. "A Taxonomy of Religious Experience." In *Religion and Society in Tension.* Chicago: Rand McNally & Company, 1965. This taxonomy arranges types of religious experience according to intensity. The types are confirming, responsive, ecstatic, and revelational. Glock and Stark classify mystical experience as one kind of ecstatic experience.

Goleman, Daniel. *The Varieties of the Meditative Experience.* New York: E. P. Dutton, 1977. A sympathetic account of meditation from someone who practices it. Part Two contains a useful survey of meditation in various religious traditions.

Jung, C. G. *Psychology & Religion.* New Haven, CT: Yale University Press, 1938. This book contains Jung's Terry Lectures at Yale, in which he presents a condensed account of his views of religion.

Kessler, Gary E. "Religious Experience: What Is It and What Does It Prove?" In *Philosophy of Religion: Toward a Global Perspective,* 150–209. Belmont, CA: Wadsworth Publishing, 1999. A collection of writings that present different views concerning religious experiences and mysticism.

Otto, Rudolf. *The Idea of the Holy.* Translated by J. W. Harvey. New York: Oxford University Press, 1958. Here you will find Otto's classic account of the numinous experience.

Proudfoot, Wayne. *Religious Experience.* Berkeley: University of California Press, 1985. This book contains an insightful analysis of Schleiermacher's and others' views. Proudfoot argues that the cognitive dimension of religious experiences is vital for understanding them.

Rahula, Walpola. *What the Buddha Taught,* 2nd ed. New York: Grove Press, 1974. While dated in some ways, this is still one of the best introductions to early Buddhism.

Schleiermacher, Friedrich Daniel Ernst. *On Religion: Speeches to Its Cultured Despisers.* Translated by J. Oman. New York: Harper and Row, 1958. Schleiermacher argues that the essence of religion is in experience and is an expression of our "sense and taste for the infinite."

Stace, W. T. *Mysticism and Philosophy.* Los Angeles: Jeremy P. Tarcher, 1960. Stace discusses his famous distinction between introvertive and extrovertive mysticism.

Teresa of Avila. *The Interior Castle.* Translated by Kieran Kavanaugh and Otilio Rodríquez. New York: Paulist Press, 1979. In this book you can accompany Teresa as she travels to the center of her soul to meet the "God within."

Teresa of Avila. *The Life of Saint Teresa of Avila by Herself.* Translated by J. M. Cohen. London: Penguin Books, 1957. This is Teresa's famous and influential spiritual autobiography written for the discerning eyes of those who would judge her mystical authenticity.

James, William. *The Varieties of Religious Experience: A Study in Human Nature.* New York: Simon & Schuster, 1997. These Gifford lectures by James are full of wonderful quotations that illustrate a wide variety of religious experiences. Few commentators notice the subtitle of this influential and much analyzed work.

Zaehner, R. C. *Mysticism: Sacred and Profane.* London: Oxford University Press, 1961. Zaehner objects to Stace's typology and adds the category theistic mysticism.

INTERNET RESOURCES

www.pbs.org/splithorn/shamanism.html   Here you will find general information on shamanism, additional resources, and background on the PBS film *The Split Horn: Life of a Hmong Shaman in America,* along with a film clip.

http://plato.stanford.edu/entries/mysticism   This site from Stanford University provides a survey of the topic of mysticism and various philosophical views concerning its significance.

http://digital.library.upenn.edu/women/teresa/letters/letters.html   At this site there are translations of sixty letters written by St. Teresa to a number of important and influential people of her day, including King Philip II of Spain.

CHAPTER 8

Explaining Evil

Elie Wiesel was born in Romania in 1928, and just shy of his fifteenth birthday, he and his family were rounded up by the Nazis because they were Jewish. His family was murdered, but he survived to write about his experiences and to bear witness to the evil of the Holocaust.

In one of his books, simply called *Night*, he tells of his journey into a night of incomprehensible fear, pain, suffering, and death. Shortly after arriving at Auschwitz, men and women were separated. He watched his mother and sisters disappear into the crowd of other female prisoners. Little did he know that he would never see them again.

As he walked in a line with his father, he saw flames. Another prisoner said:

> Do you see that chimney over there? See it? Do you see those flames? . . . Over there—that's where you are going to be taken. That's your grave, over there. Haven't you realized it yet? You dumb bastards, don't you understand anything? You're going to be burned. Frizzled away. Turned into ashes.
>
> He was growing hysterical in his fury. We stayed motionless, petrified. Surely it was all a nightmare? An unimaginable nightmare?[1]

Wiesel could not believe that they would burn people in his day and age. Europeans are modern, civilized people, he thought. Besides, humanity would never tolerate it. People would not stand by and let such a horrible thing happen. He voiced these thoughts to his father, who told him, "Humanity is not concerned with us," and began to weep.

Prisoners at Buchenwald Concentration
Camp, 1945.

His body was shaking convulsively. Around us, everyone was weeping. Someone
began to recite the Kaddish, the Prayer for the dead. I do not know if it has ever
happened before, in the long history of the Jews, that people have ever recited
the prayer for the dead for themselves.[2]

There is so much pain and suffering in the world, and so much of it seems
pointless. Why is a baby tortured and murdered? Why did the horrible events
of September 11 occur? What brings someone to blow up a building, killing
many innocent people? Nearly every day newspapers describe cases of what
we can call *moral evil*, that is, suffering and pain inflicted on others by human
beings. Much of it seems so senseless.

Watch television and you will see graphic accounts of natural disasters
like floods, earthquakes, and tornadoes. Just one example is a report of an
earthquake in western India that killed thousands of people. Many were buried
alive and died slow, agonizing deaths. These are cases of *natural evil*. As if it
were not enough to live in a world of appalling moral evil, we live in a world

filled with natural evil as well. Why? What is the point of all this human suffering and pain? If we add to this the pain inflicted on other-than-human animals, it truly seems that we live in a senselessly painful universe.

There are magnitudes of pain and suffering. A toothache is one thing, the Holocaust is another. We can understand toothaches. And we can understand the causes of many natural disasters. But as it becomes harder and harder to understand pain and suffering, and as it seems so much of it is without good purpose, the problem of evil emerges. If I asked you to define evil, many of you would probably respond by saying that it is intense, pointless suffering.

Humans want explanations; we want to know why things happen. Knowing why reassures us that we live in a **nomos,** that is, an orderly world operating according to understandable laws. Such a world has meaning and purpose because we can understand why things happen by understanding the laws according to which they operate. However, many things that happen are **anomic.** They seem random, without explanation, and they threaten the meaning a *nomos* provides. Unexplainable evil, or at least what seems to be unexplainable, is anomic. It threatens the very *nomos* by which we make sense of things. It has cosmic implications, because the orderly universe in which we think we live may dissolve into chaotic meaninglessness, unless we can find a satisfactory theodicy.

In its narrow and theological sense, a **theodicy** is any proposed solution to the problem of evil that reconciles the existence of an all-good and all-powerful God with the evil that exists in the world. In its broad sense, a sense in which social scientists often use it, it refers to any ideological (religious or secular) explanation of anomic events. Here I will use the word mostly in its broad sense to refer to any attempt to make sense of evil. However, near the close of the chapter we will turn our attention to theological theodicies characteristic of monotheism.

A theodicy can overcome anomie because it seeks to answer what we can call the existential "why" rather than the scientific "why." There are many scientific explanations for events that produce great pain and suffering. We know what causes earthquakes and floods. We even know why some people commit vicious crimes. However, the "why" that evil makes us ask is not the scientific "why," it is the existential "why." Why did this evil thing happen to me, to my friends, to my family, to my society? Why did the World Trade Center collapse when all those innocent people were inside?

The Azande, an African tribe, build large granaries high off the ground so mice and other animals cannot get to the grain. Sometimes people sit under these granaries to get some shade. Occasionally these granaries collapse, killing and injuring the people under them. If you ask the Azande why this happens, they will say it is witchcraft. A witch did it! The Azande know perfectly well that these granaries collapse because termites weaken the structures. They know the answer to the scientific "why." What is puzzling to them is the existential "why." Why did it collapse just now, killing my father or sister? Given their worldview, which includes belief in witches, witchcraft makes a good theodicy for them. It explains why some particular person suffered or died, and it reinforces the plausibility of their worldview.[3] It restores *nomos*.

Religions play a central role in resolving the problems that arise from evil. Anomie in general and evil in particular are two of the greatest challenges religions must face. If a religion is to maintain its plausibility and continue to provide meaning and purpose to human life, it must face the problem of explaining evil. It must find ways to reassure people that in spite of anomic events, there still exists an overarching *nomos*. If a religion cannot reassure people that life makes sense, even in the face of horrible evil and death, it cannot survive. In this chapter we will look at the different kinds of theodicies constructed by religions to reassure people that their lives have meaning and serve a purpose, even in the face of the anomic threat that evil poses.

We begin with two case studies; the first looks at the Hindu notion of karma and the second at the development of messianic movements among Muslims. After comparing these cases, we turn to the task of constructing a typology of theodicies relying on the work of two important sociologists of religion: Max Weber and Peter Berger. From types, we turn to functions and explore how theodicies aid us in maintaining a meaningful existence. A section is devoted to the traditional theological problem of evil and some of the philosophical problems it raises. I think you will find the closing case particularly interesting because it deals with one of the oldest and most obvious kinds of theodicy called dualism. According to dualism, a perfectly good god is not responsible for the evil in the world; an evil god is responsible. Life is given meaning and purpose as people are enlisted in the fight against evil on behalf of good. This is an ancient story about the conflict between the good guys and the bad guys that is still played out in secular forms. It can be found in novels, television, and movies as well as religions.

8.1 TWO CASE STUDIES

Karma

Karma can mean, among other things, the law of cause and effect governing our lives. It states, as does the Bible, "as a man [person] sows, so shall he [or she] reap." The doctrine of karma is coupled with the idea of samsara, the wheel of rebirth. How we behave in our previous lives determines what we reap in this present life. Likewise, what we do in this life will determine our next reincarnation. The wrong we do will return to haunt us, and the good we do will return to make our next life better. Our only hope of escaping our karma is to somehow break out of *samsara* and stop the endless rounds of death and rebirth.

In classical Hinduism the ideas of karma and *samsara* were linked to both the caste system and the idea of *dharma*, or the duty appropriate to one's caste. Progress between this life and the next largely depends upon fulfilling one's caste obligations in this life. Good karma results from following one's *dharma*, and bad karma results from failing to fulfill one's *dharma*. The *Chandogya Upanishad* illustrates the idea of karma in relation to caste when a sage says:

> Now, people here whose behavior is pleasant can expect to enter a pleasant womb, like that of a woman of the Brahmin [priests], the Ksatriya [warrior] or the Vaisya [merchant/farmer] class. But people of foul behavior can expect to enter a foul womb, like that of a dog, a pig, or an outcaste woman. (5.10.7)[4]

There are different theories about how karma works. One important variety is the naturalistic or nontheistic view. The law of karma, according to this view, operates blindly, impersonally, and automatically. It is like a natural law of physics. If we jump off a cliff, we will fall because of the physical force of gravity. Physical laws do not really care what we do. Whether we jump or not, the power of physical laws is still effective. Indeed they are not even aware of us or who we are. Nevertheless if we jump, we will fall. We can bank on it. So too with the law of karma, but instead of being a physical law, it is a moral law. Our moral actions will automatically lead to the corresponding consequences. If we steal in this life, someone will steal from us in our next reincarnation.

In addition to naturalistic views, there are also theistic ones. According to the theistic theory, some superhuman divine agent oversees the law of karma by linking the actions in one life with those in another. Since there are different varieties of theism within Hinduism, exactly how this is done depends on how people think of the divine in relation to the law of karma. If they think that the law of karma depends upon the divine will, then it is a law that a divine being might break if deemed necessary. If they think that even the divine is subordinate to the law of karma, then the deity cannot intervene in its operation. In this view, God is the implementer of a law that cannot be changed, even by God.

To simplify our discussion, we will focus on the naturalistic or nontheistic interpretation of karma. I think the implications for a theodicy in the broad sense are clear. There is no reason to blame someone else for our misfortunes. If we now lead a life of suffering and pain, it is our own doing. We got ourselves into this mess, and only we can get ourselves out of it. We have no excuses, no deity to blame. However, the law of karma does reassure us that it is a *just* world after all. Sooner or later in this life or the next, we all get what we deserve.

Recall the creation myth of the Primal Man we studied in Chapter 4. By deriving the various castes in hierarchical order from the Primal Man, this sacred story reinforced the divisions and the norms of classical Indian society. The doctrine of karma does the same. It is a powerful appeal to our own self-interest that reinforces fulfilling our social obligations to those above and those below us on the social ladder. It is in our best interests to meet our social and ethical obligations as defined by the priests (Brahmin) for our caste. Disobedience of *dharma* (duty) is the basic offense against our own clear interests in improving our lot in this life and the next. If we are ultimately successful in moving up the caste ladder, we will finally have an opportunity to escape this samsaric world with all its pain and suffering.

The Mahdi

Eschatology refers to ideas about the last things. These "last things" may refer to the end of this world and human history as we know it or may refer to the end of an era or period of history that will be followed by a "heaven on earth." Typically, religions associate eschatology with a time of judgment, when good people will be rewarded and evil people punished. Hence eschatological movements can function as theodicies, reassuring the faithful that however unjust and evil things appear now, in the end, justice and goodness will reign supreme.

One type of eschatology is associated with **millenarianism.** This idea appears in the New Testament Book of Revelation in reference to the final struggle between God and Satan and the coming of the Messiah to reign for one thousand years. Scholars of religion often use the term to describe a variety of non-Christian and Christian **apocalyptic** movements that expect some kind of redeemer or messiah shortly, who will defeat Satan in battle and begin a utopian age of peace, joy, and harmony.

In Chapter 7 we looked at some of the basic beliefs found in Islam. However, we did not distinguish between the two main branches of Islam: *Sunni* Islam and *Shia* Islam. Most Muslims belong to the Sunni branch, but a significant minority belongs to the Shia branch. While both of these groups share much in common, they part company when it comes to ideas about who should be the religious and political ruler on behalf of Allah here on earth.

The story of how the Shia movement started is complex, but at its heart is the Shia claim that only members of Muhammad's family should be considered his legitimate successors. The Sunni reject this claim and argue that any descendent of the tribe to which Muhammad belonged can rule. Ali, the fourth caliph (ruler) after Muhammad, was assassinated along with his two sons Hasan and Husain. The Shia consider them martyrs to the holy cause of Islam.

The word *Shia* does not designate one group, but several. The largest Shia sect is called Twelver Shia because it traces the religious and political leaders (called **imams** by the Shia) to the twelfth in succession, whose name was Muhammad al-Mahdi. He vanished in 874, and thereafter the Twelvers believe that he went into a type of supernatural hiding called *occultation*. They also believe that he, along with Jesus, will return as the Messiah of the last days.

Twelver Shia has a complex theory of the Imam. In every age there is a human who represents Allah on earth and who designates a successor. All Twelvers are required to acknowledge the Imam of their age because they believe that the institution of the Imam is a covenant between Allah and humans. Twelvers regard imams as free of sin. They are doorways to Allah and convey what Allah wills directly to the faithful. Unlike some other schools of Islam, the Twelvers believe that Allah is essentially good and cannot will evil and that humans have freedom to obey or disobey Allah's will. They deny, in other words, a widely held Islamic belief that Allah predestines (determines) all things. It is not surprising, given these ideas, that from time to time people arose claiming to be the Mahdi ("meh-dee," meaning "rightly guided one"), the Messiah of the end times.

In the Sudan, in North Africa, a millenarian Mahdist movement arose, led by Muhammad Ahmad ibn 'Abd Allah (1834–1885). He proclaimed himself to be the long-awaited Mahdi of the last days. Popular lore in the Sudan included stories about a mahdi or messianic figure who would be sent by Allah to rescue the community from oppression and restore Islamic justice. The Sudan had been under colonial rule for some time, and the people, longing for freedom from outside rulers, readily joined a Mahdist movement that offered them hope.

Muhammad Ahmad proclaimed that the **jihad,** or "struggle by the sword," against the enemies of Islam was second only to the rule concerning the recitation of prayers five times a day. He also added to the traditional Five Pillars of Islam the requirement that his followers profess faith in him as the Mahdi. As his Mahdist movement became more powerful, Ahmad declared a holy war against the Egyptians and Turks who ruled the Sudan at the time. His eschatological vision included, after securing the independence of the Sudan, the conquest of Egypt, Arabia, Syria, and Turkey. He preached that a time of justice, well-being, and the glorious triumph of "true Islam" under his leadership lay just around the corner of history.

Many of the upper classes of the Sudan were offended by Muhammad Ahmad's claims to be the Mahdi, but the peasants flocked to his support. They found his egalitarian policies that allowed slaves to fight alongside their masters attractive. More attractive still was the promise that he would defeat the foreign forces ruling the Sudan, thereby lifting the powerless and suffering peasant class to a position of power.

This Sudanese Mahdist uprising, which started in 1881, attracted the attention of the whole world when, in 1885, a garrison controlled by the British defender of Khartoum, General Charles George "Chinese" Gordon, was overrun after a long siege. The Mahdists killed Gordon, and the prophecies of Muhammad Ahmad seemed about to be fulfilled. An independent Sudanese state was established, and the Mahdists came into power.

In the summer of 1885 Muhammad Ahmad died. His followers were undaunted and erected a shrine over his grave, declaring him to be a saint worthy of veneration. His shrine became a pilgrimage site, even though Ahmad himself had outlawed saint veneration.

The Mahdists continued in power until 1898, when the British sent an expedition to avenge the death of Gordon. The British campaign was a success, and the Mahdist movement in the Sudan collapsed. Like so many other eschatological and millenarian movements, the promised end of evil and suffering was not realized. Yet the Mahdist movement left an important political legacy because the notion of the Mahdi now became a symbol that could be used to mobilize the masses against foreign oppression and encourage them to fight for national liberation. We still feel the echoes of this nineteenth-century movement in the beginning of the twenty-first century as militant Islamists seek to restore political power.

8.2 COMPARISON

The karma theodicy and the eschatological theodicy of the Mahdi are different in important respects. The karma theodicy assumes reincarnation, and the eschatological theodicy does not. The karma theodicy places the responsibility for evil squarely on the shoulders of human beings. We suffer because we deserve to suffer. Likewise only we can make things better by learning from our karma and doing better this time around. The eschatological theodicy of Madhism attributes evil to Satan and helps us live with present suffering by offering a promise that in the end Allah will reward the faithful and punish the wicked. But this coming time of compensation is not so much due to human effort as is the case with the karma theory, but due to a messianic figure who will come to save us. We must, however, be willing to follow him even unto death.

Both theodicies have a vision of a just world, but it is a very different vision. According to the karma account, the world is just because justice is a by-product, so to speak, of the law of karma. This law is simply the law of cause and effect with a moral twist. Such a law creates justice by making evil actions reap evil effects and good actions reap good effects, at least eventually. According to the eschatological account, the world is just because there is a divine being who will someday make it just by rewarding those who deserve rewards and by punishing those who deserve punishments.

Both these theodicies explain why bad things happen to good people, although in different ways. The karma theory says that bad things happen to good people because of their karma. The eschatological theory says that bad things happen to good people because trial and suffering brought about by Satan are the lot of the faithful as they await the time of deliverance.

These theodicies also tell people that they should not despair. Despair is appropriate only if there is no hope. The karma theodicy holds out hope for improvement for those willing to do their duties, and the eschatological theory holds out hope for the eventual redemption of those who are faithful. Both serve to reinforce the morality taught by the respective religions that espouse them.

The karma theodicy is, however, more conservative than the eschatological theodicy. The duties people should fulfill, on the karma account, are the conventional duties of society that are appropriate to one's class and traditionally taught by religion and culture. The morality reinforced by eschatological theodicies is usually counter to the conventional morality of the corrupt and evil world in which people now live. It may be proclaimed as the original morality taught by the founding prophets and corrupted over the centuries, or it may be an entirely new morality, appropriate to the end times. In the case of the Sudanese Mahdist movement, it was both. Muhammad Ahmad called on his followers to return to the pure Islam originally proclaimed by the Prophet Muhammad *and* to follow a revised set of pillars based on his present divine inspiration. He went so far as to drop the pilgrimage to Mecca from the traditional list of five to make room for jihad, understood as holy war.

Both of these theodicies deal with the anomic nature of evil by reminding people of a *nomos*, or purposeful order, that makes life meaningful and worthwhile. Because the karma theodicy does not require a god to make it work, it never has to face the question of why a perfectly good divine being who cares for creation permits evil to occur. The eschatological theodicy of the Mahdi must face this challenge. But however it answers that question, it assures people that there is ultimately a divine purpose to what goes on in this sinful and wicked age.

8.3 TYPES OF THEODICIES

There are many different types of theodicies, and like any typology, the number of types increases as the distinctions become more refined. Here I wish to examine four broad types. These types are not unrelated, and many of them appear, in one form or another, in the same religious tradition. Even so, one or another of them tends to dominate particular traditions. Also, these theodicies are not exclusively religious. Frequently they have their secular counterparts.

Karma Theodicies

In our first case study, we have already looked at one form of karma theodicy. The case we analyzed presupposed the existence of a soul that transmigrates from body to body. This soul carries with it the karma of previous lives so that when bad or good things happen to someone in this life, they are happening to the person who deserves them. However, not all karma theodicies assume there is a soul. Indeed one form, found in Theravada (Way of the Elders) Buddhism, denies there is a soul (the so-called no-self doctrine) and still supports a theory of karma. How can this be?

As we saw in Chapter 7, part of Buddha's enlightenment experience was the realization that there is no soul substance underlying what we call a person. This realization, if true, means that clinging to the objects of our desires makes no sense. If selfish clinging is the cause of suffering, as the second Noble Truth proclaims, then suffering can be eliminated once we realize that acting selfishly gains us nothing in the absence of a real, substantive self or soul.

Even though Theravada Buddhism denies the existence of a soul substance, it still supports a theory of karma. Thus Nagasena, a Buddhist monk, explains to a king how the apparent inequalities of life can exist:

> "Venerable Nagasena," asked the King, "why are men not all alike, but some short-lived and some long, some sickly and some healthy, some ugly and some handsome, some weak and some strong, some poor and some rich?"
>
> "Why, your majesty," replied the Elder, "are not all plants alike, but some astringent, some salty, some pungent, some sour, and some sweet?"
>
> "I suppose, your Reverence, because they come from different seeds."
>
> "And so it is with men! They are not alike because of different *karmas*."
> (Milindapanha)[5]

While both Hindus and Buddhists appeal to the law of karma to make sense of the good and evil that humans experience, this appeal appears much harder to make for a Buddhist who denies the existence of the soul. If the soul is not reborn in a new body to reap the consequence of past actions, how can the new person be significantly related to the previous person?

Different schools of Buddhism give different answers to this problem, but one common answer is found in the claim that karma itself is reborn. Thus Nagasena quotes the Buddha to the effect that

> "Beings each have their own *karma*. They are . . . born through *karma*, they become members of tribes and families through *karma*, each is ruled by *karma*, it is *karma* that divides them into high and low."[6]

A favorite Buddhist analogy uses a lamp and a flame to illustrate this idea. If the flame from one lamp is used to light another, and another, and another, though each lamp and flame is different (like each of our bodies and personalities are different in different lives), the flame (karma) provides a causal connection.

For Buddhism, reality does not consist of static and unchanging substances, but it consists of events. Events do not come into existence without previous causes. Events are the effects of previous actions (remember the word *karma* means action) and, in turn, are causes of subsequent events. So there is a network of cause and effect between all events, and it is no different with those events we call persons.

This may not solve all the problems that arise when Buddhists try to combine the no-soul teaching with a theory of karma, but it does remind us that it is not necessary to believe in transmigrating souls in order to believe that karma explains why inequalities and apparent pointless suffering exist. According to this theodicy, people have nowhere to hide. There is no God or Satan to blame. People cannot escape their responsibilities for the mixture of good and evil that makes up the world.

Eschatological Theodicies

Eschatological theodicies attempt to make experiences of what seem to be pointless pain and suffering meaningful by promising that someday things will be made right and justice will triumph. There are two types of eschatological theodicies: this-worldly and otherworldly. As the names indicate, a this-worldly eschatological theodicy claims that things will be made right in this world, and an otherworldly eschatological theodicy claims that things will be made right in some other world such as heaven.

The case of the Mahdist movement in the Sudan is one example of a this-worldly eschatological theodicy. Another example comes from what anthropologists call *cargo cults*. This term refers to religious and sometimes political movements that seek to bring about a time of wealth, cooperative living, and all that is imagined to be good. Melanesia is particularly noted for its cargo cults, but there are similar movements in Africa and the Americas.

These cults usually arise in times of rapid socioeconomic and religious change associated with colonialism. Under colonial rule, people often experience poverty and other sorts of deprivation. Exchange, the normal means for acquiring wealth, does not work because colonial rulers and missionaries show little interest in native goods. A way of obtaining the kinds of goods that Europeans want has to be found. Otherwise there can be no exchange. Hence these cults search for the "road to cargo," and look forward to a time when the ancestors will return, the colonial masters will depart or share their wealth. Typically a prophet or messiah figure emerges in these movements. He or she claims to have a message from the ancestors or from God about the road to cargo, and this stimulates cargo-cult development.

In the New Hebrides (now Vanuatu), for example, a movement began in 1940 and was led, in turn, by three prophets, each named Jon Frum. People thought these prophets to be manifestations of the indigenous spirit Karaperamun. These prophets encouraged cooperative work and revived practices outlawed by the Presbyterian missionaries. Positive experiences with American troops during World War II led some members of the Jon Frum cargo cult to build model airfields so the planes filled with cargo could land. They spoke of Jon Frum as "king of America" and believed he would soon return. Cataclysmic events such as the leveling of mountains would accompany his return, and he would establish a reign of bliss in which there would be no need for work, no sickness, and the natives would get back their youth.

The primary weakness of this-worldly eschatological claims is that they can be disconfirmed when the hoped-for time of a paradise on earth does not arrive. When the prophecies of a better time to come do not come true, these movements often dissolve, reset the dates for it to happen, claim it is really here but hidden, or that the time of bliss is really otherworldly, not this-worldly. Otherworldly theodicies have the advantage of making disconfirmation virtually impossible because the long-awaited rectification of injustice and evil happens after death.

Otherworldly eschatological theodicies abound in the three missionary religions of Christianity, Islam, and some schools of Mahayana (Greater Vehicle) Buddhism. Typically these theodicies teach that there will be a reward for the faithful after death in a blessed paradise and a punishment for the unfaithful in hell. As the Christian hymn says, "we are but strangers here, heaven is our home." We might add, "and we hope hell is not."

Both the Bible and the Quran refer to a day of judgment when all people will be judged for their beliefs and actions in this life. This judgment day signals the end of human history and the restoration of justice. The living and the resurrected dead will appear before God for consignment to damnation in the never ending fires of hell or to an eternal paradise with God. In Christianity, the day of judgment marks the second coming of Christ who will punish evil and redeem the righteous.

Hell is the final abode of the wicked and place of everlasting torment. On a popular level, hell is often pictured as a place under the earth where graphic tortures take place. However, among some theologians, there is a tendency to see hell not so much as a place, but as a state of endless separation from God, the only true Good. Hence it symbolizes the frustration of the goal of human life, which is to achieve happiness and meaning. It is, if you will, a truly pointless evil because there is no hope that the suffering might one day stop. It is a condition of permanent anomie.

Some have found this severe doctrine of an eternal hell too difficult to accept. Surely if evil is pointless suffering, then God must not be responsible for the worst example of it, namely, hell! Modifications have tried to take the sting out of this teaching by making hell a temporary state. This is done when hell is reconceived as a kind of purgatory where sinful souls atone for their evil deeds and, once cleansed, move on to a happier state. In some Mahayana Buddhist schools, there are no eternal hells, but different levels and kinds of purgatories into which those with bad karma may be reborn. Sooner or later they will be purified and move on to different kinds of heavens until permanent release from all suffering is achieved. Only liberation can be permanent, not suffering.

Other religions, like Roman Catholic Christianity, combine a doctrine of hell with a doctrine of purgatory. For most people, especially those who have not committed the unforgivable sin against the Holy Spirit, forgiveness and hence salvation is always possible once they pay the price for sin. Here there is hope, even beyond the grave in that part of hell where purgation takes place.

Heaven or paradise is the postdeath abode of the blessed. In Christianity it is pictured, on a popular level, as a celestial city with streets paved with gold where those who are saved offer eternal praises to the Trinity. In Islam paradise is usually referred to as "the garden," which is both the first home of Adam and Eve before their sin and the last home after the death of the faithful. This garden is supposed to have four or seven levels and to contain rivers, shade trees, fruits, jeweled couches, flowing fountains, and all things necessary for the bliss and peace of those who dwell there.

Opinions vary among both Muslim and Christian theologians about how literally to take all this detail. Many argue that such descriptions are symbolic of all things beautiful, pleasing, and good. The true joy of paradise is living in the eternal presence of God. It marks the fulfillment of human existence, which is worth all the temporary sufferings we may endure in our earthly lives.

Theodicies of Participation

A theodicy of participation deals with evil, suffering, and misfortune by relativizing such events. It reassures us that in the grand scheme of things our individual suffering is of little significance. Our lives as individuals have less value than some greater reality in which we participate. If we keep that in mind, we will be able to bear evil and suffering.

There are many different versions of this kind of theodicy depending on how people think of the "greater reality" and how they understand the process of participation. What is perhaps its oldest form encourages people to transfer their sense of identity to the family, clan, or larger social unit, including the ancestors. For example, in traditional Chinese religions identity formation involves coming to understand oneself as part of a larger family unit that includes both the living and the dead. Undergoing this sort of socialization process leads people to subordinate their own self-interests to the more enduring interests of the ongoing family. We are, this theodicy teaches, only one very small part of a much larger process of life stretching back and forward into endless time. Fidelity to the family, especially the revered ancestors and living elders, is the overriding value. All else, including our own identity and suffering, becomes insignificant in comparison.

This sort of theodicy operates in many religions, including the religion of the Australian Aborigines. What is of paramount importance to the living is to keep the memory of the ancestors alive, to perform the rituals they taught in the Dreamtime, and to carry out family, clan, and tribal obligations. In a very real sense a person becomes the group. We are, this theodicy teaches, small pulses of a life process that encompasses all of space and all of time.

A similar kind of theodicy operates among mystics. Here the social unit is replaced by nature, the One, the divine, or the "suchness" of the process we call reality. We might dip into almost any of the mystical literature in the world and find passages that speak of a mystical, self-transcending participation in an ultimate reality that is far more important than the momentary evils that may afflict people. Indeed, from this more inclusive viewpoint, not only do such evils seem less important, but they do not seem to be evils at all. In the grand scheme of reality, they are unreal nothings.

Rabia (d. 801) was a slave-woman who became a Sufi mystic. To her the love of Allah was all that really mattered. She declared herself ready to suffer the pangs of hell if it would glorify her one true love, Allah. And Rumi (d. 1273), another influential Sufi mystic, so lost his own sense of individual identity that he could declare

> What to do, O Muslims? For I do not recognize myself;
> Not a Christian I nor Jew, Zoroastrian nor Muslim.
> Not of the East am I nor West, nor land nor sea;
>
> . . . . . .
>
> Not of this world am I nor the next, not of heaven nor hell;
>
> . . . . . .
>
> My place is no place, my trace has no trace;
> Not body nor soul, for I belong to the soul of Love.
> One I seek, One I know, One I see, One I call.
> *He is the first, He the last; He the outward, He the inward.*[7]

The theodicy of participation can also take secular forms. Soldiers are trained to identify with their nations to the point of suffering death so the nation lives on. Some people identify so deeply with the value of humanity and its greater good that, paradoxical as it seems, they are ready to risk their own lives to save the lives of others.

The sort of self-transcendence discussed here can be evaluated both negatively and positively. Negatively perceived, it may seem little more than masochism. Some people denigrate and devalue their individual identity to the point that they willingly invite pain, suffering, and even death for the sake of that "greater reality" with which they identify. When the individual becomes nothing, when family, nature, or God become everything, and when the individual finds ultimate happiness in what is other than him- or herself, this is, or at least is very close to, the heart of the masochistic attitude.

Viewed from a positive perspective, self-transcendence for the sake of a greater good appears altruistic. It may even be the pinnacle of unselfishness. People often think of heroic self-sacrifice as the noblest of acts. We frequently praise those who put the happiness of others before their own pleasure. Most of us are taught from a very early age that selfishness is bad and unselfishness is good. We think a community of purely selfish people to be no true community at all.

However we may evaluate theodicies of participation, the point is that self-transcendent participation can aid people in making sense of anomie. The theodicy of participation, like the other kinds, can legitimate experiences of anomie by helping us believe we have meaning and purpose. An added benefit is the assurance that we are not alone in our suffering.

Dualistic Theodicies

Dualistic theodicies face the problem of explaining evil head-on by claiming that some sort of superhuman force is responsible for evil. This kind of theodicy comes in various shades ranging from limited dualism to absolute dualism. In its limited form, some superhuman evil force has less power than some superhuman good force. Both Christianity and Islam, for example, assure us that Satan is both a force responsible for evil and a force that God has already defeated, although the final battle is yet to be fought. In its absolute form, the two superhuman forces of good and evil have equal power, and the outcome of their battle is not certain.

Dualistic theodicies are often combined with apocalyptic themes proclaiming a final conflict at the end of history between good and evil. Often this conflict is symbolized as a horrible war or battle between the power of light (good) and the power of darkness (evil).

There have been many different dualistic religions in the history of both the West and the East. Their attraction is obvious from the viewpoint of the human need to explain what appears to be pointless suffering. What better way to explain all of the vast turmoil, pain, inhumane acts, and suffering we encounter in this world than by attributing anomie to a superhuman force of great evil?

Types of Theodicies

1. Karma theodicies
2. Eschatological theodicies

   a. This-worldly
   b. Otherworldly

3. Theodicies of participation
4. Dualistic theodicies

8.4 THE THEOLOGICAL PROBLEM OF EVIL

At the outset of this chapter we distinguished between two different kinds of problems associated with our experience of evil. The first we referred to as the broad problem of making sense of evil, and the second as the narrow or theological problem of evil. It is now time to turn our attention to the theological problem and some of its possible solutions.

The theological problem of evil appears in a monotheistic context. It arises from the apparent incompatibility of the existence of one divine creator of this world who is all-good (omnibenevolent), all-powerful (omnipotent), and all-knowing (omniscient) with the existence of evil. As the Scottish philosopher David Hume (1711–1776) put it, "Is he [God] willing to prevent evil, but not able? Then he is impotent. Is he able, but not willing? Then he is malevolent. Is he both able and willing? Whence then evil?"[8] Thomas Aquinas (1225–1274), a brilliant Roman Catholic theologian, said that the existence of evil is the *best* argument against the existence of God.

Philosophers and theologians distinguish between two different kinds of arguments about God and evil. The first is called the deductive or logical argument, and the second is named the inductive or evidential argument. J. L. Mackie (1917–1981), an English philosopher, put the deductive argument like this:

> In its simplest form the problem is this: God is omnipotent; God is wholly good; and yet evil exists. There seems to be some contradiction between these three propositions, so that if any two of them were true the third would be false. . . . However, the contradiction does not arise immediately; to show it we need some additional premises, or perhaps some quasi-logical rules connecting the terms "good," "evil," and "omnipotent." These additional principles are that good is opposed to evil, in such a way that a good thing always eliminates evil as far as it can, and that there are no limits to what an omnipotent thing can do. From this it follows that a good omnipotent thing eliminates evil completely, and then the propositions that a good omnipotent thing exists, and evil exists, are incompatible.[9]

This deductive or logical problem of evil is a problem only for people who believe that there is a God as defined by Mackie. This is neither a scientific problem that might be solved by some sort of experiment nor a practical problem that might be solved by some sort of action. It is a logical problem involving the clarification and reconciliation of a number of different beliefs.

The inductive or evidential problem of evil does not rely on the mere existence of evil to try to prove God does not exist. It does not argue that evil per se is logically incompatible with God's existence. Rather it points to the degree, variety, or amount of evil that does exist and argues that this kind of evil makes it highly improbable that God exists. If a wholly good, all-powerful, and all-knowing creator God exists, we would expect much less suffering, or less variety of suffering, or less intense types of suffering in the world than is the case.

William Rowe, a contemporary American philosopher, states the inductive or evidential problem like this:

1. There exist instances of intense suffering which an omnipotent, omniscient being could have prevented without thereby losing some greater good or permitting some evil equally bad or worse.
2. An omniscient, wholly good being would prevent the occurrence of any intense suffering it could, unless it could not do so without thereby losing some greater good or permitting some evil equally bad or worse.
3. There does not exist an omnipotent, omniscient, wholly good being.[10]

Notice that this inductive argument is not purely logical but relies on empirical evidence. If there were no instances of intense suffering that could not be justified on the grounds that they lead to a greater good or prevent a greater wrong, then this argument would lose its force. This is not to say that instances of intense human or animal suffering are good. In themselves they are evil, even if they are instrumentally good because they lead to a greater good or prevent a greater evil.

What might a greater good be that justifies God's permitting intense suffering to exist? One kind of answer that people give to this question is punishment for sin. God would not be an all-good God if he did not punish sin. So evil is justified on the grounds that it is good to punish sin. The Christian theologian St. Augustine (354–430) suggested this answer when he said that "evil is either sin or the punishment for sin."

Many people have found this answer rather harsh. It smacks of a "blame the victim" mentality. Its plausibility becomes even more questionable when we think of instances in which innocent babies burn to death. Then there are cases of apparently really good people suffering intense pain and horrible deaths, not to mention innocent animals who can hardly be guilty of sin. Here something like reincarnation can help, because it would claim that the innocent in this life were not so innocent in previous lives. This would turn this sort of theodicy into a karma theodicy, only with God as the adjudicator of karmic effects. Augustine, however, could not adopt this idea because he did not believe in reincarnation.

If this kind of theodicy (let us call it the recompense theodicy) is to work, then sooner or later people must bring in the issue of free will. If my sin is not freely done, then I am guilty of nothing and deserve no punishment. So perhaps free will is the greater good that explains why God permits instances of evil? This is sometimes called the "free will defense." This kind of theodicy says, in effect, a world in which human beings have freedom of choice, even if it sometimes leads to sin and evil, is better than a world in which there is no free choice.

If this is true, then it might well explain the existence of moral evils caused by humans, but it does not explain natural evils like the intense suffering caused by hurricanes, floods, earthquakes, and the like. How could our sins cause such things? We might also wonder, if God is all-powerful, why God cannot create free human beings who do not sin? Is it not the case that we seem to be both free to make choices, yet genetically and environmentally limited in important ways? Perhaps an omnipotent God has the power to create humans who can make genuinely free choices, yet are limited in what they can do. One of those limits is that they cannot inflict intense and senseless pain and suffering on themselves or others. It appears that the free will theodicy is, at best, quite limited in its ability to justify the existence of evil.

Some have claimed that the greater good that God brings about by permitting evil is better human beings. John Hick (see "Suggestions for Further Reading") has called this a "soul-making" theodicy because it holds that any world leading to personal moral development must include the experiences of pain and loss. God's purpose in creating this world is to aid us on our road to spiritual and moral growth, not to give us a paradise of constant pleasure in which we will be as comfortable as possible. Evil is for our own good.

While this soul-making theodicy, like the theodicies of recompense and free will, has some initial plausibility, it becomes more difficult to maintain the more specific we become about the sorts of evils we are talking about. If we grant that some experiences of pain and suffering help build our character for the better, how much pain and suffering is necessary? This world in which we live contains a large amount of intense pain and suffering, much of which appears pointless. Think of the last century alone: two world wars, Hitler, the Holocaust, the gulags of Stalin, the massacres by Pol Pot, Milosevic's ethnic cleansing, AIDS, terrorism, starvation, and on and on it goes. Would not a world with either less suffering or less intense suffering do as well when it comes to building character?

All of these monotheistic theodicies (recompense, free will, soul-making), if persuasive, would be satisfactory answers to both the logical and evidential problems of evil. If we can show that there is a good reason for evil of whatever type to exist, then we can show that there is neither a logical contradiction between the existence of God and the existence of evil, nor is there decisive evidence against God's existence.

The theological theodicies we have been considering attempt to hold God's qualities of omniscience, omnipotence, and omnibenevolence constant and still defuse various versions of the problem of evil. However, another move in this debate is possible. We might, for example, modify our under-standing of omnipotence in such a way that the problem of evil in both its deductive and inductive forms disappears. This is exactly what process the-odicy tries to do.

According to process theologians and some process philosophers, change or process constitutes all reality, including God. (You may wish to compare this to the Buddhist doctrine of impermanence.) However, not any old sort of process is the order of the day; rather, this process is social. The world consists of actual entities, ranging from the smallest forms of energy to God, that freely respond to the activity of other actual entities that in turn respond. Reality is a marvelous dance of mutually responsive energy, and no other actual entity, including God, can wholly determine the dance ahead of time.[11] Of course partial determination takes place as in any society of interacting beings, but in this vision of reality, total determination is simply not possible. The dance is too complex.

This theory implies that even omnipotent power or the greatest possi-ble power of which we can conceive is not total. God cannot create a stone that God cannot lift because it is simply not logically possible to do so. It would be a contradiction to say God has the power to create an unliftable stone or the power to do other contradictory things like creating square circles. Likewise, according to process theology, it is not possible for God to totally control every event that happens in a world of free relationships among entities. As one contemporary process theologian named Schubert Ogden puts it, God does not have all the power that there is "but only all the power that any one individual could conceivably have consistent with there being other individuals who . . . must themselves also have some power, however minimal."[12]

If this process view of omnipotence is correct, then God cannot elimi-nate all degrees and types of evil, let alone all evil. God can only minimize evil while creating as many possibilities for good as possible. This picture of God, some argue, is much closer to the biblical picture of God freely inter-acting with his free creatures with love, forgiveness, and mutual respect than to the picture of a God with infinite power, which some philosophers and theologians paint.

While this picture of a God limited in power is attractive to some, oth-ers find it unacceptable. A limited or finite God who is not in full control of his creation and whose will can not only be frustrated but also defeated by evil may not be a God worthy of worship. In the end, does such a God have enough power to secure our salvation? Could we ever be sure of that?

If one way to try to solve the monotheistic problem of evil is to modify the definition of God, another way is to deny the existence of evil. If evil does not exist, the problem of evil and the need for any kind of theodicy evaporates. But how can someone deny what seems so obvious to all of us—that there is evil?

We learned of the Hindu theologian Shankara and his school named Advaita Vedanta in Chapter 3. As you may recall, Shankara taught a radical nondualism. Only Atman/Brahman exists; all else either does not exist or only appears to exist. Among the "all else" is evil. Since we do experience what we take to be pointless suffering, evil's existence is apparent, but it is not real. It seems to exist, but does not really exist. It is *maya*, a trick or illusion that arises out of ignorance concerning our true self.

We find very similar ideas in the West, as the teachings of Mary Baker Eddy (1821–1910), the founder of Christian Science, indicate. According to her book, *Science and Health with Key to the Scriptures*, God is Mind or Spirit and is the only true reality because God is Truth. If this is so, she reasons, then illness, disease, pain, suffering, and even death only *seem* real, as the contents of a dream might seem to be real as long as the dream lasts. Evil is an illusion, a bad dream, something that, in the last analysis, does not really exist. She writes in *Science and Health*:

> the only reality of sin, sickness, or death is the awful fact that unrealities seem real to humans . . . until God strips off their disguise. They are not true, because they are not of God. We learn in Christian Science that all inharmony of mortal mind or body is illusion, possessing neither reality nor identity though seeming to be real and identical.
> The Science of Mind disposes of all evil.[13]

The keys to this debate are the words *real* and *evil*. What is it for evil to be real? Neither Shankara nor Mary Baker Eddy deny that evil is "real" to our minds. They only deny that it has a reality independent of what we think and imagine. Nevertheless to claim that evil does not exist outside human experience but only in human experience does not get us very far along the road to a satisfactory theodicy because evil still exists at least as a psychological reality if not a metaphysical one. To be told while you are suffering that you are not *really* suffering seems small comfort.

Monotheistic or Theological Theodicies

1. Recompense
2. Free will
3. Soul-making
4. Restricting God's power
5. Denying the existence of evil

8.5 HOW THEODICIES WORK

Our discussion in this chapter has centered around the idea that a theodicy can overcome anomie because it seeks to answer the existential "why." But why do humans need an answer to the existential "why?" Why is the scientific answer insufficient?

There are many things we fear, but some of our most basic fears are of being alone and of living a pointless life. We also fear intense pain and suffering, but we know that some of us may have to endure pain at some point in our lives. Believing that we are not alone and that suffering makes sense or has a point makes dealing with suffering easier than trying to cope totally alone and in despair. Theodicies assure us that we are not alone and that there is a point to suffering. They provide comfort in difficult circumstances.

On a more cosmic scale, theodicies provide us with assurances that the universe in which we live makes sense. Anomic events like evil threaten the meaningful order (*nomos*) we so desperately want. Theodicies tell us that in spite of anomic threats, the *nomos* continues. Theodicies help maintain macrocosmic as well as microcosmic meaning.

What is necessary for a theodicy to give comfort and maintain a sense of cosmic meaning? Not all theodicies work all the time for all people. Perhaps the idea of karma does not work for you because you have difficulty believing in rebirth. Perhaps we live in such a fragmented and individualistic world that theodicies of communal and family participation seem rather old-fashioned. Perhaps theodicies of mystical participation or punishment for sin seem odd in our scientific age. Perhaps we have seen too many bad things happen to too many good people, and so most theodicies have a hollow sound. They seem like the ideas of people scrambling to patch leaks in the cosmic boat while it is sinking.

If theodicies are going to work, they must seem plausible and they must legitimate by explaining and justifying the way things are in the world. Their power to legitimate is directly connected to their plausibility. Religions need plausible theodicies to legitimate their worldviews. The plausibility required is both intellectual and emotional. Theodicies must make sense to our minds and to our hearts.

From a sociological point of view, theodicies become plausible to us through a process of socialization. We are taught in thousands of ways as we grow up in a religion and in a society that its theodicies answer the problem of evil. Socialization processes are never perfect, so doubts may remain. But when we need explanations, when we or a loved one suffers intense and apparently pointless pain, we often fall back on the answers we have been taught in spite of our doubts. We do, after all, need some kind of comfort.

The need for comfort is illustrated by two kinds of responses to evil that we have not yet discussed. The first has been called a "theodicy of submission," but it is not really a theodicy because it gives up trying to make intellectual sense of evil and recommends that we simply submit to the mystery of divine rule. It is a kind of antitheodicy because it denies there is an adequate rational explanation for evil. This is equivalent to claiming that a theodicy is not possible. There is no rational explanation, at least none we can now grasp.

The Book of Job in the Hebrew Bible provides a good example of this sort of response to evil. Job is visited with unspeakable horrors because Satan bets God that if Job suffers enough he will stop believing in God. Job's friends employ the theodicy of recompense to help Job see that his apparently undeserved suffering is really punishment for sin. However, Job protests that he is righteous, not sinful. His suffering is undeserved.

The recompense theodicy is no longer plausible to Job, yet he continues to seek an answer. Finally God tells Job to stop whining and realize that God is God, the Sovereign Ruler of the whole universe. God challenges Job by saying, "Dare you deny that I am just or put me in the wrong that you may be right?" (Job 40:8). Job finally submits to God's power and majesty. He admits his ignorance of God's purposes, he admits his self-centered absorption in his own suffering, and he repents in "dust and ashes" for ever daring to question God's justice.

Submission to divine mystery may be one way to bring the hunt for theodicy to a close after all the rational answers have proved implausible. However, for some, submission will not work; only protest will do.

Elie Wiesel, whose dramatic account of his Holocaust experiences begins the chapter, does not, in spite of all the evil he and other Jews have experienced, want to give up belief in God. For Jews to stop believing in God means that Hitler wins in the end. True, Hitler did not succeed in destroying the Jewish people, but if Jews lose their faith, he will have succeeded in destroying the Jewish faith, the heart and soul of a Jew. Wiesel wants to believe, but he does not want to buy into hollow theodicies that are offensive to those who suffered and he does not want to simply submit to the mystery of divine power. He wants to protest God's actions; he wants to put God on trial and question God about God's guilt and responsibility.

In his play *The Trial of God*, Wiesel tells a tale about the aftermath of one of many *pogroms* (organized and deliberate massacres of Jews), which took place in Russia in 1649. God is put on trial for permitting the massacre, and Berish, one of two survivors, acts as prosecuting attorney. Sam, the defense attorney, lists all the usual reasons God has for permitting evil, including the assertion that the ways of God are simply beyond human understanding. Berish will buy none of it and says, "I lived as a Jew and it is as a Jew that I shall die—and it is as a Jew that, with my last breath, I shall shout my protest to God."[14]

You may recall the irony of Wiesel's account of Jews saying the kaddish (prayer for the dead) as they were about to be killed. Why pray to a God who will not save you from intense and apparently pointless suffering? Though the kaddish is a prayer of faith, it is also, in this instance, a prayer of protest. Wiesel recalls that he learned from his teachers that a good Jew may oppose God as long as he does so in order to defend God's creation. In our language we can say, "in order to defend God's *nomos*."

This "theodicy" of protest is, paradoxically, an antitheodicy. When all the usual theodicies no longer seem plausible, when they fail to offer comfort, when submission to mystery seems a cop-out, and when atheism appears to offer only despair, perhaps protest is all the believer has left to prevent the floodgates of anomie from opening.

Antitheodicies

1. Submission
2. Protest

REVIEW QUESTIONS

1. Distinguish natural from moral evil, *nomos* from *anomie*, and theodicies in the broad sense from the theodicies in the narrow sense by giving an example of each.
2. How does the answer to the existential "why" given by the karma theodicy differ from the answer given by the eschatological theodicy?
3. The Melanesian cargo cults are illustrations of what kind of theodicy? Be specific.
4. Distinguish dualistic theodices from theodices of participation.
5. Clearly state in your own words the difference between the deductive and the inductive problem of evil.
6. Of the different solutions offered to the *theological* problem of evil, which seems most plausible to you and why?
7. What is an antitheodicy, and why do you think that some people find it attractive?
8. Explain in your own words how theodices work.
9. Imagine a world in which no theodicy is plausible or helps people deal with evil and suffering. Would you like to live in such a world? Why or why not?

RESEARCH CASE—MANICHAEISM

All religions are **syncretistic** to one degree or another. They combine and blend elements from different sources as they move from one location to another and survive historical changes. Manichaeism ("man-i-kee'iz-uhm") is a blend of many different elements.

Manichaeism is a religion based on the teachings of Mani (The Living), who was born in Babylonia in 216 of Iranian parents. He probably grew up in a Christian community that practiced adult baptism. In 228 Mani received his first revelation by an angel who was his "heavenly twin" and who came to release Mani from the "error of the sectarians." A second revelation in 240 caused him to publicly break from the baptist community, and he began to preach that purity comes through knowledge, not through bathing.

Mani was the author of at least seven scriptural documents preserved now only in fragments. In these texts his heavenly twin angel teaches through him that there exist two opposing principles, light and darkness. Light symbolizes good and is associated with the Father of Greatness, and darkness symbolizes evil and is associated with the Prince of Darkness. There are three stages to the conflict between light and darkness: a preliminary stage in which both powers are separate, a stage in which both become mixed and engage in a battle for the control of the universe, and a final stage in which light and darkness will return to their separate abodes. Humans now live in the second stage, and they are particles of divine light trapped in material bodies. Eternal rounds of reincarnation in the prison house of our corrupt and polluted bodies are our lot until we come to know our true light-selves. This knowledge releases us from the bonds of matter and the snares of the Prince of Darkness.

The story of how the second stage came to be is a sordid story of violence, cannibalism, and sex. The world in which we live was created as a result of the first clashes of the Father of Light and the Prince of Darkness. This account includes a story of how the Primal Man and his sons (five elements of light) were devoured by demons. These battles resulted in a division of the universe into a *lower reign*, including the earth and under the control of Prince of Darkness, and an *upper reign* controlled by the Father of Light. These cosmic battles also generated monsters. Primordial matter caused the demons Ashaglun and Namrel to eat the monsters and then to mate, bringing Adam and Eve into existence. The Prince of Darkness wants Adam and Eve along with their offspring to mate as much as possible, thereby producing as many bodies as possible to trap the light. But a Savior named Jesus the Splendor is sent from above, arouses Adam from his ignorant slumber, and reveals to him the divine origins of the light within (the soul).

Mani was commissioned by his twin angel to undertake a worldwide mission. He proclaimed the religion he founded to be a universal religion containing a message for all people. He also claimed to be the final prophet in a line of prophets that included the Buddha, Zarathustra, and Christ. He traveled in the Middle East, perhaps as far as India. His religion, spread by a traveling merchant class, achieved success throughout much of the Roman empire. It traveled along the Silk Road as far as China, where it survived until the thirteenth or fourteenth century.

The Manichaean church was made up of two classes: Elect and Auditors (Hearers). Auditors belonged to the church only by serving the Elect, who made up the true church. Manichaean pictures, found in central Asia, show Auditors kneeling in front of male and female Elects. The Elect wore white robes, observed ascetic rules, and lived in monasteries like Buddhist and Christian monks. Some had no fixed dwelling. They wandered around like foreigners in a strange and alien land. The Auditors were obligated to offer them alms and hospitality.

Manichaeans practiced an ethic of nonviolence, and the Elect were expected to lead chaste lives, while the Auditors were to practice strict monogamy. People were instructed to pray four times a day, fast on Sundays, and give a tenth or a seventh of their earnings to the church. They were to confess their sins weekly and annually at a collective ceremony called the Bema that was celebrated in the memory of Mani's suffering and his struggle to bring liberating knowledge to the world.

Agriculture was thought to harm the divine light by trapping it in matter. Because preparing bread and vegetables polluted those who did it, the Auditors prepared the food for the Elect, and when the Elect ate it, they released the "captive light," thereby becoming "saviors of God."

Mani died in prison during the reign of the Sassaniam emperor Bahram I (274–277). Although Manichaeism no longer survives (there are, however, attempts to revive it), its ideas are still influential in many different forms, ranging from the religious to the secular. The dramatic story of the battle between the forces of darkness and the forces of light still attracts audiences.

QUESTIONS ON THE CASE OF MANICHAEISM

1. How did Manichaeism "solve" the problem of evil? Besides dualism, what aspects of other kinds of theodicies appear in its teachings?
2. What sort of social conditions would need to be present for Manichaeism to have such wide appeal in the ancient world? Have you ever felt like you did not belong here, that you were an alien in a strange world, a world to which you did not really belong? Why?
3. Why do you think the symbolism of light and dark was used to represent good and evil, spirit and matter, and why do you think the same kind of symbolism persists to this day?
4. How does Manichaeism legitimate an ascetic and celibate lifestyle?
5. Do you find the Manichaean theodicy plausible? Why or why not? How would you modify it, if you could, to make it more plausible?

Fieldwork Option: Interview at least six people about their views on evil and how it might be explained. Analyze their responses based on information provided in this chapter.

SUGGESTIONS FOR FURTHER READING

In addition to the material found in the notes, the reader may wish to consult the following for more information.

Berger, Peter L. "The Problem of Theodicy." In *The Sacred Canopy: Elements of a Sociological Theory of Religion.* Garden City, NY: Doubleday & Anchor, 1967. Berger presents a sociological analysis of various types of theodicies. Much of my discussion is based on Berger's ideas.

Griffin, David. *God, Power, and Evil: A Process Theodicy.* Philadelphia: Westminster Press, 1976. As the subtitle implies, Griffin explains and defends a process theodicy.

Herman, Arthur L. *The Problem of Evil and Indian Thought.* Delhi: Motilal Banarsidass, 1976. Herman offers a careful discussion of the history of the problem, the Indian doctrines of rebirth, including the "karma thesis," along with a philosophical critique.

Hick, John H. *Evil and the God of Love.* London: Macmillan, 1966. Hick provides a clear and spirited defense of the soul-making theodicy.

Humphreys, Christmas. *Karma and Rebirth.* London: Curzon Press, 1983. Humphreys, a British convert to Buddhism, provides a vigorous defense of karma as the best answer to the problem of evil.

Jung, C. G. "Answer to Job." In *Collected Works,* vol. II. 1938. Translated by R. F. G. Hull. Princeton, NJ: Princeton University Press, 1958/1969. Here you will find Jung's classic psychoanalytic study of Job and the problem of evil.

Livingston, James C. "Theodicy: Encountering Evil." In *The Anatomy of the Sacred.* 3rd ed. Upper Saddle River, NJ: Prentice Hall, 1998. Livingston provides a well-organized and clear discussion, which has strongly influenced my own.

Ormsby, Eric L. *Theodicy in Islamic Thought.* Princeton, NJ: Princeton University Press, 1984. Ormsby describes and explains Islamic thinking about the problem of evil.

Plantinga, Alvin. *God, Freedom, and Evil.* Grand Rapids, MI: Wm. B. Eerdmans Publishing, 1977. The philosopher Alvin Plantinga provides a logical and lucid modern defense of the free will position.

Reichenbach, Bruce R. *The Law of Karma: A Philosophical Study.* Honolulu: University of Hawaii Press, 1990. Reichenbach provides a careful study of karma in both the Indian and Buddhist contexts.

Rubenstein, Richard. *The Cunning of History.* New York: Harper and Row, 1978. Rubenstein discusses the meaning of theodicy in the context of modern genocide.

Weber, Max. "Theodicy, Salvation, Rebirth." In *Sociology of Religion.* Boston: Beacon Press, 1964. Weber first used the term *theodicy* in the broad sense and developed a useful typology that Peter Berger (see above) elaborated in *The Sacred Canopy.*

Widengren, Geo. *Mani and Manichaeism.* Translated by Charles Kessler. New York: Holt, Reinhart and Winston, 1965. Widengren has packed this book with information about Manichaeism. Some of it is dated, as recent scholarship has shown, but it still provides an excellent foundation.

Worsley, Peter. *The Trumpet Shall Sound: A Study of "Cargo" Cults in Melanesia.* New York: Schocken, 1968. Worsley provides more information about the Jon Frum movement and others like it.

INTERNET RESOURCES

http://plato.stanford.edu/entries/evil   This article in the *Stanford Encyclopedia of Philosophy* critically explores some of the basic arguments developed by philosophers and theologians concerning the problem of evil with a good bibliography that will take you deeper into the issues.

http://www.smithsonianmagazine.com/issues/2006/february/john.php This site provides a good introductory article on the cargo cult centered on Jon Frum in Vanuatu (formerly the New Hebrides).

http://en.allexperts.com/e/m/mu/muhammad_ahmad.htm.   At this site you will find a brief biography of Muhammad Ahmad's life and some background on the Madhi movement he led in the Sudan.

CHAPTER 9

Religion and Morality

Hᴏw sʜᴏᴜʟᴅ ᴏɴᴇ ʟɪᴠᴇ? The Greek philosopher Socrates (470–399 ʙ.ᴄ.ᴇ.) said that this is the most important question humans can ask of them-selves. Should we live according to God's commands, submitting our own will to the divine will? Should we live a virtuous life centered on creating social harmony? Should we follow the Golden Rule, doing unto others as we would have them do unto us? Should we order our lives by some moral natural law that is built into the structure of the universe? Should we live a life dedicated to the well-being of all living things and the world in which they live? There are many different answers to the question about how we should conduct our lives.

Humans, who are controlled less by instincts than other animals, have the freedom to select different lifestyles. This freedom is not absolute. It is limited. But the limits are constantly changing as cultural, social, scientific, and technological changes occur. We cannot ask and answer the question about how we should live once, but we must keep asking and trying to answer it as we mature and as new moral problems arise.

In an important sense we might view religions as elaborate and complex answers to the question about how we should live. These answers are moral in the very broad sense of providing norms or values for the conduct of life. This moral viewpoint is based on a distinction between what *is* the case and what *ought* to be the case. We often distinguish between what is real and what is ideal. The real is what is the case, and the ideal is what ought to be the case. Religions take into account the gap between how we do live and how we ought to live. They try to close this gap as much as possible by creating a vision of the good life and by urging people to make how they do live conform ever more closely with how they ought to live. Religions seek to make the ideal real.

We can think of **morality** as a set of norms designed to regulate and govern the conduct of humans with one another, with other living creatures, and with their environment. Technically *ethics* is the philosophical study of morality, although the word is often used interchangeably with morality. Here we will, for the most part, use the words *ethics* and *morality* interchangeably.

Religions are connected to morality in many different ways. Religions *identify* moral norms. They tell us what is morally right and what is morally wrong. Religions also *legitimate* moral norms. They justify them by telling us why we should consider them moral and thereby see ourselves under some obligation to follow them. Religions also *motivate* people to shape their lives according to a set of religiously transmitted norms. They do this in a variety of ways, including preaching, telling moral tales, offering saints and moral heroes as examples, instilling guilt when norms are broken, and promising just retribution. Religions also help *renew* moral commitments by instilling a sense of hope and providing opportunities for forgiveness and for membership in groups working to build moral communities.[1]

From what I have said so far, it would appear that religion is primarily a conservative moral force. It endorses and supports the conventional moral norms as they are culturally and religiously transmitted. However, religions also *criticize* moral norms and often endorse radical revisions in conventional morality. Religious prophets may condemn conventional morality in the name of a higher morality. For example, Martin Luther King, Jr., a Christian preacher, condemned segregation laws and the conventionally accepted attitudes they embodied in the name of a higher moral standard of human equality. We cannot naively assume that because something is legal, it is also morally good.[*]

I will elaborate on these themes as we discuss the nature of morality, how religions identify and legitimate moral norms, and how they use retribution and guilt to motivate and renew moral commitments. We will start with two cases. The first analyzes the divine command theory of ethics. There are different versions of this theory, but most assert that what is morally good is what God commands, and what is morally wrong is what God prohibits. Our second case introduces a religious tradition originating in China that we have so far not had an opportunity to discuss. It is called Confucianism and is so permeated with a concern for developing virtue that some have claimed it is not really a religion at all, but a moral philosophy.

---

[*] See Chapter 10 and the case "Truth and Reconciliation."

The research case at the end of the chapter also introduces a religion that we have not discussed before. It is called Jainism, and it originated in northern India about the same time as Buddhism (sixth century B.C.E.). You may have already heard of one of its central teachings called **ahimsa** ("ah him'suh"), which is often translated as "nonviolence."

Relations Between Religion and Morality

1. Religion identifies moral norms.
2. Religion legitimates moral norms.
3. Religion motivates people to follow moral norms.
4. Religion motivates people to renew their moral commitments.
5. Religion criticizes some moral norms in the name of a higher morality.

9.1 TWO CASE STUDIES

Divine Command Theory

The divine command theory of ethics is common to many religious traditions, especially the monotheist faiths of Judaism, Christianity, and Islam. We will focus on Islam in our analysis and explore the Islamic idea of *Sharia* ("sha-ree'ah"), which is often translated as "divine law," but literally means a path to water. It refers to the entire body of moral, ritual, and legal directives that Islam claims is ordained by Allah. The *Sharia* is the answer Islam gives to Socrates' question about how we should live.

Al-Ashari (d. 935), the founder of an Islamic school of theology named after him, argued that Allah is an "Overwhelming Monarch" who is subject to no one and no thing. If this is so, then

> nothing can be wrong on God's part. For a thing is wrong on our part only when we go beyond the limit set for us and do what we have no right to do. But since the Creator is subject to no one, nothing can be wrong on His part.
>
> Question: Then lying is wrong only because God has declared it to be wrong.
>
> Answer: Quite so. And if He declared it good, it would be good; and if he commanded it, there could be no opposition to it.[2]

Al-Ashari was arguing against a position associated with a rival theological school called the Mutazila. These theologians had argued that there was a rational basis for good and evil. If we were to ask both of these theological schools whether something is good only because God commands it, or whether God commands something because it is good, the Asharites would answer that God's commands and prohibitions are the *only thing* that make something right or wrong. The Mutazila theologians would answer that God commands something *because it is good*. In other words, God knows that something is good or bad and commands or prohibits it accordingly. God does not command lying but prohibits it because lying is morally wrong. Its wrongness can be established on rational grounds, or so Mutazila theologians argued.

Al-Ashari opposed the Mutazila view. He boldly declared that even lying would be good *if* God commanded it. In other words, morality is based on the divine will alone. It makes no difference what human reason and rationality may say about it. The basis of morality is not in human reason, but in Allah's will.

Al-Ashari's position is a good example of a strong form of the divine command theory of ethics, which states that we find the foundation of all morality in God's will. In other words, the meaning of good is equivalent to what God commands, and the meaning of wrong is equivalent to what God prohibits.

This is more than just an arcane theological debate. There are serious and important practical implications. Al-Ashari advocated a divine command theory because he wished to protect God's absolute sovereignty and power. If God commands something because it is good, limits are placed on divine power. There are things God can command and things God cannot. What these things are can be determined by human moral reason. This implies, al-Ashari argued, that human reason determines what God can or cannot do.

The Mutazila school opposed the Asharites on this issue because they believed that such a strong version of the divine command theory reduces morality to a matter of blind obedience. If divine fiat or command determines what is right or wrong, the consequences of what people may do and their intentions for doing it have no moral validity. Surely this is contrary to our rational intuitions. Would we call people morally good if they really wanted to lie, but did not do so only because God prohibited it? Would not people be like children who did what was right only because their parents, who have greater power, required it, not because they really wanted to do it? We might say that what such children do is good, but we would hardly call them morally good because their actions amount to mere conformity with the wishes of a greater power.

The Asharite position, the Mutazila theologians argued, makes the ground of morality arbitrary. If God should command lying instead of honesty, then lying would be good, given the Asharite version of the divine command theory. Let's say God should have a change of heart and decide that honesty should be forbidden and lying commanded. If this is possible, Asharite theory hardly seems like a firm foundation for morality. Of course it could always be argued that God's will is eternally the same, so God's will about honesty and lying would never change. However, if we are to avoid limiting God in any way, we must allow for the logical possibility that God's will might change and turn morality as we now know it on its head.

Identifying the basis of morality with God's commands raises the issue of where these commands can be found. They can be found, according to Islam, in the *Sharia*, or divine law. While we have been using the word *morality* to talk about the divine command theory, we must keep in mind that *Sharia* is a much broader concept. Muslims do not make sharp distinctions among what is legal, what is religious, and what is ethical or moral. The *Sharia*, as the totality of divine law, contains religious duties such as prayer along with moral and legal duties. As the Sunni tradition of Islam developed, it specified four sources of *Sharia*. The first and most obvious source is the Quran, the Holy Scripture containing the infallible revelations of Allah to Muhammad. The second source is the *Sunna*, or "customs," of the Prophet Muhammad derived from his words and actions. Some of this material has been recorded in the Hadith, which Muslims believe contains the authentic accounts of what the Prophet said and did. Muslims consider both the Quran and the *Sunna* of Muhammad as divinely inspired sources.

The Quran and the *Sunna* do not explicitly address every situation. So Muslims often appeal to a third source of *Sharia* called analogical reasoning. Analogies are drawn between new situations and the material found in the Quran and *Sunna*. If the analogy is close, a trained interpreter of the law can deduce what should be done in new situations. A fourth source of divine law is called *ijma*, or consensus of the community. This does not mean that the whole Muslim community votes on what should be done in situations not covered by the other three sources, but that a consensus is reached by those who are learned (*ulama*) and whose views are respected and widely accepted.

These religious authorities both interpret the *Sharia* and administer it. The *ulama* have often been necessary for Islamic governments to succeed because their cooperation provides a stamp of approval that legitimizes a ruler's decisions. Their lack of cooperation often spells death to a regime—witness the role of the Ayatollah Khomeini (d. 1989) during the Iranian revolution against the Shah. The *ulama*, however, have also been criticized for being too conservative, too rigid in their interpretations, and out of touch with the needs of Islamic peoples in the modern world.

Four Sources of *Sharia*

1. Quran
2. *Sunna*
3. Analogical reasoning
4. Consensus of the community

Because the *Sharia* is rooted in a divine command theory, we would expect it to be rather static, inflexible, and unable to cope with a new and changing world. However, as our discussion of the four sources of *Sharia* shows, it is a dynamic system that has been changing and evolving since the earliest days. Large numbers of Muslims take it very seriously not only because they consider it one of the most impressive aspects of their religion, but also because it makes Islam a comprehensive religion—that is, one that integrates all aspects of life from diet and dress to business and prayer.

Not every government of Islamic countries has used the *Sharia* to administer the country. So, alongside the *Sharia*, secular laws reflecting different viewpoints have arisen. Nevertheless, the attempts of recent Muslim revolutionaries (often called fundamentalists) to restore *Sharia* as the sole system of law in Islamic countries indicates the importance of *Sharia* to Islamic identity.

Confucian Virtue

Our second case comes from Confucianism, which today numbers a little over 5 million adherents. Confucianism is an English term denoting a wide range of Chinese schools of thought that in one way or another were inspired by and dedicated to the ideas of the First Teacher, also known in English as Confucius. Historians map at least six major transformations of Confucianism. Here we will be concerned only with the beginning, or classical, phase.

The classical era refers to the time when the founders of the Confucian tradition developed and transmitted a body of writings that later scholars used as a source for their thinking. The founders are Confucius (551–479 B.C.E.), Mencius (372–289 B.C.E.), and Xunzi (also spelled Hsün-tzu and pronounced "shuhn-dzuh") who flourished between 298 and 238 B.C.E. The basic literature consists of the *Five Classics* and the *Four Books*. The *Four Books* include *The Great Learning, Doctrine of the Mean, Analects,* and *Mencius.* I will rely heavily on the *Analects,* which are a collection of Confucius's sayings and dialogues with his pupils.

Biographical information is uncertain, but tradition tells us that Confucius was from the nobility and lived at a time when Chinese society was close to chaos and its leaders corrupt and ineffective. When he was three, his father died, and at nineteen he decided to seek a career in government. Ultimately, however, he was to make his name as an educator, not a politician. His reputation in China became so immense that on the popular level he was eventually deified, while among scholars he was venerated as the First Teacher.

What exactly did he teach? Again the evidence is uncertain, but as far as we can tell from the *Analects* he taught *de* (*te*), usually translated as "virtue." This may be a misleading translation because in English, *virtue* is usually associated with morality. This is not the case in ancient China. Virtue (*de*) is a broad concept more akin to excellence and power. People can become excellent at many different things, from sports to study. Not all excellence is moral excellence, but moral excellence is vitally important for living a good life. With excellence comes power, and Confucius was particularly concerned with gaining the power to live life well. D. C. Lau, a noted Confucian scholar and translator of the *Analects*, remarked that the unspoken assumption behind Confucian teaching is "that the only purpose a man can have and also the only worthwhile thing a man can do is to become as good a man as possible."[3]

It seemed obvious to Confucius that good people live good lives and create good societies. Therefore education should focus on developing good people—people whose character exhibits virtue or excellence. In light of this, it is not surprising that one of his central ideas is *ren* (*jen*). *Ren* has been translated in a variety of ways: "human excellence," "love," "benevolence," "humaneness," and "kind-heartedness." It is a difficult notion to grasp in a single English word, and Confucius does not give an explicit definition of it. *Ren* is not something we are, but something we can become by cultivating our social, aesthetic, cognitive (thinking), and moral powers. It refers to what we might call "ideal human nature." It is humanity at its best, having realized its full positive potential.

What is such an ideal character like? The ideal character has many qualities such as wisdom, piety, kindness, and respect. A person with these qualities—a person who is a cultivated gentleman, sage, and scholar—acts on the principle of *shu*. (In early Chinese Confucianism, only males had the opportunity to reach the Confucian ideal.) *Shu* means seeing someone else as being like yourself. It is often translated as "reciprocity." In response to a question about whether there was a single principle that one could act on all of one's life, Confucius responded, "Wouldn't it be likening-to-oneself (*shu*)? What you do not yourself desire, do not do to others" (*Analects* XV.24). This has sometimes been called the negative Golden Rule, but that is misleading. *Shu* is closely associated with another principle called *zhong* (*chung*), which means doing your best for others. Reciprocity (*shu*) combined with doing your best for others (*zhong*) articulates a positive, not a negative, principle for living. These principles of *shu* and *zhong* should govern the *five primary relations*: between parent and child, ruler and minister, husband and wife, older and younger siblings, and friend and friend.

There are, however, additional virtues that characterize the good life in its fullest sense. One of these is *li* (pronounced "lee"). *Li* is often translated as "propriety," but it is a broad concept that can mean order, ritual or rite, custom, manners, etiquette, worship, and ceremony.

Humans, Confucius taught, should behave appropriately in all their relationships. The models for appropriate behavior came, according to Confucius, from the traditional rites and customs handed down from the past Golden Age. Confucius thought of himself as a traditionalist, not an innovator. Tradition is important in his view because it provides an external check on what we may subjectively believe to be the right way to act and is a repository of the wisdom of the past with regard to proper conduct.

Confucius's traditionalism is evident in his views of another virtue worth cultivating, the virtue of *xiao* (*hsiao*), which is pronounced "shee-ow". This is the traditional Chinese virtue of filial piety (as it is often translated). This translation is misleading, however, because filial piety usually refers to the obligation sons and daughters have to obey their parents, in particular their father as the head of the household. There can be little doubt that *xiao* has been and is interpreted in this narrow sense. As we might expect, this narrow understanding promoted sexism and child abuse by placing nearly absolute power and authority in the father. However, in its broadest sense, *xiao* involves the practice of kindness, honor, respect, and loyalty among all family members (an ideal seldom achieved in practice).

Confucius placed emphasis on *xiao* because he believed that a strong family is the basis of a strong society. The family is the microcosmic (smaller) version of the macrocosmic (greater) social order. Society ought to be thought of as one large family. It is a short step from this idea to the more radical notion that the whole of humanity ought to be treated like family, with kindness, honor, and respect. We are still a long way from realizing the "family of humanity."

Daoist critics of Confucius accused him of confusing the ritualistic aspects of life with the moral aspects. Confucius's ideas, they argued, made proper manners and blind obedience to elders far more important than any other virtue. Some contemporary critics have even said that Confucius really had no idea of morality, in any modern sense of the word. However, Confucius does talk about *yi* (pronounced "yee" and sometimes spelled *i*), which can be translated as "rightness or what is fitting." D. C. Lau maintains that *yi* should be thought of as Confucius's concept of morality. In one sense, Lau argues, the whole of Confucius's thought should be seen as one long meditation on "what is fitting." If Lau is right, then morality is a central Confucian concern.

Recent commentators argue that we should not ignore the aesthetic dimension of Confucian thought. Ethics has to do with moral value; aesthetics has to do with the value of beauty. The Confucian concern with balance, harmony, and appropriateness reflects aesthetic values, but there is no reason why they cannot also reflect moral values. The division between moral and aesthetic value is something Confucius probably did not recognize. For him to call an action right was not only to pass a moral judgment but also an aesthetic judgment. Moral order is aesthetic order. The good and the beautiful, as Plato would say, are one.

The Confucian vision of the ideal world is one in which the world is like a home shared by all. Trust among all prevails, and "all people love and respect their parents and children . . . there is caring for the old . . . sharing replaces selfishness and materialistic greed . . . and the door to every home need never be locked and bolted by day or night" (*The Record of Rites*, Book IX, one of the *Five Classics*).

> ## Basic Confucian Ideas
>
> 1. *Ren* refers to benevolence or acting kindly toward others.
> 2. *Shu* and *zhong* refer to not doing to others what you do not want done to you and doing what is best for others.
> 3. *Li* refers to propriety, or acting appropriately.
> 4. *Xiao* refers to familial love and respect.
> 5. *Yi* refers to doing what is fitting (morality).

It is clear that education plays a key role in the process of becoming a virtuous person. Knowledge of the past is a clue to proper action in the present. Since becoming a virtuous person or developing good character is a process, it is something we must learn how to do. Hence, proper instruction and good education are the keys to developing *ren*.

But what about religion? Where does religion fit in? When Western scholars first encountered Confucianism, they wondered about what they had found. Was it a religion, a kind of philosophy, or a form of social ethics? Interestingly, the early Christian missionary-scholars called the most important Confucian texts "classics" rather than "scriptures." This indicates that they felt some uncertainty about how best to describe Confucian literature in Western terms. "Classic literature" might be religious, ethical, political, philosophical, or all of these. By labeling it this way, they avoided a definitive judgment.

There is no doubt that observing the rites and rituals centered on ancestor veneration and honoring rulers were and still are important to Confucianism. The Confucian "family" as we have seen, goes far beyond what we normally think of as the family to potentially include the whole of humanity. Even if we concentrate on the notion of family in the biological sense of people related by blood, this family extends backward and forward in time. In Confucian thought, it includes those who are living, those yet to come, and those who have died. It is not that Confucius believed in life after death. He appears to have expressed agnosticism on that issue. However, religious rites honoring the rulers and the dead ancestors were important because they reinforced social harmony and promoted the cultivation of virtuous character.

Confucius did speak about the Mandate of Heaven, which allowed rulers to rule. Once the Mandate was withdrawn, the ruler ceased to have a legitimate right to rule. He also spoke of the Dao as a guide to the right path to follow. Among Daoists, the Dao was the way of nature, and while Confucians did not often speak of it in this naturalistic sense, it often seems implicit that the right way to live is also the way nature intended humans to live. In other words, the path of virtue is also the path of nature.

This blending of ethics and naturalism does not appear to be very religious to those who think of religion as primarily having to do with supernatural gods. But the Dao is a superhuman force, and if it is also an ethical force, it becomes far more than the usual view of nature as a collective term for processes that are not artificial or created by humans. Humans do not produce the Dao, the Dao produces humans. And the Dao is ethical in the sense that it can be the path to right living.

Tu Wei-ming, a contemporary scholar involved in the development of what is today known as New Confucianism, addresses what he calls "the intriguing issue of transcendence." Since divine transcendence is associated with such religions as Judaism, Christianity, and Islam, is transcendence at "all relevant to the Confucian mode of being religious?" He writes:

> Confucian religiousness begins with the phrase "ultimate self-transformation," which implies a critical moment in a person's life as well as a continuous process of spiritual cultivation. For us to be actively involved in ultimate self-transformation, we must make a conscious decision to do so. Since being religious is tantamount to learning to be fully human, we are not religious by default but by choice.[4]

Note that Tu uses "spiritual cultivation" instead of "moral cultivation." It is clear that, at least for him, Confucianism is more than morality; it is spiritual. The morally right way to live is also a spiritual way to live.

9.2 COMPARISON

A comparison of our two cases requires, at the start, a distinction between a **duty ethics** and a **virtue ethics.** According to duty-based ethics (sometimes called deontological ethics), our primary moral obligation is to do our duty. An ethics of duty centers on rules, commands, and prohibitions that spell out what our duties are. According to a virtue-based ethics, our primary moral guides are not rules, commands, laws, and the like, but people who exhibit moral excellence, or an ideal moral character. Duty ethics are based on commands to "do this," while virtue ethics are based on admonitions to "become this."

From what we have learned about Islamic ethics and Confucian ethics, I think it is clear that the most obvious difference between the two centers on the difference between an ethics of duty and an ethics of virtue. Islamic morality is based on law (*Sharia*), and the Islamic tradition has developed an elaborate system of jurisprudence (ways of interpreting and applying law) in order to determine what the law is in this or that situation. Confucianism did not develop systems of law or procedures of jurisprudence. Rather, its focus was and is on education designed to develop the right kind of person. Confucian ethics is confident that the right kind of person (the virtuous sage) will do the right kind of things in any given situation. Islamic ethics is confident that people need rules, laws, and regulations to guide them.

This primary moral difference between Islam and Confucianism is somewhat overstated. There are clear elements of a virtue ethic within Islam, indicated by the reliance on the example of the Prophet and the *Sunna* in general as a source of *Sharia*. There are also clear elements of a duty ethic in Confucianism insofar as developing *ren* amounts to a moral obligation. However, the emphasis on virtue in the Islamic case is embedded in and supported by an elaborate legal system. In Confucianism the emphasis on duty is embedded in a system of education and moral transformation centering on learning what is fitting, on ceremonies, and on cultivating harmonious relationships in the family and in society at large. Islamic ethics seeks to produce the obedient person, and Confucian ethics seeks to produce the wise and virtuous person who practices *ren* (humaneness) naturally and spontaneously.

At the start of this chapter we spoke of the relationships between religion and morality in terms of (1) identifying, (2) legitimating, (3) motivating, (4) renewing moral commitments, and (5) criticizing some moral norms. Try your hand at comparing Islam and Confucianism with respect to these relationships. I will share some of my ideas about these issues below.

If we examine the ways in which Islam and Confucianism (1) identify and (2) legitimate moral norms, I think we can see some further differences between a duty ethic and a virtue ethic. Islam, as we have seen, recognizes four ways of identifying moral norms; two (the Quran and the *Sunna*) are based on divine revelation, and two (analogy and consensus) are based on human reason and the faith that Allah is rightly guiding the community of believers. Confucianism identifies moral norms by developing a notion of the ideal human being in relationship with the whole human family. The Islamic *Sharia* is ultimately justified by Allah's revelation. Other factors such as human reason play a role (although some Islamic schools have been highly suspicious of its use). Confucianism legitimates moral norms not by appealing to divine revelation of a personal God, but by appealing to the Mandate of Heaven, the Dao, and the harmonious and peaceful society that virtuous people create.

Islam and Confucianism also (3) motivate moral commitment in different ways. Islam motivates much like a military organization motivates its troops. There are rewards and punishments promised in this life and the next as well as powerful processes of socialization instilling in people a sense that a life of submission and obedience is the best way to live. In Islam, one does not submit to human laws and human moral norms, but to divine laws and divine norms. Confucianism motivates primarily by example and social pressure. It offers a model of the virtuous person and says in effect, "Don't you want to live like this?" It instills family values so deeply into the fabric of society that great shame results from acts of disloyalty and failure to obey those whose family status is greater than one's own.

Islam (4) renews moral commitments by offering the possibility of repentance, divine forgiveness, and divine mercy. Allah offers another chance to those who sincerely repent. Confucianism is generally optimistic about human nature or the human heart (although there are those like Xunzi who are not). People are basically good because people have been created by Heaven, and it is basically good. It may take a long time to cultivate this basic goodness, and there are bound to be failures along the way. But the message is clear, "Keep trying, keep learning, keep practicing, and someday you will succeed."

How do Islam and Confucianism (5) criticize moral norms? Islam is a prophetic religion born of a radical critique of the prevailing polytheism of its day. Its prophetic history makes it suspicious of human laws and human norms. However, like so many other religions with a strong prophetic foundation such as Judaism and Christianity, as time goes by and power is obtained, a particular set of values, norms, and laws become "the right way" to do things. This "right way" often goes unquestioned until it becomes so abusive or oppressive that calls for reform emerge. Islam can be both conservative and revolutionary.

Confucianism, in contrast, appears to be conservative and traditional. The golden past is sacred. Tradition tells the Confucianist what to do. As Confucius said, he came to teach nothing new but to preserve and pass on the tradition of virtue learned from the sage-kings of the Golden Age. This does not mean that there are no resources within Confucianism for criticism of conventional morality. Recent developments in Confucianism are testimony to its ability to produce change through criticism. However, these "new" movements often claim to be returning to the pure teachings of the past that have become distorted or corrupted. The past, not the future, remains the primary guide.

There is a prophetic motif in Confucianism that we should not overlook. It is the Mandate of Heaven. This Mandate permits a ruler to rule as long as he or she rules virtuously. This means the Mandate can be lost. When it is, the people have the right to revolt and overturn the ruling regime. Historically, Confucianism has been so closely tied to government patronage that Confucian-led revolts seldom occurred. The study of the classical literature of Confucianism was required for all government officials, and it was the basis for the civil service examinations in China for centuries. This situation encouraged Confucian support for whatever regime was in power. But, at least theoretically, the prophetic threat of the loss of the Mandate always remained.

9.3 IDENTIFYING AND LEGITIMATING MORAL NORMS

We have examined how Islam and Confucianism identify and justify moral norms using the ideas of God's commands and the virtuous sage. They do this in other ways as well, and one of the most common ways centers on the idea of natural law.

The central idea of natural law theories is the notion that morality is built into the structure of the universe. If, as Islam claims, an ethical God created the universe, we might expect that such a God used moral norms when creating nature. Confucianism, while not appealing to a moral creator God in order to legitimate its morality, nevertheless refers to the Mandate of Heaven. If a ruler does not rule with justice and mercy, the Mandate of Heaven to rule is lost. Here nature (the Mandate of Heaven) and morality intersect.

Within Christianity, Thomas Aquinas (1225–1274) offered a version of natural law theory that became and in some circles remains a widely influential way for people to identify and justify moral norms. Natural law theory instructs us to ask, "Is it (whatever 'it' may be) natural?" If the answer is yes, it is morally good, and if the answer is no, it is morally wrong.

Borrowing from both Stoic philosophy and Aristotle, Thomas argued that all reality can be divided into "natural kinds," and each of these kinds is distinguished from other kinds by a unique essence. This essence tells us what are the natural ends, or outcomes, for each kind. For example, the natural end for an acorn is to develop into an oak tree. The virtue, excellence, or goodness of an acorn is to achieve this outcome. Aquinas was primarily concerned with humans, not acorns, and whether or not their actions fostered or hindered their development toward their natural ends. For example, he argued that suicide is morally wrong because it is contrary to our natural inclination for self-preservation and life. Likewise, monogamy within marriage is morally right because it best promotes the natural human end of reproduction and proper child care.

Perhaps some of the most controversial applications of natural law theory, especially in the modern world, center on sexuality. Roman Catholicism, using natural law theory, has condemned as immoral any use of artificial methods of birth control. Homosexuality has been declared immoral on similar grounds. If the natural end of humans is to reproduce, any sexual activity that is not conducive to reproduction is morally wrong because it is "unnatural." Roman Catholicism takes the same approach to abortion. Because the natural end of a human embryo is to become a human being, aborting that embryo is unnatural because it stops this natural developmental process, just as a squirrel that eats an acorn stops its natural development into an oak tree.[5]

According to Aquinas, natural law is derived from the eternal law of God by which God governs the universe. Only God can know the complete eternal law, but humans, through the use of reason, can derive natural law from this eternal law. Human law is, then, an extension of natural law in particular cases. It follows that the laws by which societies govern themselves should reflect natural law as closely as possible. There will always be disagreements over specific applications, but the general principles should be clear enough. Following this line of reasoning, Pope Leo XIII argued in the encyclical letter *Immortale Dei* of 1885 that since both "nature and reason" command all people to worship God, it should be a public crime for people to act as if there were no God. A state with human laws that shows no concern for religion is, therefore, immoral. It should, Pope Leo concluded, be one of the chief duties of the state to "favor religion, to protect it, to shield it under the credit and sanction of the laws."[6]

Certainly much Islamic thinking about the state and human laws would agree with this natural law approach, and it can be found in other religions as well. As you may recall from your research case "The Primal Man," ancient Hinduism regarded the various castes and their duties (*dharma*) as built into the structure of the universe. The notion that duties and castes were natural allowed those in power not only to identify what is moral and what is not, but also to justify it. Hence the *Laws of Manu* asserts that the duty of husbands to control their wives is an "eternal duty." In other words, it is *natural* for wives to be dependent upon their husbands.

It is clear that notions of natural law can, at times, conflict with the rule of reciprocity. If we applied the rule of reciprocity to the issues of the relationship between husband and wife or to matters relating to sexuality, we could come to very different conclusions from those resulting from natural law theory. The rule of reciprocity requires equal treatment of men and women, it requires equal treatment for the theistic and the atheistic citizens of the state, and it requires equal treatment for heterosexuals and homosexuals. Natural law theory, at least for some people, runs counter to that conclusion. Is there some kind of deep contradiction in religious ethics? Can we support the Golden Rule and notions like "do what is best for others" together with notions like natural law?

9.4 WHAT ARE THE ELEMENTS OF A RELIGIOUS MORALITY?

We have already defined morality as a set of norms or rules designed to regulate and govern the conduct of humans with one another, with other living creatures, and with their environment. While this definition was useful for beginning our discussion, we need to revisit the issue on a deeper level. What is it about certain norms and rules that make them moral rather than mere custom? Traffic rules regulate our lives with others, and they should be obeyed, but are traffic rules on the same footing as rules like "Be honest"? What makes some rules moral and others not?

In his book *Religion and Moral Reason*, Ronald M. Green identifies three essential elements to religious morality. The first is a "method of moral reasoning" that involves "the moral point of view." The second is a "set of beliefs affirming the reality of moral retribution." And the third identifies ways to overcome "moral paralysis and despair."[7]

Green suggests that the moral point of view is a "radical impartiality" that is utilized when we make moral decisions. This means that before we make a decision that is truly moral we must look at the situation not only from a self-serving or egocentric standpoint, but also from a universal, impartial, and fair standpoint. To be impartial is not to favor one party over another. What counts morally is not what we desire, but what would be right for any person to do. This is why, Green argues, so much of morality counsels self-discipline, delayed gratification, self-sacrifice, and self-denial. It is not that our own self-interests are not important or even that they are less important than the interests of others; it is that when it comes to morality, our own self-interest is not the only thing to be considered.

Green thinks that the impartiality required by the moral point of view is captured in versions of the Golden Rule found in most major religious traditions. To do unto others as you would have them do unto you requires the ability to transcend self-interest and take into account the point of view of someone else. This rule requires consistency in our actions and prohibits us from doing things we would not want others to do to us.

The idea of impartiality is built into Islamic notions of morality. The best judge is the impartial judge. The *Sharia* emphasizes the need for objective judgment, and the Hadith holds up the decisions of Muhammad in resolving disputes as the models of impartiality and fairness.

The Confucian principle of *shu* (reciprocity) recognizes the need for impartiality in moral judgment. Confucius also captured the fairness and balance of interests required by moral judgment when he said that the virtuous "man does not set his mind either absolutely for anything or absolutely against anything. The sole measure of them all is morality and justice" (*Analects* IV). This idea is reinforced by Mencius, who writes, "Try your best to treat others as you would wish to be treated yourself, and you will find that this is the shortest way to benevolence (*ren*)" (*Mencius* VII.A.4).

Of course it is often very difficult to be truly impartial in our judgments. Self-interest and prejudice can creep in at any point. Confucius recognized this when he claimed that becoming truly virtuous was not an easy thing to do. And Islam recognizes this in its claim that only Allah is a truly impartial, fair, and unbiased judge. Only the divine can have a perfectly moral point of view. By basing morality on a divine command or on the judgment and actions of the truly virtuous person, both Islam and Confucianism recognize the need for impartiality. Who could be more impartial than God or a perfectly virtuous person?

The problem with the Golden Rule is that it is possible to imagine someone who is prepared to do what we normally take to be immoral and gladly permit others to do the same. For example, a person who is terminally ill who steals money in order to go out in a blaze of self-indulgence might well say that anyone else in the same situation is entitled to do the same. Confucius understood the limitation of *shu* (reciprocity) and added the principle of *zhong*—doing what is best for others. Allah is not only a just God, but a merciful one as well.

There is more to the moral point of view than impartiality. Justice, the impartial application of law, must also be tempered by mercy and compassion. Impartiality sounds cold and impersonal. Religions also speak of love, compassion, and mercy. Sometimes we need to go beyond being fair in order to do what is best for others.

Retribution

It is time to turn our attention to the second element Green identifies as a component of religious moral reasoning—"a set of beliefs affirming the reality of moral retribution."

Retribution conveys the idea of recompense, return, and just deserts. It takes many different forms in religion, such as the law of karma and judgment day. It is intimately tied to the ideas of merit, reward, and punishment. It permeates much religious thought. How many of us believe that God will reward us with eternal life if we are morally good, or with eternal punishment if we are morally bad? How many of us think that judgment day is "payback time"? How many of us cheer at the movies when the bad guy gets killed? How many of us have said on one occasion or another, "What goes around, comes around"? If a villain has committed a horrible crime, we expect him or her to meet a horrible end. Why?

One reason is that we want to see justice done. It gives us a sense of cosmic satisfaction. Another reason runs deeper than satisfaction. It derives from the moral point of view. If being moral requires self-sacrifice, why make that sacrifice? Why should we sacrifice our self-interest and desire just so someone else is treated fairly? In short, why be moral? In particular, why be moral if morality requires the subordination of our own pleasures, our own desires, and our own short-term joys in order to be fair to others? Others may not be moral at all. They may not live their lives according to a moral point of view, and who is to say that they are any worse off?

Retribution tries to answer the question, Why be moral? Whether it takes the form of karma, judgment day, or the threat of the removal of the Mandate of Heaven, retribution means that the righteous will be rewarded and the unrighteous punished. Those who risk their lives, those who sacrifice their lives, and even those who lose their lives for the sake of righteousness will someday gain an even better life.

It is not surprising that religions, which identify the moral point of view with self-sacrifice, should also develop theories of retribution. It is also not surprising that this way of answering the question, Why be moral? is plagued with ethical difficulties. If the moral attitude is one of impartiality and compassion for the other, and if we should do what is morally right because it is right, then fear of punishment or hope of reward should not motivate our desire to be moral. If retribution is the only answer religions offer to the question of why be moral, that very answer violates the moral point of view by appealing to self-interest.

We are now in a better position to understand why religions also offer, to use Green's terms, "a series of 'transmoral' beliefs that suspend moral judgment and retribution when this is needed to overcome moral paralysis and despair." This is the third element of religious morality that Green identifies.

Overcoming Moral Failure

Religions recognize the need to overcome moral failure when they speak of love, compassion, forgiveness, and reconciliation. We will discuss a concrete case of the application of these ideas in the next chapter when we examine the work of the Truth and Reconciliation Commission in South Africa. For now we need to point out that although religions often proclaim very noble moral ideals, they also recognize that few people can live up to them. Therefore they provide ways to overcome the guilt associated with moral failure.

Ways of dealing with moral failure are necessary in order to renew moral commitments because, as Green points out, moral failure can lead to despair and moral paralysis. Deep despair is, as the Christian philosopher Soren Kierkegaard said, "the sickness unto death."[8] It is a sickness that can push one into a downward spiral leading to a total lack of hope for the future. Yet providing people hope for the future is one of the psychological strengths of religion. At the same time, reminding people of their moral failures is an important motivating strategy. How can religion provide both hope for the future and motivate people to renew their moral commitment to live up to what are often impossible moral ideals of perfection?

Religions have devised many different ways of dealing with this problem. Rituals of confession, repentance, forgiveness, and purification provide a few examples. Such rituals offer hope to the hopeless, and the public nature of many of these rituals acknowledges the communal nature of morality. The presence of public witnesses reinforces the power of such rituals to provide occasions for moral renewal.

If you have ever attended a Christian worship service, chances are a portion of the service required those present to publicly and communally confess their sins of "thought, word, and deed." This is usually followed by assurances of forgiveness and God's mercy. In Judaism Yom Kippur or the Day of Atonement is one of the most solemn days in the Jewish festival cycle. People go to synagogue to spend a good portion of the day asking God to forgive their sins and grant renewed life for the coming year. Neither food nor drink is allowed from sundown to sundown.

Frequently, doing penance for one's failures can take more severe forms. These can range from human and animal sacrifices to self-flagellation. Penitential rituals may include elements found in mourning rituals such as wearing rags and smearing oneself with mud or ashes. In the United States the Penitente Brotherhoods are probably the most famous example of severe penitential rituals. These brotherhoods have been active for over four hundred years in southern Colorado and northern New Mexico. During Holy Week, they engage in acts of self-flagellation and mock crucifixions in order to identify with the redemptive suffering and pain of Jesus.

Religious Moral Reasoning
1. Developing a moral point of view
2. Believing in moral retribution
3. Overcoming moral paralysis and despair

REVIEW QUESTIONS

1. What is a norm, and why is this concept central to notions of morality?
2. How does the way in which Islam legitimates moral norms differ from the ways in which Confucianism legitimates moral norms?
3. What is the basic problem with the divine command theory of ethics?
4. Briefly define the following terms: *Sharia, Sunna, ren, shu,* and *zhong.*
5. Describe natural law theory and how it relates to questions of morality.
6. According to Green, what are the basic elements of religious moral reasoning?

RESEARCH CASE—JAIN NONVIOLENCE

A man falls into a deep well. He grabs the branch of a tree growing from the side of the well and hangs on for dear life. Looking below he sees in the pit beneath poisonous snakes waiting for him. Looking up he sees two mice, one black and one white, gnawing at the branch he is desperately clutching. He soon realizes that when they gnaw through he will fall. He is in a dangerous predicament and begins to search for a way out. A beehive on the tree that is now shaking begins to drop bits of sweet honey near him. Forgetting his terrible situation he reaches for the sweet drops of honey, loses his grip on the branch, and falls.

Jainas ("jinas"—followers of or children of the victor or *jina*) tell this parable to illustrate an important point about how humans should live. The man in the well represents the soul, which can fall to its death at any moment. The mice symbolize our lives. The white mouse represents the days, and the black mouse represents the nights. Time is slowly eating away at our lives, and most of us, instead of seriously seeking to escape our danger, reach for fleeting experiences of enjoyment and pleasure (the drops of honey). By doing so we lose our chance to get on the right path that will lead us out of the cycles of rebirth and suffering.

We will return to the issue of the "right path," but first some contextual information will aid our understanding. Jainism is a religion originating in India. Jainas date the start of their religion in a distant past when the first of twenty-four great people, or saints, became Tirthankaras or "ford finders." This title indicates that these great saints found the place to cross the river of life, with its countless cycles of rebirth, to the other side, the side where rebirth ceases.

There is no historical evidence for the existence of all twenty-four of these saints, but the last two, Parshava and Mahavira, are historical figures. Many historians credit Mahavira with founding Jainism, but he was probably developing and passing on the teachings of his predecessor, Parshava.

Mahavira (great hero) lived at about the same time as Siddhartha Gautama was developing Buddhism and in the same geographic region of north India. Hence it is not surprising that there are strong parallels between Jainism and Buddhism. In fact the life story of Mahavira as told by Jainas has a remarkable similarity to the life story told by Buddhists about Shakyamuni. However, each of the main branches of Jainism has a different version.

Mahavira's birth, like the birth of many religious founders, is portrayed as miraculous.

> [When] the Venerable Ascetic Mahavira was born, . . . [there] rained down on the palace of King Siddhartha [his father] one great shower of silver, gold, diamonds, clothes, ornaments, leaves, flowers, . . . sandal powder and riches.[9]

In his search for enlightenment, he renounced secular life and undertook a life of ascetic practices. Mahavira's renunciation was marked by pulling out the hair on his head (a practice still followed by those who become monks or nuns) to indicate that he did not hold his body in high regard. His enlightenment was marked by gaining great powers of wisdom and insight.

> When the Venerable Ascetic Mahavira had become a Jina [victor] and Arhat [saint], he was a Kevalin [liberated one], omniscient and comprehending all objects; he knew and saw all conditions of the world, of gods, men, and demons: whence they came, whither they go, whether they are born as men or animals or become gods or hell beings . . . he the Arhat for whom there is no secret, knew and saw all conditions of living beings in the world, what they thought, spoke or did at any moment.[10]

His first sermon after his enlightenment was on *ahimsa*, which is usually translated as "nonviolence," but literally means "desiring to do no harm to others." Even though the teaching of *ahimsa* is found in Buddhism and Hinduism, it has become a distinctive hallmark of Jainism. No other religion has devoted as much time and attention to *ahimsa*. The universe is filled with various forms of life, and violence to any in thought, word, or deed stains one's soul.

Sometime after Mahavira's death, his disciples, like so many other disciples, split into differing groups, which in turn split into subgroups. The two main groups are the Digambara (sky-clad) and the Shvetambaras (white clothes). As we might guess from these names, a major issue that divided the community was the wearing of clothes. The Digambaras advocate the practice of nudity, and the Shvetambaras advocate wearing white clothes.

To the outsider this may seem like a trivial issue, but behind it stands a debate about what true renunciation involves. This is important because renunciation is part of the "right path" that leads to liberation from the bondage of rebirth. It also has important social implications.

Apparently Mahavira willingly ordained women as ascetics, and evidence indicates that at the time of his death, women ascetics outnumbered men by a ratio of two and a half to one. The Shvetambaras hold that the nineteenth Tirthankara, named Malli, was a woman. The Digambaras claim Malli was a man. They argue further that it is improper for women to go around nude; therefore, women cannot achieve liberation until they are reborn as men. The Shvetambaras not only claim that one of the Tirthankaras was a woman, but also that women do not have to be reborn as men in order to receive liberation. Indeed, according to the Shvetambaras, women can also be teachers of the right path.

In order to understand the right path and the role that the practice of *ahimsa* plays in it, we need to know something about Jain metaphysics. According to Jainism, all of reality can be divided into three basic categories: matter, sentient beings (beings that can sense), and that which is neither material nor sentient. Matter falls into the category of *ajiva* (non-soul), while sentient beings are *jivas* (souls).

The universe consists of three levels: heaven, earth, and below the earth. Each of these is divided into numerous subcategories arranged hierarchically. *Jivas* can take the form of a celestial or heavenly being (god), a human being, an animal, a plant, or a demigod inhabiting the underworlds. Transmigrating souls can move in and out of these different forms. The goal of life is for a *jiva* to rise to the crescent-shaped apex of the universe beyond the highest heaven. Here the Tirthankaras dwell in purity, their *jivas* permanently liberated from the cycle of rebirth. They dwell even above the gods, their souls perfectly clear of any material stain.

Jainism, like Buddhism and Hinduism, teaches that karma keeps us trapped in the cycle of rebirth. However, Jainas understand karma quite differently from Buddhists and Hindus. Karma is material in nature and its particles become attached to *jivas* anytime they do anything. Some actions produce a greater amount of karma than others. Killing, engaging in violence, or desiring to do harm produce a very large amount of karmic material. The soul becomes darker and heavier the more karma particles it accumulates, sinking, eventually, to the very bottom of the universe. Bondage to matter

A Jain Devotee, 1993

must be broken if souls are to ascend to a life of purity and bliss, free from all suffering and concern. But since karma is accumulated no matter what a sentient being does, how on earth (pun intended) can the soul ever free itself from this horrible bondage?

It is here that the idea of the right path comes in. There are three jewels: *right insight* (viewpoint or faith), *right knowledge,* and *right conduct.* Right insight is a flash, a glimpse that the soul has of its true destiny. This insight starts it on the path of liberation. Right knowledge is coming to know the true nature of the universe and human life. Right conduct consists of five basic principles, the first of which is the most important. These are *ahimsa* (desiring no harm), truthfulness, nonstealing, sexual purity, and nonpossession.

For the purposes of this case, our interest centers on the ethic of *ahimsa.* This ethic automatically means that all Jainas are vegetarians, and the taking of animal life is taboo. Even taking plant life is considered undesirable, and should be done sparingly. Matters of diet become significant because the devotee must avoid harming souls wherever they may be found. Killing and eating meat, fish, and fowl is, of course, completely out of bounds. Certain forms of vegetables, such as eggplant and root vegetables (potatoes and onions), are to be avoided as well because they are teeming with microcosmic life-forms. Water should be strained and boiled before drinking, and monks and nuns should sweep the ground on which they walk and recline, lest any life-forms such as ants might be killed. Meals are to be eaten before sunset to avoid lighting lamps and thereby attracting insects to their deaths. Some ascetics avoid bathing in order not to harm any life-forms living on their bodies or in water.

Ahimsa has implications concerning acceptable occupations. Hunting, fishing, and butchering are clearly unacceptable, and farming, while allowed, is dangerous. Hence many Jainas become doctors, lawyers, and merchants. Even though there are strict rules about wealth and possessions, the latent function of *ahimsa* has resulted in a prosperous community because the acceptable professions often attract wealth. The *Acaranga Sutra* on Good Conduct says:

> the sage who walks the beaten track (to liberation), regards the world in a different way. "Knowing thus (the nature of) acts in all regards, he does not kill," he controls himself, he is not overbearing.[11]

We have been talking about *ahimsa* almost exclusively in terms of not doing physical harm. But the last comment about not being overbearing and the admonitions to practice *ahimsa* in thought, word, and deed point to a broader meaning. The political potential of *ahimsa* was realized when Gandhi started a nonviolent campaign, which resulted in overthrowing the British colonial system in India. Martin Luther King, Jr., adopted it as an effective tool in the fight to overturn segregation laws. Today many Jainas and others attracted to the *ahimsa* teaching are applying the concept to ecological concerns, environmental issues, and the fight for global peace and justice. Not doing harm has become more than just a part of a right path to individual spiritual well-being.

There are a little over 4 million Jainas in the world today. Most live in India, but there are significant immigrant communities in England and North America. Although the Western world knew next to nothing of Jainism until it was introduced at the World's Parliament of Religions in 1893, it is drawing increased attention as we struggle in the twenty-first century to find ways to preserve all forms of life on this earth in the face of a looming ecological catastrophe. Vasudha Narayanan, a scholar of Jainism observes:

> Many Jains now give broader scope to the interpretation of non-violence and associate it with contemporary issues such as civil rights, national security and nuclear warfare. It is in these areas that the Jains see the large-scale challenge of violence. They see their tradition as one that offers a vision not just for the liberation of the soul, but for the survival of human beings, and indeed, this planet.[12]

QUESTIONS ON THE CASE OF JAIN NONVIOLENCE

1. Compare the case of Jain ethics to the first case on Islamic *Sharia*. What are the differences and similarities?
2. Compare the case of Jain nonviolence to the second case on Confucian virtue. Do you think there are more differences than similarities? Why or why not?
3. If souls are not physical realities and cannot be killed because they are eternal, why should Jainism be so concerned with physical harm such as killing? Answer this question first from an insider's viewpoint and then from an outsider's viewpoint.
4. Even though these were not discussed in this case, do you think Jainism has mechanisms for dealing with violation of ethical rules? If so, what do you think they might be like? How would you go about checking your hypothesis?
5. Do you find a "moral point of view" expressed in the ethic of *ahimsa*? Is *ahimsa* ultimately motivated by selfish concerns about karmic impact on one's own *jiva*?

Fieldwork Option: Visit a Jain temple and write a participant observation report.

SUGGESTIONS FOR FURTHER READING

In addition to the material found in the notes, the reader may wish to consult the following for more information.

Aslan, Reza. *No God but God: The Origins, Evolution, and Future of Islam.* New York: Random House, 2006. See Chapter 6 for a brief but clearly written introduction to the development of Islamic theology and law.

Berthrong, John H. *Transformations of the Confucian Way.* Boulder: Westview Press, 1998. This book provides a developmental survey of Confucianism from its beginnings through the modern age.

Carmody, Denise Lardner, and John Tully Carmody. *Christian Ethics: An Introduction Through History and Current Issues.* Englewood Cliffs, NJ: Prentice Hall, 1993. The authors present a clear and concise overview of Christian ethical thought.

Cort, John. *Jains in the World: Religious Values and Ideology in India.* New York: Oxford University Press, 2001. Cort discusses Jain ideology, asceticism, temple worship, celebrations, and much more.

Fingerette, Herbert. *Confucius—The Secular as Sacred.* New York: Harper and Row, 1972. This is an illuminating interpretation of Confucius and his ideas.

Green, Ronald M. *Religious Reason: The Rational and Moral Basis of Religious Belief.* New York: Oxford University Press, 1978. This advanced and tightly argued book relies heavily on Kant, who tries to show that the basis of religious moral views is rational.

Jaini, Padmanah. *Gender and Salvation: Jaina Debates on the Spiritual Liberation of Women.* Berkeley: University of California Press, 1991. Jaini traces the ins and outs of the debate about women and liberation in the Jain tradition.

Kessler, Gary E. "How Are Religion and Morality Related?" In *Philosophy of Religion: Toward a Global Perspective*. Belmont, CA: Wadsworth Publishing, 1999. This is an introductory overview of some issues and a collection of essays dealing with various topics, such as the divine command theory, liberation theology, and women's rights.

Lovin, Robin W., and Frank E. Reynolds, eds. *Cosmology and Ethical Order: New Studies in Comparative Ethics*. Chicago: University of Chicago Press, 1985. The editors argue that it is a mistake to isolate ethics from its cosmological background and that a comparative perspective is essential for understanding different religious ethical systems.

Morgan, Peggy, and Clive Lawton, eds. *Ethical Issues in Six Religious Traditions*. Edinburgh: Edinburgh University Press, 1996. This helpful collection of essays discusses how Hinduism, Buddhism, Sikhism, Judaism, Christianity, and Islam deal with different ethical issues ranging from marriage and the family to global issues of poverty and ecology.

INTERNET RESOURCES

www.cs.colostate.edu/~malaiya/jainhlinks.html   This page contains a comprehensive index of links to sites on Jainism. Topics range from the fundamentals of Jainism, to Jain songs and prayers, to Jain texts.

www.princeton.edu/~humcomp/alkhaz.html   Al-Khazina is an interactive database for the study of Islamic culture developed for use in university courses.

www.sacred-texts.com/cfu/index.htm   This site provides access to James Legge's 1893 translations of key Confucian texts including the *Analects*.

CHAPTER 10

Religion and Politics

CAN TERRORISM EVER BE justified? Can it be *religiously* justified? Until recently many people assumed that the motivation and justification for violent terrorist acts were primarily political. The rise and expansion of jihadist* terrorism in recent years has also led many people to assume that Islam, unlike other religions, is a violent religion. However, anyone familiar with the history of religions knows that Islam has no monopoly on violent terrorism. All religions have spawned violence and inspired terrorist movements.

The extreme wing of the Christian anti-abortion movement has justified the killing of doctors and the bombing of clinics where women can exercise their legal rights to medical procedures that end a pregnancy. In the first century, a Jewish terrorist movement engaged in violent acts against the occupying Romans in order to drive them from their holy land. Christians have engaged in violent crusades aimed at Muslims, and Muslims have returned the favor. The Protestant Reformation set off years of religious warfare between different Christian groups in Europe. Asian religions such as Hinduism and Buddhism also have inspired violence, including terrorist violence, at various times in their history.

---

* I use the word *jihadist* to refer to what many call Islamic fundamentalism, or extremism in order to distinguish it from mainstream moderate Islam. For more on jihad, see "Just War and Holy War" in section 10.3.

But what makes terrorism different from other forms of violence? The word itself comes from a Latin word that means "to cause to tremble." And it was first used to name the violence of the state against its citizens. But whether terrorism is the violence of the powerful against the less powerful or the violence of those with little power against the state, many agree that there are two unique characteristics of the sort of violence we usually call terrorism. Grant Wardlaw describes them as follows:

> There are two unique conditions [of terrorism]. The first is that the violence committed constitutes an act of terror only when the target group (those being coerced) is distinct from the immediate victims (those being bombed, shot, or held hostage). The second is that the act must create in the target group a condition of extreme anxiety or fear, which is the lever by which pressure is applied (or is intended to be applied) to coerce acquiescence to the terrorist's demands. Thus, an act of violence which is aimed only at a particular immediate victim (be it an individual or group) is not an act of terrorism.[1]

Often the goal of terrorism is purely political. But sometimes it is a mixture of both religious and political motives, justifications, and goals. Religious terrorism differs from other types in so far as it is embedded in an explicitly religious ideology that invokes the blessings of superhuman powers and asserts the absolute righteousness of its cause.

Our first case focuses on one type of religious terrorism—the terrorism of Osama bin Laden. I select this case not to single out Islam, which historically has prided itself as a religion of peace, but because al-Qaeda is the most notorious terrorist group of our time, and Osama bin Laden has paid particular attention to articulating a religious as well as a political rationale for his terrorism.

Our second case transports us to a very different political and religious world. If bin Laden's brand of Islam recognizes no distinction between religion and politics, the American experiment with the "separation of church and state" struggles to articulate in legal language and rulings how religion and government are not only different but how they should ideally relate to each other. The First Amendment to the Constitution of the United States articulates two principles. The first is that the state or government should not establish any particular religion as the religion of the state, and the second guarantees the citizens of the state freedom of religion. Precisely what these two principles mean in practice and what happens when they clash will be the focus of our second case.

After comparing these two very different cases, we will explore some patterns and issues that have arisen in the long history of the interaction of religion and politics, including ideas of holy war and theocracy. We end with a case in which religion played a significant role in helping a deeply divided society bring to light the atrocities of state terrorism and reconcile bitter enemies.

10.1 TWO CASE STUDIES

Inside the Mind of a Religious Terrorist

Osama bin Laden, the most notorious terrorist of our age, was one of five people who signed, in 1998, a *hukm* or considered judgment that reads in part:

> To kill the American and their allies—civilians and military—is an individual duty incumbent upon every Muslim in all countries . . . so that their armies leave all the territory of Islam, defeated, broken, and unable to threaten any Muslim. This is in accordance with the words of God Almighty: "Fight the idolaters at any time, if they first fight you"[2]

Osama bin Laden (and his terrorist organization al-Qaeda) is by now a household name throughout the world. Yet many people still do not know very much about him and even less about what motivates him and how he justifies violent acts in the name of Islam and God.

Osama bin Muhammad bin Laden was born in Saudi Arabia in 1957. His father was a Yemeni immigrant who made a fortune in the construction business and became a close friend of the al-Saud family, which rules Saudi Arabia. In 1980 at the age of twenty-three he went to Peshawar on the Afghanistan and Pakistan border to set up a base (*al-qaeda*) to train Arab recruits for the war in Afghanistan against the Russians. In 1989, after the defeat of the Soviets, bin Laden returned to Saudi Arabia convinced of two things: (1) the Americans could not be trusted because they abandoned Afghans to civil war after the Soviets left, and (2) a great world power (the Soviets) could be defeated by a dedicated band of soldiers whose motivation was deeply religious.

After Saddam Hussein invaded Kuwait, bin Laden offered the Saudi government the services of the Arab Afghan veterans he had organized to fight the Soviet Union. The Saudi royal family refused his offer and, to add insult to injury, invited some half-million American and other foreign troops to use the sacred land of Arabia as a staging area for invading Kuwait and driving the Iraqis out. Bin Laden was outraged and deeply offended by the Saudi decision. He regarded it as nothing short of a sacrilege.

Terrorists are not born terrorists. They learn to become terrorists—not only by experience but also by internalizing an ideology. Two streams of thought helped bin Laden construct his particularly violent interpretation of Islam. The first was Wahhabism, which bin Laden learned while growing up in Saudi Arabia. It is named for Muhammad ibn Abd al-Wahhab, an eighteenth-century advocate of Islamic revival. Al-Wahhab taught that the Quran should be interpreted literally, a view not supported by all Islamic scholars, and he denounced as unbelievers and polytheists any who disagreed with him. He emphasized that jihad primarily meant "holy war" even though there was by no means a consensus in the tradition about its primary meaning (see section 10.3). Further he taught that jihad should be an obligation of all

Muslims, contrary to much of the Islamic tradition that taught it was permissible for only some Muslims for defensive purposes. He also claimed it should be a war against all unbelievers even if they are Muslim in order to establish a "true" Islam along with a purified Islamic state.

After bin Laden went to university to study business so he could work in his father's construction company, he became more interested in Islamic studies than business courses. Some of his classes in Islam were taught by Dr. Abdallah Azzam, who advocated a militant global jihad, arguing forcefully that struggle (the original meaning of jihad) against the corrupting influence of secularism and atheism was the duty of every Muslim. With fiery rhetoric Assam proclaimed "Jihad and the rifle alone: no negotiations, no conferences, and no dialogues."[3]

Another one of bin Laden's professors in Islamic studies was Muhammed Qutb, who was the brother of the famous and influential Sayyid Qutb. Sayyid Qutb, until his execution in 1966, was a leader in the militant wing of the Egyptian Muslim Brotherhood. He too advocated militant jihad and reinterpreted the classical notion of ignorance or *jahiliyyah*, which Prophet Muhammad used to characterize the polytheism of pre-Islamic Arabia, as applying to the present. Qutb used the idea of ignorance to divide the whole world into two opposing camps. One camp has the exclusive inside track on the true knowledge of God. It is the *Dar-ul-Islam* ("home of truth"). The opposed camp is one of ignorance and unbelief, which constitutes the *Dar-ul-Harb* ("home of hostility"). According to Qutb, you are either for Islam or against it, in one home or the other. There is no middle ground.

Bin Laden's university courses in Islam taught him that an uncompromising, global, and violent jihad was the best means for regaining the past glory of Islam. Western dominance in the Middle East and the rule of hypocritical so-called Muslim leaders stole this glory. He learned to think of the world in black and white terms. There is the home of truth and the home of hostility to truth. The Wahhabi influence taught him to read the Quran as a book of eternal truths that could be "literally" applied to contemporary events. He also learned that "true believers" must have absolute certainty that they are right and that those who disagree are not merely wrong, but constituted a danger to the "truth." The God of mercy and forgiveness that is found in the Islamic as well as Christian traditions was replaced in his mind by the God of stern justice and wrath, a conception that is also found in both traditions. The righteous anger of the One God with all and every deviation from the "truth" captivated bin Laden's thoughts and inspired him to cast himself as the fearless defender of the Divine Truth. And he found a following among disillusioned youth.

In 1996 bin Laden returned to Afghanistan shortly before the Taliban took control. While he did not always get along with the Taliban, they allowed him to reopen his training bases for young Arab men who wished to prepare themselves for jihad, now understood almost exclusively as holy war. In 1998 he instigated the bombing of the American embassies in Tanzania and Kenya, which resulted in some two hundred deaths. President Clinton launched a missile attack on one of his bases in retaliation but failed to kill him. Bin Laden orchestrated the infamous September 11, 2001, attacks on New York and Washington three years later in which some three thousand people were killed and many more injured.

Not long after these attacks, the Bush administration announced the "war on terror," and the United States invaded both Afghanistan and Iraq, killing thousands of people and plunging Iraq into a civil war that has killed thousands more. Since then, bin Laden's popularity has increased among young, activist Muslims. More "holy warriors" have taken up the call to jihad, and al-Qaeda has become a global terror network.

Bin Laden has made no secret of his motivation, and he has not shied away from entering debates about the morality of his use of violence. For bin Laden, Islam is a comprehensive way of life. Hence there is no distinction between religion and politics. Church and state are not, as in modern secular societies, separate. To ask whether his motivations, justifications, and goals are primarily political or religious makes no sense, given the context in which he thinks. His goals are both, and, more importantly, bin Laden thinks they *ought* to be both.

Reading contemporary events as God's punishment and attacking those who disagree as hypocrites is characteristic of the "true believer" mentality, be it Islamic or Christian. On September 13, 2001, only two days after 9/11, Pat Robertson interviewed Jerry Falwell on a broadcast of *The 700 Club*. Both agreed that the terrorist attack on September 11 showed that God had lifted his protection from America because it has "insulted God at the highest levels of our government."[4] They cite banning prayer and Bible reading in public schools, along with not allowing children to "read the Commandments," as examples of insulting God. Bin Laden, Pat Robertson, and Jerry Falwell may seem like strange bedfellows, but their thinking is remarkably similar. Just as bin Laden views the presence of foreign troops on Saudi soil as divine punishment for abandoning true Islam, so Robertson and Falwell consider September 11 as divine punishment for abandoning true Christianity.

It may not be surprising that "true believers" of whatever faith read current events in light of their beliefs in divine punishments, but it may be surprising to find President George W. Bush using the same logical fallacy of "black and white" as bin Laden. On November 6, 2001, President Bush said that in the "war against terrorism" there is no room for neutrality. "You're either with us or against us in the fight against terror."[5] In October of the same year, bin Laden asserted, echoing his teachers, that hostility toward Islam has split the world into two camps. "I tell you that these events have split the entire world into two camps: one of faith, with no hypocrites, and one of unbelief—may

God protect us from it."[6] Just as Bush sees no middle ground in the global fight against terrorism, so bin Laden sees no middle ground in the global jihad against unbelief.

Bin Laden explicitly makes reference to Bush's either/or comment, citing it as evidence that Bush agrees with him about the nature of the struggle. Bin Laden also cites Bush's use of the term *crusade* as proof that the West is waging a war against the religion of Islam. He comments, "The odd thing about this is that he [Bush] has taken the words right out of our mouth."[7] This proves to bin Laden that he is right in characterizing his terrorist activities as "self-defense."

On October 14, 2002, a letter from bin Laden appeared on the Internet.[8] This letter is important because it tries to lay out a logical and systematic argument for jihad against America. The letter is addressed to Americans, and in it he offers detailed answers to two basic questions:"Why are we fighting and opposing you?" and "What are we calling you to do, and what do we want from you?" The answer to the first question is, according to bin Laden, "very simple." We fight, "because you attacked us and continue to attack us."[9] This "very simple" answer is then elaborated in numerous subsections covering some four pages in which he explains who the "us" is and the "attacks" to which he is referring.

First on the list of those attacked is Palestine followed by Somalia, Chechnya, Kashmir, Lebanon, Iraq, Afghanistan, and the lands of the Arabian Gulf. He also includes on his list Muslim countries whose rulers support the United States and have not instituted the rule of *Sharia*. The rhetoric becomes more strident and is peppered with words like *oppression, tyranny, crimes, killing, expulsion, destruction,* and *devastation* to indicate what he believes Israel has done to the Palestinians with U.S. support. "The blood pouring out of Palestine," he says, "must be equally avenged."[10]

His list of examples of U.S. aggression (direct or indirect) toward Muslims culminates in a moral justification for his "defensive jihad" against Americans. He appeals to both religious and rational principles to show that violence in response to violence is morally justified.

> These tragedies and calamities are only a few examples of your oppression and aggression against us. It is commanded by our religion and intellect that the oppressed have a right to respond to aggression. Do not expect anything from us but jihad, resistance, and revenge. Is it in any way rational to expect that after America has attacked us for more than half a century, that we will then leave her to live in security and peace?[11]

He even claims, contrary to Islamic tradition, that violence against innocent civilians is justified because America is a democratic country, and the American people have chosen their leaders, thereby consenting to their aggression. Thus all Americans, civilian and military, are fair game because all

Americans have the blood of innocent Muslim men, women, and children on their hands.

The first part of the letter concludes with a summary of bin Laden's argument in support of his aggression. He claims divine permission for his "defensive jihad":

> God, the Almighty, legislated the permission and the option to avenge this oppression. Thus, if we are attacked, then we have the right to strike back. If people destroy our villages and towns, then we have the right to do the same in return. If people steal our wealth, then we have the right to destroy their economy. And whoever kills our civilians, then we have the right to kill theirs.[12]

What may surprise readers who think of bin Laden as a crazed and fanatical terrorist is his careful justification for engaging in terrorism. His argument is based on the *lex talionis* or law of reciprocity (sometimes characterized as "an eye for an eye and a tooth for a tooth"), which is acknowledged by Christians, Jews, and Muslims according to their scriptures. He recognizes that under normal conditions his support of Muslim violence against Americans would not be justified, and hence he needs to carefully point out that so-called normal conditions do not exist. In short, the Americans started this fight, so Muslims have a right to fight back.

His answer to the second question ("What are we calling you to do, and what do we want from you?") provides some hints at the answer to why he has chosen the path of violence, rather than, let's say, the path of dialogue. Bin Laden says that he is calling Americans to convert to Islam. This section of the letter is really addressed to his critics within the Islamic community who point out that Islam requires that you offer your enemies a chance to convert before you take violent action against them. He is here offering, if only rhetorically, that chance to convert.

He says he wants the United States "to stop your oppression, lies, immorality, and debauchery."[13] Americans should reject "fornication, homosexuality, intoxicants, gambling, and usury."[14] He finds it sad that he must tell America that it is the "worst civilization witnessed in the history of mankind" because America makes its own laws, thereby contradicting the Absolute Authority of the True Lord to establish rightful laws. Americans exploit the sexuality of women, pollute the environment, allow Jews to control the media and the economy, and dropped nuclear bombs on Japan. Further, Americans are hypocrites, which is something particularly abhorrent to a "true believer" like bin Laden. They claim, he says, to support democracy yet reject democratic elections in places like Algeria when the outcome favors the Islamic party. They claim to trust in God yet behave like pagan polytheists and act unfairly by permitting Israel to have weapons of mass destruction but not others. America also claims to support international law yet ignores it when it conflicts with the self-interest of the United States. It claims to champion human rights yet runs prisons like Guantanamo. He calls on Americans to be honest with themselves and recognize they are a nation "without principles or manners."[15] He advises America to pack its bags and get out of Muslim lands; otherwise, it can expect to have its soldiers sent back in body bags and suffer more attacks.

After this "friendly" advice, as he characterizes it, he calls on America to deal with the Muslim community on the basis of mutual interests. If America does not do the things he demands, then it must prepare to fight the "Islamic Nation of Monotheism, Honor, Martyrdom, and Victory." It is a nation, he says, that "desires death more than you desire life."[16] In other words, he wants Americans to know that Islam is a formidable foe that is far superior in all respects to America, and America's fate will be the same as the "Soviets who fled from Afghanistan to deal with their military defeat, political breakup, ideological downfall, and economic bankruptcy."[17]

Separation of Church and State

That portion of the First Amendment to the U.S. Constitution (see section 2.3) that deals explicitly with religion consists of two phrases that seem, on the surface, clear enough. The first is called the Establishment Clause, and it *forbids* Congress from making a law that establishes a state religion; the second, called the Free Exercise Clause, forbids Congress from "prohibiting the free exercise of religion." For its day, this was very radical. Up until then, no country in the history of the world had restrained governments from endorsing an official religion or church, and none guaranteed its citizens the liberty to believe or not believe as they saw fit. This idea was rooted in John Locke's notion of religious toleration, an idea Locke introduced into English law after Europe was nearly destroyed by the Wars of Religion that broke out after the Protestant Reformation. It was also rooted in the idea of freedom of conscience, one of the fundamental principles articulated by Protestant theology in its struggle with Roman Catholicism over the issue of religious authority.

While the Establishment Clause and the Free Exercise Clause seem clear enough, the discerning reader can smell trouble brewing. What happens when the two principles (No Establishment and Free Exercise) clash? How should the courts adjudicate such cases? For example, does paying for the services of a priest or rabbi or imam out of tax money for military personnel constitute "establishment"? One could argue that it does. However, one could also argue that not providing such services for people in the military deprives them of the possibility of practicing their religion freely. In this case it seems that to satisfy one demand necessarily means one must violate the other.

Further problems arise when we ask what is meant by that little word *religion*. Does it refer (as it did to most of the Framers of the Bill of Rights and the Constitution) to the various, mostly Protestant, sects that dotted the American landscape, or did it mean something more abstract and less institutionally identifiable? Words change their meaning over time in part because circumstances change. Religious diversity in America even at the time the Bill of Rights was written was one of the many factors convincing the Framers that endorsing one sect could lead to political trouble and deep national division. Religious diversity has increased over time due to large immigrations of Jews, Muslims, Roman Catholics, Asians, as well as home-grown religious groups like the Latter-day Saints, Jehovah's Witnesses, Christian Scientists, and many more. Atheists have also increased in number, and while they normally do not form "churches" for obvious reasons, is it not the case that their freedom of conscience *not* to believe must be respected if we are to live together in some kind of civil harmony?

To simplify a long and complex history of legal views on the meaning and application of the First Amendment, we can divide the often warring camps into two dominant groups. One is typically called "separationist" and the other "accommodationist." These views are not absolute or monolithic but represent a continuum from extreme to moderate.

Kathleen Sullivan represents one sort of separationist view when she says:

> The affirmative implication of the Establishment Clause is the establishment of the civil public order. . . . All religions gain from the settlement of the war of all sects against all. . . . The price of this truce is the banishment of religion from the public square.[18]

Richard Neuhaus states one kind of accommodationist view when he writes, "The naked public square is the result of political doctrine and practice that would exclude religion and religiously grounded values from the conduct of public business."[19]

Sullivan's position is supported by the argument that if the United States adheres to a strict "no establishment" position, the freedom of individuals to believe as they wish is also upheld. Neuhaus's viewpoint is supported by the argument that claims restricting freedom of religion to the private domain of personal individual belief restricts its freedom in the public sphere, leaving, to use Neuhaus's image, the public square religiously naked or devoid of any meaningful religious viewpoint. This amounts to an undue burden on religious faith because it prevents believers from sharing their faith with others and from seeking legislation that supports their values.

There have been some key cases decided by the Supreme Court that indicate the ways in which the Court has struggled to reconcile the prohibition against Establishment with the Free Exercise Clause and to define the scope of government regulation in religious matters. One obvious issue with respect to "free exercise" is whether it covers only belief or whether it also extends into the realm of action. In 1879 the case of *Reynolds v. United States* came before the Court. Reynolds was a Mormon who had two wives. Mormons, at that time, believed that plural marriage (polygamy) was ordained by God and acted on that belief by taking multiple wives. The Court ruled that plural marriage was illegal. It acknowledged that Reynolds and other Mormons were free to *believe* as they wished, but they were not free to *act* as they wished. The state should not regulate religious belief, but it should regulate religious action when such actions were "in violation of social duties or subversive of good."[20]

It was not until 1940 in the case of *Cantwell v. Connecticut* that the Court seriously engaged the belief/action distinction again. A Jehovah's Witness was arrested for playing on a phonograph an anti-Catholic message in a Roman Catholic neighborhood. Lower courts found this illegal because it was a violation of a "breach of the peace" ordinance. Surprising many, the Supreme Court reversed the lower court ruling on the grounds that it specifically targeted religious behavior. They imported from free speech rulings the idea of a "clear and present danger." Since Cantwell's actions did not present a clear and present danger and since they were religiously motivated, they were protected by the Free Exercise Clause. The Court had now put itself in the uncomfortable position of trying to decide which religious actions might be allowed and which proscribed, on what grounds, and, more importantly, what was religious and what was not. It seemed to be precisely in the place the Framers did not want the government to be—deciding what constituted religion.

The answer that eventually emerged from the adjudication of several different cases focused on the *function* of a belief and not its content.[21] Does a particular belief—let's say, someone refusing to go to war on grounds of conscience alone, without any explicit religious component—function in the lives of those who hold an anti-war conviction the way that religious beliefs function in the lives of the explicitly religious? Is a sincerely held, deep conviction, without the trappings of religious belief or church membership, enough? So far the answer has been yes. Thus the Free Exercise of Religion Clause has come to be understood as the "free exercise of conscience," thereby considerably broadening the scope of the idea of religion. Ironically the Framers almost used the word *conscience* rather than *religion* when drafting the First Amendment. Had they done that, a lot of time and effort might have been saved.

In 1963 (*Sherbert v. Verner*) the Court faced the free exercise issue again. A Seventh-day Adventist had been fired and denied unemployment compensation because she would not work on Saturdays, which is the Sabbath Day for Seventh-day Adventists. The Court ruled that this was an unconstitutional limitation on Sherbert's freedom to practice her religion because it placed on her an "undue burden" solely because of her religious convictions. Other cases added to what became known as the *Sherbert* test. This consists of asking and answering three questions. Does a state regulation place an undue burden on the plaintiff? Does the state have a compelling interest in the matter? Are there alternative means the state could use to achieve the purpose of the regulation without seriously burdening the plaintiff?

In 1971 the Court formalized, in the case of *Lemon v. Kurtzman,* what came to be known as the *Lemon* test. In that case the Court ruled that it was unconstitutional for taxes to be used to support certain nonpublic schools. The majority ruled that for a program funded by public taxes to be constitutional, it had to meet three tests: its *purpose* must neither inhibit nor advance religion; its primary *effect* should not be to inhibit or advance religion; and it must be free of "entangling alliances" between religion and the state.

With the belief/action distinction in place along with the *Sherbert* and *Lemon* tests, most legal scholars had concluded that the Court had set clear guidelines for legislation dealing with freedom of religion. They did not foresee that the Court would begin chipping away at the *Lemon* test in the 1980s. In *Lynch v. Donnely* (1984) the Court ruled that a Christmas display in a public park *that had* (a Christmas tree, a Santa house, reindeer, carolers, clowns, candy canes, and a crèche scene of Mary, Joseph, and the baby Jesus) was legal because it did not violate the Establishment Clause. It did not because the display was primarily secular in purpose. Justice Sandra Day O'Connor concurred with the majority but wrote a separate opinion in which she did not invoke the *Lemon* test. Noah Feldman summarizes her reasoning this way:

> The reason that government should not get involved in the endorsement or disapproval of religion was that doing so would make some people less equal than others. The goal of government in its engagement with religion should not be secularism; it should be equality. The crèche did not violate the Constitution, O'Connor concluded, because in the context of the display, it did not make anyone feel like an outsider to the political community. By invoking egalitarianism, O'Connor could avoid the Court's strained suggestion that the crèche was secular while still allowing it to remain on display.[22]

The *Lemon* test still stood, however, because the majority in their reasoning had employed it. It was not until *County of Allegheny v. ACLU Greater Pittsburgh* (1989) that the test was completely dropped in favor of O'Connor's government "neutrality and equality" test. This 1989 case was almost identical to the *Lynch* case of 1984. It centered on the legality of the display of a crèche in a courthouse in Pennsylvania. In this case, however, the Court found the display illegal because it violated the Establishment Clause. The Court now found itself in the embarrassing situation of finding the public display of a crèche legal in one instance and illegal in another. The way out was to de-emphasize the *Lemon* test of "secular purpose" and adopt O'Connor's test of neutrality and equality. In short, the majority argued that the crèche was legal in the first instance because its purpose and effect were secular not religious, but it was illegal in the second instance because the implied governmental support did not show neutrality toward all religions and did make some citizens (non-Christians and atheists) feel excluded from the civic community. In other words, it failed O'Connor's "neutrality and equality" test.

Not long after the Court began to move away from the *Lemon* test, it abandoned, much to the dismay of legal scholars, the *Sherbert* test as well. In 1990 a case (*Oregon Employment Division v. Smith*) involving the religious use of an illegal drug came before the Court. Two Native Americans were fired as drug abuse counselors by the state of Oregon after admitting they used peyote as part of the central sacramental ritual of the Native American Church. Justice Antonin Scalia, writing for the majority, declared that the law making peyote illegal was not targeting any "specific religion," and the state was not obliged to prove a "compelling interest" because the law prohibiting the use of peyote had been legislated appropriately.

Clearly, given this brief history of some of the Supreme Court decisions relating to the First Amendment, sorting out how the separation of church and state should legally work has not been an easy task. And it is not likely to become any easier in the future. Christian evangelicals, emboldened by the political victories of Republicans in recent years, have made an all-out attack on what they claim is a government endorsement of a "religion" they call "secular humanism," thereby violating the Establishment Clause. They have made some headway insofar as the Court has abandoned talk of "secular purpose" and adopted the language of neutrality and equality. Not to be deterred, the Christian conservatives have now adopted the position that they are a persecuted minority, the government is denying them their *equal* religious rights, and the public square is not *neutral* but prejudiced against their version of Christianity. Hence whether one uses the language of "secular purpose" (*Lemon* test) or the language of "equality/neutrality" (O'Connor test), conservative Christians claim that the Court is restricting their religious freedom.

Two recent results of these kinds of arguments have been controversial rulings on the legality of educational voucher systems and "faith-based" charities. In both instances public tax dollars have been spent to support religious home schooling and religiously based programs that many argue amount to a violation of the Establishment Clause. The Christian conservatives also convinced the Court to outlaw a medical procedure used in some late-term abortions even if the mother's life is in danger. Many claim, on both sides of the abortion debate, that this is the first step that could lead to overturning *Roe v. Wade* (1973), the Court decision that made abortion legal. However, Christian conservatives have been unsuccessful at getting prayer and Bible reading reinstated in public schools, as well as at making it legal to display religious symbols (like the Ten Commandments) in public places.[23] Clearly, there will be more tough decisions relating directly or indirectly to the First Amendment that the Court will be making in the future.

At the same time as the political power and influence of Christian conservatives has increased, the United States has become more diverse religiously. Hence the divide in America has grown between those who believe the First Amendment establishes a separation of church and state and those who believe that it should accommodate people of the Christian faith. There are extremes on both sides of this divide. On the one hand, the extreme Christian right (see section 10.3 below) believes the country was founded as a Christian nation, and the laws of the land must recognize that. The extreme secularists believe that the country was founded to be as purely secular as possible, and the laws should embody secularity. Is there any way to bridge the gap?

10.2 COMPARISON

These two cases focusing on the reasoning of one religiously motivated terrorist and on the arguments about the First Amendment could not be more different. I have selected them precisely because they are so different. Their stark contrast exposes how different assumptions of the relationship of the religious to the political realm can lead to very different political situations. Osama bin Laden assumes, in keeping with one strain of the Islamic tradition, that there is no difference between religion and politics. Hence the government, if it is to be a true government, must embody and support Islamic law and morality. The First Amendment assumes, in keeping with one strain of political thinking, that religion and politics should be kept separate, but there should be no undue political suppression or support of religious beliefs and actions. The first position maintains that a perfectly just and peaceful society can be realized only on the basis of a particular interpretation of God and his laws. The second position maintains that while no society can ever be perfectly just and harmonious, the best hope for achieving these goals can only be realized by the separation of church and state and working out, through a rational legal process, what that might mean in concrete cases.

While the thinking behind bin Laden's rhetoric reveals a black-and-white mentality and while the political rhetoric of politicians and conservative Christians may share such rhetorical flourishes, the language of Supreme Court decisions is usually nuanced and accommodating of conflicting interests. Thus the thinking behind the Court decisions is what we might call "legal rationality." It is part of the way in which legal thought has developed in both English and American jurisprudence. Reasons that presumably any reasonable person could understand, if not totally accept, are given for conclusions that are logically consistent and agree with previous law as well as the standards of logical reasoning. The language of the "public legal square," as we might call it, is used, rather than the language of a "private sectarian ideology."

There is, I should point out, a long tradition of Islamic jurisprudence with its own standards and rules of thinking. Osama bin Laden does invoke this tradition when he appeals to reason and the universal nature of the *lex talionis* (law of reciprocity) that even an unbeliever, he thinks, must recognize. But such talk is deeply embedded in a tradition of divine authority, as his references to God indicate. He invokes both reason and revelation in his argument justifying his "defensive jihad" thereby reflecting both the revelatory and rational sources of *Sharia* (see section 9.1). While the justices of the Supreme Court do recognize the authority of the U.S. Constitution, they recognize that claims to divine authority for their decisions is way out of the bounds of what is considered rational discourse in a secular legal system. This is one reason why Christian conservatives, when they enter the debate in the public square, realize that they must appeal to concepts like fairness and rights to convince the Court to rule in their favor.

I should note two more things before leaving these cases. First, the historical and cultural conditions that gave rise to Osama bin Laden and extremist Islam are very different from the historical and cultural conditions that gave rise to the U.S. Constitution. The idea of limiting the power of one religious sect to control the laws of society is built into a tradition of Enlightenment thinking. The Enlightenment was an influential intellectual movement of eighteenth-century Europe that championed the authority of human reason. Its motto was "think for yourself." In addition, the religious wars that nearly destroyed Europe after the Protestant Reformation led to increased support for ideas like religious tolerance. It was better, many thought, to learn to live with those you disagreed with on religious matters than to kill one another. Both of these traditions (The Enlightenment and toleration) are largely foreign to the history of Islam. Certainly, during the Golden Age of Islam (roughfully the tenth to the twelfth centuries), a culture of great tolerance, brilliant scientific thought, and rational discourse on religious matters developed within Islam. But for a number of complex reasons it did not have the power or the range of influence that Enlightenment thinking had in the West. Instead the political upheavals of colonialism and the scramble to exploit the oil resources of the Middle East gave rise to a number of anti-Western movements including Wahhabism and the Muslim Brotherhood. It is these recent movements that have promoted the radical Islamist ideas that so influence bin Laden.

Second, we should not ignore the brief reference to "mutual interest" bin Laden makes in his letter. This reflects the widespread feeling that Americans are arrogant and do not respect others. If they did, they would deal with Muslims on the basis of mutual interests. It is difficult to know how sincere bin Laden is in this statement, but it does provide some reason to hope that one day reason will prevail in dealing with those with whom we disagree. If bin Laden sincerely believes that we have "mutual interests" with Muslims, then the hard task of talking to one's enemies and reaching mutual agreements diplomatically might some day replace war and terrorist violence as the way in which international disputes are settled.

10.3 PATTERNS OF POLITICAL ENGAGEMENT

There are many different patterns that have emerged in the relationship between religion and politics. The article on "Church and State" in *The HarperCollins Dictionary of Religion* identifies four such patterns found primarily in the West.[24] The first is state or government domination of religious institutions (*state over church*). This pattern is characterized by the exercise of civil power over religion, sometimes to the point of deciding religious doctrines and making appointments of religious officials. England from the sixteenth through the nineteenth century provides an example.

A second pattern reverses the relationship. Religious institutions dominate the government (*church over state*). Civil government is subordinated to religious interests, and religious leaders assert, usually on the basis of divine authority, their right to decide both religious and civil matters including the laws and the appropriate punishments for breaking the laws. In the Middle Ages the Roman Catholic Church in Western Europe claimed this role, although in practice tensions with various kings over the right to rule often checked the civil power of the church. Also the sixteenth century saw Calvinism, a variety of Protestantism, assert the right to rule civil authorities in parts of Switzerland, and again in the Massachusetts colony in America, the Puritans exercised civil control.

In both patterns (state over church and church over state), one religious institution or church was recognized as the true religion, and no dissenters were allowed. If dissenters became too troublesome, they were forced to conform or were banished. In extreme cases they were executed. The civil, social, and religious tensions and conflicts that these two patterns caused eventually contributed to the idea of somehow separating the power of religious institutions from the power of the state.

A pattern widely adopted in Europe became known as *toleration*. This pattern refers to a situation in which there is one official church recognized by the government and supported by public taxes, but other religious groups are permitted to organize and worship freely. In other words, one church is official, but other churches are tolerated. For example, in Scandinavian countries like Sweden, the Lutheran Church is the officially recognized church, but other churches are allowed to exist. In contemporary England, the Anglican Church is the official church of the state, and the queen is recognized as its official head, but other churches are permitted to practice, and their members are allowed to worship as they see fit.

The fourth pattern is *separation of church and state*, which was eventually adopted in America. In the Constitution itself there is only one reference to religion. Article VI states that "No religious Test shall ever be required as a Qualification to any Office or public Trust under the United States." In other words, a person cannot be denied or given any public office based on their religious beliefs or lack thereof. In part this was a reaction to the situation among the Puritan-dominated colonies that did require religious tests for office. In spite of this, unofficial "religious tests" often existed among the voting citizens and are evident even today when you hear people say that they would not vote for an atheist, or agnostic, or Muslim, or Jew for president. In practice there has been and still is a *de facto* test favoring Christians for public offices. This idea of not officially requiring people to be of this religion or that became spelled out in more detail in the Bill of Rights attached to the original Constitution as amendments. We discussed in our second case above the First Amendment prohibiting an established religion and guaranteeing religious freedom.

We should add at least one more pattern to the four discussed above. That pattern is *withdrawal*. To withdraw from worldly politics in order to better serve a transcendent superhuman power without social or political entanglements appears in the New Testament and among early Christians. Jesus's claim that his "kingdom is not of this world" reflects a withdrawal attitude, and early Christians, while obedient to Rome, saw it as an alien political power with no ultimate significance. This attitude changed dramatically when Christianity became the official religion of that once alien empire. The People's Temple led by Jim Jones (see the case on Jonestown in section 11.1) also exhibits this pattern. Some of you may also think of the Amish communities that minimize interactions with a society and government that they are willing to obey, but in which they are not willing to fully participate.

Patterns of Political Engagement

1. State over church
2. Church over state
3. Toleration
4. Separation
5. Withdrawal

In the rest of this section I will focus on three topics that provide good examples of the ways in which religion and politics can relate. These examples supplement the two cases with which I opened this chapter and provide more instances of how some of the patterns discussed above manifest themselves in practice.

Just War and Holy War

Politics is messy and often violent. The violence, particularly the bloodshed and suffering of war, can pose problems for religions, especially those that preach peace and love of neighbor. The radical pacifism of some statements by Jesus such as "love your enemies, do good to those who hate you, bless those who curse you, pray for those who abuse you" (Luke 6: 27–28) indicated to early Christians that violence in response to violence was not what their Lord wanted them to do. However, when Christianity became the official and established religion of the Roman empire with all its wealth and power, it was clear that some theory of when war was justified needed to be developed.

St. Augustine (d. 430) developed the ideas of Cicero (d. 43 B.C.E.), a Roman statesman, and laid the foundations for what has come to be called "just war theory." The basic elements, later elaborated by other Christian theologians, were two: conditions required before war is permissible (*jus ad bellum*) and rules of engagement or the conduct of war itself (*jus in bello*). Different theologians and philosophers have provided different lists of conditions for *jus ad bellum*, but chief among most is the requirement that war is the "last resort" waged in order to protect citizens of the state from actual or imminent harm. Typically the rules of engagement (justice in war or *jus in bello*), once a war considered just was being waged, required proportionality of response and a prohibition against killing innocent noncombatants.

In 1095 Pope Urban II called Christians to invade the Holy Land and recapture the land taken from them by the Muslim "infidels." This was the beginning of a series of campaigns later called the Crusades and viewed by the Christians as a holy war. The idea of a just war now fused with the idea of a holy war blessed by God, waged in His name, and on the authority of God's representative on earth, the pope.

The historical circumstances of the rise of Islam were quite different from those of Christianity. The Prophet Muhammad was, from the beginning, both the spiritual and political head of the community of followers that accepted his message. When the early Muslim community came in conflict with others, it was natural and expected that Muhammad would lead them into battle. Therefore the necessity arose very early on to develop some kind of understanding of how war is to be waged so that it conformed to the ethical standards that Muhammad was preaching.

In its broadest sense, jihad refers to the duty of every Muslim to make a sincere effort to submit to Allah's law and spread belief in Allah throughout the world. This "sincere effort" does not necessarily imply military warfare, as the notions of the "jihad of the tongue" or "jihad of the pen" indicate. The broader interpretation of *jihad* rests on a passage of the Quran, which reads, "Call men to the path of your Lord with wisdom and kindly exhortation. Reason with them in the most courteous manner. Your Lord best knows those who stray from His path, and those who are rightly guided" (16:125ff). In other words, faithful Muslims have an obligation to use forms of peaceful persuasion.

In the Quran, jihad is presented as the obligation to command good and forbid evil, most particularly with respect to the struggle of the faithful against persecution and idolatry. "Let there become of you a nation that shall speak for righteousness, enjoin justice, and forbid evil" (3:104). When this struggle for righteousness and justice takes the form of warfare, the Quran speaks of killing (*qital*) in addition to jihad.

Based on a passage in the Hadith of the Prophet, Muslim scholars make a distinction between the "lesser jihad" and the "greater jihad." The lesser jihad is military struggle (war), and the greater jihad is the struggle of believers to live faithful lives, to do good, avoid evil, and to peacefully spread the truth of Allah as revealed to Muhammad. Clearly it is wrong to equate jihad exclusively with the notion of a holy war.

Nevertheless, we must note that "jihad by the sword" is not forbidden, and Muslim jurists agree that military action against unbelievers is justified. But when is it justified? What conditions make "jihad by the sword" a moral and spiritual obligation rather than "jihad by the tongue?"

Among classical Sunni jurists, during the time when Islam was rapidly expanding, jihad by the sword was justified in order to expand Islamic territory, but not to make converts per se. Hence the Sunni jurists developed and elaborated an extensive set of rules governing when it is appropriate to wage jihad by the sword and how to conduct the resulting war. Shiite jurists disagreed with the Sunni position and argued that, at least during the occultation of the Twelfth Imam (see Chapter 9), military action could be used only in defending established Islamic lands, not in capturing new land.

Contemporary Islamic thought on jihad moves in two different directions. One stresses a broad interpretation (the "greater jihad") that enjoins all believers to engage in self-discipline, education, and social reform in order to "command good" and "forbid evil." The second direction stresses jihad by the sword. However, within this second tendency there are disagreements about when jihad by the sword is justified. Some claim that the sword can be used only for defensive wars, not wars of expansion. Others argue that the sword can be used in the struggle to replace secular Islamic states with "true" Islamic states based on the *Sharia*. Osama bin Laden has introduced yet another position. According to him, the sword can be used against civilian populations as well as military personnel of non-Islamic and secular Islamic nations when such nations constitute a threat to the religion of Islam.

Civil Religion

Have you ever thought that the fervor of patriotism seems very close to the intensity of religious faith? Have you ever wondered why both religion and politics can be conversation stoppers or spark arguments, even at parties? Have you ever noticed that stories told about the great heroes and revered leaders of a nation bear a close resemblance to myths (sacred stories)? Have you ever surmised that the significant holidays of a society such as Memorial Day and the Fourth of July in the United States might be very similar to religious rituals? Have you thought about why, when a nation goes to war, nationalistic pride swells, and flags—the symbol of a nation—seem to magically appear as backdrops for political leaders when they address the public in serious if not pious tones about matters of grave importance or celebrate victories over the enemies who threaten the welfare and well-being of the nation?

If you have thought and wondered about these things, you may have been glimpsing what scholars call civil religion. **Civil religion** is the set of beliefs and rituals that unite the diverse elements of a society into a unifying ideology. It is a subtle and nearly invisible glue connecting individuals into a common bond with a shared sense of oneness and values. It is no specific, identifiable religion or denomination but a generic brand that expresses through symbols and ceremonies the patriotism, national pride, and idealized sacred narrative of a people. Emile Durkheim (see Chapter 3) wrote that a "society is not constituted simply by the mass of individuals who comprise it, the ground they occupy, the things they use, or the movements they make, but above all by the idea it has of itself."[25]

If we ask what is the idea that American society has of itself, part of the answer is bound to reflect a vaguely Christian Protestant outlook that includes a belief that the nation has a unique destiny "under God" as long as it stays true to the motto inscribed on its money, "In God We Trust." The civil religion of America presents a pantheon of saints, heroes, and martyrs and includes, among others, a patriarchal wise First Leader (George Washington) and a savior martyr (Abraham Lincoln) who kept the ideal of a united nation alive during a bloody civil war along with the hallowed war dead that are eulogized and thanked in Memorial Day ceremonies. And the birth of the nation is celebrated every Fourth of July with rousing music, flag-waving, marches, fireworks, hot dogs, beer, and patriotic speeches. A central event of its festival calendar is the quadrennial inauguration of a president elected by the people to serve the people and lead the nation on into a glorious future of greatness. Civil religion elevates democracy to the level of a sacred ideal, a God-given gift of incalculable worth, even though in reality less than fifty percent of U.S. citizens actually bother to vote.

America is religiously diverse. There are over six hundred Protestant Christian groups alone. In addition there are Catholic, Orthodox, Unitarian, Episcopalian, Latter-day Saint, Muslim, Hindu, Neo-Pagan, Buddhist, Jain, Native American, and many more—not to mention a considerable number of atheist and agnostic groups. If civil religion is to somehow symbolize the unity of the citizens, then the "God" that is featured must be general, vague, and generic. In 1954 the Knights of Columbus, a Roman Catholic group, campaigned to have the words "under God" added to the original Pledge of Allegiance that had been written in 1892 by a Baptist minister who was a Christian socialist.[26] This addition succeeded because the "God" referenced was left unspecified, and many Americans thought of the country as locked in a Cold War with "Godless Communism." Adding "under God" seemed to make it clear that we were pious while our enemy was not.

Largely because of increased religious sentiment stirred up by the Civil War that many feared would tear the nation apart, the motto "In God We Trust" began to be added to American money in 1864. It was not until 1956 that Congress passed a law making it the national motto.[27] The patriotic fervor of the Cold War again played a part underscoring that American civil religion is often most visible during times of national crisis.

Phillip Hammond maintains that whatever the shape of American civil religion, the real heart of it appears as what he, along with others, call the "religion behind the Constitution." Hammond writes:

> It is this unifying potential of the religion behind the Constitution, more than its symbolic role in the religion *of* the Constitution, that comes closer, in my view, to revealing a possible American civil religion. Americans are free to accept or reject the *symbolism* of the Constitution, for example, but they are not free to accept or reject its *authority.* One ceases to *be* an American citizen in any meaningful sense if one rejects the Constitution: exile or heavily insulated social isolation are the only options, the extremist militia groups being a case in point.[28]

America is not the only nation with a civil religion. Scholars have identified distinctive civil religions in such nations as Japan, South Africa, Israel, and the former Soviet Union. In all cases, however, the civil religion is a "religion" in which all citizens participate whether they think of it as a religion or not. The political and patriotic life of a nation becomes so fused with quasi-sacred symbols and ceremonies that their religious dimension remains largely invisible.

Theocracy

Theocracy is a political theory that subordinates human rule to the rule of God. Of course, God does not directly rule, but his agents, who claim divine appointment usually based on scriptural interpretations, rule in his place. Today we tend to think of theocracies as largely part of a distant past or as vaguely Islamic. There are very few theocracies currently in the world, even among Muslims, but the power of the theocratic ideal still spawns political movements. As we saw in our first case, part of Osama bin Laden's motivation is a theocratic impulse to establish global rule of Allah's revealed law, the *Sharia*. It may come as a surprise that there is a homegrown theocratic movement on American soil that has already made significant inroads into democracy and among conservative, evangelical Christians. If we believe the following statistics, we are not talking about a weird fringe group among American citizens.

> George Barna, a respected evangelical pollster, defines "evangelicals". . . narrowly as a fundamentalist subset of born-again Christians. By his measures, almost 40 percent of Americans are born-again Christians, but only 7 percent are true evangelicals. Among both cohorts, there is substantial support for amending the United States Constitution to make Christianity the country's official religion—66 percent of evangelicals endorse the idea, as do 44 percent of other born-again Christians.[29]

Those who support such an amendment are a force that threatens not only freedom of religion in America, but portends a possible theocracy. Some of them are, as Chris Hedges characterizes them, "American Fascists" who are waging war on American democracy in the hopes of establishing a theocratic state.[30]

Hedges uses strong language, and not all who advocate making Christianity the official religion of the United States are necessarily theocrats. Most have in mind something like the pattern of toleration we discussed above. Christianity would be the official privileged religion receiving tax dollars, but other religions would be allowed to exist. They would be tolerated. But they would not be officially sanctioned, nor would they get government support.

Some, however, go further. George Grant, former executive director of D. James Kennedy's Coral Ridge Ministries, comes about as close to advocating a Christian theocracy as one can get, without using the word. In his book *The Changing of the Guard: Biblical Principles for Political Action*, he wrote:

> Christians have an obligation, a mandate, a commission, a holy responsibility to reclaim the land for Jesus Christ—to have dominion in civil structures, just as in every aspect of life and godliness.
> But it is dominion we are after. Not just a voice.
> It is dominion we are after. Not just influence.
> It is dominion we are after. Not just equal time.
> It is dominion we are after.
> World conquest. That's what Christ has commissioned us to accomplish. . . .[31]

D. James Kennedy, who is a member of and leader in the Presbyterian Church in America, founded Coral Ridge Ministries. This is a schismatic sect that broke from the mainline Presbyterian Church because of its "liberalism." Kennedy's television show, called *The Coral Ridge Hour*, airs on over six hundred TV stations and on the Armed Forces Network. The National Religious Broadcasters Hall of Fame inducted Kennedy into its ranks in 2005. He was an original board member of the Moral Majority and is nearly as influential as Jerry Falwell and Pat Robertson, although not as well known.

Kennedy is a leading popularizer of *dominion theology*, which stems from the writings of R. J. Rushdoony. Rushdoony wrote many books, but his core work is a massive and dense three-volume tome titled *Institutes of Biblical Law.* He advocates the replacement of civil with biblical law. He also supports the abolition of public schools, all social services, and the death penalty for blasphemers, gay people, and "unchaste women" on the basis of his reading of the Old Testament. The basis for citizenship in the "true" state is obedience to the law of God as laid down in the Bible. He asserts that the:

> Bible is not a devotional manual: it is a battle plan and a prescriptive word, a command word, and therefore a law word. The "spiritual" preachers deserve not even a yawn: they are putting the church into the sleep of death. God's servants will declare, "Thus saith the Lord," and His word covers every aspect of our lives, our work, our family life, our sexuality, politics, economics, farming, business, social and personal lives, and all things else.[32]

At the heart of dominion theology is an interpretation of Genesis 1:28, which states that God gave Adam and Eve dominion over "every living thing that moves upon the earth." If one points out that this command was given to Adam and Eve, not to Christians, Kennedy has a ready answer:

> Would God be saying to unregenerate people today that they are to rule the earth? I don't think so. He is speaking to those of us who have been recreated into the image of God and who are being refashioned by him.[33]

In other words, contrary to what the text literally says, God is speaking to born-again Christians and commanding them, as a sacred duty, to establish dominion over all things. Kennedy is echoing Rushdoony's claims that "true Christians" are the "new chosen people of God," that they are summoned to "create the society God requires," that there can be "no tolerance in a law-system for another religion," and that revealed law is the "only means whereby man can fulfill his creation mandate of exercising dominion under God."[34] Sounding very much like Osama bin Laden talking about Islamic law (see above), Rushdoony passionately asserts:

> To defy the law and treat it with contempt, to place oneself above the laws of God and man [sic], is to be at total war with God and man [sic], and the penalty is death.
>   Wherever a society refuses to exact the required death penalty, there God exacts the death penalty on that society . . .[35]

Dominionism is at the center of a movement called Christian Reconstructionism. Reconstruction theology is based on the premise that it is the duty of Christians to transform the secular, godless, and materialistic society of the United States into a theocracy. These ideas are based on a postmillennial view of Christ's Second Coming, which maintains that Jesus will return to earth only after Christians have "reconstructed" society to conform to Christian standards as they see them: in other words, *their* interpretation of the Bible, and *their* interpretation of Christianity, and *their* views of morality, should rule American society—indeed, should rule the world.

But how can you sell these ideas of Christian rule and theocracy to an American public steeped in the traditions of democracy and First Amendment guarantees of freedom of religion? Gary North, one of the key leaders in the Christian Reconstructionist movement, explained how in a 1981 article published in *The Journal of Christian Reconstruction*. He wrote that Christian conservative activists have to get involved in secular institutions in order to "smooth the transition to Christian political leadership. . . . Christians must begin to organize politically within the present party structure, and they must begin to infiltrate the existing institutional order."[36] By 1992 half the delegates to the Republican Party convention were evangelical Christians. The official platform of the Texas Republican Party pledged to "dispel the myth of the separation of church and state."[37]

Pat Robertson, one-time presidential candidate and popular Christian TV personality, makes clear in his book *The New World Order* that the Christian agenda should be to throw out of office liberal secularists, establish control of the political parties, and, eventually, establish Christian control of the United States.[38] Gary DeMar, author of textbooks widely used in Christian home schools, asserts "Only the Christian has a rightful claim to the earth and all its potential."[39] DeMar also makes clear to students that sinful humans have no claim to human rights so Christians have no obligation to work for the promotion of human rights. A popular and widely used Christian textbook, *America's Providential History*, claims that the "spirit" of the Constitution is Christian, belittles secular environmentalists, and tells students that a Christian's duty is to create material wealth.

Running throughout much of the literature churned out by Christian theocrats, dominionists, and reconstructionists are claims that the Founders of the United States intended this to be a "Christian nation" and that Christians are now a persecuted minority in their own land. They argue that their rights are being denied by liberal, secular humanists. And even though they have not been able to overturn the Supreme Court's rulings on prayer in public schools, the legality of abortion, or achieve a constitutional amendment to ban gay marriage, they have made some inroads into government. In fiscal year 2005, eleven percent of all federal competitive service grants went to faith-based organizations, and thirty percent of American schools taught abstinence-only sex education. Perhaps most importantly, they claim credit for getting an evangelical, born-again Christian, George W. Bush, elected to the White House twice even though he has not given them all they could wish for and have prayed for.

Conspiracy theories are popular on both the left and the right of the political spectrum, but we cannot lump all evangelical Christians into the same political bag. Among their politically active base views range widely—all the way from extreme militants such as those willing to bomb abortion clinics to those who think that involvement in politics is a mistake because it corrupts the Christian faith by making people hungry for power. At one time evangelicalism inspired abolition of slavery, the right to vote for women, and many different social reform movements seeking justice for all, be they Christians or not. Most have been strong supporters of the separation of church and state, valuing their freedom to worship as their conscience directs them. The National Association of Evangelicals, a group representing some thirty million members, issued a position paper in 2004. The document, "For the Health of the Nation," called upon evangelicals to seek justice for the poor, to protect human rights, to seek peace, and to protect God's creation."[40]

From the point of view of religious studies, the more militant political right of the Christian evangelical movement—theocracy advocates, dominionists, reconstructionists—can be understood as rather typical revitalization movements (see section 5.3). These movements arise out of fear that their way of life, culture, religion, and power are threatened. They literally fear for their lives. Attempts to revitalize the community of the faithful may range from magical rituals (such as the Ghost Dance among Native Americans), through militancy (such as Islamist terrorism), to political activism (conservative Christians). History is littered with such movements because times change, and while it is understandable that change can be very threatening, the attempts to control change and somehow force history to move in a particular direction often do not succeed. Typically revitalization movements idealize the past by attempting to rewrite history to celebrate the purity and power of their mythic ancestors and to empower the faithful to believe that all will turn out well for them. Does it work? Will reality overtake the idealization? It takes a lot of money and energy to keep the historical truth from emerging.

REVIEW QUESTIONS

1. Explain bin Ladin's justification for his terrorist actions and the role that the *lex talionis* plays in his thinking.
2. Do you think that terrorism can ever be justified? Why or why not?
3. What role did the diversity of Protestant sects play at the time the Bill of Rights was written, and how does the increase of religious diversity today complicate church/state relations?
4. What are the *Sherbert* and *Lemon* tests, and why are they important in interpretations and applications of the First Amendment?
5. Do you think that the Establishment Clause and the Free Exercise Clause of the First Amendment are inherently contradictory in practice, if not in theory? Why or why not?
6. Based on your reading of the two cases with which the chapter opens, what would you add to the comparison provided in section 10.2 and why?

7. State the differences among the five patterns discussed at the start of section 10.3.
8. Explain just war theory and how it relates to the idea of holy war.
9. What is American civil religion? Provide an example from your own experience.
10. Do you think that the Founders of the United States intended it to be a Christian nation? Why or why not?

RESEARCH CASE—THE TRUTH AND RECONCILIATION COMMISSION

Imagine a country in which a native population had been conquered, subjugated, and brutally repressed for more than a century. Imagine a country controlled and dominated by a government that passed laws that systematically discriminated against a large segment of its people—denying them the right to vote, segregating them to ghetto enclaves, denying them adequate health care, education, employment, and opportunity for advancement. Imagine a country controlled by a religious ideology that justified such oppression in the name of God. Add a large dose of racism to this mix by imagining the dominant class as white and the subjugated class as black.

Now imagine this same country dismantling the apartheid laws that supported such a racist and unjust system. What do you think might happen? Do you think a peaceful transition to justice and equality might be possible? Do you think revenge, violence, and "getting even" would sweep such a country—creating a widespread bloodbath and social chaos? Would you guess that the same religion that supported the repression could now inspire forgiveness, reconciliation, and help facilitate a peaceful transition to a new social and legal order that included all segments of the population?

If you have not already guessed it, I am talking about South Africa and its remarkable transformation from an unjust and repressive police state to a just and free society. Religion, in this case the Christian religion, can be a force for both evil and good. Our final case will focus on how some remarkable people, in particular Anglican Archbishop Desmond Tutu, who headed the Truth and Reconciliation Commission (TRC), helped to facilitate such a transformation.

Desmond Tutu became Archbishop of the Anglican Church in South Africa in 1986. He did not have an opportunity to freely vote until 1994. That election brought Nelson Mandela and his African National Congress (ANC) Party to power. Mandela, who had long opposed and resisted the white-dominated government, had been in prison for twenty-seven years and was finally released in 1990. This was an opportunity for a new beginning, and Mandela had the wisdom to create a commission (TRC) to uncover the truth about past atrocities perpetrated by the previous white-dominated government and to find a way to reconcile the people of South Africa so they could move forward in creating a new, just society. He appointed Desmond Tutu, who had been awarded the Nobel Peace Prize in 1984 for his efforts to bring peace and stability to a nation racked by civil strife, to head the TRC.

The TRC was designed to find a third way between the extremes of creating a Nuremberg-type tribunal to punish people for past crimes against humanity and an attempt to bury the past by forgetting it or by offering blanket amnesty. The idea was to grant amnesty to people in exchange for a complete disclosure of their past crimes in public before the commission. Also, the possibility of reparations was offered to the victims of government atrocities provided they appeared before the commission to tell their stories of abuse and suffering.

This approach to the political situation of a country embroiled in civil strife and government abuse of human rights reflects, according to Archbishop Tutu, the African ideal of social harmony called *ubuntu* and the Christian ideals of confession of guilt, forgiveness, and reconciliation. He writes:

> We are bound up in a delicate network of interdependence because, as we say in our African idiom, a person is a person through other persons. To dehumanize another inexorably means that one is dehumanized as well. . . . Thus to forgive is indeed the best form of self-interest since anger, resentment, and revenge are corrosive of the *summum bonum,* that greatest good, communal harmony that enhances the humanity and personhood of all in the community.[41]

Although the TRC recognized that most people think of justice as retributive (getting even), and many would be disappointed that it did not pursue that goal, the commission, under Tutu's leadership, focused on restorative justice. The healing, forgiveness, reconciliation, and social stability restorative justice can provide is in the long run better for the nation as a whole. Restorative justice, Tutu believes, is more in keeping with the teachings of Jesus than revenge and retribution.

The pursuit of restorative justice meant that people had to learn to forgo the self-righteous pleasure of demonizing the perpetrators of violence, recognize the capacity in all of us for evil, and acknowledge that we live, as Tutu put it, in a "moral universe." If this path was not pursued, he feared that the country would be "choking with a lust for revenge."[42]

Restorative justice does require the satisfaction of certain conditions. Among them are the following:

1. The act for which amnesty was required should have happened between 1960 and 1994.
2. The act must have been politically motivated.
3. The applicant had to make a full disclosure.
4. The rubric of proportionality had to be observed.[43]

Archbishop Tutu (right) with President Mandela.

As the atrocities of the past came to light, it became apparent that forgiveness and reconciliation would not be easy. Horrible stories of the police abducting people, torturing them, sexually abusing them, and having barbeques as they burned the bodies nearby left a sense in many that the former whites in control of the government had somehow become so corrupt and inhumane that they hardly seemed like human beings. Yet these were "ordinary citizens" sworn to uphold the law, carrying out their "duties" as they dehumanized and brutalized their fellow human beings. What they failed to realize is that they were also dehumanizing themselves.

The white-dominated government and police force felt fully justified. They viewed their victims as "terrorists" and "Communists," and through the distorted prism of racist ideology, as less than human. The Dutch Reformed Church to which most of the white ruling class belonged contributed to that ideology by preaching that the Bible provided a divine justification for racism and apartheid. They cited the story of the Tower of Babel and the curse of Ham as proof that God had ordained the separation of races.

Although pressure began to mount from other countries, both the Thatcher government in Britain and the Reagan government in the United States at the time were so caught up in the "War on Communism" that they were lukewarm to the idea of sanctions against the anti-Communist government of South Africa. They viewed it as an ally in the Cold War. Archbishop Tutu reports a less-than-productive meeting with President Reagan shortly after winning the Nobel Peace Prize in 1984, in which the president was "shocked" by the fact that Tutu's passport listed his nationality as "undeterminable at present."[44] Eventually public pressure resulted in some sanctions that contributed to the demise of apartheid.

Other factors also contributed to the racist ideology of apartheid. For one thing, this arrangement economically benefited the white ruling class. Blacks provided cheap labor for the mines, for agriculture, and for domestic service. People were willing to assume that judges were infallible, that what was legal was also moral, and that conformity to what those in authority wanted was not only the highest virtue, but also their patriotic duty. When the attitude of "my country, right or wrong" begins to grip the collective thinking of people, the stage is set for abuse of those who disagree with governmental policies.

In reflecting on what he learned as chair of the TRC, Archbishop Tutu credited his theological understanding of the gospel of Jesus with providing a guiding set of principles. Security cannot be guaranteed by the barrel of a gun. Forgiveness is the only way to reconciliation, but reconciliation is not cheap, and the forgiveness must be neither a forgetting or a sentimentalizing. Genuine forgiving means giving up your right to "pay back." Only then can it liberate both the victim and the victimizer from the guilt and ghosts of the past. "Confession," writes Archbishop Tutu, "forgiveness, and reparation, wherever feasible, form part of a continuum."[45]

The TRC discovered that the simple task of telling one's story had a positive and healing effect. But it was a very difficult and a very courageous act. Can you imagine appearing in public and confessing how you tortured and murdered women, men, and young boys? Saying "I am sorry" is never easy, and looking at the family of one of your victims while you say so is extremely difficult. Can you imagine appearing in public and recounting how you were tortured and sexually abused at the hands of the police? Reliving such past events even in narrative form can bring back memories that most people would find traumatic, to say the least. This is one reason why the TRC provided counseling before, during, and after an appearance.

The result of this very difficult process was the rehumanization of those who had been dehumanized, be they victims or victimizers. That "terrorist" now became someone's son, and those whom the "monsters" tortured and killed now became someone's husband, wife, or child. Throughout the process, Desmond Tutu was guided by the conviction that " God wants to show that there is life after conflict and repression—that because of forgiveness there is a future."[46]

QUESTIONS ON THE CASE OF THE
TRUTH AND RECONCILIATION COMMISSION

1. Do you think that religious ideas of confession and forgiveness can provide a way to reconcile enemies even in a political context? Why or why not?
2. What is the most significant thing you learned from this case?
3. Do you think that Archbishop Tutu's theological biases resulted in an unrealistic idealization of the process of telling the truth and the resulting reconciliation?
4. Compare this case to the first two cases with which we opened this chapter. How are they the same, and how are they different?
5. What pattern of the five relationships between religion and politics (see section 10.3) do you think this case best exemplifies? Why?

Fieldwork Option: Interview at least six people about their understanding of the First Amendment and how well they think the Supreme Court has decided First Amendment cases such as prayer in public schools. Summarize and analyze the results and, if possible, present them to the class for general discussion.

SUGGESTIONS FOR FURTHER READING

In addition to the material found in the notes, the reader may wish to consult the following for more information.

Bellah, Robert. "Civil Religion in America." *Daedalus,* 96 (Winter 1967), 1–21. This is the seminal article that sparked much of the research in American civil religion. The other articles in this issue also deal with civil religion from various perspectives.

Chidester, David. *Patterns of Power: Religion and Politics in American Culture.* Englewood Cliffs, NJ: Prentice Hall, 1988. Part I analyzes three "systems of power"— theocracy, democracy, and civil religion—in the interaction between religion and politics in America, and Part II explores "zones of conflict" between religion and politics.

Esposito, John L. *Unholy War: Terror in the Name of Islam.* Oxford: Oxford University Press, 2002. Esposito provides detailed information on the idea of jihad and its development in the Islamic tradition.

Gibson, James L. *Overcoming Apartheid: Can Truth Reconcile a Divided Nation?* New York: Russell Sage Foundation, 2004. This book reports on post-apartheid attitudes in South Africa and concludes that without the process of the Truth and Reconciliation Commission, the chances for a successful democratic society would have been severely diminished.

Howe, Mark deWolfe. *The Garden and the Wilderness: Religion and Government in American Constitutional History.* Chicago: University of Chicago Press, 1965. The author argues that there is a religion "behind" the First Amendment that embodies Protestant ideals of freedom of conscience and worship.

Juergensmeyer, Mark. *Terror in the Mind of God: The Global Rise of Religious Violence.* 3rd ed. Berkeley: University of California Press, 2003. This is a perceptive study of the culture and logic of religious violence.

Pewdahzur, Ami. *Suicide Terrorism.* Cambridge, MA: Polity Press, 2005. The focus of this book is primarily on Palestinian suicide bombers and their motivations.

Prothero, Stephen. *American Jesus: How the Son of God Became a National Icon.* New York: Farrar, Straus and Giroux, 2003. An engaging study of how American culture combines the sacred and secular by creating different images of Jesus.

Selengut, Charles. *Sacred Fury: Understanding Religious Violence.* Walnut Creek, CA: Rowman and Littlefield, 2003. Selengut's study explores different approaches to understanding religious violence, including terrorism.

Urban, Hugh. "Politics and Religion: An Overview." *Encyclopedia of Religion.* 2nd ed., volume 13. Detroit: Thomson Gale, 2005, 7248–7260. This article is an excellent introduction to religion and politics in various religions. Helpful articles on specific religions follow. The bibliography will lead you into the relevant literature.

INTERNET RESOURCES

www.pbs.org/wgbh/pages/frontline/shows/binladen   *Frontline* provides basic information about Osama bin Laden and the al-Qaeda movement he founded.

www.religioustolerance.org/reconstr.htm   This Web connection offers useful information about Christian Reconstructionism including dominion theology, along with a bibliography for further reading.

http://www.doj.gov.za/trc   Here you will find the home page of the Truth and Reconciliation Commission along with links to other useful sites.

CHAPTER 11

Organizing the Sacred

To organize in a social sense is to create order and stability in a community. Organization is necessary if a group of people focused on what they consider sacred is to flourish and survive. The creation of a stable order involves a process of institutionalization. To institutionalize is to establish a social order on a more permanent basis. Sociologists of religion are particularly interested in how and why religious groups establish themselves and what effect this has on both religion and society. How do religious ideas and practices become embodied in groups? How do these groups function? How do they maintain authority, motivate people, and inspire appropriate kinds of behavior?

All groups, religious or not, have certain characteristics. Sociologist Robert L. Johnstone defines a group as

> two or more interacting people who (1) share common goals or aims that stem from common problems and a desire to resolve them; (2) agree upon a set of norms they hope will help them achieve their common goals; (3) combine certain norms into roles that they expect persons within the group to fill and carry out in the interests of the group; (4) agree (often only implicitly) on certain status dimensions and distinctions on the basis of which they create one another; and (5) identify with the group and express or exhibit some degree of commitment to the group, what it proposes to do, and how it proposes to do it.[1]

According to Johnstone, groups that hope to function successfully must meet the challenges posed by five functional prerequisites. We can identify these as (1) recruitment and reproduction; (2) socialization; (3) production of satisfactory levels of goods and services; (4) preservation of order; and (5) preservation of a sense of purpose.[2]

Members of groups die or leave, so groups need a more or less steady supply of new members. This is often achieved in religious communities by encouraging members to have large families and/or by encouraging members to recruit new members. New members must be socialized into the group. They must be trained and educated in the beliefs and practices of the community. New members must be brought to believe sincerely that what the community teaches is not only good for them and their children, but also good for others. Hence groups must provide the sorts of goods and services that people want or have become convinced that they need. There are many different ways to preserve and create order. All of them involve such things as the adoption of codes, laws, rules, constitutions, governance structures, and systems of authority.

The last functional prerequisite that Johnstone identifies (maintaining a sense of purpose) is, perhaps, the most important. We have been stressing how religion provides meaning and purpose to human life by creating a sense of identity and a sense of belonging to something larger than ourselves. If sacred communities fail to maintain a sense of common purpose, they fail to provide that meaning, identity, and belonging that people want. If humans are, as some claim, basically social animals, then people not only *want* their groups to maintain a sense of common purpose, but also *need* them to do so.

Five Functional Prerequisites of Groups

1. Recruitment and reproduction
2. Socialization
3. Production of satisfactory levels of goods and services
4. Preservation of order
5. Preservation of a sense of purpose

In this chapter we will examine certain aspects of religion that are of particular interest to sociologists. We begin with two case studies. One focuses on Tibetan Buddhism, a religion whose existence is increasingly precarious in its homeland. The other examines a new religious movement that failed tragically, ending in mass suicide, the ultimate antisocial act.

We shall also be concerned with examining the dilemmas faced as religions become larger and more successful, types of authority, the role that scriptures play in maintaining a group, and how gender roles are played out in religious groups. Religions, of course, do not exist in a social vacuum. They are parts of a larger society that affects religious groups, and religious groups affect that larger society.

We close the chapter with a research case on Shinto, the indigenous religion of Japan. This case provides a chance for you to exercise your new skills in the sociological analysis of religion.

11.1 TWO CASE STUDIES

Tibetan Buddhism

Tibet, an inner Asian land located west of China on the Himalayan plateau, is overwhelmingly Buddhist. Not much is known about Tibet before the seventh century. According to early chronicles, kings, the first seven of whom were believed to have descended from the heavens by means of a ladder or cord, ruled Tibet. These kings created a system of law and social order that they believed reflected the cosmic order. The king, as a descendent of heaven, was not only the protector of the cosmic and social order, but also its manifestation on earth. The welfare of the people depended on the welfare of the king.[3]

This cult of divine kingship included the belief that the king had a great power of special significance. The king was the embodiment of the essence of the divine ancestor, which was reborn in each successive king. The king ruled along with a head priest representing the priestly class and a chief minister representing the clan nobility. Power was distributed in a hierarchical fashion connecting heaven, king, priest, nobility, and finally, peasants.

The first Tibetan king to support Buddhism was Tri Songdetsen (754–797). He invited to Tibet the Indian Buddhist abbot Shantarakshita and the great master of tantric meditation Padmasambhava. The first Buddhist monastery was established at Samye about 779.

Teams of translators set about translating Buddhist scriptures into Tibetan. Some of the texts they translated are called *tantras*. The tantras set forth a broad range of techniques for attaining enlightenment designed to shorten the eons-long path described in earlier Buddhist literature. These tantras often recommend actions that run directly counter to the conventional rules for proper monastic conduct, including eating meat and having sexual intercourse. *Left-handed* tantra takes these techniques literally, while *right-handed* tantra understands them symbolically. When the translators came to the Sanskrit word for *teacher* (guru), they translated it with the Tibetan word *lama*. Henceforth Buddhist monks who attained the rank of teacher were called lamas.

Although Tibetan Buddhism derives many of its monastic rules and practices from Theravada (Way of the Elders) Buddhism, Tibetan Buddhists also drew on the ideas associated with Mahayana (Great Vehicle) Buddhism. One of the most important features of Mahayana is its emphasis on the bodhisattva as a person who makes a vow to become a buddha in the future in order to lead all beings out of the samsaric realm of suffering. To become fully enlightened, a bodhisattva must develop infinite compassion.

Avalokiteshvara ("ah-wah-loh-ki-tesh' wah-rah"), who is said to be a manifestation of the compassion of all buddhas, is highly revered in Tibet. His famous mantra *om mani padme hum*[*] is widely used in meditation and prayer. As followers of Avalokiteshvara, Tibetan Buddhists refer to their type of Buddhism as the Buddhism of compassion. Tibetan Buddhists also refer to themselves as followers of Vajrayana (Diamond Vehicle). This vehicle emphasizes the tantric approach to the Mahayana path. It is also called the Thunderbolt Vehicle because, it is said, it can cut the length of time required to achieve buddhahood (which is traditionally reckoned as 384×10^{58} years) to three years and three months!

The monastery was an institution of great power and influence before the Chinese Communist takeover in 1959. The largest Buddhist monastery in the world, with some ten thousand monks (in 1959), was Drepung. The power and influence of monasteries extended to both the political and economic spheres. The three most important monastic seats around Lhasa, the capital city, could exercise near veto power over major government policies. Monasteries owned large tracts of productive land and acquired substantial wealth.

The Dalai Lama ("dahl'ee lahm'ah") is a title for the most influential spiritual leader (and at one time, political leader) of Tibetan Buddhism. The faithful consider him to be an emanation of Avalokiteshvara. Some schools of Tibetan Buddhism regard each Dalai Lama to be a reincarnation of the previous one, thereby continuing a lineage that allegedly extends back to the creation of the Tibetan people by the Bodhisattva of Compassion.

Monks, whether novice or ordained, were held in great respect and had high social status. Becoming a monk provided one of the few paths to social advancement. Monks who made it to the higher levels of scholar, teacher, or meditator attracted substantial patronage. Tibetans saw (and still see) Buddhism as symbolic of their country's identity, and they viewed the institutions of monastery and of monk as the manifestation of Tibetan spirituality. These two institutions validated Tibetan identity as a spiritual people.

In pre-Communist Tibet, a substantial part of the male population were monks (10 to 15 percent by some estimates), and a smaller part of the female population were nuns (perhaps 3 percent). The nuns lived in six hundred covenants, the largest of which was home to about one thousand women.

---

[*] The exact meaning of this mantra is in dispute. Some regard it as meaning something like "O you who hold the jewel and the lotus [have mercy upon us]." If it does mean this, it probably is a prayer addressed to Avalokiteshvara since "Jewel Lotus" was one of his/her many names.

While monks could advance to full ordination, nuns could not (although recent efforts have been made to change this situation). Being a nun carried little status, and parents usually did not encourage their daughters to pursue the life of a nun. Regardless of low social status, becoming a nun provided an opportunity (for many, the only opportunity) to escape bad marriages or marrying entirely.

Despite the lower status of nuns and the obvious patriarchal nature of traditional Tibetan society, there were and still are many important female divinities. The goddess Tara is one of the most commonly invoked deities. It should also be noted that nuns did become meditation masters and played important roles as mediums conveying messages from various deities. Avalokiteshvara is represented in both male and female form.

Given the importance of monastic Buddhism in Tibet, it was only natural that as the monarchy declined, political authority shifted to the lamas. Monarchs can pass their power on to their biological descendents, but monks cannot. So by the fourteenth century a form of succession developed in which political and religious power was passed on via the institution of the *incarnate lama,* or *tulku.* Incarnate lamas are technically buddhas because they are manifestations of the third buddha body called the "emanation body." Their rebirth is considered entirely voluntary, and hence their return is celebrated as an expression of great compassion.

Tibetan Buddhism adopted the practice of identifying successive rebirths of great lamas. This institution of the incarnate lama has become a central part of Tibetan society because it assures that power and authority can be passed from one generation to the next. Potential incarnate lamas must pass a test by recognizing personal items of the previous lama. This test is an impressive way of reinforcing the truth of reincarnation and hence, the truth of Buddhism.

The thirteenth through the fifteenth centuries saw the founding of a number of different monastic lineages. Here, we will be primarily concerned with the Geluk lineage.

The Geluk lineage traces its line of authority to Tsong Khapa (1357–1419), a monastic reformer and a creative interpreter of Buddhist philosophy. His disciple, Gendundrup (1391–1474), was identified as the first Dalai Lama. The Gelukpas established monastic universities throughout Tibet. It is this lineage that eventually came to dominate much of the religious and political life of Tibet. The Mongols, after their conversion to Tibetan Buddhism, became powerful patrons of the Geluk lineage and, in 1642, established the fifth Dalai Lama as ruler of Tibet. Now religious and secular power was combined into a single authority.

In the early 1950s the Chinese Communists invaded and occupied Tibet. The atheism of Communism came into immediate conflict with the faith of the Tibetans. A popular uprising against the Chinese occupation forces began on March 17, 1959. It was ruthlessly put down, and the fourteenth Dalai Lama

Tibetan Lamas Debate Meaning of Scripture at Labrang Monastery

was forced to flee. He escaped to India, and many of his followers fled to India as well. Today over 100,000 Tibetans live in exile, and Tibet itself remains a Chinese colony.

Since 1959 there has been violent suppression of the Tibetan religion, which peaked during the Cultural Revolution when thousands of monasteries and temples were destroyed. It is estimated that between 1959 and 1979, one million of the six million ethnic Tibetans have died as a result of Chinese policies. From the Chinese point of view, their invasion and occupation of Tibet is a liberation of the Tibetan people from centuries of feudal and religious domination. The people see it very differently.

Since 1979 the Chinese have relaxed their more oppressive policies due to international attention and their own desire to attract the tourist dollar. Some monasteries and temples have been rebuilt, and some Tibetans have returned to the monastic way of life, although their numbers are carefully regulated by the Chinese. The Tibetan community in exile is expanding and attracting both European and American converts. The present (fourteenth) Dalai Lama won the Nobel Peace Prize and gives talks worldwide on the inner peace that Buddhist practice can give.

At one time, Westerners saw Tibet either as a backward place dominated by crude superstitions and magical practices or as an ideal community (Shangri-La) of happy people uncorrupted by the modern world and possessing ancient wisdom of great value. Contemporary scholarship is painting a more balanced and complex picture.

Past monastic practices in Tibet pursued a program of "mass monasticism." The monasteries enrolled as many monks as possible and expelled as few as possible. Many monks were illiterate and followed no rigorous course of study. Quantity, not quality, was emphasized. Monastic leaders thought that having as many monks as possible was a sign of the truth of Buddhism. This policy led to corruption and lax standards. From time to time there were attempts—some successful, some not—to reform the monastic system. Today the situation is very different.

As monasticism is revived in Tibet, the Chinese have been careful to stress the religious rather than the political nature of Tibetan Buddhism. Monks are forbidden to have any political power or influence. The exiled Tibetan community has come into close contact with other religions, cultures, and democratic rather than theocratic political systems. The Dalai Lama stresses that he is a simple Buddhist monk committed to the practice of compassion. It will be interesting to see what happens to Tibetan Buddhism in general and the monastic system in particular if the fourteenth Dalai Lama is ever allowed to go home.

I visited Drepung monastery in 1999. There were about six hundred monks living there and three or four very elderly nuns living in shacks outside the walls. Children can no longer be enrolled, and the Communist government forbids enrollment below the age of eighteen. Nevertheless, I did see some monks who appeared younger. The government does not support the monastery, so it has had to devise its own means of raising funds from various sources, including tourist money and alms from lay Tibetans. Money is not distributed equally, but according to points earned by monks in different work units.

The immediate future of the monastery will, to a large extent, depend on whether the monks are willing to concentrate on religious matters alone and forgo political activities. Ninety-two monks from Drepung alone were arrested for participating in ten antigovernment demonstrations between 1987 and 1993. The monks in this monastery and others have a long history of involvement in politics. The Chinese government's attempt to persuade and intimidate Drepung's monks in order to uncouple religion from nationalistic politics has not yet worked as well as the Chinese would like. What has motivated the monks in the past has been a combination of religion and nationalistic concerns. A crucial question is whether strong motivation can be maintained on religious grounds alone.

Jonestown

Around five o'clock in the afternoon on November 18, 1978, in Jonestown, Guyana, 918 people died. According to their leader, the Reverend Jim Jones, these people committed an act of "revolutionary suicide." As the news reports of the tragedy spread across the globe, people were understandably shocked and dismayed. How could this happen? Why did it happen? The media was quick to use the word *cult* to characterize what Jones and his followers called the Peoples Temple.

The word *cult* had become a dirty word with the public. It suggested brain-washing, kidnapping, weird rituals, bizarre beliefs, fanatical followers, and crazy leaders. Once the label was in place, the standard assaults against founders of new religious movements or alternative religions (terms more neutral than *cult*) soon followed. Jim Jones was portrayed in the news as a "fake," a "fraud," a "sexual pervert," and a "crazy man." How could there be any other explanation?

The student of religion is challenged by such extreme cases to make sense of them from a scholarly viewpoint. Media reports on religion are seldom well informed and often misleading. As students of religion we must probe behind the standard media accounts and ask questions that lead to a deeper understanding. If Jim Jones was so obviously insane, why did these people follow him even unto death? On a tape recording of the final minutes of the tragedy, a man who is apparently a member of the Peoples Temple says, "And I'd like to say that I thank Dad [a title of affection for Jim Jones] for making me strong to stand with it all and make me ready for it. Thank you."[4] Why would a crazy man who is telling his followers to commit revolutionary suicide be called Dad and thanked?

The facts of the case of Jim Jones and Jonestown are easy enough to document since they are a matter of public record. What is not easy to understand is the event Jones called "revolutionary suicide," a term he borrowed from Huey Newton of Black Panther fame.

The story begins when James Warren Jones was born on May 13, 1931, in Lynn, Indiana. Lynn is a small farming community and a seat of both Christian fundamentalism and Ku Klux Klan activity. Jones's mother had Cherokee blood, and his family was considered poor white trash. He apparently felt alienated from society because of the social status of his family. They lived on the margins of Lynn society. According to some, this early experience of alienation became an ongoing problem in Jones's life and explains his moves from one place to another seeking acceptance from society as a whole.

In 1951, Jones, who had married, moved to Indianapolis and, in 1952, became pastor of a Methodist church and director of a racially integrated community center. His outspoken views in favor of the civil rights movement and his public support of Martin Luther King, Jr., resulted in an invitation to leave. While in Indianapolis Jones became interested in Communism and its vision of a just, classless society. He found an affinity between socialism and the Christian concern for social justice.

In 1956 he started the Peoples Temple Full Gospel Church, an integrated but mostly black congregation. At the Peoples Temple, he preached what he called "apostolic socialism" citing Acts 4:32–35, for support, which says:

> Now the company of those who believed were of one heart and soul and no one said that any of the things which he possessed was his own, but they had everything in common.
>
> And with great power the apostles gave their testimony to the resurrection of the Lord Jesus, and great grace was upon them all. There was not a needy

person among them, for as many as were possessors of lands or houses sold them, and brought the proceeds of what was sold and laid it at the apostles' feet; and distribution was made to each as any had need.

Jones and his congregation strove to live according to the Marxist maxim (a maxim they also considered Christian), "From each according to his ability, to each according to his need." With his message of apostolic socialism Jones combined a ministry of faith healing and revival-style preaching. He explained his ability to heal by claiming that he was a manifestation of the "Christ Principle."

> I have put on Christ, you see. I have followed after the example of Christ. When you see me it's no longer Jim Jones here. I'm crucified with Christ, nevertheless I live, yet not I, but Christ that lives here. Now Christ is in this body.
> You will not get Christ's blessing in Jim Jones' blessing until you walk like Jim Jones, until you talk like Jim Jones, until you act like Jim Jones, until you look like Jim Jones. How long will I be with you until you understand that I am no longer a man, but a Principle. I am the Way, the Truth, and the Light. No one can come to the Father but through me.[5]

Jones warned people that a race war, genocide, and finally, nuclear war were at hand. He predicted a nuclear holocaust to occur on July 15, 1967. He labeled American capitalistic culture "Babylon." There is no evidence that he was not sincere in what he preached or that he personally enriched himself. The evidence does indicate that he was so convinced of the looming catastrophe that he began searching for a place his congregation could move in order to escape nuclear war. His plan was to survive the war and, after Babylon had been destroyed, emerge to rebuild a Christian socialist society.

In 1961, the Peoples Temple became affiliated with the Disciples of Christ, and in 1964, Jones was ordained a minister in that denomination. His millenarian beliefs and his dualistic views of a coming battle between the forces of good (Peoples Temple) and the forces of evil (Babylon) reinforced his belief that nuclear war was at hand. This belief led him to move to Ukiah, California, one of the places that had been identified by *Esquire* magazine as "safe" from nuclear attack.

By 1967 Jones had established an important religious and civic presence in California. He became chairman of the Ukiah Legal Services Society and foreman of the Mendocino Grand Jury. By 1972 he had founded churches in San Francisco and Los Angeles. He published a widely circulated newspaper and had a half-hour radio program. In 1973 he leased 27,000 acres of undeveloped land in Guyana, South America, which was another place identified by *Esquire* as "safe" from nuclear attack.

His combined congregations in California grew so large that the *Sacramento Bee* reported, "Peoples Temple ranks as probably the largest Protestant congregation in Northern California."[6] Jones was named by *Religion in Life* as one of the one hundred outstanding clergymen in the United States. In 1976 he received the Humanitarian of the Year award from the *Los Angeles Herald*. In 1977 he was given the Martin Luther King Humanitarian of the Year award and became chairman of the San Francisco Housing Authority.

What was not reported in the papers, at least not at that time, was the fact that Jim Jones was having sexual relations with a number of young white women and with some men. In 1972 Grace Stoen, a member of Peoples Temple, gave birth to John Victor Stoen, and her husband, Tim Stoen, acknowledged that Jim Jones was the father. Tim Stoen stated in an affidavit:

> The child, John Victor Stoen, was born January 15, 1972. I am privileged beyond words to have the responsibility for caring for him, and I undertake this task humbly with the steadfast hope that said child will become a devoted follower of Jesus Christ and be instrumental in bringing God's kingdom here on earth, as has been his wonderful natural father.[7]

Eventually Grace and Tim Stoen defected separately, leaving the child with the Peoples Temple. The child became the focus of a bitter custody battle, and the Stoens used the press and government agencies to spark investigations of the Temple. Sensationalized news stories from defectors began to appear, and soon both the Treasury Department and the Internal Revenue Service started an investigation, thereby confirming Jones's belief that the Peoples Temple was being persecuted. Jones sensed it was time to leave, and in the summer of 1977 he, along with over one thousand members of the Temple, moved to Jonestown, their "promised land" deep in the heart of the Guyanese jungle.

The defectors and parents of Peoples Temple members formed a group (primarily whites) and named themselves Concerned Relatives. Their stories of sexual, financial, and physical abuses appeared in an article in *New West* (August, 1977).[8] The Stoens initiated legal proceedings to gain custody of John Victor. In 1978 they filed suit, asking for damages of over $56 million. Other lawsuits by other defectors followed. The Social Security Administration asked the U.S. embassy in Guyana to check on the members of Jonestown who received Social Security checks. Consul McCoy visited Jonestown three times between 1977 and 1978. He interviewed seventy-five people, none of whom wanted to leave. McCoy later said, "Anyone who says it was a concentration camp is just being silly. For the old people, and the people coming from the ghetto, it was relatively better."[9] In spite of positive reports, the U.S. Postal Service stopped delivering or rerouting Social Security checks. Since the Temple held all assets in common, this threatened the economic survival of Jonestown. Options began to narrow.

In a book by Catherine Wessinger, Rebecca Moore is quoted:

> Jonestown residents were caught in a "vise" consisting of lawsuits filed by Tim Stoen and Concerned Relatives, investigations and actions by federal agencies

that threatened the continued existence of Jonestown, dismay caused by internal dissension, highly negative press stories, and fears that their status in Guyana was precarious because of the Guyanese political situation. The Jonestown residents had no place to go to escape the multiple pressures. Jim Jones could not return to the United States, where lawsuits and a criminal complaint were pending against him. African American residents of Jonestown did not see returning to racist America and ghetto life as a viable option. The white members did not want to be disloyal to the blacks and their shared ideal of multiracial justice and harmony.[10]

Jones's increasingly radical millenarianism did not help matters. He declared the so-called deity of traditional Christianity to be a "Buzzard God" and asserted he was a messiah sent by the True God, the "Principle of Socialism," to rescue people from their bondage to capitalism. He claimed he was previously incarnated as Moses and then again as Lenin. He claimed the King James Version of the Bible was written by white men to justify the oppression of people of color and to subordinate women. He declared that the United States was the Antichrist and that a pitched battle of good versus evil would soon begin.

In November of 1978 Congressman Leo Ryan went to Jonestown at the urging of the Concerned Relatives. He brought with him some of the people the members of Jonestown hated most: representatives of the American government, of the press, and of the Concerned Relatives. After visiting Jonestown, Congressman Ryan informed Jones that his report would be basically positive. He saw neither evidence of force being used to keep people there nor any evidence of "brainwashing." He recommended that Jonestown increase its contacts with the outside world. A man wielding a knife attacked Ryan, and he and his party rapidly departed for the airstrip with those members of Jonestown that decided to go with him.

At the airstrip, Ryan's party was attacked, and he along with four members of his party were killed by some members of Jonestown. About an hour later, Jones began the "White Night"—an event that had been previously rehearsed. The White Night referred to mass suicide. Most died by taking a fruit drink mixed with cyanide and tranquilizers. It appears that most died voluntarily. Two hundred and sixty small children and infants had been given poison, many of them by their parents. Livestock, dogs, and fishponds had also been poisoned along with the supply of drinking water. Most of the dead were American citizens, most were black, and most were family groups.

The decision to commit mass suicide was not the decision of Jim Jones alone, as the tape of the last minutes shows. Christine Miller, a sixty-year-old black woman, argued with Jones, claiming that suicide was not a proper response. Jones's power and influence had been declining since the move to Jonestown. His healing power had been replaced by medical health care. The mostly young white women who formed the inner circle of leaders used their administrative skills to run Jonestown. As Jim Jones's mental health deteriorated, the community's will to succeed as a socialist collective became stronger. Once it was clear that they could not succeed, most decided to die for their ultimate concern rather than let their ideal die.

There had been warnings. In the summer of 1978 a member of Jonestown named Mike Prokes wrote to the *San Francisco Examiner*, "We have found something to die for, and it's called social justice. We will at least have had the satisfaction of living that principle, not because it promised success or reward, but simply because we felt it was the right thing to do."[11] Before Ryan's trip to Guyana, defectors, including Grace Stoen, briefed the U.S. State Department on the possibility of mass suicide in Jonestown. In the end, these warnings did not stop the tragedy.

Annie Moore, a nurse, apparently was the last person to die. She wrote a final letter that concluded:

> Jim Jones showed us all this—that we could live together with our differences, that we are all the same human beings. Luckily, we are more fortunate than the starving babies of Ethiopia, than the starving babies of the United States.
>
> What a beautiful place this was. The children love the jungle, learned about animals and plants. There were no cars to run over them; no child molesters to molest them; nobody to hurt them. They were the freest, most intelligent children I had ever known.
>
> Seniors had dignity. They had whatever they wanted—a plot of land for a garden. Seniors were treated with respect—something they never had in the United States. A rare few were sick and when they were, they were given the best medical care. . . . We died because you would not let us live in peace. Annie Moore.[12]

Those are some of the facts. What do they mean? How can they be explained? The tendency of both popular and a few scholarly explanations is to focus on Jim Jones. He is the culprit that explains it all. He suffered from extreme alienation, an overinflated ego, paranoia, obsessions with sex, and much more. The bulk of the press made him out to be a "wrathful, lustful giant" with extraordinary powers to brainwash people.

From a sociological viewpoint, I think this explains very little. It certainly does not explain why hundreds of adults voluntarily followed Jones into death. They were not zombies who had lost their will. They argued with Jones and with each other about the best course of action. Our focus needs to be on the community and the racist, capitalistic society it was fleeing.

Catherine Wessinger, using Tillich's idea of religion as an ultimate concern, argued that the collective had become, for most of the members of the Peoples Temple, their ultimate concern. An ultimate concern is something for which people are willing to lay down their lives. We do not find it incomprehensible when people willingly lay down their lives for their nation (soldiers do it all the time) or their families. The Peoples Temple was family and nation for the citizens of Jonestown. The story about how it became that for these people is long and complex. It has to do with the ideology Jones preached (millenarianism and apostolic socialism), U.S. racism, idealist fantasies of a perfect society, and the natural desire of people to believe that they have given their lives to a righteous cause.

Jonathan Z. Smith offers some partial explanations. He points out parallels between the history of religion and Jonestown. The members of Peoples Temple were not the first, and would not be the last, to commit mass suicide in the name of religion. Jim Jones even reminded a member of that during the final minutes, when a member claimed that this had never been done before. It has been done before, Jones emphatically asserted. Indeed it had, and it usually happened when people found themselves in desperate situations and believed the pure community they had been building had become corrupted. Paradise, utopia, the perfect society in the making had been invaded and profaned by the arrival of Congressman Ryan and others. People from the polluted, racist, capitalistic "outside" had crossed over the boundary to the pure, nonracist, socialist "inside." Jones actually uses the word *invasion* to characterize Ryan's arrival.

If we couple the violation of boundaries with the sense that there are no good alternatives, we can see how desperate people might take their own lives. Some of their members had killed Ryan and others. They knew it was only a matter of time before the law would show up. At one time they had hoped to go to Russia if Guyana did not work out. On the tape of the final minutes we hear Jim Jones saying, "It's too late for Russia." "There's no plane." So "Let's get gone. Let's get gone. Let's get gone."[13]

The causes of this tragedy are much more complex. But Wessinger's and Smith's theories are a step in the right direction. They do not rely on simplistic explanations that focus on one person as the culprit that caused all this. They help us make the bizarre and shocking more familiar. They help us understand that perhaps we too, if we had the same experiences and were in the same situation, might also opt for "revolutionary suicide."

11.2 COMPARISON

I think we will find it helpful, as a way of organizing our comparative discussion, to focus on the five functional prerequisites of groups discussed in the introduction to this chapter. Once again I ask you to try your hand at comparison based on the information you have. Note the differences and similarities between Tibetan Buddhism and Jonestown with respect to

1. Recruitment and reproduction
2. Socialization
3. Production of goods and services
4. Preservation of order
5. Preservation of purpose

Again, you may compare your comparison to mine, noting the differences and similarities. Since the information you have is limited, there are bound to be differences because my account draws on additional information.

Recruitment and Reproduction With respect to recruitment and reproduction, I think it is clear that monastic communities like the Tibetan Buddhists that require vows of celibacy cannot fill their ranks by reproduction. The only option available is recruitment. In the pre-Communist days (what I will call traditional Tibet), recruitment was no problem when it came to monks because of the high social status enjoyed by monks and the willingness of most Tibetan families to send their sons off at an early age to become monks. In occupied Tibet we might think enrollment of new monks would be more difficult, but it is not. Though monks have been killed and imprisoned, children are prohibited by law from joining, and caps are placed on enrollments, still, all available positions are filled.

For the Tibetan Buddhist diaspora (those spread around the world), adding new members, including both monks and nuns, has proved not to be a problem, especially in Europe and the United States. The Dalai Lama is immensely popular and attracts new members by his evident spirituality and wisdom. Also, the International Campaign to Free Tibet is a popular cause, attracting those who are interested in righting what they see to be a social injustice.

The Peoples Temple relied on both recruitment and reproduction. If the Peoples Temple had survived the White Night, there would have been another generation ready to fill its ranks as adult members. Its most successful recruitment came among families, African Americans, and whites who were concerned about issues of social justice and racism. The social situation in the United States in the 1960s and early 1970s created favorable conditions for recruitment. People were concerned about civil rights and nuclear war. There were also a number of communal movements interested in experimenting with socialism. Jones himself had great charisma (a quality of persons that attracts others), and the close bonding that occurred among members attracted many who were lonely and isolated.

We can only speculate on how long the Peoples Temple could have kept going if the tragedy at Jonestown had not happened. It is clear at present that Tibetan monastic Buddhism is so ingrained in Tibet that if Tibet did become a free nation, it would flower once more. It is hard to say whether Communist "reeducation" programs will have a major impact on Tibetan religious attitudes over the long haul. Perhaps the greatest threat comes from the Chinese resettlement programs in which ever more Chinese are being relocated in Tibet and more and more Tibetans are being forced to move outside their traditional homeland.

Socialization   How did these two groups socialize their members into the ideology and practices of the group, and how well did they do it?

In traditional Tibet, the socialization process began early, and therefore had a greater chance of success. If someone has almost complete power and influence over a child, getting him or her to accept the ideology and practices of a group is simply a process of gradual education. In contemporary Tibet, socialization may prove more difficult because new monks must be eighteen to be admitted. Yet the socialization process has already begun in the home, and the motivation to fight for the nation in addition to the religion provides a fertile field supporting the socialization process.

Renunciation also plays a major role in the socialization process. A monk takes vows to renounce the world outside the monastery. These vows, while they do not require complete separation from family and friends, isolate monks from their previous lives and focus their attention on building new bonds with the new community they have joined.

The socialization process in the Peoples Temple was much more difficult than it was in traditional societies that support monastic ideals. The appeal to Christian teachings helped. Early members were predisposed to join Protestant Christian churches because of the religious environment in which they grew up. The added message of socialism and antiracism was also appealing, not only to the ethically concerned and marginalized members of American society, but also to the ethically sensitive and perhaps somewhat guilt-ridden whites. There were education classes and, of course, Jim Jones's preaching, but the most effective form of socialization appears to be the close bonds—indeed, family-like atmosphere that pervaded the group. Jim Jones was called Father and Dad. The sexual bonds that formed between Jones and the "inner circle" of white women also provided a powerful means of socialization. Near the end, when Jones was sinking deeper into paranoia, this inner circle helped keep Jonestown running.

When the end neared, what alternatives did people have? If they gave all their money and property to the group, if they broke with former family and friends and moved to a foreign land, how could they exit? Members of the Peoples Temple, though not monks and not taking vows of renunciation, did in their own way renounce the outside world. And equally important, the outside world renounced the Peoples Temple.

Americans like churches, but they do not like cults. Label something a cult and it immediately becomes strange, different, even somewhat sinister. Once the press used that word for the Peoples Temple, their acceptance by and even success with the general population of California began to diminish. No longer were they a well-intentioned group fighting for social justice and a truly integrated religious community. Now they were dangerous. Now they might not even be "Christian" anymore. As the hostility and suspicion of those outside grew, the fear and desperation of those inside mounted. In the end, there was little left of their former lives in capitalist, racist America that members found attractive.

Both the monastic system of Tibet and the Peoples Temple used similar socialization processes, relying heavily on education and renunciation. The main difference is the attitude of the society at large. Tibetan monasticism has been and still is strongly supported by the general population, but communal and utopian movements in America (of which there have been many) have always been looked on with a suspicious eye. Social status in America is definitely not increased by joining a fringe movement.

Production of Satisfactory Levels of Goods and Services   The third functional prerequisite of a successful group is producing satisfactory levels of goods and services. There are two levels of goods and services: economic and intellectual/emotional. In traditional Tibet, the monasteries were very wealthy, but individual monks were often quite poor. They were given insufficient funds to live on, so they had to devise ways to supplement their income. Shelter was usually provided, and some food, but the monasteries spent much of their money on religious festivals and other related activities. In contemporary Tibet, individual monks are much better off, getting sufficient or nearly sufficient funds from the money-making enterprises of the monastery. However, goods and services are not distributed equally, but divided according to "work points" earned.

On the emotional and intellectual level, communal life and strong bonds of friendship unite the monks. In traditional Tibet, few monks entered the rigorous education program, but one was available. There were various sorts of degrees possible, ranging from what we might call undergraduate through graduate levels. Buddhism is an intellectually and emotionally challenging religion. Its philosophy and theology are complex and difficult to grasp, there is an almost endless amount of literature to master, and its meditation practices can be very difficult. The faithful engage in relentless self-examination and are constantly seeking personal and moral improvement.

The Peoples Temple was a socialist commune, so all resources were held in common. They were not distributed according to work done, but according to need. At its beginning and at its end it was financially unstable. But it enjoyed several years of prosperity in California. Few appeared to complain about the lack of material goods.

For most members, the intellectual and emotional needs, not economic needs, were primary. Emotionally, the Peoples Temple was able to provide a sense of family. People saw themselves as related in a grand project to create a perfectly integrated society. Their kinship was in their common cause. Although Jones's theology appears to be rather simplistic, and little emphasis was put on philosophical or theological education, many of the white members were college educated. However, it was not the intellectual challenge that attracted them and kept them in the Temple, it was the emotional satisfaction they received from the belief that they had dedicated their lives to a righteous cause.

Preservation of Order   The fourth prerequisite requires rules, regulations, organization, and structure. The structure of Tibetan monasticism is hierarchical, with the abbots and *tulkus* enjoying more power than other monks. Like all monastic orders, it had its rules and regulations about work and religious practice. Some people worked in the kitchen, some in the fields, others on construction, and some studied. Drepung had its own judicial system. Expulsion was always possible for major offenses but, in traditional Tibet, seldom used.

The Peoples Temple maintained order to the end. People lined up by families to receive their toxic cocktail. Children were poisoned first, then the adults. The bodies of families were found lying together on the ground. It appeared to be for the most part a very orderly process. Four individuals, including Jones, died of gunshot wounds, and approximately seventy bodies had puncture wounds, which suggests the poison may have been injected. Whether it was injected voluntarily or not could not be determined.

An inner circle of Jones's advisors maintained order in the Temple and in Jonestown. They managed the affairs of the community, from financial to medical. The inner circle was mostly white and mostly female. There appears to have been a constant fear of defection, the worst of sins. Things began to fall apart when the Stoens left. More followed, and eventually, near the end, a few of the inner circle left too. The boundaries between the order inside and the order outside were clearly drawn. To step from the outside in, caused joy. To step from the inside out, threatened not only disorder, but also the very existence of the community.

Tibetan monasticism was more highly organized than Jonestown. It had to be because it was much larger. Even so, both were hierarchical (in spite of Jones's egalitarian preaching), and both were organized in ways that facilitated getting work done. The members of the Temple would regularly meet (often in all-night sessions) to discuss problems in the community, courses of action, and how to improve their communal life. Jones created order by having what, in effect, amounted to town meetings. The organization of Jonestown appears far more democratic than the organization of Tibetan monasticism, an organization that is feudal in comparison.

Preservation of a Sense of Purpose   The ideologies and practices of both groups reinforced a shared sense of purpose. This sense of purpose was threatened when the Communists invaded Tibet and the Ryan investigative group invaded Jonestown. Invasion, perceived or real, always threatens the expectation that common goals will be reached. In the case of Tibetan monasticism, the invaders demanded that the purpose change. The monks are to abandon, under penalty of law, all political and nationalistic causes. From now on, the monasteries are to pursue exclusively religious goals. Only the future will show whether this revised purpose can be maintained. It is very difficult to separate religion from politics, especially in a nation where the two have been entwined for centuries.

Some might claim that the mass suicide at Jonestown shows that in the end, the Peoples Temple failed in maintaining a sense of purpose. That is certainly true for the defectors. But it may not be entirely true for those who died. They clearly believed that they were leaving this earth to continue the cause elsewhere. The world was not ready for them and their ideals, so they simply had to go somewhere else, just as the community had moved from place to place on this earth. Unfortunately, we know little about their views of the afterlife. In 1973, Jones used the word *translation* to talk about being "translated to a distant planet." The language of death used by Jones and others near the end was spatial—"Let's get gone," "stepping over," "you have to step across," "this world was not our home." Whatever the specifics of their view of life after death, it seems clear that they expected to continue their grand experiment in integrated socialist living someplace else. Most probably died with their sense of purpose intact.

11.3 THE DILEMMAS OF INSTITUTIONALIZATION

Among the novels by Fyodor Michaelovitch Dostoevsky (1821–1864), the great Russian novelist, is one titled *The Brothers Karamazov* (published in 1880). Within that novel is a section called the "Grand Inquisitor," which Sigmund Freud called "one of the peaks of the literature of the world."[14] Dostoevsky imagines that Christ has returned during the Spanish Inquisition and that he is arrested and questioned by the Grand Inquisitor of the Roman Catholic Church. The Inquisitor, who recognizes Christ, asks him why he has come back and informs him that his return is dangerous to the stability of the church he has founded. The Inquisitor tells Christ, "I swear, man is weaker and baser by nature than Thou hast believed him!" The Grand Inquisitor also says to the returned Christ, "We [the Roman Catholic Church] have corrected Thy work and have founded it upon *miracle, mystery* and *authority*."[15]

Max Weber gave the subject of Dostoevsky's literary essay a sociological term. He called it the "routinization of charisma." In time, the original creative surge of the founder of new religious movements is made "routine." Weber thinks this is necessary if the movement is to survive. It must institutionalize and thus create a bureaucracy.

Thomas O'Dea, a sociologist of religion, has noted that the routinization process typically presents religious organizations with **five dilemmas.**[16] The first he called the "dilemma of mixed motivation." In its beginning stages, a new religious movement exhibits a kind of single-minded focus on what it takes to be its main goal and message. As it grows in size and as subsequent generations move into leadership positions that carry rewards, power, and honor, people may begin to ask why people want positions of leadership. Do they seek these positions because of their concern for the mission of the group or because of the prestige associated with leadership positions? Perhaps their motivation is mixed. We might wonder about the motivation of Dostoevsky's Grand Inquisitor. The Inquisitor acknowledges, in the course of his inquisition of Christ, that Christ came to give humans freedom. But freedom, he says, is too much for ordinary humans to bear. So instead of freedom, the church has given them what they want and need—miracle, mystery, and authority.

O'Dea's second dilemma is the "symbolic dilemma." Religions must convey their messages in symbols. Rituals often embody these symbols in concrete action. Initially the rituals remind the early members of important and meaningful experiences. Over time, as the group grows and becomes more routinized, the rituals and symbols may seem increasingly meaningless and strange. Ritual activity becomes a matter of mere formality, taking on a hollow, sometimes even magical, tone. Often the symbols become so dead and the ritual activities so formal, that sectarian movements develop with the goal of revitalizing the beliefs and practices of the group.

The third dilemma centers on problems associated with developing an "administrative order." As an organization grows in complexity, new offices and positions need to be created. A bureaucracy forms. Bureaucracies need to elaborate policies and rules to cover new situations. However, the more they do that, the more flexibility they lose. So the Grand Inquisitor represents an elaborated bureaucracy with its own policies and procedures. He no longer has the flexibility of allowing Christ to go free, even though he recognizes him. It is his responsibility to question and, if necessary, punish those deemed dangerous to the Roman Catholic Church.

The "dilemma of delimitation" refers to the conflict between the need for concrete and specific rules of behavior and the moral spirit of the religion. New situations arise, new rules must be created to apply to these new situations, and soon legalism sets in, making general guidelines hard-and-fast laws. The focus shifts from the "spirit of the law" to the "letter of the law." For example, too easily the admonition to love one's neighbor can get side-tracked into debates about who exactly is my neighbor and precisely what does love mean. As definitions pile up and hairs are split, the life gets slowly squeezed out of what starts as a simple command to help people in need. Meanwhile the hungry go unfed and the homeless go without shelter.

The last dilemma O'Dea refers to as the "dilemma of power." Voluntary religious organizations normally want people to join and to remain adherents because of a sincere conviction that their beliefs are true. However, these organizations are sometimes tempted to use manipulative methods, even coercion, to gain and retain members. The later days of the Peoples Temple are a good example. As defections increased, Jones and other members of the group began to feel ever more threatened. The greater the perceived danger from a declining membership, the greater the manipulation by those in charge. Also, some religions have resorted to coercion (more or less extreme) rather than conversion in order to build their numbers. The hard sell of some televangelists and door-to-door proselytizers is another example of the "conversion versus coercion" power dilemma.

The success of religious organizations often depends on how well they solve these five dilemmas. Success, however, does not always smell so sweet when compromises have to be made.

Five Dilemmas of Institutionalization

1. The dilemma of mixed motivation
2. The symbolic dilemma
3. The dilemma of administrative order
4. The dilemma of delimitation
5. The dilemma of power

11.4 TYPES OF AUTHORITY

What is the probability that some group of people will obey specific commands? Why should any of us believe or do what someone else tells us to believe or do? Why do people sometimes sacrifice their own self-interest in order to obey others? There are many kinds of authority, but here I wish to focus on the different types of authority enjoyed by religious leaders.

According to Max Weber, there are three basic types of religious authority: charismatic, traditional, and legal-rational. Jim Jones is an example of a charismatic leader. His authority was a product of a particular type of relationship that he was able to establish with people by the sheer force of his personality. He was able to inspire loyalty in people. He had a certain quality that enabled him to attract devoted followers and inspire high levels of emotion and commitment.

Weber notes that charismatic authority is revolutionary. It is based on a break with tradition. It provides a new vision of the way the world should be. A religious leader whose authority is based in charisma can get people to change their customary beliefs and do things that their tradition has told them not to do. Jim Jones was able to inspire belief in apostolic socialism among people who had been socialized into capitalism, and he was able to get them to follow him even when it involved a high cost—their own lives. The Jesus portrayed in the New Testament had charismatic authority, as did Buddha, Moses, and Muhammad. All leaders of new religious movements rely on this kind of authority to get something that is religiously novel started.

Once a religion is up and running and once it survives long enough, traditional authority replaces charismatic authority. This sort of authority is usually informal in the sense that there is no formal rule or law authorizing a person or group to exercise authority. For example, it is customary and traditional in Tibet to recognize the authority of certain Buddhist lineages, but there is no law that requires it.

Traditional authority is closely related to what Weber labels legal-rational, but a legal-rational authority is one based on formalized rules, regulations, and laws. These have been thought out and are the result of conscious calculation—hence Weber calls them "rational." For example, professional clergy such as ministers, rabbis, and priests have legal-rational authority because they occupy an office or position that is established as authoritative by the formal rules of some particular religious group.

Professional clergy also enjoy traditional authority because it is customary to see them as authorities in certain matters. There are, of course, many different kinds of clergy, and it is possible for new positions to be created by legal authority that are not necessarily traditional. So when some religious groups began to ordain women as professional clergy, a new position of authority for women was created by new rules, but it was not traditional in many religious organizations to ordain women.

Some religious leaders can have all three types of authority. Martin Luther King, Jr., was a charismatic religious leader who was also head of the Southern Christian Leadership Conference (SCLC) and a Baptist minister. His positions as head of SCLC and as a minister were based on legal-rational authority. But his clergy status was also based on traditional authority because in the black community it is traditional to acknowledge the authority of Christian ministers.

Whatever type of authority a religious leader may enjoy—charismatic, traditional, legal-rational—in the end, some group of people must acknowledge the authority of another group by following their commands. If no one followed, no one could lead.

Types of Authority

1. Charismatic
2. Traditional
3. Legal-rational

11.5 SCRIPTURE

Scriptures are social events. Communities of faith create holy writings for communities of faith. Once sacred scriptures exist, they become another source of authority that influences in turn the communities of faith that produced them. Such communities also continue to shape their scriptures by adding or subtracting material and by evolving new interpretations to fit changing circumstances.

Scriptures function in many ways, but one important way involves establishing a worldview. This worldview, or way of seeing the world and its history, provides a map for understanding life—its origin, meaning, and purpose. This worldview becomes a framework for interpreting subsequent events. For example, numerous Christian groups have been searching for "signs" of the end times in order to prepare for the Second Coming of Jesus. Without a worldview that incorporates the notion that history will at some point come to an end, being on the lookout for signs of the last days makes little sense.

Before written documents, oral traditions (some of which end up in scriptural collections) shape and are shaped by developing communities of faith. Before there was writing, stories, sayings, sermons, prophesies, myths, hymns, moral rules, ritual instructions, and the like existed only when spoken and heard in a communal setting. Even after scriptures (what is written) had come into existence, they were often known only when heard because the majority of believers were illiterate. Only the elite could read and write. Even when literacy became widespread, the oral/aural (spoken/heard) mode persisted as scriptures were read, chanted, sung, and memorized in ritual settings. Whether scriptures are oral or written, communities are quite literally created when people recognize a common source of authority.

In 1987, the national television network of India presented in serialized form the *Ramayana*—a sacred text of epic poetry recounting the exploits of Rama ("rah'muh"), an incarnation of the god Vishnu. This series turned out to be immensely popular. There was an estimated audience of over 100 million, and much of India came to a standstill as people stopped what they were doing to watch an episode. For a moment in time, the diverse people of India became a single community.

Each year the towns and villages of India produce a play reenacting the story of the *Ramayana*. These performances (called *Ramlila* or "play of Rama") last anywhere from nine to thirty days and, in the richer villages, can be very elaborate productions. Because of these ritualized presentations, many Hindus are able to memorize and recall many verses without ever having read the text itself. Through the play, the audiences of the Ramlila become bound in a community of common experience and knowledge. The influence and authority of the *Ramayana* is thereby reinforced. It is quite natural to think that this scripture must be significant if all these millions of people take it seriously (or should I say playfully?).

Hearing is so important in the formation of Hindu scriptures that all the vast amount of sacred literature produced over many generations is divided into two types: *shruti* (that which is heard) and *smriti* (that which is remembered). The classification *shruti* is reserved for all texts that have a nonhuman origin, and the classification *smriti* is used for all texts that have human authors. The four Vedas (*Rig, Sama, Yajur,* and *Atharva*) are *shruti* texts. They are the most sacred texts and became the **canon** (rule or standard) for classifying all other literature as sacred. If an epic poem like the *Ramayana,* for example, acknowledges the authority of the Vedas and claims its teachings are consistent with Vedic teaching, it is admitted into the canon of sacred scripture, even though it has a human author. The Vedic canon was closed (meaning nothing more could be added) about the fourth century B.C.E.

If texts classified as *smriti,* or remembered, have human authors, who are the nonhuman authors of *shruti* texts like the Vedas? Many of us would probably say, because of the influence of Jewish, Christian, and Islamic traditions on our society, that God or gods reveal the Vedas to humans. While we can say that the Vedas are revealed, they have no authors, divine or human.

The Vedas embody the *Vac,* which is the eternal sacred and cosmic word/sound that brings into being the entire creation. The sounds that the words of the Vedas embody are eternal. The Vedas have no beginning or end. Seers who have developed special spiritual abilities at the beginning of each world cycle hear these sounds. The eternalness and authorless nature of the Vedas enhances their authority because there are no possible changes that might occur, and there is no author (divine or human) that might make a mistake in the course of revealing their content. The Vedas can be trusted because they have none of the defects associated with texts produced by humans. Their authority is eternal and absolute. Some scholars believe that the *shruti* theory of the Vedas was developed in opposition to the canons of Buddhism and Jainism since neither of these religions recognized the authority of the Vedas.

The Christian Bible is made up of two major divisions called the Old Testament and the New Testament. The Old Testament consists of many of the texts found in the Hebrew scriptures, or Tanakh, whose canon took shape over many centuries and combined both oral and written material from different historical periods and different authors. Hebrew scriptures contain twenty-four books divided into three main parts: the Law, the Prophets, and the Writings. The Protestant version of the Old Testament is nearly identical to the Hebrew scripture but, because of different ways of dividing the books, consists of thirty-nine books. The versions of the Old Testament found in Roman Catholic and Eastern Orthodox traditions include seven more books as well as additions to the books of Esther and Daniel.

The Christian recognition of the sacred authority of the scriptures of another religion (Judaism) testifies to the strong bond between these religions.

It is rare when one religion accepts as authoritative the scriptures of another tradition. However, this acceptance of Hebrew scriptures did not come without a fight. A priest named Marcion (ca. 140) developed an early version of the Bible that completely excluded the Hebrew scriptures. Marcion was a dualist, and he sharply distinguished between the god of judgment, punishment, and wrath and the god of mercy, forgiveness, and love. Marcion identified the first god with the Hebrew deity and accordingly rejected Hebrew scriptures. He identified the second god with the Christian deity and therefore created the first New Testament, consisting of an abridged version of the Gospel of Luke and an edited version of Paul's letters. His charismatic movement produced many early martyrs.

Another group of Christians, the group that finally emerged as the victors over rival Christian groups like the Marcionites, accepted the Hebrew scriptures as they were constituted about the end of the first century and fought against Marcion's interpretation of the Christian message. However, they accepted the Hebrew scriptures only as an *old* testament to the acts of God. They claimed that there was now a *new* testament to the acts of God that made the meaning of the old clear. This new interpretation centered on the recognition of a human being named Jesus as a messiah or christ sent by God in the last days before the establishment of God's kingdom.

The New Testament canon contains twenty-seven books—four gospels witnessing the religious significance of the life and death of Jesus the Christ, the Acts of the Apostles who were the first followers of Jesus, twenty-one letters, and a book called Revelation. The story of how this particular collection came to be is complex and cannot be recounted in much detail here. Suffice it to say that different churches recognized different books as sacred, and out of the vast amount of material and after much struggle and political infighting, a canon was settled on by representatives of those churches that had the most power. The fact that some Syrian churches omit the letters of Second Peter, Second and Third John, Jude, and Revelation testifies to the fact that the canon of the New Testament is not completely fixed. However, the New Testament as it is generally known in Protestant, Roman Catholic, and Eastern Orthodox Christianity became authoritative by the end of the fourth century. This brief history of the formation of the Christian canon demonstrates clearly the way in which scriptures are creations of communities of faith.

Note that all the books included in the New Testament identify human authors. From a Hindu point of view, they would all be *smriti*, not *shruti*. However, in the Gospel of John, Jesus is identified with the *Logos*, the word by which God created the whole universe. Like the Hindu *Vac*, this creative Logos is eternal and cosmic. This idea opened up the possibility of understanding the Bible to be the word of God in a derivative sense. The Logos is the true "Bible" or divine word, and the human Bible testifies to it insofar as its various human authors testify correctly.

Perhaps the constant battles Christians have fought about what writings should be included in the canon and about how best to interpret them arise, in part, because "what is remembered" by human authors can be mistaken. The insistence of some Protestant groups on the dictation theory of revelation, the inerrancy of scripture, and its literal interpretation testifies to the fact that it is always difficult to claim absolute authority for texts written by humans on the basis of what they remember. The notion that God through the Holy Spirit literally dictated the words of scriptures to the human authors, and the claim that what the authors heard was accurately written down is, from the Hindu perspective, an attempt to move a *smriti* text closer to a *shruti* text. However, unlike Hindu notions of *shruti* and the eternal *Vac*, the eternal Logos heard by the authors of the Christian New Testament has a divine source.

The stories of how the scriptures came to be in religions other than Hinduism and Christianity are different. But most, if not all, when viewed from a sociological perspective, constitute stories of conflict, struggles for power, and the creation of communities.

11.6 GENDER

We begin with some definitions. First let us take *sexism* to mean discrimination against persons because of their sex, and any ideology that maintains that one sex (be it male or female) is superior to the other. Sexism manifests itself in subtle and not so subtle ways. One of the more obvious ways involves sex roles. Sex roles encompass tasks assigned on the basis of sex, rather than ability. For example, women might be forbidden to be priests in some religions just because they are women, regardless of their abilities to perform successfully in that role.

Another way sexism manifests itself is in concepts of gender. While the word *gender* is often used to refer to biological qualities designated by the terms female and male, it can also be used to refer to ideas people have of the nature of females and males. In this sense, gender refers to concepts of femininity and masculinity. Every society creates concepts of gender— that is, concepts of femininity and masculinity based on some socially constructed notion of the nature of males and females. For example, women might be thought of as nurturing and nonaggressive by nature. These qualities become feminine qualities, and if a female acts contrary to gender stereotyping, she is often thought of as odd or overly masculine. When she is a child, her playmates will often call her a tomboy. Likewise men might be thought of as unemotional and aggressive by nature, and if a male acts contrary to gender expectation, he may be called a sissy. We are all socialized at a very early age to accept the gender ideas of our society uncritically and to engage in gender stereotyping.

I have referred occasionally throughout this book to the relationship between gender and religion. With respect to females, these references have more often than not shown that women have been and still are portrayed in negative ways, especially in patriarchal religions that insist on the superiority of males. The examples of sexist attitudes found among religions that we have noted can, unfortunately, be multiplied by the thousands. This situation is more than unfortunate because such negative notions of females are given divine sanction in sacred texts and religious teachings. In other words, the human origin of gender concepts is obscured by claiming this is the way the gods intended things to be. Restricting female opportunities and placing them under the dominance of males now becomes not something that humans invented and hence can be changed, but something the divine invented and hence cannot be changed. By obscuring the cultural origin of gender, religious promotion of sexist views becomes doubly harmful. If a female wants to be a priest, or a rabbi, or a Quranic scholar, she may be told that such a desire is an affront to God and amounts to sin. Not only does she want something her society does not want her to have; she wants something that God does not want her to have.

In Hinduism, Judaism, Christianity, Buddhism (the list could go on), women are frequently portrayed as sources of pollution, especially during menstruation. In traditional Hinduism, women could not be educated in the Vedas, they were instructed to view their husbands as gods, and to serve their sons with absolute devotion. Traditional Hinduism taught them and still teaches them that their highest goal in life is to marry and give birth to a son. When their husband dies they are to throw themselves on his funeral pyre as a supreme act of devotion. This practice (called *suti*) is no longer legal, but it still sometimes occurs in rural regions and was practiced in India until the nineteenth century.

In Orthodox Judaism, women were and are forbidden to study Torah, to become rabbis, or to assume any religious roles reserved for males. To this day many Orthodox Jewish men speak this prayer in the morning, "Blessed art thou, O Lord our God, King of the Universe who has not made me a woman." An infamous saying in I Timothy 2:11–15 (a letter attributed to the Apostle Paul but most likely not written by him) set the stage for twenty centuries of the subordination of women in Christianity. The author of Timothy says:

> Let a woman learn in silence with all submissiveness. I permit no woman to teach or to have authority over men; she is to keep silent. For Adam was formed first, then Eve; and Adam was not deceived, but the woman was deceived and became a transgressor. Yet woman will be saved through bearing children, if she continues in faith and love and holiness, with modesty.[17]

The gender bias is clear, and the author backs his sexism with his interpretation of Torah, thereby invoking divine sanction for his views.

As we have already seen, some Buddhist groups taught that women could not be enlightened as long as they remained women. Nirvana was possible only after women were reincarnated as men. Buddhist monks had fewer monastic rules to follow than nuns did. Nuns, no matter how old or experienced, were instructed to serve the youngest and newest monks. They were told that they were on the bottom of the monastic hierarchy.

These examples of giving sacred justification for female subordination are not the whole story. The relationship between gender and religion is far more complex than these few examples illustrate. We need to distinguish religion in the texts from religion in the real world. The texts may say one thing, but practices may be quite different. For example, some Southern Baptist women have told sociological interviewers that while the Bible does teach that women should be subordinate to their husbands, this particular teaching does not really apply to them or to their situations.

There is an increasing amount of data on gender and religion, but how to interpret that data is often problematic. For example, in Hinduism, goddesses are worshiped and often given more powers than the many gods. Some Hindu tantric texts assert gender equality and teach the harmony of feminine and masculine forces in both the universe and in society.

Reform Judaism, in contrast to the Orthodox variety, encourages women to study Torah and ordains them as rabbis. There is a long and influential tradition in Judaism that emphasizes verse twenty-seven in the first chapter of Genesis and claims it supports gender equality. The verse reads, "So God created humans in his own image, in the image of God he created them; male and female God created them."

As noted above, some scholars maintain that Paul is not the real author of the first letter to Timothy and hence did not pen the sexist words quoted earlier. They certainly seem to be incompatible with what he wrote in Galatians 3:28 about there being "neither Jew nor Greek, . . . neither slave nor free, . . . neither male nor female in Christ." Evidence indicates that women played an active leadership role in the early church, and that Jesus most likely treated both men and women equally. Today many Protestant denominations ordain women, and even in the Roman Catholic Church, women are becoming "pastoral associates." They perform practically every function of a priest except celebrating the mass.

Nancy Schuster Barnes, a Buddhist scholar, maintains that "Doctrinally, Buddhism has been egalitarian from its beginnings. The same teachings were given by the Buddha to his female and male disciples, the same spiritual path was opened to all, the same goal pointed out."[18] She goes on to argue that sometime between 300 B.C.E. and 200 things began to change. Monks challenged the spiritual capacities of women, and male Buddhists made an effort to prove that women were inferior to men.

Still, there have been and are religions in which women serve in leadership positions. There are also religions founded and developed by women. According to Susan Sered, the existence of religions in which women are dominant raise at least two questions.[19] First, how might religions founded by or directed by women be different from male-dominated religions? Second, how might male-dominated religions change as women assume a greater leadership role?

Sered has tried to answer these two questions by collecting data on several groups in which women have dominated in the past or do now dominate the spiritual scene. Among the many groups she studied are ancestral cults among Black Caribs in Belize, matrilineal spirit cults in Thailand, Christian Science, Shakerism, and Korean shamanism.

She selected these groups because they are all dominated by women, there is no discrimination against women with respect to leadership opportunities, members are self-aware that their group is primarily "a women's religion," and there is also awareness that the group is independent of larger, male-dominated religions. She found three sets of factors that, when they combine, are likely to influence the development of women's religions (a religion dominated by females).

The first condition she calls "gender dissonance." This is an experience "in which culturally accepted notions of gender are either highly contradictory and/or rapidly changing."[20] The second condition is that there is a strong and noticeable cultural emphasis on the maternal role. The last condition is the existence of a high degree of personal, economic, and social autonomy or independence for women.

Three Conditions Influencing the Rise of Women's Religion

1. Gender dissonance
2. Focus on women's maternal roles
3. A high degree of autonomy from men

Women's religions exhibit, according to Sered, three kinds of developments. First, emphasis will be placed on activities and issues that traditionally fall to women as bearers and caretakers of children. Second, explicit attention will be paid to the issue of patriarchy and its effect on women's lives.

These two kinds of development are not particularly unexpected. What is unexpected is the third feature of women's religions. Sered found that the effects of gender on the form and content of the religions studied are not all that different from men's religions. Religions, whether dominated by men or women, will "worship supernatural beings, perform rituals of thanks and appeasement, utilize techniques that induce altered states of consciousness, and provide devotees with persuasive explanations for the ultimate conditions of existence."[21]

Three Characteristics of Women's Religions

1. Focus on women's issues surrounding the role of being mothers
2. Explicit attention to the issue of patriarchy
3. In form and content similar to male-dominated religions

REVIEW QUESTIONS

1. Compare the ways in which Tibetan Buddhism, Peoples Temple, and any religious group you know about engage in socialization. Be as precise as you can.
2. Give your own example of two of the five dilemmas of institutionalization.
3. If you belong to a religious group, what type of authority does the leader of that group have? Support your answer with evidence. If you do not belong to a religious group, what type of authority would be most appealing to you and why?
4. Does the fact that scriptures are the creation of communities of faith undermine their authority? Why or why not?
5. Do you agree that many of the world religions are sexist? Why or why not?

RESEARCH CASE—SHINTO

[At one time] the Sun Goddess [shocked by the misdeeds of her brother, Valiant Male Kami], opened the heavenly rock-cave door and concealed herself inside. Then the Plain of High Heaven became completely dark, and all manner of calamities arose.

Then the 800 myriads of kami gathered in a divine assembly, and summoned Kami of the Little Roof in Heaven and Kami of the Grand Bead to perform a divination. They hung long strings of myriad curved beads on the upper branches of a sacred tree, and hung a large-dimensioned mirror on its middle branches . . . Kami of Heavenly Strength . . . stamped on an overturned bucket which was placed before the rock-cave. Then she became kami-possessed, exposed her breasts and genitals. Thereupon the 800 myriads of kami laughed so hard that the Plain of High Heaven shook with their laughter.

The Sun Goddess, intrigued by all this, opened the rock-cave door slightly . . . Then Kami of Heavenly Headgear said, "There is a kami nobler than you, and that is why we are happy and dancing." While she was speaking thus, Kami of the Little Roof and Kami of the Grand Bead showed the mirror to the Sun Goddess. Thereupon, the Sun Goddess, thinking this ever so strange, gradually came out of the cave, and hidden Kami of Grand Bead took her hand and pulled her out. Then as the sun Goddess reappeared, the Plain of High Heaven was naturally illuminated.[22]

This ancient myth of Japan is from the *Kojiki*, which was first put together in 712. The *Kojiki*, along with the *Nihongi* (720), constitute two of the most highly revered books of Shinto. I say "highly revered" because Shinto has no official scripture. The major theme of the *Kojiki* is the origin of kingship. Book One contains a creation myth. According to this account, Japan originates through the activity of two married kami, Izanagi and Izanami, who are descendents of the first five heavenly kami. Izanagi and Izanami also create many other kami. The Kami of Fire kills Izanami, and her husband descends to the underworld to find her. When Izanagi returns to earth, he needs to be purified, and the result is the birth of Amaterasu, the Sun Goddess mentioned in the story. She is the ancestor of the imperial family of Japan, and Book Two recounts the story of how her great-grandson becomes the first emperor of Japan. In this way the imperial line is placed in a context that goes all the way back to the sacred beginning of Japan.

Literature on Japanese religion usually describes Shinto ("shin-toh") as the native religion of Japan. It has no founder and arose spontaneously out of people's response to the forces of nature that were called kami ("kah-mee"). This description is partly true, but in fact there is no name for the ancient religion of Japan because it was so intermixed with the culture that no name was needed. Without a name, it was not even singled out as a religion. It was part of everyday life. The name *Shinto*, which means the "way of the kami," came about when Buddhist missionaries from China brought the "way of the Buddha" to Japan. Only when this happened did the need for a name for the indigenous "religion" of Japan arise.

The word *kami* is often translated into English as "god." This too is misleading. Kami are sacred and hence possess extraordinary powers that pervade everything in heaven, earth, and the underworld. They are associated with the sun, thunder, rain, wind, animals, ancestors, and great people such as the emperors. In ancient Japan the word *kami* is used as an adjective, not a noun, to designate anything mysterious, superhuman, or sacred. In other words, kami are any power deemed worthy of worship and to whom prayers and offerings can be made because they have some sort of power over human affairs.

Scholars today distinguish many different kinds of Shinto, including Folk or Popular Shinto, Domestic or Home Shinto, Sect Shinto, State Shinto, Imperial Household Shinto, and Shrine Shinto. Shinto exhibits great variety, and the use of one word to refer to this variety should not fool us into thinking that there is only one kind of Shinto.

Popular Shinto refers to the kind of Shinto practiced in the everyday life of the Japanese people, and *Domestic Shinto* refers to the practices that center on the home altar. *Sect Shinto* is the name for a number of different splinter groups that became independent religious organizations. In pre–World War II Japan, there were thirteen official sects.

State Shinto was banned in 1945 by the new constitution that Japan had to accept as part of the conditions of surrender to the American occupying forces. It was mandated because many believed that State Shinto promoted the worship of the Japanese nation and the emperor, which in turn supported the military regime that led Japan into World War II. *Imperial Household Shinto* refers to rites conducted at the three shrines within the palace grounds. These shrines are for the exclusive use of the imperial family. *Shrine Shinto* is the most prevalent type of kami-based faith and, as the name implies, indicates the ritual practices conducted at the many Shinto shrines throughout the country.

Seasonal festivals are celebrated at local shrines, and they typically have something to do with agriculture, the primary financial base of the countryside (although this is changing as Japan becomes ever more urban). Also, priests conduct worship services at the local shrines, which typically consist of purification rites, an offering to the kami, prayer, and a symbolic feast. Usually, purification of pollution and evil is accomplished by individual worshipers symbolically rinsing the mouth and pouring clear water over the fingertips. The minimum requirement for worshiping the kami is periodic presentation of offerings. Many believe that the kami and particularly the ancestral spirits will be unhappy and bring misfortune if a devotee fails to observe this duty. As a rule the formal prayers recited by the priest open with words of praise for the kami and include petitions for favors, thanksgiving, a recitation of gifts offered, and the status and name of the priest. They usually close with words of awe and respect. At the end of a worship service, ceremony (like a wedding), or festival there is a sacred feast (often symbolic) called the *naorai,* which means "to eat together with the kami."

Our discussion will concentrate mostly on State and Shrine Shinto. However, we do need some general knowledge of the historical development of Shinto. No religious faith stands still. It is dynamic and changing, filled with new developments, interpretations, literature, rites, and much more.

During the early period, reverence for the forces of nature and shamanistic practices were widespread. Nature kami, both male and female, abounded.

There were no shrine or temple structures, but different areas in nature were sites of religious practice. Many of the shamans were female, and they often interpreted the will of the kami for the people. Today, girls serve as ceremonial assistants to male priests.

Two centuries before the Heian period (794–1185), Chinese culture and religious practices entered Japan. During this period Confucian family values, Daoist views on living in harmony with nature, and Buddhist beliefs and practices became mixed with Shinto so closely that it became almost impossible to separate them.

The Kamakura period (1185–1333) saw struggles for political power emerge among the *shoguns* (regional rulers) as the power of the royal court weakened. Political instability and the struggles of this feudal age made eschatological forms of Buddhism attractive. People came to believe that they were living in the end times and the world would soon end with a great catastrophe.

The Tokugawa period 1600–1868 saw the emergence of a strong central government emphasizing the need for peace, law, and order. During this period several different religious trends developed. The ritual practice of the imperial court, which maintained a formal schedule of complex rituals honoring both the buddhas and the kami, became increasingly important. Both Shinto and Buddhist priests serviced many of the shrines, and hence the shrines became both Shinto and Buddhist places of worship.

During the Meiji period Japan developed into a modern nation-state. A constitutional government was created with the emperor as its head. It provided for a legislature and the separation of religion and the state. A new capital was founded in Tokyo, and a formal tax system was established. This period is usually called the Meiji Restoration because the leadership of Japan wanted to restore both imperial rule and a purified Shinto. Tax money was used to support Shinto shrines, and Shinto became the official "religion" of the Japanese nation. There was an intensified campaign against Buddhism, and the government decreed that Buddhist statues and priests had to be removed from Shinto shrines.

However, Buddhism was so entrenched in Japanese culture that this purification effort failed to be totally effective. Between 1872 and 1875 the government had a Department of Religion that included both Buddhism and Shinto. In 1882 the government formally recognized State Shinto, and to get around the part of the constitution that recognized the separation of religion and the state, the government proclaimed that legally State Shinto was not a religion. Shinto was now described as the embodiment of the values and traditional institutions of the Japanese people. In creating State Shinto and proclaiming that it was not a religion, the government had to create Sect Shinto as a religion. The government did this by setting the official number of sects at thirteen. These sects were not supported with tax money. Thus the illusion was created that religion and the state were officially separate.

In one sense this was not an illusion. The government-supported State Shinto bore little resemblance to traditional Shinto. Because of the word *restoration*, many people both inside and outside Japan have been convinced that the official Shinto of the Meiji period was simply a continuation of past practices and beliefs. This is not so. State Shinto supported patriotism to the nation as represented by the emperor, who was proclaimed chief priest. During most of the previous history of Shinto, Japan was not a nation-state. It had no central national government, and various clans governed the provinces. The allegiance of the people was more to their clans and local villages than to a centralized government.

Shrine Shinto was completely transformed by these new developments. The state underwrote the construction of new shrines, promoted the cult of the kami of the Ise shrine as the highest ancestors, and created a cult of the war dead associated with the ritual activities of various shrines. The effect on popular Shinto by this massive state intervention was immense. It produced a unified institutional and symbolic system where there had been only localized and diverse cultic life at largely independent shrines.

Helen Hardacre, author of one of the best books on State Shinto, argues:

> The creation of even the semblance of a comprehensive, national organization for Shinto dates to 1900. Before that the worship of its deities, the kami, was carried out on a localized basis, and its priests were organized not in a national priesthood . . . but in independent sacerdotal lineages managed by a small number of large shrines . . . or by purely local arrangement and on a rotating basis among male members of the community. Thus in an institutional sense, Shinto has no legitimate claim to antiquity as Japan's "indigenous religion," however frequently the claim is made.[23]

Some people are under the impression that Shinto was a key player in the growing militaristic state, and that it bears major responsibility for promoting the nationalistic and patriotic values and attitudes that eventually led to the Second World War. This is not the case. The military power that came to control the government used Shinto to promote its imperialistic ambitions. However, it must be noted that practically all of the religious traditions in Japan supported the war effort. The Shinto priests of the various local shrines offered no objections. Sect Shinto offered no objections, nor did the various Buddhist sects.

Hardacre remarks

> the creation of a cult of the war dead . . . tapped Japan's oldest and most affectively laden area of religious life, the cult of the dead and the ancestors. The people sought religious explanations for the multitudinous deaths in war of Japanese youth. Officiating at public memorial rites, Shinto priests . . . inevitably affirmed and glorified Japan's wars. Thus it was not that Shinto itself became an

"engine of war,". . . but that it idealized as the highest good a role as the state's obedient servant. And its greatest service to the state has concerned memorialization of the war dead.[24]

After Japan surrendered to the Allies in 1945, American soldiers occupied Japan. A military government was set up, but one of its purposes was to create a new democratic constitution and return home rule as soon as possible. The separation of church and state was an important part of this new constitution. However, the provisional, occupying government of Japan understood religion to be something like a church, and so, in adopting the idea of the separation of church and state, they were not sufficiently sensitive to the Japanese religious scene. The Japanese interpreted the idea of separation to mean the cessation of using public money to support the various Shinto shrines and sects (an interpretation approved by the occupying forces), but what should be done when other circumstances arose?

On January 7, 1989, Emperor Hirohito died. Normally, Crown Prince Akihito would be enthroned the next day. But this ceremony was delayed until 1990 while debates raged about how Article 89 of the Japanese constitution should be interpreted. That article explicitly states that "no public money or other property shall be expended. . . for benefit or maintenance of any religious institution or association." Article 89 would appear to prohibit funding for the traditional Shinto enthronement ceremony. There was no purely secular ceremony to mark royal succession. A solution was reached when the government cleverly divided the occasion into a religious part that was paid for out of the royal family funds and a public secular ceremony funded out of the public purse. So the public enthronement ceremony got state support, but the "Daijosai" rite did not. The Daijosai is the occasion when the new emperor assumes spiritual power by spending part of the night in a Shinto shrine. Though the Daijosai was funded out of the imperial court budget, we might wonder whether these careful distinctions between secular and sacred made any real difference since the court budget comes from public funds.

In postwar Japan the political culture has become more pluralistic, and there have been a number of protests against the state's past and present attempts to control Shinto and manipulate religion in support of the interests of the state. The Union of New Religions has been one voice in opposing any state support of Shinto. Shrine Shinto has had to make it on its own without state support, and the lack of state support has not destroyed it, as many predicted. In 1946 the Association of Shinto Shrines was founded. It invited all the local shrines to affiliate, and most of them did. The association is administered by a board of councilors, composed of representatives from forty-six regional associations. The association has six departments, which provide a number of services to member shrines including mutual aid, teaching, and research. This association is closely connected with Kokugakuin University, which is the only Shinto institution of higher education in Japan. In sociological terms, Shrine Shinto reinvented itself as a denomination.

On the local level, priests and committees made up of representatives of the worshipers manage the shrines. Usually they are incorporated, own their own land and buildings, and raise their own funds. Also, many new religions have developed in postwar Japan that mix elements from various sources and help fill the shelves of the new religious marketplace that has taken root after state support ceased. Religiously Japan is now a free market.

QUESTIONS ON THE CASE OF SHINTO

1. Write a three-paragraph interpretation of the meaning of the myth of the Sun Goddess that opened the case. Compare your interpretation with another student's and discuss the differences.
2. Given the fact that goddesses have been and are worshiped in Shinto, that in the early period many shamans were females, and that in recent times the priesthood has been reserved for males, would you say Shinto is sexist or not? What further information would you need to settle the issue?
3. In what ways do you think Shinto functions to provide meaning and purpose to the lives of the Japanese? In your answer, be sure to note the different kinds of Shinto and how they might function to provide meaning and purpose.
4. Do you think the Allies were right to insist that State Shinto be abandoned? In general, do you think conquerors have the right to change the religion of the countries they conquer? Why or why not?

Fieldwork Option: Formulate a hypothesis about why so many religions appear to discriminate against women; then devise a questionnaire to test your hypothesis and administer it to at least six people. Summarize and analyze the results and, if possible, present them to the class for a general discussion.

SUGGESTIONS FOR FURTHER READING

In addition to the material found in the notes, readers may wish to consult the following for more information.

Bellah, Robert. *Tokugawa Religion: The Values of Pre-Industrial Japan.* Glencoe, IL: Free Press, 1957. A classic sociological study of Tokugawa Shinto.

Boyarin, Daniel. "Gender." In *Critical Terms for Religious Studies,* edited by Mark C. Tylor, 117–135. Chicago: University of Chicago Press, 1998. Boyarin presents a study of the concept of gender in relationship to religion that summarizes and integrates a number of different theories.

Carmody, Denise. *Women and World Religions.* Nashville: Abingdon, 1979. Carmody synthesizes a lot of information from around the world into a readable book. The student is also directed to an ongoing series edited by Arvind Sharma and

Katherine K. Young, called *The Annual Review of Women in World Religions*, published by the State University Press of New York.

Chidester, David. *Salvation and Suicide: An Interpretation of Jim Jones, the Peoples Temple, and Jonestown*. Bloomington: Indiana University Press, 1991. This well-written and detailed account is sympathetic (some would say too sympathetic).

Coward, Harold, ed. *Experiencing Scripture in World Religions*. Maryknoll, NY: Orbis Books, 2000. This helpful collection of essays focuses on the role of scripture in Judaism, Christianity, Islam, Hinduism, Sikhism, and Buddhism.

Goldstein, Melvyn C., and Matthew T. Kapstein, eds. *Buddhism in Contemporary Tibet: Religious Revival and Cultural Identity*. Berkeley: University of California Press, 1998. This collection of essays provides a wealth of information on what is going on today with respect to religion in Tibet.

Hamilton, Malcolm. *Sociology and the World's Religions*. New York: St. Martin's Press, 1998. This book brings together and summarizes a vast range of sociological research on both tribal and world religions.

Kessler, Gary E. *Shinto Ways of Being Religious*. New York: McGraw-Hill, 2005. An introductory collection of primary sources with explanatory commentary surveying the historical development of Shinto.

Nelson, John K. *A Year in the Life of a Shinto Shrine*. Seattle: University of Washington Press, 1996. This study provides detailed information on what goes on in a Shinto Shrine during a one-year cycle.

Powers, John. *Introduction to Tibetan Buddhism*. Ithaca, NY: Snow Lion Publications, 1995. Powers discusses the Indian background, Tibetan history and culture, doctrines and practices, and the various schools of Tibetan Buddhism in a clear and sympathetic way.

INTERNET RESOURCES

www-rohan.sdsu.edu/~remoore/jonestown   This site about Jonestown is sponsored by the Department of Religious Studies at San Diego State University. It provides pictures, articles, archival material, three different versions of the so-called death tape, and much more. You will also find a link to the New Religious Movements Web site at the University of Virginia.

www.bbc.co.uk/religion/religions/shinto   This BBC site provides basic information about Shinto, including its history, beliefs, and festivals.

www.tibet.com   This is the official home page of the Tibetan government in exile with links to a variety of resources.

CHAPTER 12

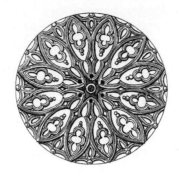

Human Existence
and Destiny

THE AMERICAN psychologist and philosopher William James (1842–1910), in his book *The Varieties of Religious Experience*, claimed that there was no unique or special religious feeling. However, he did think there were common features of what he called the "intellectual content" of religious experiences:

> there is a certain uniform deliverance in which religions all appear to meet. It consists of two parts:
>
> 1. An uneasiness; and
> 2. Its solution.
>
> 1. The uneasiness, reduced to its simple terms, is a sense that there is *something wrong about us* as we naturally stand.
> 2. The solution is a sense that *we are saved from the wrongness* by making proper connection with the higher powers.[1]

Although James seems to think these two parts characterize all religions, they do not. They do, however, characterize **religions of salvation**, which teach that things are not as they should be and need to be transcended or changed. We can contrast salvation religions with **religions of sanctification**, which teach that things are as they should be, and the religious task is to maintain this situation. Christianity is a clear example of a religion of salvation, and the religion of the Australian Aborigines is a good example of the sanctification type.

This distinction between religions of salvation and religions of sanctification is not absolute. These are ideal types, because in the muddy waters of the real world, religions often combine elements of both salvation and sanctification. Many religions offer descriptions of what is wrong and how it can be put right as well as descriptions of what is right and how it can be maintained. In this chapter, however, our main concern will be with religions of salvation.

It is not surprising that many religions find things wrong with the way things are. In a previous chapter, Elie Wiesel and others vividly reminded us of some of the things that are wrong. Our own experiences of life and the societies in which we live often convince us that things are not right. The fact that we are all headed toward death is enough to make many of us dissatisfied and uneasy with the human condition. If we add this uneasiness about death to experiences of physical and mental illness, moral failure, anxiety, frustration, loss, and alienation, we can easily understand the human desire for salvation—for healing, for making whole, for restoring health, for overcoming death, for, in short, making things right.

The very structure of human consciousness invites dissatisfaction. We are self-conscious creatures. We are aware, and we are aware that we are aware. Lurking behind our experiences of the world, there is always an I—the ego, or self—that remains, or at least appears to remain, the subject of our experiences. Consider the simple experience of seeing this book and then becoming aware that you are seeing this book. Even when we make that subject who is aware of this book an object of our thoughts, a "new" I, or subject, pops up. We might now say, "I am aware that I am aware of seeing this book." If there were enough time, this process might go on forever. I am aware that I am aware that I am aware that I am aware that I am seeing this book. That last sentence is potentially endless.

Why should this invite dissatisfaction? It invites dissatisfaction because it separates us from the things we wish to know. Objects, such as books, are "out there," and we are "in here." What we can know about the "out there" is limited by our consciousness. A division between subject and object plagues us. We can never know the book as it is in itself. We can only know it as it appears to us.

The division between subject and object also pertains to our selves. Division, and hence alienation, is built into the structure of consciousness because we can never turn around fast enough to catch our selves being ourselves. We forever elude ourselves. We cannot gaze on ourselves in leisure. At best, we can catch a glimpse of our selves receding to become a subject of yet another level of awareness. So there is alienation from the living and nonliving things that we believe exist outside of us, and there is an internal alienation buried deep within the very structure of self-consciousness.

According to some religious, psychological, and philosophical perspectives, this inner and outer alienation breeds anxiety and uneasiness—a sense that there is something wrong about our lives. If we assume that humans seek to know themselves, others, and the world in the most intimate way possible, then the subject/object division that is created by self-consciousness can only frustrate that goal. Separation from loved ones leaves us feeling uneasy. Separation from our selves and the world in which we live makes us feel still more uneasy. Some psychologists hold that this is the basis of "free-floating anxiety"—as James would have it, a general sense that there is something wrong.

Self-consciousness also opens up the possibility of transcendence and enjoyment. We come to realize, the more we explore self-consciousness, that we can go beyond our immediate selves. We can take trips into fantasylands, imagine ourselves as different people, think about the past, and contemplate the future. Our contemplation of the future, however, soon brings before us death, the potential loss of self-consciousness. We might, when deeply depressed and alienated, contemplate the loss of self-consciousness as a release from all our cares and anxieties. We find refreshing our momentary loss of self-consciousness in sleep. Then we wake up, and the preciousness of awareness contributes to our fear of a permanent sleep from which we never wake. We can and do both welcome death and fear its arrival because while it provides what may be the ultimate transcendence of self-consciousness, it also threatens the existence of all awareness.

In one sense the experience of self-awareness traps us in a subject/object dualism, and in another sense that experience makes it possible to go beyond our present conscious situations. Perhaps our hopes for something better (for a "solution") can be found in this ability to go beyond. But what is it to "go beyond"? Does transcendence mean a new, purified, and immortal self-consciousness free from alienation; does it mean an end to all consciousness in an eternal nothingness; or does it mean a merging into a greater divine whole? Perhaps it means waking up to a new way of seeing things, a way that sees things as appropriate and right just the way they are.

We will begin with two case studies. One case focuses on Sikhism ("sek'iz-uhm"), a religion that started in India and has now spread throughout the world. The other case focuses on Christianity, a religion that has developed a number of different varieties in its nearly two thousand—year history.

These case studies will provide us with an opportunity to analyze more carefully what religions claim is wrong with human existence, the ways they recommend to overcome this wrongness, and their different views of human destiny. A medical analogy may help. Just as a doctor diagnoses a disease and offers a cure, many religions offer a diagnosis of the human condition and offer a cure. The Four Noble Truths of Buddhism, discussed in Chapter 7, provide a good example of this sort of structure. We will close with a research case highlighting a particularly influential form of Japanese Buddhism, called Zen (meditation) Buddhism.

12.1 TWO CASE STUDIES

Sikhism

Have you ever seen men and perhaps some women wearing turbans and dressed in white? If so, you may have seen some members of a religion called Sikhism. There are some 23 million Sikhs spread throughout the world, many of them living in the United States and Canada.

Sikhism originated in the Punjab region of northwest India. The word *sikh* is derived from a verb meaning "to learn." The first Sikhs were the disciples (learners) of Guru (teacher) Nanak (1469–1539). Eventually these learners of Guru Nanak evolved into members of a distinct religion with its own scriptures, beliefs, and practices.

Nanak was born about forty miles from Lahore, which is located in present-day Pakistan. He was strongly influenced by the bhakti (devotional) tradition as it was found among both Hindus and Muslims, and he traveled about singing hymns in praise of the one God. At twenty-nine, Nanak had a mystical experience in which God told him, "I am with thee. Through thee my name will be magnified." Nanak interpreted this experience as an instruction from God to go into the world to pray and to teach others how to pray. He opened his mission with the pronouncement, "There is no Hindu, there is no Muslim."

The history of Sikhism is complex, and as with all religions, changes were introduced as it evolved. Ram Das (1534–1581), the fourth guru, made the office of guru, or teacher, hereditary and founded the city of Amritsar, now regarded as the sacred center of the faith. The fifth guru, Arjun (1563–1606), compiled the writings and hymns of the first four gurus into a scripture called *Adi Granth*. The sixth guru, Hargobind (1595–1644), created a small army of Sikhs who were sworn to fight for justice and religious liberty. Guru Gobind Singh (1666–1708), the tenth guru, introduced an initiation rite involving nectar (*amrit*) stirred with a double-edged sword and the wearing of five symbols. They are uncut hair, a comb, a sword, a steel bracelet, and short trousers. This rite initiates Sikhs into a core community called the Khalsa. Male members replace their caste names with Singh (lion), and women abandon their caste names for Kaur (princess). One aspect of the symbolism of the dress and the name change is to eliminate class identity by raising everyone to the status of a warrior, the class of Guru Nanak.

The four sons of Guru Gobind Singh were killed in battles with the Moghuls. It is said that he took this as a sign that with him the line of individual gurus had come to an end, and he passed on the guruship to the whole community and to the writings of the *Adi Granth*, which now became known as the *Guru Granth Sahib*.

The Sikhs teach that Akal Purakh (their name for God, meaning "the being that is beyond the limitations of time") is beyond the categories of male and female, although they often use male pronouns when speaking of God. In essence God is not only beyond all gender distinctions, but also beyond all characteristics and hence beyond human understanding. However, God does manifest himself/herself as a personal being who transcends his/her creation and is present in it (immanent). God is the divine Guru, the inner teacher who saves people by grace. The Mool Mantra (basic sacred chant) that prefaces every Sikh prayer goes like this:

> There is One God
> His Name is Truth.
> He is the Creator,
> He is without fear and without hate.
> He is beyond time Immortal.
> His Spirit pervades the universe.
> He is not born,
> Nor does He die to be born again.
> He is self-existent.
> By the guru's grace shalt thou worship Him.[2]

Sikhs affirm the doctrines of rebirth and karma. There is, they teach, an eternal soul (*jiva*) that can inhabit many different kinds of bodies. Its rebirth is decided by its actions. The soul reaps in its next birth what it sowed in its previous births. The bodies the *jiva* can inhabit range from inanimate rocks to human bodies. Guru Arjun in the *Guru Granth Sahib* states:

> In so many incarnations, you were a worm and an insect; in so
> many incarnations, you were an elephant, a fish, and a deer.
> In so many incarnations, you were a bird and a snake. In so
> many incarnations, you were yoked as a ox and a horse.
>
> Meet the Lord of the Universe—now is the time to meet him.
> After so very long, this human body was fashioned for you.[3]

People wander through rounds of rebirths for a variety of reasons, but the fundamental reason is selfishness born from being separated from God, the source and creator. Humans are self-centered rather than God-centered. People are obsessed with themselves and thus remain largely unaware of the Truth. Preserving the self at all costs becomes their struggle, and so they become aggressive, proud, and a slave to their desires and impulses. This leads to lust, anger, envy, and attachments to worldly things. In short, *jivas*, or souls, belong to God and with God, but now live alienated or separated from him because of self-centeredness.

Selfishness and all its spin-off vices can be overcome only by "walking according to *hukam*, the will of God, as preordained." *Hukam* is a complex concept with different but related senses. It means God's order, his commandments, and the rules according to which the created universe runs. It is an expression of God's will, which ultimately underlies all that happens—life and death, joys and sorrows, reincarnations, and our final release or liberation. God is responsible for everything, and the *jiva* must overcome its self-centeredness by learning to submit to *hukam* without complaint. Living in a human body is itself a gift of God because it is only while in this body that people have a chance for release.

How do humans learn to move from self-centeredness to God-centeredness? While human effort is partially involved, it is primarily by God's grace. A living spiritual teacher or guru can facilitate this grace, or free gift.

The doctrine of guruship is one of the most distinctive aspects of the Sikh tradition. In ancient Hinduism, gurus, or spiritual teachers, were taught knowledge of the sacred Vedas. Many gurus were from the priestly class. Spiritual power was thus concentrated in the highest Hindu class. However, a parallel tradition in India maintained that the authority of the guru did not lie in class or in knowledge of the Vedas but in personal enlightenment. This "guruship of enlightenment" was combined with a sense of mission, a mission to teach any sincere seeker regardless of gender, rank, class, or caste. Guru Nanak was a teacher in this egalitarian tradition, and he added to it the notion that God is the ultimate Guru or Primal Guru (often called the "Sat Guru," or true teacher).

The ten human gurus of the Sikh tradition all emphasized that only God was the Guru, and they were but faithful messengers through whom the divine Word (*shabad*) was revealed. They believed that this Word appeared as a sound that became articulate in the words they spoke, chanted, and sang. The hymns not only speak about God, they embody divine sounds, which have the power to enlighten and transform.

Once grace awakens and enlightens the soul, making an effort to serve humanity and to live according to God's truth is imperative. This means living a life in service to others and in devotion to God. Devotion to God is manifested both inwardly by praying and meditating on the Name (*Nam*) of God and outwardly in acts of communal worship and charity. Sikhs believe that meditation, communal worship, and concentration on the divine *Nam* are sufficient for attaining the "realm of Truth." Ascetic practices and elaborate rituals led by priests are not necessary. The poet Bhai Burdas sums up the Sikh ideal practice:

> At dawn a Sikh wakes up and practices meditation, charity and purity.
> A Sikh is soft-spoken, humble, benevolent, and grateful to anyone
> who asks for help.
> A Sikh sleeps little, eats little, and speaks little, and adopts
> the Guru's teachings.
> A Sikh makes a living through honest work, and gives in charity; though
> respected a Sikh should remain humble.

Joining the congregation morning and evening to participate in singing hymns, the mind should be linked to the gurbani [divine sound] and the Sikh should feel grateful to the Guru.

A Sikh's spontaneous devotion should be self-less for it is inspired by the sheer love of the Guru.[4]

The goal of this kind of life is God-realization, which is often characterized as union with God. This union is sought and hopefully can be achieved in an individual's present life, not in some afterlife. Those who achieve this union or oneness with God still must work out their past karma in this life. So they go on living in a body. However, they will accumulate no additional karma, and thus, after death, their souls will live in the divine presence and they will never again be reborn.

There are many references to heaven and hell in Sikh literature, but these seem to be states, rather than places. More importantly they are part of the ongoing process of reincarnation. If we die with good karma, we merit a certain kind of heaven, and if we die with bad karma, we merit a certain kind of hell. But these states are temporary, not eternal. Only union with God will bring eternal and final bliss. However, the Sikhs' mystical devotionalism is not world rejecting, but world affirming. They do not separate themselves from society, work, and affairs of the world. They do not become monks or nuns, but marry, raise children, and engage in honest work and public affairs.

Christianity

The designation "Christian" was first used, as far as we know, in Antioch around 135. It was used to name an emerging religious movement made up of Jews and Gentiles who worshiped a "Christos," named Jesus of Nazareth, who was executed by the Romans as a political criminal in Judea in the first part of the first century of the common era (C.E.).

"Christos" is the Greek translation of the Hebrew title Messiah, which refers to someone anointed by God for a special mission. The kings of ancient Israel were often given this title, and even the Persian King Cyrus, who liberated some of the Jews from exile in Babylon, was called Messiah or Christ. By the first century C.E. some Jews believed that a new messiah would arise to deliver the Jews from the hands of the Romans. The debate about the new messiah spawned various Jewish sects. The first disciples (learners) of the Jewish teacher (rabbi) named Jesus formed one of these Jewish sectarian movements.

When Jesus died and the hoped-for deliverance from Roman rule did not materialize, his first followers were devastated, and some thought that they may have been mistaken about who Jesus was. However, a story soon circulated that Jesus was not dead, but had risen from the dead. Various followers swore they had witnessed this miracle, and some even claimed to have seen the resurrected Jesus rise into heaven after appearing to various followers.

This story explained why the end of the present age and the delivery from Roman rule did not occur before Jesus died or with his death. The time was not right. When it was, Jesus would return in a "Second Coming" with a divine army of angels and defeat not just the Romans, but all the "demons" like them that ruled this sinful world.

This story, or the "Good News" (gospel), about the life, teachings, death, and resurrection of Jesus had appeal beyond the Jewish community. Eventually more Gentile learners joined this Christian movement, as the Romans called it. The Roman name stuck, and the Christian movement eventually became a new religion distinct from its parent religion, Judaism. However, its Jewish roots remained deep—so deep that Christians claimed to be the true fulfillment of Jewish law and prophecy. They even took over from Judaism the designation of the "Chosen People of God."

Crucial to this process was the creation of a scripture, or canon, of official documents. Different groups preferred different writings. Eventually, however, the majority settled on a Greek translation (called the Septuagint) of the Jewish scriptures, which they now called the Old Testament, and a collection of writings called the New Testament.

The Old and New Testaments (usually called the Bible) became the scriptural foundation of Christian teachings and eventually assumed the status of divine revelation among the growing congregations. The Bible was designated the word of God because it bore witness to the divine creative Word (Logos), which, according to the Gospel of John, became incarnated in Jesus the Christ (Messiah).

The story of how Christianity spread from Judea to Syria, then into all parts of the Roman empire and beyond, eventually to become the largest religion in the world, is too complex to recount here. But today, as in the beginning, there is no single entity or group to which the term "Christian" refers. Instead, there are *Christianities* with widely variant organizational and ritual structures, not to mention beliefs and histories. Christianity has proved to be a creative religion, developing new and different forms as it moves through history and cultures. Even though at times it appears rather rigid and unwilling to change, Christianity has proved amazingly flexible.

According to Christianity, what is wrong with human existence as presently lived is that it is lived in sin. Generally, sin is any thought or action that has a negative impact on the spiritual health of persons, or on their ethical interactions with other persons and the environment. In the New Testament, the Greek word translated as sin is *hamartia*, which means wandering from the path or missing the mark. It was commonly used for an arrow that has gone astray and missed its target.

Hamartia is described in many different ways. Christians often think of it as idolatry. Idolatry is more than the worship of gods other than the one preferred by Christians. It is trusting in something that is less than ultimate. The idolater's loyalty and devotion is completely given to people, things, institutions, or ideologies that are not ultimate (and hence not divine), but are passing fancies of the human imagination.

Christians also describe sin as rebellion against God's will. This view is inspired by the story of the disobedience of Adam and Eve in the Garden of Eden, a disobedience that constitutes the original, or archetypal, sin. Sin is transgression, the failure to follow God's will in thought, word, and deed. This failure to obey God is rooted in selfishness and the elevation of one's own will over the divine will.

Sin is also linked to temptation. In Genesis, the temptation of Adam and Eve by a snake (much later identified as Satan or the Devil) comes from outside human nature. Evil is there, in the environment, waiting to lure people into selfish and disobedient acts. However, temptation also arises within humans themselves. Humans are created, according to Genesis, out of "the dust of the ground." Hence, the "temptations of the flesh" are an ever present cause for concern. Yet, according to the Bible, humans are also created in the image of God.

Christians have disagreed over exactly what this image is, but there seems to be general agreement that humans have a dual origin. They are creatures of God, like all other aspects of creation, but they are closer to God than all other creatures. Under the influence of Greek philosophy, some Christians have talked about this dual origin in terms of body and soul, the material and spiritual components of human nature.

Some Christian theologians also describe sin as alienation or separation from God, symbolized by the expulsion of Adam and Eve from Eden. Some forms of early Christianity adopted the widespread religious symbols of light and dark to paint a picture of sparks of the divine light (souls) separated from God by the material darkness (body) of the world. Theories of sin as bondage or enslavement to both matter and Satan also emerged from this metaphor of separation.

Closely associated with the interpretation of sin as separation is the view that the original sin of Adam and Eve was a "fall" from divine intimacy and grace in which the "image of God" was damaged. Christians debate precisely how much damage resulted from this first sin of Adam and Eve. Roman Catholic theologians generally argue that the divine image was not lost by the "fall into sin," but it was flawed and damaged in significant ways. Protestant theologians usually argue that original sin affected human nature more severely than Roman Catholics think.

Roman Catholic moral theology distinguishes between different kinds of sin, for example, venial sins and mortal, or deadly, sins. Venial sins are less serious than mortal sins and do not result in eternal unhappiness. Mortal sins turn the soul from God and deprive it of God's forgiving grace and eternal happiness. Thomas Aquinas argued that a sin must cause grave injury to the self, or to the community, or to God and his purposes for creation to qualify as mortal. Such sin must also, according to Aquinas, come from a moral agent who is aware of the wrongness of the sin, but does it anyway.

rule. Dividing the whole of humanity into two categories, the saved and the damned, has inspired rejoicing on the part of some and anxiety among those who think they are damned.

In one way or another, for good or bad, these stories in both their sacred and secular versions form the passion play in which billions of people have lived and died. Christian stories of sin, atonement, and salvation, along with similar stories told by many other religions, provide meaning and hope to humans who often despair of finding any great truths by which to live and, unfortunately, sometimes provide justifications for perpetuating unjust power.

Christian Atonement Theories

1. Ransom
2. Satisfaction
3. Moral example

12.2 COMPARISON

Both Sikhism and Christianity describe the human condition in remarkably similar terms. Both agree that the root of our troubles resides in our separation from God. This separation results in selfishness, which in turn leads to all the other sins that keep God and humans apart. However, beyond the obvious similarities, there are important differences.

So far I have been doing the comparisons of the opening cases for you. You have advanced enough in thinking about religion to try your own hand at comparing these opening cases. I will help by providing categories that you can use and offering some suggestions.

A. Fall and Reincarnation   There is no doctrine of the fall in Sikhism, and there is no doctrine of reincarnation in Christianity (although some Christian theologians have suggested this idea from time to time). How is this fact significant for understanding the differences relating to salvation found among Sikhs and Christians?

B. Devil   Do you find it significant that there are no teachings about a devil or Satan in Sikhism? Why?

C. Grace   While both Sikhs and Christians acknowledge that humans cannot save themselves and thereby affirm the necessity of grace, they disagree about how God's grace is delivered. Describe how they differ on this issue.

D. Devotion   Both Christianity and Sikhism think of the way, or road, to salvation primarily in terms of a life of devotion. For both, devotion involves similar activities of worship, hymn singing, praying, meditating, and the like. However, Sikhism has no priesthood and no sacraments in the sense of visible vehicles of grace, such as baptism and a sacred meal. Do you find this fact an indication of a significant difference? Why or why not?

E. Scripture   What role does scripture play in both the Sikh and Christian traditions with respect to the issue of salvation?

F. Gifts   In both traditions the ancient notion of exchanging gifts is represented, although in different ways. In Christianity what does God give? In Sikhism what does God give? Be specific. What do the devotees in both traditions give in return?

G. Heaven and Hell   While both Christians and Sikhs hope for union with God and see this as the final human destiny, their views of heaven and hell differ radically. How do they differ?

It may have occurred to you as you were making these comparisons that from a psychological and sociological viewpoint we might describe both the Sikh and Christian views of human existence and destiny in terms of elaborate schemes of social control. These schemes are designed to reinforce socially acceptable, well-ordered, and conventional moral behavior. Such behavior affects the power structures and distribution of wealth found in the cultures where Christianity and Sikhism had the most success.

Social control, however, is only part of the story. These schemes of control also provide meaning and hope to people. They are not merely the effects of social conditions, but they also create social conditions by their ability to empower and mobilize people in just causes.

12.3 RELIGIONS OF SALVATION AND SOCIETY

The sociologist Max Weber was particularly interested in religions of salvation because of their possible social consequences. The need for salvation arises, Weber thinks, as humans attempt to resolve discrepancies between the actual situation they find themselves in and some imagined ideal situation. Humans wish to live an ideal life, but they find their actual lives less than ideal. What can they do?

Religions of salvation try to resolve this gap between the real and the ideal in many ways. Weber believed that most of these ways would fit into one of two patterns. One strategy is to escape from the awareness of life's imperfections. This Weber called *mysticism*. The other strategy is to gain mastery over the world in order to bring it into conformity with the ideal. This Weber called *asceticism*. Weber is using the words *mysticism* and *asceticism* in a very broad sense to encompass, on the one hand, all religious attempts to escape imperfection and, on the other hand, to designate all religious attempts to transform imperfections into perfections. Because the word *asceticism* is usually used to designate individual practices of self-denial, I will use the term *world-transformation* to designate what Weber calls asceticism.

Although Weber did not relate this insight to the biological phenomenon called "flight or fight," I think we can readily see the parallels. Just as all animals exhibit a flight or fight reaction when faced with situations they consider dangerous, religions of salvation, when faced with the evils of life in this world, either try to escape these evils or fight these evils. Mystical views of salvation represent the flight strategy and world-transforming views represent the fight strategy.

Weber was particularly interested in salvation strategies that try to change the world. If world-transforming strategies did have significant social impact, then Karl Marx's assertion that religious ideologies are largely by-products of economic conditions might well be false or, at least, only half the story. Weber further noted (although critics have questioned whether he was right about this) that the change from medieval feudalism to capitalism accelerated in Europe around the time of the Protestant Reformation in the sixteenth century. According to Weber, capitalism was more likely to gain a firm footing in Protestant countries. This suggested to Weber that Christian Protestantism, or at least some forms of it, may have strongly influenced and reinforced the rise of capitalism.

In a controversial and influential book titled *The Protestant Ethic and the Spirit of Capitalism* (1905), Weber argued that the Protestant movement started by John Calvin did have an important influence on the rise of capitalism. Calvin taught that God created human beings in order that they might glorify him. Everything people do should somehow add and not detract from God's glory. Just as our heavenly life will be one of constantly glorifying God, so too should our earthly life.

Calvin also developed the concept that ordinary work was a divine calling and an appropriate way to glorify God. Prior to Calvin, the Protestant reformer Martin Luther (1483–1546) developed the notion of calling, or vocation, in opposition to Catholic teachings. Luther, a former German monk, accused the Roman Catholic Church of perverting the Christian gospel. One of its many perversions was to draw a sharp distinction between the clergy and the laity in such a way that the life of the clergy, especially the life of monks and nuns, was elevated in spiritual value over the life of the laity, who were largely merchants and peasants. If one truly wished to glorify God, the Roman Church taught, then one should withdraw from the evils and temptations of the world and work for the church full time.

The teaching that religious callings (vocations) have more spiritual value than secular work obviously had its advantages in recruiting the best and the brightest to work for the Roman Church. Luther's assertion that secular work was just as much a calling from God as was religious work unleashed a flood of social energy by destroying one of the keystones of the feudal system and empowering both the merchant and peasant classes with a newfound dignity. Calvin focused that energy by arguing that whatever one's vocation may be, sacred or secular, the work should be well done. Hard, devoted work glorified God, and sloppy, lazy work detracted from God's glory.

In addition to the concept of living for the glory of God and the broadening of the notion of vocation, Calvin added a third idea, the idea of predestination. Christianity had long taught that God chooses in advance those who will be saved. They were called "the elect." Calvin portrayed God as assigning from all eternity, salvation to some (the elect) and, by default, damnation to others.

Calvin's understanding of predestination was motivated in part by his desire to protect the absolute sovereignty of God as well as to reject the whole Roman Catholic apparatus of salvation. No church, no sacraments, no priests would do a person any good when it came to matters of salvation. Nothing will prevail on God to change his mind. God has either elected you or he has not: end of story.

Of course Calvin taught that we should still go to church, worship, listen to sermons, work hard, and lead a moral life because this glorified God, and giving God glory was the sole purpose of living. Combining Calvin's understanding of predestination with the obligation to glorify God resulted in an extreme sort of individualism: You are on your own religiously. No church or pious community can help. Nothing can help you in any way to move from the list of the damned, if you are unfortunate enough to be there, to the list of the elect.

If extreme individualism was one social consequence of this view of salvation, another was anxiety about fate. Granted that this side of death there is no way of knowing for sure whether we are among the elect or not, there might be signs from which we could infer our fate. What might these signs be? This is the question that burned in the back of the good Calvinist's mind.

According to Weber, the signs of election include success in work, accumulation of wealth, and a morally upright life. Surely God could not have abandoned those who work hard, thereby glorifying God by their fine examples? If we do not engage in idle chatter, unproductive recreation, or sleep too much instead of work long and hard and late, surely we must be among the elect?

Calvin, by combining the ideas of predestination, calling, and living a life glorifying God, produced what Weber called "ascetic Protestantism," but what we can call "world-transforming Protestantism." This kind of Protestantism played a role, Weber thought, in the rise of capitalism because it reinforced the sort of work ethic demanded by capitalism and led to the accumulation of surplus wealth that could be invested.

There have been many criticisms of what some call the **Protestant ethic thesis.** Exploring them here, however, would take us too far afield. If we assume that there is at least some truth in what Weber says about the social and economic consequences of world-transforming Protestantism, we can see how religions of salvation, or at least certain versions of them, might have profound effects on social history.

We are also in a better position to understand the economic success that many Sikhs have achieved. In many ways Sikhism is like world-transforming Protestantism. Guru Nanak rejected the caste system of India and the traditional Vedic reliance on a priestly elite. He encouraged his followers to live and work hard in the world, not to abandon it by becoming monks or nuns. He showed how the traditional householder stage of life had spiritual value. People need not leave their family obligations to seek enlightenment. It can be found here and now, in the midst of family and work. As humans, we now have the opportunity to sing the praises of God and to glorify him in all that we do.

There are some important differences between Calvinistic forms of world-transforming Protestantism and what we might call world-transforming Sikhism. Perhaps the most important is the doctrine of reincarnation. Nanak's God, like Calvin's, controls all things and saves us by his grace, but, if we are Sikh, we need not be overly concerned with this because we will get another chance to obtain union with God (although we may not if we squander our opportunity as a reincarnated human being). We do, however, have to be concerned about securing a better rebirth; so hard work, a moral life, and pious practices are very much worthwhile. As we sow, so shall we reap. As we invest, so shall we gain.

12.4 WHERE ARE WE GOING?

We have seen that different religious traditions interpret the "unease" and "wrongness" of which William James spoke in many different ways. Likewise the remedies for overcoming the wrongness, for making what James called the "proper connection," vary and have different social implications. Here we focus specifically on the results of making that proper connection. I will call that result *salvation*.

The English word *salvation* comes from the Latin *salus*, meaning "whole" or "healthy." Salvation, in a general sense, is connected to a state of being that is safe from destructive forces (anomie or lawlessness). It is a result of being delivered from the wrongness of human existence. The ways in which the wrongness is characterized determine the ways in which salvation is characterized. So salvation may be described as deliverance from pain, suffering, loss, death, sin, punishment, bondage, ignorance, and so on. Gerardus van der Leeuw, an early phenomenologist of religion, described the essence of salvation as power experienced as good. What counts as good, of course, depends on what counts as evil or bad.

Of the many different types of salvation, we will discuss four: limited, unlimited, this-worldly, and otherworldly.[6] Limited salvation refers to the overcoming of specific problems such as illness, danger, and other threats to our well-being. These may be physical or psychological, but most often they are a combination. Limited salvation does not last. Our enemies can attack again, even though we have been delivered before. Illness can return, even though we were healed before. Despair, dread, anxiety, and fear can be temporarily overcome, but that deliverance may not last.

Unlimited or absolute salvation refers to a final and complete overcoming of all unease and wrongness. It is final because, unlike limited salvation, the problems will never return. In the state of absolute salvation, sin and death no longer occur, the rounds of reincarnation (*samsara*) finally end, and a complete release from all attachments (nirvana) is achieved or graciously granted.

This-worldly salvation refers to saving states that happen this side of death and in the world in which humans live and die. It should not be confused with limited salvation because for some religions there is the possibility of ultimate or final salvation in this world. So, for example, truly liberated persons in Sikhism, Hinduism, and Buddhism no longer accumulate karma. They remain in the world only because it takes time to "burn up" the remaining effects of past karma. Different religions often regard "living saints" as enjoying complete salvation. In some traditions, the only salvation that exists is this-worldly, not otherworldly. In these traditions salvation amounts to getting the "right understanding" of life, the world, and death. Part of that right understanding is the realization that there is no life after death. This is the last attachment humans must give up before their salvation can be complete.

Otherworldly salvation refers to after-death states. Once again, we should not confuse this with absolute salvation. Life immediately after death may be and often is thought of as incomplete. We may have to go through purgatory, pass through purifying hells, or await the final day when our body will be resurrected to join our soul in some heaven. Heavens are often arranged hierarchically from incomplete to complete. Immediately after death we might enter a lower (even the lowest) heaven and work our way up to higher levels.

Types of Salvation

1. Limited
2. Absolute
3. This-worldly
4. Otherworldly

Frequently, salvation is equated with enjoying some kind of immortality or life after death. We must be careful here and remind ourselves that not all kinds of life after death are necessarily enjoyable. There are hells and purgatories, which, presumably, we want to avoid if possible. But there are also unavoidable states that are not enjoyable. The early Greeks thought of life after death as survival in an underworld that they called Hades. Life in Hades was not particularly enjoyable. It was a "ghostly" survival. Shades of our living selves wandered about in a cold, dark, and largely lifeless world. It was much like living in a cave, with no hope of ever again enjoying the green, living, and sun-drenched earth. An early Hebrew notion of life after death is similar. The ancient Hebrew equivalent to Hades was Sheol. It existed under the earth and was thought of as a kind of cavern or pit. Life there was a sort of twilight existence and without pleasure. It was not desirable in any respect and so unwelcome that Job could say to his friends, "Let me alone, that I may find a little comfort before I go whence I shall not return, to the land of gloom and deep darkness." (Job 10:20b–21).

Do not misunderstand. Hades and Sheol are not places of punishment. They are morally neutral. They are simply places where the dead live. The Egyptians probably introduced the idea of the afterlife as reward or punishment for deeds done in this life. According to the Egyptian *Book of the Dead,* Osiris judges the person that has died, weighing a person's heart on a scale against the "feather" of Maat, the god of truth.

According to the Egyptians, what survived was a person's *ba,* or life force, which existed apart from the body, but nevertheless had needs that must be met while in the body. Accordingly, they buried the mummified corpse with whatever was needed in order to continue living the "good life." The mystery cults of Greece introduced the idea of an immortal *psyche* (life force) as the vehicle of survival. The Persians, however, could not imagine some disembodied existence as desirable, so they introduced the notion of resurrection of the body. But what sort of body is resurrected? Is it the physical body? If so, how could that be immortal since it is flesh, and all flesh decays? Perhaps it was a transformed body—a body that was no longer physical but spiritual.

The idea of the resurrection of a spiritual body made its way into the New Testament. St. Paul writes in I Corinthians 15:40–44:

> There are celestial bodies and there are terrestrial bodies; but the glory of
> the celestial is one, and the glory of the terrestrial is another. . . . So it is with
> the resurrection of the dead. What is sown is perishable, what is raised is
> imperishable. It is sown in dishonor, it is raised in glory. It is sown in weakness,
> it is raised in power. It is sown a physical body, it is raised a spiritual body. If
> there is a physical body, there is also a spiritual body.

Over time Judaism, Christianity, and Islam put these ideas of judgment, soul-immortality, and resurrection together in different ways. There were controversies over whether judgment took place at the time of death, or later. Whether the dead "sleep" until the resurrection or whether the soul departs for paradise awaiting its spiritual body. Within Christianity, by the medieval period, the prevailing popular view envisioned judgment at the time of death resulting in the soul either going to eternal damnation or eternal paradise. Then, when Christ returns, there will be a general resurrection of the bodies of those who "died in Christ," now transformed from physical to spiritual bodies.

All these ideas of judgment, immortal souls, and resurrected bodies center on the notion of *individual immortality*. We, as individuals, somehow survive death and enjoy, if "saved," life in a paradise of glory and bliss. Similar ideas are found in Pure Land Buddhism, various Hindu sects, and Chinese popular religion. There are also, however, *nonindividualistic* views of life after death. In some Hindu schools, for example, life after death is characterized by metaphors such as salt dissolving in water and rivers flowing into the ocean. At death the individual completely merges with the one true reality, Brahman. In this view, salvation is *moksha*—release or liberation from individuality, not the timeless continuance of individual existence. *Moksha* is, perhaps, the ultimate overcoming of the subject/object dualism that we discussed at the beginning of this chapter. Because individual consciousness is so prized in the West, *moksha* may appear decidedly negative. But according to at least one influential Hindu interpretation, it is not negative at all but the realization of full and complete, absolute consciousness. Shankara calls it being (*sat*), consciousness (*chit*), and bliss (*ananda*).

Still other nonindividualist views locate immortality in some larger unit like the tribe, community, race, or nation. We spoke of this in Chapter 8 as a theodicy of participation.

In Buddhism, views of what happens after death vary a great deal by school and sect. Presumably Buddha himself refused to speculate because it was beyond the abilities of mere mortals to know or describe.

> When a monk does not look on the soul as [eternal] he refrains from such views and clings to nothing in the world; and not clinging he does not tremble, and not trembling he attains Nirvana. He knows that rebirth is at an end, that his goal is reached, that he has accomplished what he set out to do, and that after this present world there is no other for him. It would be absurd to say of such a monk, with his heart set free, that he believes that the perfected being survives after death—or indeed that he does not survive, or that he does and yet does not, or that he neither does nor does not. Because the monk is free his state transcends all expression, predication, communication, and knowledge. (*Digha Nikaya*, 2.64ff)[7]

Nirvana is the extinction of all attachments, even attachments to ideas like an immortal soul. To posit a future life in some paradise is to invite craving and attachment, which is the cause of suffering. To be free is to cling to no views about a possible afterlife because once we have views we cling, and once we cling we become attached, and once we become attached we are locked into suffering and the samsaric lives of seemingly endless rebirths.

Just as in Christianity, controversies developed as Buddhism expanded. According to some schools, the monk who has realized nirvana ceases to exist when he dies. Nirvana is, in other words, a psychological state of freedom. According to others, the monk who has realized nirvana becomes, after death, one with true reality, which is empty of all substance. And, as we have seen in the case of Pure Land Buddhism, some sects hold that at death the enlightened go to live with Amida Buddha in a perfect paradise.

> This world Sukhavati, [the Pure Land], Ananda, which is the world system of the Lord Amitabha [Amida], is rich and prosperous, comfortable, fertile, delightful and crowded with many Gods and men. And in this world system, Ananda, there are no hells, no animals, no ghosts, . . . and none of the inauspicious places of rebirth. And in this our world no jewels make their appearance like those which exist in the world system Sukhavati.
>
> And that world system Sukhavati, Ananda, emits many fragrant odours, it is rich in a great variety of flowers and fruits, adorned with jewel trees, which are frequented by flocks of various birds with sweet voices. . . . And jewel trees have . . . many hundreds of thousands of colours. They are variously composed of . . . gold, silver, beryl, crystal, coral, red pearls or emerald. Such jewel trees, and clusters of banana trees and rows of palm trees, all made of precious things, grow everywhere in this Buddha-field. (*Sukhavativyuka*, 15–16).[8]

Compare this description of the Pure Land with Islamic and Christian descriptions of heaven: It is said that gates to Allah's palace in paradise are made of "green emerald," and the soil smells of the finest "musk and saffron." There are jewels everywhere and wonderful fruit trees of which the righteous will eat. In the New Testament book of Revelation (20:15ff), the "New Jerusalem" has gates of pearls, streets of "pure gold," and the foundations of its walls are adorned with every kind of jewel: jasper, sapphire, agate, emerald, onyx, amethyst, beryl, topaz, and more.

While the goal of salvation may be invisible, religions have found ways to make it at least symbolically visible with descriptions of palatial paradises, perfect tranquility, absolute bliss, perfect joy, and more. What humans have considered "living the good life" is reflected in their elaborate visions of life after death.

REVIEW QUESTIONS

1. What is the primary difference between religions of salvation and religions of sanctification?
2. Explain how the experience of self-awareness can lead to both alienation and the sense that humans can go beyond or transcend alienation.

3. What are the most striking similarities between Sikhism and Christianity? Present reasons to support your answer.
4. Explain the Protestant ethic thesis. Do you think that religions have economic consequences? Why or why not?
5. Define and give an example of unlimited, otherworldly salvation. How does unlimited otherworldly salvation differ from unlimited, this-worldly salvation?

RESEARCH CASE—ZEN BUDDHISM

There are three major forms of Buddhism, and within each, there are numerous schools and sects. Out of the many different groups that early Buddhism comprised, only one remains active today. It is called Theravada (Way of the Elders) Buddhism. This form of Buddhism places emphasis on the disciplined life of the monk and generally views the path to enlightenment as a matter of individual effort. Buddhas are ideal examples of humans who have become enlightened. Today Theravada Buddhism is primarily found in such Southeast Asian countries as Sri Lanka, Thailand, Laos, and Cambodia. Mahayana (Great Vehicle) Buddhism predominates in China, Korea, Vietnam, and Japan. It developed out of early Buddhism sometime around 100 B.C.E. and places emphasis on buddhas as savior figures whose aid is necessary for enlightenment. Vajrayana (Diamond or Thunderbolt Vehicle) is a third type of Buddhism found mostly in Tibet, although at one time it was more widespread. It developed in the sixth century and its Tibetan form in the seventh century. Vajrayana emphasizes both individual effort and the aid of various buddhas. It teaches that enlightenment is beyond all oppositions, such as *samsara*/nirvana, male/female, self/other, effort/grace, sacred/profane.

Zen Buddhism is a Japanese school within the Mahayana tradition that was imported from China, where it is called Chan Buddhism. The word *Zen* means "meditation," and it is characteristic of this school to emphasize the life of meditation as an essential feature of the Buddhist path.

There are two main sects of Zen Buddhism—Rinzai Zen, introduced to Japan by the monk Eisai (1141–1213), and Soto Zen, introduced to Japan by Dogen (1200–1253). Rinzai Zen claims enlightenment is a sudden experience that can be induced by the practice of *koan* **meditation.** A *koan* is a short paradoxical question given by a master to a student designed to shock the student out of dualistic modes of thought. Some famous *koans* are "what is the sound of one hand clapping?" and "does a dog have the Buddha nature?"

Soto Zen emphasizes gradual enlightenment and the practice of *zazen* or "sitting meditation." In *zazen* practice, the meditator assumes the lotus, or cross-legged, position with the buttocks elevated by means of a cushion so that the back is straight and the head is erect. The hands are folded on the lap. The seated meditators empty their minds and go into deep meditative states usually by concentrating on their breathing. According to Dogen, *zazen* should not be thought of as a method for attaining enlightenment but a way of expressing the innate enlightenment (Buddha-nature) we all possess. Dogen claims we are already enlightened, but we do not yet realize it. If we undertake *zazen* with the faith that we are already buddhas, then, as we forget ourselves in meditation, the Buddha-nature will gradually unfold in all aspects of our lives. Our entire life will become one of selfless, compassionate service.

Ritualized chanting and rites paying homage to buddhas also play a role in Zen practice. Typically, each day at a monastic temple begins with ritualized acts of worship followed by periods of meditation and work. At sunset another worship service takes place. Worship itself is an act of meditation and should be done "mindfully," that is, with complete attention. Today, in many Zen centers, *koan* practice, *zazen*, mindful work, and mindful worship may be combined in different ways.

D. T. Suzuki (1870–1966), who aroused much interest in Zen Buddhism in the United States, asserted that *satori* is the essence of Zen. *Satori* is the Japanese Zen term for enlightenment. Suzuki interpreted it as

> an intuitive looking into the nature of things in contradistinction to the analytical or logical understanding of it. Practically, it means the unfolding of a new world hitherto unperceived in the confusion of a dualistically-trained mind. Or we may say that with *satori* our entire surroundings are viewed from quite an unexpected angle of perception. . . . Logically stated, all its [the world's] opposites and contradictions are united and harmonized into a consistent organic whole.[9]

There is and has been much debate over *satori* with regard to both its nature and its effects. It is apparently a flashing, momentary, and seemingly spontaneous intuition much like a sudden discovery or insight. Suzuki emphasized its transforming effect:

> All your mental activities will now be working in a different key, which will be more satisfying, more peaceful, more full of joy than anything you ever experienced before. The tone of life will be altered.[10]

If the basic problem with human life is suffering because of cravings and attachments, then the effects of *satori* gradually lead to learning to live a joyous, peaceful life of compassion. Such a life is possible once selfishness is overcome. Craving things for ourselves and becoming attached to things that please us make no sense once we overcome dualistic thinking. Once we have seen reality in its deepest sense, we realize there is no real difference between others and ourselves. We are all interconnected parts of the ongoing flow and dance of what we call the universe.

In 1949 a laywoman named Nakayama Momoyo wrote about her life before and after Zen practice. She told of her struggles as a single mother in prewar and wartime Japan and how she became overwhelmed with grief when her son died. During a Zen retreat of intense *koan* meditation, she underwent an experience she later recounted in the following manner:

> "Gong!" rang the temple bell, and suddenly, I cried out and returned to myself. It was attained! "Heaven and Earth are of one piece. The universe and I are one body. I am the Buddha! We're jointed in one!" . . . Apart from buddha mind, there is nothing. That is joy. This too is joy. My life is full in this vast, delightful and pure world. In one of my teacher's lectures she spoke the lines,
>
>> My clear dew mind
>> Is a ruby
>> When amongst the autumn leaves.
>> It's because my mind is clear or colorless that it can adapt to any and all circumstances.
>
> Because of the kindness of the buddhas and patriarchs [Zen masters who transmitted the enlightenment experience "mind to mind"], a life worth living, a life that requires only the slightest effort, has begun.[11]

Although *satori* is a dramatic and transforming experience, many Zen Buddhists emphasize the practice of meditation, not *satori*, as the essence of Zen. Suzuki's emphasis on satori reflects a Rinzai bias. The Soto emphasis on gradual enlightenment and the importance of regular meditation practice is what, in the long run, counts the most in changing a person's life. The desire for the dramatic and sudden experience of *satori* can become yet another selfish ego trap.

QUESTIONS ON THE CASE OF ZEN BUDDHISM

1. How does Zen Buddhism solve the problem of suffering?
2. How do you think *koan* and *zazen* practices work?
3. Is "salvation" in Zen this-worldly or otherworldly? Support your answer with reasons.
4. Compare and contrast Zen with Sikhism and Christianity. In what ways are they the same and in what ways different?
5. Would you classify Zen as a salvation religion? Why or why not?

Fieldwork Option: Visit a Zendo and write a participant observation report.

SUGGESTIONS FOR FURTHER READING

In addition to the material found in the notes, the reader may wish to consult the following for more information.

Badham, Paul, and Linda Badham, eds. *Death and Immortality in the Religions of the World.* New York: Paragon House, 1987. This collection of essays examines different religious views of the afterlife along with some philosophical critiques.

Cole, W. Owen, and Piara Singh Sambhi. *The Sikhs.* Brighton: Sussex Academic Press, 1995. I recommend this careful discussion of Sikh history and beliefs.

Coward, Harold. *Sin and Salvation in the World Religions: A Short Introduction.* Oxford: Oneworld Publications, 2003. A concise and accurate survey of the ideas of sin and salvation found in the major religions of the world.

Gier, Nicholas F. *Spiritual Titanism.* Albany State University of New York Press, 2000. Gier presents an insightful comparative study of Titanism, the religious tendency to attribute to human beings divine characteristics.

Hawkins, Bradley K. *Buddhism.* Upper Saddle River, NJ: Prentice Hall, 1999. This book provides a clear and concise introduction to Buddhism.

Holm, Jean, ed. *Human Nature and Destiny.* London: Printer Publishers, 1994. This is a collection of essays about how different religions describe human nature and human destiny.

Johnstone, Ronald L. "Religion and the Economy." In *Religion in Society: A Sociology of Religion.* 6th ed. Upper Saddle River, NJ: Prentice Hall, 2001. I have relied heavily on Johnstone's discussion of the Protestant ethic thesis because it is clear and insightful.

Kasulis, Thomas P. "Nirvana." In *Buddhism and Asian History,* edited by Joseph M. Kitagawa and Mark D. Cummings. New York: Macmillan, 1987, 1989. Kasulis's article, originally published in *The Encyclopedia of Religion,* provides an overview of the many different meanings of nirvana in Buddhist thought.

Neville, Robert Cummings, ed. *The Human Condition.* Albany: State University of New York Press, 2001. This volume in the Comparative Religious Ideas Project includes essays by leading scholars on different religious views concerning the human predicament.

Pagels, Elaine. *Adam, Eve, and the Serpent.* New York: Random House, 1988. Pagels shows how certain ideas concerning sexuality, moral freedom, and human value based on the stories of Adam, Eve, and the serpent in Genesis have affected the development of Western culture.

Singh, Trilochan, et al., trans. *The Sacred Writings of the Sikhs.* New York: Samuel Weiser, 1973. This contains selections from the Sikh scripture, *Adi Granth.*

Weber, Max. *The Protestant Ethic and the Spirit of Capitalism.* Translated by Talcott Parsons. New York: Scribner's, 1958. Weber's classic statement, first published in German in 1905, is translated here.

Wilson, Brian. *Christianity.* Upper Saddle River, NJ: Prentice Hall, 1999. This book, in the *Religions of the World* series, provides a concise introduction to the history of Christianity and some of its main teachings and practices.

INTERNET RESOURCES

www.religiousworlds.com/sikh.html   At this religious world's Web site, you can locate links to information about Sikhism, much of it from an insider's viewpoint.

www.religiousworlds.com/christian.html   Here you will find links to sites with all kinds of information about Christianity along with a glossary of theological terms.

www.religionfacts.com/buddhism/sects/zen.htm   This site, with links, provides basic information about the history of Zen Buddhism and some of its practices.

CHAPTER 13

Religious Diversity
and Truth

I HOPE THIS BOOK has answered many of your questions about different reli
gious beliefs and practices. But I am sure it has left you (I know it has left
me) with even more questions. Some of these may have to do with religious
conflict and rivalry. Some questions may concern how the various religions
might be related. Other questions may have to do with religious truth. We
need to pay attention to what Mark Twain half humorously and half seriously
said in *Letters from Earth*: "Man is the only animal that has a True Religion—
several of them."

People who study comparative religions experience what some have
called "the shock of recognition."[1] They discover similarities between their
own religion and other religions. It seems that in some sense religions are not
all that different. We recognize ourselves in what others believe and do. So are
all religions equally effective paths to salvation?

Recognition of similarities is often accompanied by "the shock of difference."[2] There is no denying religious diversity. After our initiation into the
academic study of religion, we can see that the often-repeated judgment that
"all religions are the same" is too superficial given the evidence. Also, it is not
fair to others or to ourselves to pronounce all religions the same and to act as
if religious differences were not real differences or not very important. What
are we to make of this situation? Can all religions be true if real differences
separate them?

In this concluding chapter, we will tackle some of these questions. We will explore some of the reasons for religious conflict and competition. We will examine some of the many ways we have been socialized to think about the relationships among religions, and we will examine the question of religious truth. We will also return to the topic of religious tolerance introduced in the first chapter. And we will extend our abilities to understand and interpret religion by looking at the case of a relatively recent religious development called Baha'i. Baha'i advocates religious harmony and peace. What compels it to do so? Why does this message arise at this time in history?

13.1 WHY CAN'T WE ALL GET ALONG?

Rodney King asked the above question with respect to race relations, and we can ask it with respect to the relationships among and within religions. Why have religious wars been fought? Why have tens of millions of people been slaughtered in the name of some god? Why does such religiously inspired carnage continue?

Religious conflict is caused by many factors, including nationalistic expansionism, economic inequities, political instability, and long-standing ethnic hatred and prejudice. However, there is no denying that religious beliefs and prejudices have played and continue to play a major role in human conflict. There is the Palestinian and Israeli conflict in the eastern Mediterranean, where, although not all Palestinians are Muslim and not all Israelis are devoted Jews, religious factors are involved. In the former Yugoslavia, the Christian (Eastern Orthodox) Serbs have murdered their Muslim neighbors under the banner of "ethnic cleansing." We can grant that the political ambitions of Slobodan Milosevic were a key factor in this conflict, but that does not mean that religious tensions did not contribute to the sickening slaughter. The Nazis were far from Christian in their ideology, but most of gentile Germany was either Catholic or Protestant, and in spite of Jesus's admonition to love your neighbor, many of them proceeded to cooperate in and support the mass extermination of Jews. Now various groups seek to cloak their terrorism in terms of a Muslim/Judeo-Christian holy war.

A sociological theory, called *conflict theory*, postulates that conflict arises in cases of power differences. In other words, conflict between and within groups amounts to a struggle for power, wealth, prestige, and privilege. Religions are in competition. The more religions there are, and the more religions are forced by historical, political, economic, and geographic factors to interact, the more likely it is, according to conflict theory, that they will fight (often violently and viciously) over power, wealth, prestige, and privilege.

Conflict arises out of other sources besides the competition for power and influence. Conflict often stems from a sense of threat. The Peace of Westphalia in 1648 brought to a close thirty years of religious and political conflict among

Christians. According to some estimates, the population of Europe was reduced from sixteen million to less than six million due to war, disease, and economic collapse brought about by thirty years of religious warfare among Protestant and Catholic Christians.

In order to try to end the fighting, a policy called **secularization** was introduced. At that time, it was a name for the process of transferring lands and possessions from religious control to civil control. Since that time, the word has been used in a variety of different ways. One way it is used suggests that secularization marks a gradual process of the loss of social and public influence of religious organizations. Another way suggests that secularization marks a change in traditional religious patterns that involves the increased privatization of religious choice and commitment.

Although scholars disagree about whether secularization marks a decline of religion or a change, most do agree that the sources of secularization can be identified as an increased reliance on human reason as the judge of truth that characterized the modern age and the expansion of scientific modes of thought. And the **postmodern** age has called into question the presumably unbiased and objective character of human reason by showing that it is tainted by political, economic, and sexist agendas as well as the modern inclination to trust science and technology to solve all problems.

If modernism threatens religion by its elevation of science and human reason to the throne of power and judgment, postmodernism also threatens it by questioning whether there exists any final, absolute, and objective standard of judgment. Historically, at least in many religions, the divine was granted the role of final judge; not only the final judge, but the absolutely objective judge of what is true and what is false. It now appears that this so-called objective judge may be little more than a partisan of the religion that claims power in the name of the divine. The threat to traditional religion is real, and the natural human reaction to threat is to become defensive. So reactionary fundamentalist movements crisscross the landscape of our time, indicating their willingness to fight, even to kill, to preserve what they take to be the traditional and divinely ordained order of things.

The perceived threat of secularization and postmodernism to traditional religious power leaves many ready to fight. As we come into closer contact with cultures and religions very different from our own, we become even more defensive. We live in an age of increased diversity and increased contact between different cultures and religions. By some counts, two million Muslims have migrated to the United States. There are now fifty Muslim mosques in Chicago alone. Approximately one hundred thousand Sikhs live in Toronto. Christianity has spread to the most remote corners of the world. We live in a global religious village. Diane Eck, chair of the Pluralism Project at Harvard University, writes:

It is precisely the interpenetration and proximity of ancient civilizations and cultures that is the hallmark of the late twentieth century. This is the new geo-religious reality. The map of the world in which we now live cannot be color-coded as to its Christian, Muslim, Hindu identity: each part of the world is marbled with the colors and textures of the whole.[3]

There is not only a geo-religious global community in the making, but also a massive economic globalization occurring in which multinational corporations control one-third of the world's wealth, handle 70 percent of its trade, and fan out in all directions seeking cheap labor. As massive wealth accumulates in the hands of a few, the gap between rich and poor increases. This gap transcends national boundaries, and the poor of New York join the poor of Southeast Asia. Population growth is out of control, the environment is deteriorating at an increasingly rapid rate, and religions appear not only unable to do anything to stop the massive exploitation of people and the environment, but are also increasingly defensive and threatened by processes that seem to be beyond anyone's control.

Although we cannot divorce religious developments from this larger setting, we must return our focus to religious conflict. Will this increasing proximity of diverse religions create a climate in which religious conflict will increase? Or will it slowly begin to dawn on people that even if there are many reasons why we cannot get along, we have little choice but to try.

13.2 EXCLUSIVISM, INCLUSIVISM, AND PLURALISM

If we lived in a world in which there was only one religion, the question of how the different religions might be related, or which, if any, are true, simply would not arise. If we lived in a world in which religions did not recommend different paths to salvation, promote differing views of reality, and, in some cases, condemn rivals as immoral, demonic, and heretical, we might assume that religious cooperation would replace religious conflict. We do not live in such a world. We live in a world in which some religions have claimed to be the only ones that are true. Not all religions have claimed this, and different elements within religions have held different positions at different times, but the claim to exclusivity in matters of faith is common enough that it deserves a closer look.

Exclusivism

In its extreme form, **exclusivism** is the position that one religion is true both in the sense of teaching the truth about ultimate reality and in the sense of providing the only valid way to salvation. Because it would be very odd if not illogical to claim there is one true religion and it is *not* their own, people who support exclusivism mean that their own religion is the only one that is true. It follows that all other religions are false, and the people who profess them are destined for a bad end.

Although some people think that exclusivism is both a natural and logical position to assume when thinking about the different world religions in the context of a concern about truth, it is not. Some religions that focus on worshiping the spirits of nature and the ancestors of their tribe or clan need not be (and often are not) exclusivistic. Just as different people can have different ancestors, so different religions can worship different spirits. A polytheism that recognizes many different gods need not be exclusivistic. Neither is henotheism necessarily exclusivistic because while people may believe that they are obligated to worship one of the many gods, other people have no such obligation. Even monotheism need not be exclusivistic, at least with respect to other monotheistic religions. The Quran recognizes all true believers in one divine being as religiously correct, whether or not they are Muslims.

Within Christianity exclusivism has not always reigned supreme, but Christianity in much of its history has tended toward exclusivism. The reasons for Christian exclusivism are both historical and theological. There were, as we have seen, many different early groups claiming to follow the way of Jesus the Christ. As the new religious movement that was eventually designated by the name Christianity developed into a successful missionary movement, it had to face the dilemmas of institutionalization. What was unique about its message? Why should someone abandon his or her traditional religious beliefs and practices to join this new way? Why is the Christian conception of the divine better than other conceptions?

We can add to all of the above the political pressures that arose once Christianity became the state religion of the Roman empire. The emperor expected this new religion to provide a clear, unified, and distinctive message that would support the unity of the empire. So, what is distinctive about the Christian message? Different Christian groups fought bitterly over the answer to this question, and the turning point came at the Councils of Nicea and Chalcedon. Participants at these councils had to answer the question, "Is Jesus one of many different manifestations of the divine, or is Jesus the one and only unique incarnation of the divine?" The faction supporting uniqueness won the day. So bishops meeting at Chalcedon proclaimed that to be a true Christian and to be saved, one must recognize that "Jesus of Nazareth is unique in the precise sense that while being fully man, it is true of him and him alone, that he is also fully God."[4] As a result, those Christians who think that there is one and only one incarnation of the divine, and it is Jesus of Nazareth, feel obligated to reject the idea of multiple incarnations. The Hindu notion that Krishna, Rama, Jesus, and others are all incarnations of the divine, for example, becomes incompatible with Christian teaching. If we assume that only one religion can be true, then either the Christians are right or the Hindus are right. There can be no middle ground.

It appears to be a short step from exclusivism to religious intolerance, contempt for the religious practices of others, self-righteous pride, and a refusal to engage in serious dialogue with those of other faiths. Preaching for purposes of conversion is preferred over dialogue. Such things as intolerance, contempt, unjustified pride, and disrespect for others raise serious questions about the morality of exclusivism. It is easy to see how exclusivism can promote or at least support religious conflict. It is also easy to see how such a position leads to suspicion and skepticism on the part of others concerning any and all exclusivistic claims. As the philosopher and theologian John Hick remarked:

> However, a "hermeneutic of suspicion" is provoked by the evident fact that in perhaps 99 percent of cases the religion to which one adheres (or against which one reacts) is selected by the accident of birth. Someone born to devout Muslim parents in Iran or Indonesia is very likely to be a Muslim; someone born to devout Buddhist parents in Thailand or Sri Lanka is very likely to be a Buddhist; someone born to devout Christian parents in Italy or Mexico is very likely to be a Catholic Christian; and so on.[5]

It seems to be arbitrary for people to claim that the particular religion into which they happen to be born is the one and only true religion. Why has God seen fit to bless them with the saving truth by accident of birth while excluding the majority of the human race from such a blessing?

Exclusivism need not, however, be either immoral or irrationally arbitrary. Alvin Plantinga, a Christian philosopher, argues that religious exclusivism is not necessarily responsible for immoral attitudes toward others, nor is it necessarily guilty of any faulty reasoning.[6] In response to the charge that there is something morally suspect about religious exclusivism, he replies that people would not be immoral *just because* they believed that they had really good, knockdown arguments supporting their beliefs, which others, assuming they were in a position to hear and understand, would come to agree with. For example, if a scientist believes that her theory about some physical event is the only correct theory and rejects rival theories, we normally would not accuse her of being immoral. Likewise, Plantinga argues, to reject what other people believe religiously is not necessarily to hold them in contempt, to be intolerant of their right to believe, or to be prideful.

To Hick's suggestion that the accident of birth makes exclusivism intellectually arbitrary, Plantinga responds that there is no reason why the fact that someone is brought up to believe certain things to be true necessarily implies that they are false or that the person is not justified in believing them. If that were so, people brought up to believe that all religions are the same, or that they are all in some sense true, or that none of them is true would be as arbitrary in their belief as the exclusivist. Plantinga adds that some exclusivism in all our beliefs, religious or otherwise, is inevitable if we think, quite reasonably, that ideas that contradict true beliefs must be false beliefs.

Plantinga does not directly address the issue of whether exclusivism necessarily shuts off religious dialogue and hence the possibility of understanding other religious viewpoints. But he does address the issue of learning about religions other than our own. He admits that such learning may be dangerous for exclusivists because it may lead to a lessening if not an abandonment of their faith. But he quickly notes that things do not have to go this way. There are several possibilities. "A fresh or heightened awareness of the facts of religious pluralism could bring about a reappraisal of one's religious life, a reawakening, a new or renewed and deepened grasp [of one's own religious convictions]."[7]

There have been responses to Plantinga's response to those who condemn exclusivism on moral and intellectual grounds. The philosophical and theological debate is far from dead. In some circles, however, there has been a shift in thinking about the relationships among religions. This shift in thinking is called inclusivism.

Inclusivism

There are different kinds of **inclusivism**, but, as the name implies, all varieties wish to acknowledge the possibility of salvation in different religions. At the same time, inclusivists wish to assert the superiority of their own religion. How can they recognize the validity of other religions and also insist on the superiority of their own? Different religions have different ways of doing this.

Some early Christians, for example, claimed that the divine revelation to the Jews as found in the Old Testament is true and valid, but it must be interpreted in light of the new revelation of the divine in Christ. They argued that the New Testament completes and makes plain the Law and the Prophets contained in the Old Testament. The Christian scripture includes the Jewish scripture, and hence Christianity includes the truth of Judaism. Nevertheless, it goes beyond that truth by acknowledging a new revelation of the incarnation of God in Jesus, a revelation only "foreshadowed" and "anticipated" in Jewish scripture.

This same kind of argument is repeated in many religions. Muslims argue that Muhammad is the "seal" of the prophets, completing and perfecting the divine revelations given to Moses and Jesus. While Islam did not incorporate Jewish or Christian scripture in its own holy book, the Quran, it did recognize Jews and Christians as "people of the book," and it did include many of the stories from both the Old and New Testament.

Those who claim to be the last prophet always run the risk of someone else coming along later who claims to be the last prophet whose revelation includes, but supersedes, all previous revelations. The history of the development of much of the world's scriptures could be written in this manner. Each new revelation not only rejects the absoluteness of the old revelations (often thereby increasing the skepticism of outsiders), it also seems arrogant to those who follow what is now "old." Anyone who claims to have the final word on something automatically implies that what another holds dear should not be held so dearly.

Other types of inclusivism see their own religious ideas as hidden, concealed, or implicit in the religions of others. Of the many examples of this sort of inclusivism in the religions of the world, we will concentrate on the views of a Roman Catholic theologian named Karl Rahner (1904–1984) because they have been and still are influential among many Catholic thinkers as well as others. Rahner argued that if we truly believe that God intended his saving grace for all humanity and that the truth of salvation is revealed most perfectly in Christianity, then we must recognize what he called "anonymous Christians." In other words, Buddhists, Hindus, Muslims, Jews, and others who have truly and genuinely responded to God's saving grace are, in effect, Christians, even if they do not think of themselves that way. The Christian Church should not think of itself as the exclusive community of those who are saved, but as the historical vanguard expressing explicitly what is hidden in other religions. Rahner writes:

> Until the moment when the gospel really enters into the historical situation of the individual, a non-Christian religion . . . does not merely contain elements of a natural knowledge of God . . . It contains also supernatural elements arising out of the grace which is given to men as a gratuitous gift on account of Christ. For this reason a non-Christian religion can be recognized as a *lawful* religion.[8]

By a *"lawful* religion" Rahner means a historical religion that God has included in the divine plan of salvation. All lawful religions, because they occur within a historical and institutional setting, are liable to error and corruption. When religions fail to promote social justice and support or engage in destructive conflicts with others, they exhibit their human origins and frailty. This does not mean that God cannot use them to dispense grace and forgiveness. Indeed, if there were no human sin in institutional religions or elsewhere, there would be no need for grace. It does mean, however, that Christians (and others) should abandon the either/or mentality that claims a religion must either come from God or it must be a fake, a mere human invention.

Rahner's brand of inclusivism has been criticized from many sides. Christians argue that it fails to appreciate what is radically new in Christ and undermines Christian missionary work. Others argue that Rahner's position is paternalistic, arrogant, and imperialistic. In effect, it says to the devout of any religion other than Christianity that they are deceived because they think they are Buddhists (or whatever the religion might be), but in reality they are anonymous Christians. This hardly seems the best way to promote serious and honest dialogue among the world's faiths.

Rahner denies that his position undermines missionary work because if a missionary converts a non-Christian to Christianity, he turns an anonymous Christian into someone who now consciously knows what he or she truly is. This knowledge is an advance over their previous state. Rahner responds to the charges of arrogance and paternalism by maintaining that non-Christians may indeed think his brand of inclusivism is presumptuous. But they must understand that a Christian has no other choice than to see all genuine acts of divine grace as manifestations of the grace of Christ, even if others do not see them that way. Rahner concedes, as he must, that it is only fair that other religions might refer to Christians as "anonymous Muslims," or "anonymous Buddhists," and so on.

Whatever the defects of Rahner's version of inclusivism, his ideas have helped reflective Catholics to move beyond a parochial understanding of the Catholic dogma, "There is no salvation outside of the church" (*Extra ecclesiam nulla salus*). While Protestant versions of Christianity have always rejected the Roman Catholic version of this doctrine, their rejection has been related to internal fights for autonomy from the dominance of Roman Catholicism. In effect, at least among some Protestant groups, a variation of the old Catholic exclusivism that they fought so hard to overcome has become reinstated as exclusivism with respect to other religions. "There is no salvation outside of the church" is transformed into "There is no salvation outside of Christianity." Rahner's inclusivism is clearly a challenge to any and all forms of exclusivism.

Pluralism

If exclusivism holds that there is one and only one true religious path to salvation, and inclusivism holds that different religions may contain in a hidden way the true path that is most clearly expressed in only one, **pluralism** holds that there are many different true paths to salvation expressed in the many diverse religions of the world.

Perhaps the most influential advocate of pluralism writing today is John Hick, a Protestant philosopher and theologian. Hick believes that historical circumstances are now leading to a revolution in human thought about religions comparable to the Copernican revolution in astronomy in the sixteenth century. Before Copernicus's theory of the sun as the center of our solar system won wide acceptance, the Ptolemaic view of the earth as the center prevailed. "Ptolemaic" thinking about religion holds that one or another of the world's religions is at the center of religious truth. So Christianity (if I am a Christian), or Islam (if I am a Muslim), or Hinduism (if I am a Hindu), and so on is the "true center," and all other religious traditions circle around that "sun." Just as Ptolemaic astronomy was geocentric, so Ptolemaic religion is ethnocentric since accident of birth mostly determines our religious outlook. "Copernican" thinking about religion recognizes a new center around which all religions revolve. Hick refers to that center as the Real.

What is the Real? Hick uses a distinction from the philosopher Kant between *noumena* (things-in-themselves) and *phenomena* (things-as-they-appear) to develop the idea. Just as *noumena* cannot be grasped by human thought because they do not appear to thought as do phenomena, so the Real-in-itself transcends our limited human ways of talking and thinking. However, the Real-as-it-appears in the various religions can be thought about and experienced.

Hick formulates the pluralistic hypothesis as follows: "the Real (to select this term from several equally available ones) in itself is present to us, or impinges upon us, all the time and that when this impingement comes to consciousness it takes the form of what we call religious experience."[9] These historically and culturally conditioned experiences give rise to different concepts of the Real. Even though the Real-in-itself is beyond human thought, the Real as experienced in time and space is thought of differently in different human communities. In some it is named YHWH, in others Krishna, in still others Dao, or Allah, or God, or the Holy Trinity, or "that which nothing greater can be thought," or Zeus, or kami, or—I could go on and on, but you get the idea. Each finite religious tradition generates its own names and, along with those names, different conceptions of the Real.

Hick thinks that most of these conceptions fall into two camps. One camp thinks of the Real in personal terms. It is conscious, has a will, cares about people, and, in short, exhibits person-like characteristics. The other camp thinks of the Real in nonpersonal terms. It is the Absolute, the Principle, the Infinite, the Eternal, and so on. Hick contends that even though these two camps center on different conceptions of the Real, they are not mutually exclusive. They are, Hick argues, complementary.

The task of demonstrating how they are complementary is not easy. But Hick is encouraged by the fact that all the different religions that fall into the personal camp or the nonpersonal camp have developed systems that promote human spiritual and moral transformation. Hick writes that these "fruits . . . prove a common criterion by which to recognize the salvific transformation of human existence from natural self-centeredness to a new orientation centered in the Real, a transformation which takes different concrete forms with different religious cultures."[10]

This version of pluralism allows for real differences among the religions, but it argues that such differences should not lead to religious intolerance. There are many religious questions to which humans do not have definitive answers, such as whether there really is life after death or whether there is some purpose to human existence. Different religions make claims to have the answers, and their answers often conflict. But neither our ignorance of the answers nor conflicting claims to truth prevent moral and spiritual transformations from taking place in many different religious traditions. Therefore we should tolerate and live in harmony with the conflicting truth-claims.

What about the Real itself? Do we know that it exists? How could we know it if it is beyond the limits of human thought? Hick responds by saying that the existence of the Real as the center of all the religions is a *postulate* that the pluralistic hypothesis must make. If it does not, then we are left with the unattractive alternatives of exclusivism, inclusivism, or of regarding all religious experience as illusory.

Arvind Sharma, a professor of comparative religion at McGill University, has compared Hick's pluralism with the pluralism of the Hindu school of Advaita (nondualistic) Vedanta. As you may recall, Shankara, one of the leading thinkers of this school, claimed that Brahman (Being-in-itself or the divine-in-itself) is not different from Atman (consciousness-in-itself). You may also recall that *Hinduism* is a convenient word to use for a plurality of religious traditions that developed and took root in India. The religious world in which Advaita developed was already diverse, and most Indians had learned to live more or less in harmony with a wide variety of religious beliefs and practices.

Sharma points out that Hick's distinction between the Real as experienced nonpersonally and the Real as experienced personally is similar (although not identical) to Shankara's distinction between *nirguna* Brahman (the divine without qualities) and *saguna* Brahman (the divine with qualities). The divine with qualities is called Ishvara, or Lord. It is this Lord that is worshiped in the many devotional sects of Hinduism by many names such as Rama, Krishna, Shiva, the goddess Kali, Ganesha, and so on. If Shankara had been aware of the many non-Indian devotional traditions such as Judaism, Christianity, and Islam, all of whom worship a personal divine being, he would have called them worshipers of *saguna* Brahman, or the Lord, as well.

If nondualism is correct, then in the final analysis for Advaita, *nirguna* Brahman and *saguna* Brahman are identical. Hick's claim that they are complementary conceptions of the Real-in-itself would appear to imply a subordination or at least a dualism that Advaita denies. This is one of Sharma's arguments.

Sharma finds other differences between Advaitic pluralism and Hick's pluralism as well. But in spite of the divergences, he concludes that there is a "strong family resemblance" between the two. This family resemblance becomes apparent, Sharma thinks, by the Advaitic statements found in the *Yogavasishtha*:

> Many names have been given to the Absolute by the learned for practical purposes such as Law, Self, Truth.
> It is called Person by the Samkhya thinkers, Brahman by the Vedantins, pure and simple consciousness by the Vijnanavadins, Sunya [Nothing] by the Nihilists, the Illuminator by the worshippers of the Sun. It is also called the Speaker, the Thinker, the Enjoyer of actions and the Doer of them.
> Shiva for the worshippers of Shiva, and Time for those who believe in Time alone.[11]

> **Possible Truth-Relations among Different Religions**
>
> 1. Exclusivism—one and only one of the many religions is true.
> 2. Inclusivism—truth is most clearly and fully expressed in one religion, but other religions also contain truth, although in a partial or hidden way.
> 3. Pluralism—in spite of their differences, all religions contain valid experiences of ultimate reality.

13.3 CAN WE DETERMINE RELIGIOUS TRUTH?

We have been using the words *true* and *truth* vaguely. It is time for some clarification. In particular it is time to confront more directly the question of whether there are any criteria we can use to determine what is true or false religiously. If the idea of truth has something to do with verification, how might we verify the truth of religious claims?

The question of truth becomes particularly important when we look at religious diversity and the conflicting claims made by religions. Some teach a doctrine of the soul, some do not. Some teach that there is an eternal hell, others do not. Some teach that there are many gods, others do not. We could pile example on top of example. By what criteria can we sort all of this out?

When it comes to questions of truth, one major advantage that the natural sciences have over religions, especially religions that posit supernatural realities, is a generally agreed-upon methodology for purposes of verification. What is accepted as true is an outcome of checking procedures that critically examine claims to truth and test them according to the best methods available. One of those methods is experimentation. Scientific theories generate empirical hypothesis that are then tested, ideally by experiments under laboratory conditions. A key feature of experimentation is repeatability. Anyone properly trained and knowledgeable in a field of research with the appropriate resources should be able to repeat an experiment and compare the results to previous ones.

Another method is mathematics. Mathematicians do not conduct laboratory experiments, but they do use the principles of mathematical and logical coherence to test ideas and to deduce new ones. The rigor of these tests must meet the highest standards in the field and be checkable by other mathematicians.

Few religious claims, especially claims about the truth of beliefs concerning things beyond nature, appear to be testable by strict experimental methods. This should not surprise us since the experimental method was developed in science precisely to test claims about the natural world, not the supernatural world. Tests of coherence seem more promising because one can certainly ask of any religion whether its overall view of the world and how to live one's life in the world makes logical sense. But this sort of test is of limited value because something can make sense logically (for instance, the earth is flat) and be false. Further, many religions often claim that their key ideas are "mysteries." Whatever this might mean, it certainly appears to mean that we should not expect logical coherence to characterize all core beliefs. The doctrines of the Trinity and incarnation are examples in Christianity, and the claim in Madhyamika Buddhism that all views are false implies that even this view of all views is false. If it is not false, then it is false that all views are false. If it is false, then isn't Madhyamika's core claim self-defeating?

A key claim of Advaita Hinduism along with many other religions is that ultimate reality is inexpressible. It is, like the Dao or God's nature—beyond the ability of human languages to adequately express. If it is true that ultimate reality is inexpressible, then one cannot coherently express that by saying it! To call these things mysteries is to tell us very little except, perhaps, not to expect logical coherence as a characteristic of core religious beliefs about the nature of ultimate reality.

If experimental verification and logical coherence pose problems for trying to determine religious truth, then what if we could devise a more pragmatic test. The philosopher William James argued that true beliefs are those beliefs that are a good basis for action (see Chapter 2). We can know if they are a good basis by the results. If the outcomes of the action are desirable, then the action is good, and the beliefs upon which it is based are true beliefs. They are, in a word, useful. Religious beliefs provide meaning and purpose to many people's lives, and they have been doing this from time immemorial. They must have survival value, or the evolutionary process of weeding out useless beliefs and actions would have led to the end of religion eons ago.

The difficulty of the pragmatic test centers on two issues. First, the slipperiness of words like *success, good,* and *useful* poses a problem. How do we judge whether an outcome is successful or useful and hence good? To make that call we need objectively agreed-upon criteria to measure success and usefulness. Any proposed set of criteria is likely to be controversial. Experimentation and mathematical coherence have the advantage of providing ways for the community of scientists to settle controversies. It is doubtful that the pragmatic test would have the same impact on communities of faith since many beliefs might be useful to someone (such as the belief in ghosts) but not useful to others.

The second problem is more serious. The connections between true or false beliefs and successful actions are far from clear. For example, we can imagine a false belief leading to success and a true belief leading to disaster. I may believe that if I avoid walking under ladders I will get home safely, and I do get home safely. Does that mean that my belief about avoiding ladders in order to be safe is a true belief? I might believe that a plane is safe and fly on it with confidence. Let's say it is mechanically safe, but a terrorist has put a bomb on board, and the plane blows up, killing all passengers and crew. Few of us would want to argue that the explosion and resulting deaths were successful outcomes of my true belief that the plane was mechanically safe. Yet it was mechanically safe. It is doubtful that successful outcomes, even if we could agree on how to measure success, guarantee the truth of a belief.

Many people would find this discussion of the tests for the truth of beliefs quite irrelevant to the "proofs" that miracles and fulfilled prophecies provide. All you have to do is watch a few televangelists to realize that the airways are filled with appeals to miracles and fulfilled prophecies as "proofs" for the wonderful workings of the divine among humans. These appeals provide comfort to many people, otherwise they would not willingly send their money. However, do they really prove anything?

Presumably miracles and fulfilled prophecies are acts of God and not the result of natural causes. If they are the result of natural causes, they can provide no proof at all for some kind of supernatural power. So the first step is to eliminate all possible natural explanations for, let's say, someone's cancer cure and all possible natural explanations for some prophet "knowing" some future event in a sense specific enough for an objective observer to say, "Yes, that is precisely the event foretold thousands of years ago." It is no easy task to eliminate all possible natural explanations, but let's say it could be done. There is then a second step. This step is to show that a divine agent is the cause. One cannot take this second step without begging an important question. How do we know, independently of the alleged miracle or fulfilled prophecy, that its cause was a divine agent rather than a natural cause yet to be discovered or simply random chance? In other words, we would need some other kind of evidence or convincing arguments for the existence of divine agents apart from the events (miracles or fulfilled prophecies) that they allegedly caused.

This brief discussion of the problems involved in proving the truth of religious claims leads us to what for many may be a disappointing conclusion. Humans have not been able to devise tests, at this point in time, that verify beyond a reasonable doubt the central claims that many religions make. While this may be disappointing, it should not be surprising. If such tests had been successfully devised, we would not be facing the sort of disagreement among religions that we do in fact face. Also, religions would not celebrate the necessity and the virtues of faith and hope if what they taught were a matter of objectively determined knowledge. We would not have to be told that there are virtues in believing beyond the evidence if there were in fact convincing evidence.

However, perhaps this discussion is based on a false assumption. Perhaps religions and their claims are not the sorts of things to which the concepts of true and false apply. Perhaps something else is going on here. If so, what might it be?

Language Games

We do not think of civilizations as true or false, so why should we think of religions that way? Think of religions, some philosophers advise, as "language games." Just as different games have their own rules and it would be inappropriate to judge, say, a game of tennis by the rules of chess, so the religious language game, or at least some of the language games religions play, should not be judged by inappropriate rules. If the religious language game is primarily symbolic, metaphoric, and poetic, why use rules of truth or falsity? Perhaps it is more appropriate to think in terms of spiritual and moral qualities. Radhakrishnan (1888–1973), an Indian philosopher, states that we should "frankly recognize that the efficiency of a religion is to be judged by the development of religious qualities such as quiet confidence, inner calm, gentleness of the spirit, love of neighbour, mercy to all creation, destruction of tyrannous desires, and the aspiration for spiritual freedom, and there are no trustworthy statistics to tell us that these qualities are found more in efficient nations."[12]

Note Radhakrishnan's use of the word *efficiency* in this context, rather than truth. Note as well that while there are no trustworthy statistics on these matters when we compare religions to nations, there are also no trustworthy statistics when we compare religion to religion. The historical record indicates that the ability of religions to produce moral transformations in people is ambiguous.

Changing direction away from the focus on true and false to morally better or worse may be attractive in many ways, but most religions claim to teach more than morality, and for most believers matters of truth are important. However, even if we think the focus should shift from truth to moral value, the controversy over criteria errupts again. Now, rather than a controversy concerning criteria of truth, it is about what criteria to use to judge moral value.

13.4 CRITICAL TOLERANCE AND THE PRINCIPLE OF CHARITY

We spoke briefly about critical tolerance in the first chapter. It is time to return to that theme. Our first discussion was in the context of beginners in the field of the academic study of religion. While all of us have much more to learn about religions and their study, we are more informed now than we were before and hence in a better position to look at the issue of critical tolerance with more understanding.

We learned in the first chapter that tolerance does not imply that we should never make critical judgments, be they positive or negative. Religious toleration does not compel us to accept as true everything others do or believe with respect to religious matters. The concept of tolerance, or toleration (I use the terms interchangeably for the most part) presupposes some disagreement.[13] If tolerance demanded that we accept uncritically what others do and believe, it would banish disagreement and replace it with acceptance. However, if I truly respect the views of others as well as my own, and I truly disagree with them, then I need to practice critical tolerance. This does not have to imply an attitude of resignation in which I "put up" with others, even though I prefer not to. None of us want others merely to put up with us; we want others to respect us and take our views seriously. Critical tolerance does that.

Edward Langerak, professor of philosophy at St. Olaf College, Minnesota, presents a thesis in his essay "Disagreement: Appreciating the Dark Side of Tolerance" that captures part of what I mean by critical tolerance. He writes:

> My thesis is that, although we do need a conceptual framework that allows us to respect many of the views we regard as wrong, it also must allow us to judge that these respectable views are disagreeable and even that sometimes actions based on them should not be tolerated.[14]

Tolerance does not demand that we accept all religious views, let alone practices, but it does demand that we make a sincere effort to understand. What is a sincere effort to understand? Philosophers often appeal to the principle of charity, which states that interpreting what people mean should be done in such a way as to maximize the truth of what they claim. In other words, we need to put the best construction we can on what others mean. In popular speech, this means giving someone the "benefit of the doubt." For example, I may think that ancestor worship goes a bit too far, but it would be wrong to represent it as stupid, unreasonable, and even dangerous. I can understand the importance of respect for ancestors and the sense of debt we feel to those who have gone before.

The Blind People and the Elephant

It may be helpful to consider a parable attributed to the Buddha about the blind people and the elephant. His disciples, having heard a number of sectarians arguing about what is true, asked what is to be made of all this quarreling among religious sects. The Buddha replies by telling a story about a king who once faced a similar situation. The king asked his servants to bring to the palace an elephant and all the blind men they could find. He then told the servants to tell these blind men that an elephant is present and allow them to feel it. Some felt its thick legs and said that an elephant is like a pillar. Some felt its tusks and said an elephant is like a plough. Still others felt its body and said that an elephant is like a granary. Soon the blind men were arguing among themselves about what an elephant is like. The king said that the religious sectarians were like the blind men. Each blind man has partial knowledge of the elephant. But because they do not realize their knowledge is partial, they argue. Partial knowledge, the Buddha pointed out, leads to disagreements, bigotry, and even fanaticism.

This parable advises that we should think of all the different religious views as partial views. They all have some value, and they all capture part of the truth. None, however, is completely true. This parable may also imply that just as sight is beyond the capacity of those who are blind, knowing the whole of religious truth (the elephant) may well be beyond the limits of human intellectual abilities. Many religions do claim that ultimate reality is, in the final analysis, a mystery.

This story supports the practice of religious toleration, but it is critical toleration. While each blind man argues about what the elephant is like, it has not occurred to him that his experiences may be limited and not reveal the whole truth. The critical principle implied here is that religions do not contain the complete and final truth, even if they think they do. This principle advises humility about our religious claims to truth and a recognition of human fallibility. It tells us to be suspicious when some religion stakes its claim to the whole truth.

The Elephant Principle

If we resist the temptation of claiming that our religion "sees the elephant," and if we think the whole elephant is beyond the human intellect, how can we hold that all religious views are partial? We can know some view is partial only if we compare it to a whole view. But such comparison is impossible if no one sees the whole elephant. Perhaps we should not read too much into this parable. After all, it is only a story. Even so, the story appears to suggest a paradox. We cannot know that all views are partial unless we know the entire truth. But if we claim to know the entire truth, we violate the claim that all religions teach part of the truth. So what are we to do? We appear to be caught in yet another dilemma.

Perhaps we cannot do much better than to adopt the principle that all religions have a partial grasp on truth. Jainism suggests that we adopt this principle, but just because Jainism or some other religions suggest it is not reason enough to adopt it. It seems that the only justification for adopting the notion that all religions contain some of the truth is pragmatic. This view encourages religious toleration, explains why religions may disagree, and promotes interreligious dialogue. If we talk to others who disagree, if we study their religious beliefs and practices, if we listen with the principle of charity to their myths and legends, we may learn something of real value that we did not know before. We can even learn something from atheism and agnosticism if we listen. We do not have to agree in order to learn.

Valuable social benefits also result from adopting the principle (should we call it the Elephant Principle?) that all religious and antireligious views are partial. Adopting such a principle not only promotes dialogue, but also a religiously tolerant society in which "the religious beliefs, or rejection of religion, of the citizen are not allowed to affect their legal right to live, marry, raise children, worship, pursue careers, own property, make contracts, participate in politics, and engage in all the other activities normally open to citizens in that society."[15]

REVIEW QUESTIONS

1. What are some of the causes of religious conflict?
2. What does secularization mean, and how does it relate to globalization?
3. Write a dialogue among an exclusivist, inclusivist, and a pluralist. In this imagined conversation, make clear the positions of each participant, the reasons for their respective positions, and some of the objections each has to the other's position.
4. Do you think that there are presently no conclusive tests to prove some of the core claims about matters beyond the natural world that religions make? If you disagree, state what you think some of the tests for the truth of core religious beliefs might be. Be as specific as you can.
5. Explain how the concept of a language game may relate to the issue of religious truth.
6. What is the relationship between critical tolerance and the principle of charity?
7. How would you interpret the story of the blind men and the elephant?
8. I argued that there are good reasons to acccept the ideal that all, or nearly all, religions contain partial truth. Do you agree or not? Why?

RESEARCH CASE—BAHA'I

The Baha'i Faith upholds the unity of God, recognizes the unity of His Prophets, and inculcates the principle of the oneness and wholeness of the entire human race. It proclaims the necessity and inevitability of the unification of mankind . . . enjoins upon its followers the primary duty of an unfettered search after truth, condemns all manner of prejudice and superstition, declares the purpose of religion to be the promotion of amity and concord, proclaims its essential harmony with science, and recognizes it as the foremost agency for the pacification and the orderly progress of human society. It unequivocally maintains the principle of equal rights, opportunities, and privileges for men and women, insists on compulsory education, eliminates extremes of poverty and wealth, abolishes the institution of priesthood, prohibits slavery, asceticism, mendicancy, and monasticism, prescribes monogamy, discourages divorce, emphasizes the necessity of strict obedience to one's government, exalts any work performed in the spirit of service to the level of worship, urges either the creation or the selection of an auxiliary international language, and delineates the outlines of those institutions that must establish and perpetuate the general peace of mankind.[16]

Baha'i ("Bah-hi" or more properly "bah-hah'ee") is a young religion, but like so many others it has roots in the older traditional religions, especially Islam. Here we will examine its history as well as its beliefs and practices.

History   The story begins with the founding of an Islamic messianic sect of Shia Islam in Iraq and Iran in 1844. The founder and leader of this movement was called the *Bab* (gate), and his followers were known as the Babis. The Bab was said to be the gate between men and the hidden twelfth Imam. The Bab was to prepare the way for the Imam. The Baha'i faith originated in the 1860s as a faction within Babism.

The first Baha'is were followers of Mirza Husayn Ali Nuri (1817–1892). He was an Iranian Persian born to a noble family in Tehran, and he came to be known as Baha Allah (glory of God). Some of the Babis recognized Ali Nuri as a prophet whose arrival was foretold by the Bab, although other Babis, including Ali Nuri's half-brother Mirza Yahaya, rejected this assessment. Mirza Yahaya became known as Subh-I Asal (dawn of eternity), and he led a faction of the Babis that refused to recognize Ali Nuri as Baha Allah.

Why did some Babis follow Ali Nuri and not his brother? We must backtrack a bit, and pick up the story in the "Black Hole" of Tehran. When a wave of religious persecution against the Babis swept Iran after an attempt on the shah's life in 1852, Ali Nuri was thrown into the Black Hole, a notorious prison in Tehran. There he had several deeply moving and transforming religious experiences. In one he heard a voice telling him that God will use him to bring "life to the hearts of the sages." He described another experience as feeling like a torrent of water was running from the top of his head to his chest. It was, he said, like a powerful river emerging from the earth and cascading from the summit of a lofty mountain.

When Ali Nuri was released from prison in 1853, the government confiscated his property, and he was banished along with his family and others to Baghdad. There he began to have increasing influence in the Babi community of exiles. The Persian consul asked the Ottoman police to remove Ali Nuri to Istanbul. Shortly before he left, some claim he declared himself to be "one whom God shall manifest," which is the figure the Bab said would come after him. He did this in spite of the fact that in late 1847 the Bab himself claimed to be the hidden Imam who would appear in the person of the Mahdi. The new message for Muslims was that Muhammad was not the last prophet. Needless to say, this did not sit well with many Muslims.

After several months in Istanbul, the exiles were sent to Edirne in Turkey, and there Ali Nuri, now called Baha Allah, openly declared his prophetic mission and sent letters to various world leaders, including Pope Pius IX. Further troubles between the government and the Baha'is as well as the Azalis (Babi followers of Nuri's half-brother) led to banishment to Palestine. Baha Allah arrived in Acre in 1868, and to this day Baha'is consider Palestine as the Holy Land.

Baha Allah's most important work is known as the *Kitab al-aqdas* (The Most Holy Book). When he died, he designated his eldest son, Abbas Effendi (1844–1921) to be the infallible interpreter of his books and called him the "center of the covenant." Abbas Effendi received the title Abd al-Baha (servant of the glory) and became the leader of the Baha'is.

Abd al-Baha became a world traveler and persuasive missionary, traveling to Egypt, Europe, and America between 1910 and 1913 preaching the message of Baha'i. These missionary activities were consciously and carefully planned and were designed to market Baha'i as a new world faith, "destined to supersede all established religions." The early converts were largely drawn from Westerners interested in psychic phenomena, theosophy, and what we today would call New Age teachings. After Abd al-Baha died, he was buried next to the Bab in a shrine on Mount Carmel. In his will, he appointed Shoghi Effendi Rabbani (1899–1957) "guardian of the cause of God" and infallible interpreter of his own, plus his father's, writings. Shoghi Effendi was the eldest son of Abd al-Baha's eldest daughter and the author of the statement with which we began this case.

Shoghi Effendi studied at Oxford and assumed a leadership role at the administrative center of Bahaism in Haifa. He married Mary Maxwell, a Canadian, in 1936. He was responsible for creating the main administrative structure of Baha'i as well as modernizing and internationalizing the Baha'i message.

He died in 1957 without designating a successor or leaving children. To make matters worse, he had excommunicated all his living male relatives. Both he and his father, Abd al-Baha, had been explicit about the need for the Guardianship to continue through the "hereditary principle." They predicted that if this did not happen, the Baha'i faith would be "mutilated." These events provoked a crisis within the movement over authority. The way through the crisis was eventually found by utilizing the administrative system of National Assemblies that Shoghi Effendi had organized. In 1963 these National Assemblies elected the Universal House of Justice, which assumed international leadership of the movement. Members are reelected every five years and still administer the Baha'i movement. When the principle of heredity failed, what we might call the "principle of bureaucracy" carried the day. Baha'i had become a well-organized movement, and authority was passed from family descendents to the administrative mechanisms created by Shoghi Effendi.[17]

Baha'i is organized in pyramid fashion. Each local Baha'i community elects a nine-person local assembly. Each country has a National Spiritual

Assembly whose members are elected at a national convention. An international convention elects members to the Universal House of Justice. Even though the history of this movement indicates it has been plagued by factionalism, this administrative structure has proved effective in keeping the Baha'is relatively unified. In addition, severe persecution by other religions has helped to unify the faithful. The largest Baha'i community is still in Iran. Since the 1979 Iranian revolution, the old persecution of the Baha'is by some Muslims has been renewed. In 1983 the revolutionary government of Iran banned all religious activities of the Baha'is.

Beliefs and Practices   Our focus here will be on contemporary beliefs and practices. Baha'i theology has changed in many ways since its early days, as it has become more international and distinguished itself more sharply from Shia Islam. It consciously presents itself as a distinct world religion with roots in the messages of many different religions. The Baha'i Guardianship is placed directly in a long line of prophets extending back to Adam and including Noah, Abraham, Moses, Zoroaster, Buddha, Krishna, Jesus, and Muhammad. The Bab brought the old prophetic cycle (called the Adamic Cycle) to a close and began a new prophetic cycle called the Baha'i Cycle or Cycle of Fulfillment. This cycle is to last for 500,000 years, and then another new cycle will start.

At the heart of this vision is a view of revelation usually called *dispensationalism*. Religious revelation and hence religious truth is relative to different times and cultures. The essence of God is the Logos, and the Logos is one, but there are many manifestations of the Divine Logos. The divine goal is to create ever wider unity among people. Abraham unified a tribe, Moses unified a people, and Muhammad unified a nation. Jesus purified individuals, thereby preparing them for even greater unity. The task of Baha Allah was to unify the entire human race.

Each of the prophets accomplished his tasks, and the religions they spawned are not failures but successful parts of a much larger scheme. In a sense, each of these prophets was the "final" prophet, but they were final in the sense of definitive for their time and place. So Muhammad is truly "the seal of the prophets" as Muslims claim, and Jesus is the final manifestation of God as Christians assert. However, every prophet is the seal or final manifestation of those who preceded them. They are not final in the sense that there will never be any more prophets or any more revelations.

This dispensational view of revelation allows Baha'is to accept all religions as true but none as the complete and final truth. In a sense, this is a version of inclusivism since each prophet includes the truth of the previous prophets. The voyage of the human soul is an infinite voyage toward the infinite unknowable essence of God.

According to Abd al-Baha, there are five types of spirits: animal, vegetable, human, faith, and the Holy Spirit. God gives the spirit of faith, and this spirit, added to the human spirit, makes eternal life possible. Faith is essential to Baha'i spiritual life. Faith, along with hope, is what keeps humanity moving toward God.

The idea of the eternity of the soul means, for Baha'is, the eternal journey toward God. Both a heavenly paradise and an eternal hell are meant symbolically. Heaven symbolizes believers on the right path to God, and hell symbolizes the unbelievers who knowingly reject the option of faith and perform evil deeds. The path to hell leads to total annihilation unless the soul believes the divine message concerning the eventual unification of the whole human race and begins to take that path toward a new society of unity and peace.

The long passage with which this case opened is a condensed summary by Shoghi Effendi of the primary teachings. If you read it carefully, you will find an interesting mixture of progressive views (such as equality of women and men along with the desire to reduce the gap between the poor and rich) and conservative views (strict obedience to one's government). The roots in traditional Islamic teachings are obscured. Since the majority of converts today are from non-Islamic backgrounds, few realize the essentially Islamic vision that informs Baha'i thinking. Both Islam and Baha'i share the idea that history is a process directed by periodic divine interventions whose purpose is to reveal God's will in the form of *Sharia*, a comprehensive legal, moral, and social system designed to shape and regulate human behavior at all levels. The Universal House of Justice is today responsible for developing this new *Sharia* for a unified world and unified human race that Baha'i will usher in.

The Islamic (also Jewish and Christian) ideas of covenant and "rightly guided" leaders are also obscured by Shoghi Effendi's summary of Baha'i teachings. The Mahdi is the rightly guided leader of Islam, and the exclusivism of Shi'ite sectarian movements often stemmed from each sect claiming to have leaders that are rightly guided by God. This is one reason why fights over how the authority is passed on continually plagued traditional Islam as well as the Baha'i movement. A corollary of this idea is the use of excommunication and shunning of those who fail to recognize and obey the correct leadership. The Baha'is faced a crisis in leadership with the death of Shoghi Effendi in part because he had excommunicated male members of his family who rejected his authority. The Universal House of Justice has inherited the mantle of being rightly guided.

Traditional Islamic views have been greatly modified and modernized. Also, the history of the movement has been officially rewritten to incorporate Babism. Abd al-Baha characterized Baha'ism and Babism as opposites. Whereas Babism was militant, exclusivistic, willing to use violence, and generally opposed to modern progressive ideas, Baha'i was pacifistic, inclusivistic, opposed to violence, and receptive to at least some elements of modern thought. Shoghi Effendi conflated Babism and Baha'i, giving the impression that what they taught was largely the same. This served his purposes well because linking a movement closely with past movements often bolsters subsequent religious authority.

Today, as Third World converts along with Western progressive social activists fill the ranks, the admonition to obey one's government without question is sounding more and more outdated. The Universal House of Justice has recognized this, and just as past leaders have incorporated modern elements into a traditionally Islamic framework, so the present leadership is developing more social activist projects, including medical, agricultural, and literacy projects in cooperation with the United Nations.

The ritual practices of Baha'i are not elaborate. They are derived from Islam and center primarily on ritual prayer, annual fasting, and pilgrimage. All of these are *obligatory* for faithful Baha'is. Other practices, such as rites of passage, are *prescriptive.*

Ritual prayer is private, and the believer has three alternatives: to pray once in twenty-four hours, or once at noon, or three times a day. The believer is to face in the direction of the tomb of Baha Allah in Acre. Fasting takes place once a year in the last month of the solar year (March 2–20). Unless ill or pregnant, believers fast from dawn until dusk for nineteen days (there are nineteen solar months divided into nineteen days). The pilgrimage is not well defined. At first, only male Baha'is were to go to the homes of the Bab in Shiraz, Iran, and to Baha Allah in Baghdad. These have become increasingly difficult (the Bab's home was destroyed in 1979), so pilgrimages to "lesser" sites have evolved. These include the tombs of the Bab and Baha Allah outside Haifa and most recently the grave of Shoghi Effendi in London. Fairly elaborate rituals are performed at these pilgrimage sites.

There is no priesthood, nor are there any sacraments. Recently, semi-professionals, both men and women, have been appointed to protect and to spread the faith. While these individuals may be thought of as a kind of clergy, they do not perform ritual functions. Nineteen times a year on the first of each month, Baha'is come together for the Nineteen-Day Feast. These feasts, which are usually held in homes of members, involve the reading of prayers and sacred texts, discussion of administrative issues, and the sharing of food and drink. Like Muslims, Baha'is are forbidden to drink alcohol.

Although there are no mosques, there are seven temples that are showpieces used largely for public gatherings. The temples are presently located in the United States (Wilmette, Illinois, near Chicago), Germany, Australia, India, Panama, Uganda, and Samoa.

The primary rites of passage are naming ceremonies for babies, marriage, and funeral rites. Circumcision is allowed, but not mandatory. Marriages can be arranged and often are in places like Iran. However, they do not have to be. Only the consent of both parties and all living parents is required. Burial is carried out according to a complex set of regulations, and cremation is considered undesirable, but not strictly prohibited.

In origin, Baha'i belongs to the world of nineteenth-century Iran. But at significant stages of its development it has responded positively to many Western ideas and values. Its leaders, since about 1920, have faced squarely the dilemmas of institutionalization and have carefully planned and organized in order to make Baha'i a world religion. Few religions have so self-consciously managed their development. Rational organizations, conscious articulation of goals, and rational planning to achieve them sound more characteristic of businesses than religions. But as Max Weber predicted, everything in the modern world, including religion, becomes increasingly subject to rationalization and the forces of routinization.

QUESTIONS ON THE CASE OF BAHA'I

I have directed you enough. Instead of focusing on the answers to questions I ask, analyze this case on your own. Carefully reread the case, and as you read, jot down any questions or ideas that occur to you. These can be descriptive, interpretive, comparative, explanatory, and evaluative questions. They can be questions requiring more information or parallels to other cases we have already studied. Jot down tentative answers to your questions, and check out your ideas by gathering additional information or rechecking ideas and cases from elsewhere in this book. I have provided a few hints at possible lines of development in the case itself. Use your questions and notes as background information for writing a five- to seven-page paper on the case of Baha'i.

You have two choices for your paper. The first is a comparative study in which you select another religion and compare and contrast it with Baha'i. Create a useful typology for comparison to focus your research and structure your paper. For example, your typology might be drawn from any of the many typologies found in previous chapters or some combination thereof. You may find it more useful to create your own, letting it develop out of the Baha'i case.

The second choice involves creating a hypothesis and testing it against the evidence. In this paper, state a hypothesis, summarize what some of the literature has to say about the answer, explain what sort of evidence (such as statistical, historical, testimonial, primary, secondary, etc.) you gathered, whether the evidence proved or disproved the hypothesis, and areas for further research. A hypothesis is a one-sentence statement that is provisional and is adopted to explain certain facts. In other words, it is a tentative explanation that needs to be tested in light of the evidence. Examples of some possible hypotheses are (1) Baha'i is primarily Islamic in spite of its claim to be a new world religion; (2) Baha'i has failed to satisfactorily solve the dilemma of administrative order; (3) Baha'i's revisionist history with respect to the Bab is intended to create more plausible credentials for the faith. These are some of mine, and you *cannot* use them! Create your own. Have fun.

SUGGESTIONS FOR FURTHER READING

In addition to the material found in the notes, readers may wish to consult the following for more information.

Baha'u'llah. *The Seven Valleys and the Four Valleys.* Translated by Marzieh Gail. Wilmette, IL: Baha'i Publishing Trust, 1945. This is a book of mystical meditations by Baha Allah using Sufi images and symbols.

Coward, Harold. *Pluralism: Challenge to World Religions.* Maryknoll, NY: Orbis Books. 1985. Coward describes the views about religious diversity and conflicting truth claims found in Judaism, Christianity, Islam, Hinduism, and Buddhism. He closes with a helpful chapter on religious diversity and the future of religion.

Dean, Thomas, ed. *Religious Pluralism and Truth: Essays in Cross-Cultural Philosophy of Religion.* Albany, State University of New York Press, 1995. Dean has edited a collection of essays by well-known scholars on four themes relating to problems associated with cross-cultural truth in religion.

Hick, John. *An Interpretation of Religion: Human Responses to the Transcendent.* New Haven, CT: Yale University Press, 1989. In this book Hick develops his version of pluralism in some detail, including the development of an "ethical criterion."

Hick, John, and Askari Hasan, eds. *The Experience of Religious Diversity.* Aldershot, England: Ashgate, 1985. This book is a collection of essays by scholars and representatives of different religious traditions on the issues that relate to questions of truth.

Hutter, Manfred. "Baha'is." In *Encyclopedia of Religion,* vol. 2, edited by Lindsay Jones, 737–740. Farmington Hills, MI: Thompson Gale, 2005. This article provides a brief overview of Baha'i history, practices, beliefs, and organization.

Locke, John. *A Letter Concerning Toleration.* Edited by James Tully. Indianapolis, IN: Hackett Publishing, 1983. In 1689 the British philosopher John Locke published this letter in which he presents the case for what amounts to the separation of church and state. He maintains that the secular magistrate of the state is to act for the good of the whole of society as he sees it and is not to determine that good by appeal to any particular religious doctrine. This idea was revolutionary for Locke's time, but was attractive to a Europe that had recently been nearly destroyed by vicious and prolonged religious warfare.

Maceoin, Denis. "Baha'ism." In *A New Handbook of Living Religions,* edited by John R. Hinnells, 618–643. London: Penguin, 1998. Maceoin provides reliable information on history and beliefs as well as a review of sources and recent scholarship. I am greatly indebted to his discussion.

Neville, Robert Cummings, ed. *Religious Truth: A Volume in the Comparative Religious Ideas Project.* Albany State University of New York Press, 2001. These essays by different scholars explore the idea of truth as found in Chinese, Hindu, Buddhist, Jewish, Christian, and Islamic religions.

Panikkar, R. *The Intrareligious Dialogue.* New York: Paulist Press, 1978. Panikkar focuses on different models of religious dialogue and sets forth some "rules of the game."

He argues that defensiveness and attempts to prove others wrong based on one's own faith do not contribute positively to religious dialogue.

Schuon, Frithjof. *The Transcendent Unity of Religions.* New York: Harper and Row, 1975. Schuon argues that there are two levels to religion: the exoteric, or outer face, and the esoteric, or hidden face. Outwardly religions are different, but inwardly they are all united in a unity that transcends difference and discord.

Smith, Wilfred Cantwell. *Towards a World Theology.* Philadelphia: Westminster Press, 1981. It is time, Smith argues, to go beyond sectarian theology and develop theological ideas in a global context.

———. *Questions of Religious Truth.* New York: Scribner, 1967. Smith argues that religions are not true or false, but better or worse.

INTERNET RESOURCES

www.mideastinfo.com/Religion/bahai.htm   This site provides links to information about Baha'i. Much of it is apologetic, so use with care. This is a good place to find primary sources.

www.pluralism.org   Here you will find information about the Harvard pluralism project, information on different religious groups, and links to other sites.

www.wcc-coe.org/wcc/what/interreligious/index-e.html   This is the Web site for the World Council of Churches, which deals with interreligion relations and dialogue.

Notes

Chapter 1

1. Some of the material in the first two chapters was first published in Gary E. Kessler, *Ways of Being Religious* (Mountain View, CA: Mayfield Publishing, 2000). Reprinted by permission of The McGraw-Hill Companies, Inc.
2. F. Max Müller, *Lectures on the Science of Religion* (New York: Charles Scribners, 1872), 10–11.

Chapter 2

1. William P. Alston, "Religion," in *The Encyclopedia of Philosophy*, ed. Paul Edwards (New York: Macmillan, 1967), 7:141–142.
2. Benson Saler, *Conceptualizing Religion: Immanent Anthropologists, Transcendent Natives, and Unbounded Categories* (New York: Berghahn Books, 2000), 9.
3. Mary Daly, *Beyond God the Father* (Boston: Beacon Press, 1973), 19.
4. Paul Tillich, *Christianity and the Encounter with World Religions* (New York: Columbia University Press, 1963), 4.
5. Melford E. Spiro, "Religion: Problems of Definition and Explanation," in *Anthropological Approaches to the Study of Religion*, ed. Michael Banton (London: Tavistock, 1966), 96.
6. See *http://www.law.cornell.edu/constitution/constitution.billofrights.html*. Retrieved March 24, 2007.
7. Bill Bright, "Humanism: The Grand Delusion," *Worldwide Challenge* 8 (March 1981): 6
8. Tim LaHaye, *The Battle for the Family* (Old Tappan, NJ: Fleming H. Revell Company, 1982), 36.
9. Quoted in Terry Eastland, ed. *Religious Liberty in the Supreme Court* (Washington, DC: Ethics and Public Policy Center, 1993), 165.
10. The 1963 case was prompted by a Pennsylvania law that required all public schools in the Commonwealth to begin the day with a Bible reading of at least ten verses. This was usually followed by a recitation of the Lord's Prayer.
11. See *http://www.cnn.com/2003/LAW/08/21/ten.commandments/index.html*. Retrieved March 24, 2007.
12. Clifford Geertz, "Religion as a Cultural System," in *Anthropological Approaches to the Study of Religion*, ed. Michael Banton (London: Tavistock, 1966).
13. Gary Kessler, *Philosophy of Religion: Toward a Global Perspective* (Belmont, CA: Wadsworth Publishing, 1999), 3.
14. Donald S. Lopez, Jr., ed., *Buddhist Hermeneutics* (Honolulu: University of Hawaii Press, 1988), 8.
15. I am indebted to James Ross of the Sociology Department at California State University for material used in this section.
16. Quoted in Lawrence S. Cunningham, et al., *The Sacred Quest: An Invitation to the Study of Religion* (Englewood Cliffs, NJ: Prentice Hall, 1995), 13. Also see James G. Frazer, *The Golden Bough* (London: Macmillan, 1990), 50.

Chapter 3

1. Translation by Wing-tsit Chan, *A Source Book of Chinese Philosophy* (Princeton: Princeton University Press, 1963, 1991), 139.
2. Isabelle Robinet, *Taoism: Growth of a Religion*, trans. Phyllis Brooks (Stanford, CA: Stanford University Press, 1997), 26.
3. It is customary to capitalize the word *God* when speaking of monotheistic conceptions of the divine and not to do so when referring to gods and goddesses. However, some think this practice conceals a prejudice and argue that, in fairness to others, the word should not be capitalized or capitalized all the time. This issue is complicated by the fact that *God* can function as a proper name in English. For the most part I have opted to follow the custom of capitalizing God when it refers to one supreme deity and to use lowercase when referring to more than one divine being.
4. Anselm, *Proslogion*, trans. Robert Van Voorst, in *Readings in Christianity*, 2nd ed. (Belmont, CA: Wadsworth, 2001).
5. *The Bhagavad-Gita: Krishna's Counsel in Time of War*, trans. Barbara Stoler Miller (New York: Bantam Books, 1986), 100.
6. J. R. Walker, *The Sun Dance and Other Ceremonies of the Oglala Division of the Teton Dakota* (American Museum of Natural History, Anthropological Papers, vol. XVI, part II, 1917), 152–153.
7. *Authorized Daily Prayer Book*, trans. S. Singer, 9th American ed. (New York: Hebrew Publishing Company, 1912), 89.
8. *The Book of Common Prayer* (London, 1855).
9. *Upanishads*, trans. Patrick Olivelle (Oxford: Oxford University Press, 1996), 153.
10. Ludwig Feuerbach, *The Essence of Christianity*, trans. George Eliot. (Gloucester, MA: Peter Smith Publishers, 1854).
11. Peter L. Berger, *The Sacred Canopy: Elements of a Sociological Theory of Religion* (Garden City, NY: Doubleday & Company, Inc., 1967), 28.
12. Bruce Bryant Friedland, "Ganesha Ritual a Milestone for Hindus," *Jacksonville (FL) Times-Union*, September 9, 1999.
13. Robert L. Brown, ed., *Ganesh: Studies of an Asian God* (Albany: State University of New York Press, 1991), 3.

Chapter 4

1. From Barbara C. Sproul, *Primal Myths: Creating the World* (San Francisco: Harper and Row, 1979), 92.
2. There are two versions of the giving of the commandments at Sinai, and the golden calf episode is mentioned in the second version, which starts at Exodus 24:9. It is instructive to compare Exodus 19–24:8 (the first version) with Exodus 24:9 and following.
3. Mircea Eliade, *Myth and Reality*, trans. Willard R. Trask (New York: Harper and Row, 1963), 5–6.
4. *Averroes on the Harmony of Religion and Philosophy*, trans. G. F. Hourani (London: Luzac Oriental, 1961).
5. Michael Ruse, "Introduction," in *Religion and Science*, Bertrand Russell (New York: Oxford University Press, 1997).
6. *The Rig Veda: An Anthology*, trans. Wendy Doniger O'Flaherty (London: Penguin Books, 1981), 31.
7. *The Laws of Manu*, trans. Wendy Doniger with Brian Smith (London: Penguin Books, 1991), 13.
8. Ibid., 197.
9. Bruce Lincoln, *Myth, Cosmos, and Society: Indo-European Themes of Creation and Destruction* (Cambridge: Harvard University Press, 1986), 164.

Chapter 5

1. Burton Watson, trans., *Hsün Tzu: Basic Writings* (New York: Columbia University Press, 1963), 94–95.
2. Evan M. Zuesse, "Ritual," in *The Encyclopedia of Religion*, ed. Mircea Eliade (New York: Macmillan Publishing Company, 1987), 12:405. My definition is a modified form of Zuesse's definition.
3. Theodore Gaster, *Thespis: Ritual, Myth, and Drama in the Ancient Near East*, 2nd rev. ed. (New York: Gordian Press, 1975), 26.
4. Henri Frankfort, *Kingship and the Gods: A Study of Ancient Near Eastern Religion as the Integration of Society and Nature* (Chicago: University of Chicago Press, 1948/1978), 319.
5. J. B. Pritchard, ed., *Ancient Near Eastern Texts Relating to the Old Testament*, trans. S. Sachs, 2nd ed. (Princeton: Princeton University Press, 1955), 334.
6. Jonathan Z. Smith, *Imagining Religion: From Babylon to Jonestown* (Chicago: University of Chicago Press, 1982), 93.
7. The Rev. Richard E. Power, *Our Mass: A Manual for the Dialogue Mass* (Collegeville, MN: St. John's Abbey, 1956), 44–45.
8. For more information on *Black Elk Speaks*, see "Suggestions for Further Reading." Black Elk has sparked considerable controversy in the scholarly world. He participated in the Roman Catholic Church until his death and made a conscious connection between the seven major rituals of the Lakota Sioux and the seven sacraments of the Church. Some have argued that he was a genuine Christian who was only culturally attached to the Lakota religious tradition; others argue the reverse. For a careful discussion of the issues, see William A. Young, *Quest for Harmony: Native American Spiritual Traditions* (New York: Seven Bridges Press, 2002), 209ff.
9. Joseph Epes Brown, recorder and ed., *The Sacred Pipe: Black Elk's Account of the Seven Rites of the Oglala Sioux* (Norman: University of Oklahoma Press, 1953, 1989), xix. The quotes that follow are taken from this source starting with page 116.
10. Bruce Lincoln, *Emerging from the Chrysalis: Studies in Rituals of Women's Initiation* (Cambridge: Harvard University Press, 1981), 106.
11. Ibid., 108.
12. Nahum N. Glatzer, ed., *The Passover Haggadah* (New York: Schocken Books, 1953), 25. The quotes relating to the seder that follow are all taken from this source.
13. E. M. Broner, "Honor and Ceremony in Women's Rituals," in *The Politics of Women's Spirituality: Essays on the Rise of Spiritual Power Within the Feminist Movement*, ed. Charlene Spretnak (Garden City, NY: Doubleday Anchor, 1982), 237–238. Miriam, the sister of Moses, helped lead the Hebrews out of exile. She was a prophetess in her own right and is the first woman in the Bible to be given that title.

Chapter 6

1. This quote and most of the other information about Kilimanjaro come from Edwin Bernbaum's beautiful book, *Sacred Mountains of the World*. See the list of suggested readings for more information.
2. Jonathan Z. Smith, *To Take Place: Toward Theory in Ritual* (Chicago: University of Chicago Press, 1987), 11. *Tjurunga* is a name for a wide variety of powerful sacred objects. Tjilapa is the ancestor of the cat-people as well as the name for a band of Aranda Aborigines who trace their descent to Tjilapa.
3. David Chidester and Edward T. Linenthal, eds., *American Sacred Space* (Bloomington: Indiana University Press, 1995), 1.
4. Alan Watts, *Myth and Ritual in Christianity* (Boston: Beacon Press, 1969), 86. Watts's book is an informative study of Christian symbolism covering art, architecture, the church year, and much more. His approach is heavily influenced by Carl Jung's theory of archetypes.

Chapter 7

1. Today this site is marked by the Dome of the Rock located on top of the ruins of the Jewish Temple.
2. This and the following quotes come from *The Translation of the Meanings of Sahih al-Bukhari*, trans. Muhammad Muhsin Khan (Chicago: Kazi Publications, 1979), 5:144.
3. I rely here on the work of Glock and Stark. See "Suggestions for Further Readings" at the end of the chapter.
4. *The Life of the Buddha as It Appears in the Pali Canon, the Oldest Authentic Record*, trans. Nanamoli (Kandy: Buddhist Publication Society, 1972), 21.
5. *Buddhist Scriptures*, trans. Edward Conze (Middlesex, England: Penguin Books, 1959), 49.
6. Ibid., 50–51.
7. Friedrich Schleiermacher, *The Christian Faith*, trans. H. R. Mackintosh and J. S. Stewart. 2nd ed. (Edinburgh: T&T Clark, 1928), 4.
8. Not all students of Schleiermacher would agree with Otto's interpretation. But I must pass over the ins and outs of this debate here. Suffice it to say, scholars dispute Otto's "subjectivistic" interpretation of Schleiermacher.
9. Again I am relying on Glock and Stark's typology.
10. The following classification of yogas derives from Huston Smith's attempt to simplify the vast diversity of yoga practices into four main types. See his *The Religions of Man* (New York: Harper and Row, 1958), 32ff.
11. For a selection from the writings of Freud and Jung see Chapter 8 of Carl Olson's *Theory and Method in the Study of Religion: A Selection of Critical Readings* (Belmont, CA: Wadsworth/Thomson Learning, 2003).
12. Kieran Kavanaugh and Otilio Rodríguez, eds., "Introduction," in *The Interior Castle*, Teresa of Avila (New York: Paulist Press, 1979), 2.
13. Quoted in Alison Weber, *Teresa of Avila and the Rhetoric of Femininity* (Princeton, NJ: Princeton University Press, 1990), 160.
14. Ibid.
15. *The Book of Her Life, Spiritual Testimonies. Soliloquies*, trans. Kieran Kavanaugh and Otilio Rodríquez. In *The Collected Works of St. Teresa of Avila*, vol. 1 (Washington, DC: Institutes of Carmelite Studies, 1976), *Life*, Chap. 27, no. 4.
16. Ibid., *Spiritual Testimonies*, 14.
17. Weber, *Teresa of Avila*, 11.
18. Ibid., 164–165.
19. Ibid., 165.

Chapter 8

1. Elie Wiesel, *Night*, trans. Stella Rodway (New York: Farrar, Straus, and Giroux, 1960), 40.
2. Ibid., 42.
3. See E. E. Evans-Pritchard, *Witchcraft, Oracles, and Magic Among the Azande* (Oxford: Oxford University Press, 1937).
4. *Upanishads*, trans. Patrick Olivelle (Oxford: Oxford University Press, 1998), 142.
5. William Theodore de Bary, ed., *The Buddhist Tradition in India, China and Japan* (New York: Vintage Books, 1972), 25.
6. Ibid.
7. R. A. Nicholson, ed. *Selected Poems from the Divant Shamsi Tabriz* (Cambridge: Cambridge University Press, 1898/1977), 125.

8. David Hume, *Dialogues Concerning Natural Religion* (Oxford: Oxford University Press, 1935), 244.

9. J. L. Mackie, "Evil and Omnipotence," in *Philosophy of Religion: Toward a Global Perspective*, ed. Gary E. Kessler (Belmont, CA: Wadsworth Publishing, 1999), 226.

10. William Rowe, "The Problem of Evil and Some Varieties of Atheism," in Kessler, 240.

11. Alfred North Whitehead, the "father" of process philosophy would disagree with the idea of mutual transference of energy, but Charles Hartshorne, a student of Whitehead, endorses mutual transference.

12. Schubert Ogden, "Evil and Belief in God: The Distinctive Relevance of a 'Process Theology'," *The Perkins Journal* (Summer 1978): 33.

13. Mary Baker Eddy, *Science and Health with Key to the Scriptures* (Boston: The First Church of Christ, Scientist), 472–473.

14. Elie Wiesel, *The Trial of God* (New York: Random House, 1979), 157.

Chapter 9

1. See the entry "Morality and Religion" in *The HarperCollins Dictionary of Religion*, ed. Jonathan Z. Smith (San Francisco: HarperSanFrancisco, 1995), 729.

2. "Acquisition," in *The Word of Islam*, ed. John Alden Williams (Austin, TX: University of Texas Press, 1994), 153.

3. *The Analects*, trans. D. C. Lau (London: Penguin Books, 1979), 12.

4. Tu Wei-ming, *Centrality and Commonality: An Essay on Confucian Religiousness* (Albany: State University of New York Press, 1989), 116.

5. Aquinas himself permitted the aborting of embryos and fetuses up to the time of "quickening" (the time when the mother can feel the fetus move). He did this because he thought the function of the soul was to make matter alive, and hence the soul did not enter the fetus until it exhibited movement. Today the Roman Catholic Church has taken a more radical position, declaring that human life begins at conception.

6. Clyde L. Manschreck, ed., *A History of Christianity* (Englewood Cliffs, NJ: Prentice Hall, 1965), 376.

7. Ronald M. Green, *Religion and Moral Reason* (New York: Oxford University Press, 1988), 3.

8. Soren Kierkegaard, *Fear and Trembling* and *The Sickness unto Death*, trans. Walter Lowrie (Garden City, NY: Doubleday & Company, 1954).

9. *Jaina Sutras*, trans. H. Jacobi, Part I (Oxford: Clarendon Press, 1884), 251.

10. Ibid., 263–264.

11. Ibid., 46.

12. "The Jain Tradition," in *World Religions: Eastern Traditions*, ed. Willard G. Oxtoby (Oxford: Oxford University Press, 1996), 172.

Chapter 10

1. Grant Wardlaw, "Justifications and Means: The Moral Dimension of State-Sponsored Terrorism," in *The Morality of Terrorism: Religious and Secular Justifications*, ed. David C. Rapoport and Yonah Alexander, 2nd ed. (New York: Columbia University Press, 1989), 376–377.

2. Bruce Lawrence, ed., *Messages to the World: The Statements of Osama bin Laden*, trans. James Howarth (London: Verso, 2005), 61.

3. Quoted in Peter L. Bergen, *Holy War Inc.: Inside the Secret World of Osama bin Laden* (New York: Free Press, 2002), 53.

4. A transcript of the complete broadcast can be found in Appendix D of Bruce Lincoln's *Holy Terrors: Thinking about Religion after September 11* (Chicago: University of Chicago Press, 2003), 104–107.

5. Quoted in footnote 22 by Bruce Lawrence in *Messages to the World*, 113.

6. Ibid., 105.

7. Ibid., 121.

8. *The London Observer* published an English version of this letter on November 24, 2002.

9. Lawrence, *Messages to the World*, 162.

10. Ibid., 163.

11. Ibid., 164.

12. Ibid., 165.

13. Ibid., 166.

14. Ibid., 166

15. Ibid., 170.

16. Ibid., 172.

17. Ibid., 172.

18. Kathleen Sullivan, "Religion and Liberal Democracy," *University of Chicago Law Review* 59, (1992), 7.

19. Richard John Neuhaus, *The Naked Public Square* (Grand Rapids: Wm. B. Eerdmans Publishing Co., 1984), vii.

20. Phillip E. Hammond, *With Liberty for All: Freedom of Religion in the United States* (Louisville, KY: Westminster John Knox Press, 1998), 42.

21. Ibid., 50–54. Hammond here summarizes several of the relevant cases.

22. Noah Feldman, *Divided by God: America's Church–State Problem—And What We Should Do about It*, (New York: Farrar, Straus and Giroux, 2005), 204.

23. Ibid., 3–4.

24. *The HarperCollins Dictionary of Religion*, ed. Jonathan Z. Smith (New York: HarperCollins, 1995), 270–271.

25. Emile Durkheim, *The Elementary Forms of Religious Life*, trans. Karen E. Fields (New York: Free Press, 1995 [1912]), 425.

26. For a history of the Pledge see http://history.vineyard.net/pledge.htm. The original author, Francis Bellamy (1855–1931) wanted to use the word *equality* in the Pledge, but he also wanted it recited in public schools and knew some educators opposed equality for women and African Americans so that word was never included.

27. See http://www.ustreas.gov/education/fact-sheets/currency/in-god-we-trust.shtml for a history of this motto.

28. Hammond, *With Liberty for All*, 109.

29. Michelle Goldberg, *Kingdom Coming: The Rise of Christian Nationalism* (New York: W. W. Norton and Company, 2007), 9.

30. Chris Hedges, *American Fascists: The Christian Right and the War on America* (New York: Free Press, 2006), 11.

31. George Grant, *The Changing of the Guard: Biblical Principles for Political Action* (Fort Worth: Dominion Press, 1987), 50–51.

32. Rousas John Rushdoony, *Law and Society: Volume II of the Institutes of Biblical Law* (Vallecito, CA: Ross House of Books, 1986), 689.

33. D. James Kennedy, *Character and Destiny: A Nation in Search of Its Soul* (Grand Rapids: Zondervan, 1995), 59.

34. Rushdoony, *The Institutes of Biblical Law* (Dallas: Craig Press, 1973), 4, 5, 10.

35. Ibid., 326.

36. Quoted in Goldberg, *Kingdom Coming*, 14.

37. Quoted in Paul Krugman, "For God's Sake," *New York Times*, April 13, 2007.

38. Pat Robertson, *The New World Order* (Dallas: Word Publishing, 1991), 261ff.

39. Gary DeMar, *God and Government: A Biblical and Historical Study,* Vol. III (Midland, TX: Primero Resources, 1989), 129.

40. Frances FitzGerald, "The Evangelical Surprise," *The New York Review of Books,* Vol. LIV, April 26, 2007, 33.

41. Desmond Tutu, *No Future Without Forgiveness* (New York: Doubleday, 1999), 35.

42. Ibid., 118.

43. Ibid., 49–50.

44. Ibid., 237.

45. Ibid., 273.

46. Ibid., 282.

Chapter 11

1. Robert L. Johnstone, *Religion in Society: A Sociology of Religion,* 6th ed. (Upper Saddle River, NJ: Prentice Hall, 2001), 35.

2. Ibid., 37–42.

3. In addition to the information found in John Power's book *Introduction to Tibetan Buddhism* (see "Suggestions for Further Reading"), I am indebted to the discussion found in the introduction to *Religions of Tibet in Practice,* ed. Donald S. Lopez, Jr. (Princeton, NJ: Princeton University Press, 1997), 3–36.

4. This is part of an extract taken from the transcript of a tape of the final forty-three minutes at Jonestown obtained by the *New York Times* from the International Home Video Club, Inc., New York City, and published in the *New York Times,* 15 March 1979. This extract can be found in Appendix 2 of Jonathan Z. Smith, *Imagining Religion: From Babylon to Jonestown* (Chicago: University of Chicago Press, 1982), 134.

5. Rebecca Moore, *Sympathetic History of Jonestown: The Moore Family Involvement in Peoples Temple* (Lewiston, NY: Edwin Mellen Press, 1985), 155.

6. Quoted in Jonathan Z. Smith, "The Devil in Mr. Jones," in *Imagining Religion: From Babylon to Jonestown* (Chicago: The University of Chicago Press, 1982), 107. I am indebted to Smith's discussion for much of the background information on Jim Jones and Jonestown.

7. Moore, *Sympathetic History of Jonestown,* 229.

8. See Smith, *Imagining Religion,* 107.

9. Moore, *Sympathetic History of Jonestown,* 288.

10. Catherine Wessinger, *How the Millennium Comes Violently: From Jonestown to Heaven's Gate* (New York: Seven Bridges Press, 2000), 41.

11. John Hall, *Gone from the Promised Land: Jonestown in American Cultural History* (New Brunswick, NJ: Transaction Books, 1987), 254.

12. Quoted in Wessinger, *How the Millennium Comes Violently,* 51–52.

13. Smith, *Imagining Religion,* 133.

14. Quoted in the introduction by Anne Fremantle to *The Grand Inquisitor* (New York: Frederick Ungar Publishing, 1978), viii.

15. *The Grand Inquisitor,* 12, 13.

16. Thomas O'Dea, *The Sociology of Religion* (Englewood Cliffs, NJ: Prentice Hall, 1966), 90ff.

17. The last verse is controversial. I have followed the translation of the RSV. Others suggest translations like "she will be saved through the birth of the Child [Jesus]" and "she will be brought safely through childbirth."

18. Nancy Schuster Barnes, "Buddhism," in *Women in World Religions,* ed. Arvind Sharma (Albany: State University of New York Press, 1987), 105.

19. Susan Sered, *Priestess, Mother, Sacred Sister* (New York: Oxford University Press, 1994). For a more complete discussion of Sered's study, see Johnstone, *Religion in Society,* 248–250.

20. Ibid., 43.
21. Ibid., 8.
22. *Kojiki* [Records of Ancient Material], trans. Joseph M. Kitagawa, Chap. 17, in *The Great Asian Religions: An Anthology*, ed. Wing-Tsit Chan, et. al. (New York: Macmillan, 1969), 232–233.
23. Helen Hardacre, *Shinto and the State, 1868–1988* (Princeton, NJ: Princeton University Press, 1989), 5.
24. Ibid., 161.

Chapter 12

1. William James, *The Varieties of Religious Experience: A Study in Human Nature* (New York: Simon and Schuster, 1997), 393.
2. *Hymns of Guru Nanak* (New Delhi: Orient Longmans, 1969), 25.
3. From the *Khalsa Consensus Translation*, Dr. Sant Singh Khalas (www.sikhs.org/english/frame.html), 176.
4. Quoted in W. Owen Cole, "Sikhism," in *A New Handbook of Living Religions*, ed. John R. Hinnels (Cambridge: Blackwell, 1997), 331–332.
5. "Salvation," in *The HarperCollins Dictionary of Religion*, ed. Jonathan Z. Smith (San Francisco: HarperCollins, 1995), 954.
6. See D. G. Dawe's discussion of "Salvation," in *The Perennial Dictionary of World Religions*, ed. Keith Crim (San Fransico: Harper and Row, 1989), 643–646.
7. From *The Buddhist Traditions in India, China and Japan*, ed. Wm. Theodore de Bary (New York: Random House, 1969), 21.
8. From *Buddhist Texts Through the Ages*, ed. Edward Conze (New York: Harper and Row, 1954), 202–203.
9. D. T. Suzuki, *Zen Buddhism* (New York: Doubleday, 1956), 84.
10. D. T. Suzuki, *Introduction to Zen Buddhism* (London: Rider, 1949), 97.
11. Sallie King, "Awakening Stories of Zen Buddhist Women," in *Buddhism in Practice*, ed. Donald S. Lopez, Jr. (Princeton, NJ: Princeton University Press, 1995), 520–521.

Chapter 13

1. See James C. Livingston, *Anatomy of the Sacred: An Introduction to Religion*, 3rd ed. (Upper Saddle River, NJ: Prentice Hall, 1998), 420–421.
2. Ibid., 420.
3. Diane Eck, "A New Geo-Religious Reality." Paper presented at the World Conference on Religion and Peace, Sixth World Assembly, Riva del Garda, Italy, November, 1994. Quoted in Mary Pat Fisher, *Religion in the Twenty-First Century* (Upper Saddle River, NJ: Prentice Hall, 1999), 14. Note that there are two different uses of *pluralism* relevant to our topic. One is the descriptive use, which refers to religious diversity or variety. It is in that sense that pluralism is used in Eck's pluralism project. Another use of pluralism is normative. In this sense it refers to a particular theory about the relationship among religions with respect the issue of truth. In order to avoid confusion, I have used the word *diversity* instead of *pluralism* wherever possible to indicate the descriptive sense, and I have restricted the word *pluralism* to its normative sense.
4. M. Wiles, "Christianity Without Incarnation?" in *The Myth of God Incarnate*, ed. John Hick (Philadelphia: Westminster Press, 1977), 1.
5. John Hick, "Religious Pluralism," in *A Companion to Philosophy of Religion*, ed. Philip L. Quinn and Charles Taliaferro (Cambridge, MA: Blackwell Publishers, 1997), 610.
6. Alvin Plantinga, "A Defense of Religious Exclusivism," in *Philosophy of Religion: An Anthology*, 3rd ed., ed. Louis P. Pojman (Belmont, CA: Wadsworth Publishing, 1998), 517–530.

7. Ibid., 530.

8. Karl Rahner, "Christianity and the Non-Christian Religions" in *Theological Investigations* (New York: Seabury Press, 1996–1979), 5:124.

9. Hick, "Religious Pluralism," 612.

10. Ibid., 612.

11. Quoted in Arvind Sharma, *The Philosophy of Religion and Advaita Vedanta: A Comparative Study in Religion and Reason* (University Park: Pennsylvania State University Press, 1995), 224.

12. Radhakrishnan, *Eastern Religions and Western Thought*, (Oxford: Oxford University Press, 1989), 323.

13. Nick Fotion and Gerald Elfstrom argue in their book *Toleration* (Tuscaloosa, AL: University of Alabama Press, 1992) that we should reserve the use of *tolerance* to name an accepting attitude, and we should use *toleration* to indicate enduring the disagreeable. They wish to do this because one of the connotations of tolerance is a kind of begrudging endurance that others find offensive. It connotes an attitude something like, "I may not like your religion, but I will put up with it if I have to." While the authors are right about disassociating tolerance from begrudging endurance, their proposal obscures the important role that genuine disagreement plays.

14. Edward Langarek, "Disagreement," in *Philosophy, Religion, and the Question of Intolerance,* eds. Mehdi Amin Razavi and David Ambuel (Albany: State University of New York Press, 1997), 112.

15. J. B. Schneewind, "Bayle, Locke, and the Concept of Toleration," in Razavi and Ambuel, 4.

16. Shoghi Effendi, *Guidance for Today and Tomorrow* (Wilmette, IL: Baha'i Publishing Trust, 1953), 3–4.

17. There was some opposition to the transfer of authority from family to administrative mechanisms. Mason Remey, a Baha'i residing in New Mexico, proclaimed himself the heir to the Guardianship. In 1961 he designated Joel B. Marangella as his successor. Remey's group considers itself the true representatives of the Baha'i tradition, calling itself Orthodox Baha'i. They refuse to recognize the Universal House of Justice.

Glossary

agnosticism: The belief that knowledge of God's existence is not possible.

ahimsa: This idea is central to Jain ethics and is usually translated as "nonviolence." It literally means desiring to do no harm.

animism: The belief that all or most things are animated by a soul or spirit.

anomic: A word derived from the French *anomie* (Greek *anomia*) meaning "lawlessness." Emile Durkheim introduced the term to name a condition of a society or an individual when normal order (*nomos*) is dissolving or even absent. Such a condition often produces anxiety, confusion, and even chaos. *See* **nomos.**

anthropology of religion: A social scientific approach to the study of religion that uses standard anthropological methods to understand how religion is related to culture.

anthropomorphic: This word literally means "in human form" and refers to the tendency of many religions to picture gods in human form.

apocalyptic: The Greek word *apocalypse*, from which this is derived, means "revelation" and has come to refer in general to a type of literature or religious movement that alleges to reveal future events related to the fulfillment of religious hopes and dreams.

apologetics: The activity of offering a defense of one's religion.

archetypes: The word means "primary model" or "type," and Carl Jung uses it to name what he thinks are universal psychological patterns encoded in the collective unconscious of the human race.

ascetic: A person who lives an austere life of self-denial, often involving physical deprivations such as fasting, in order to intensify devotion or enhance spirituality by becoming independent of physical needs and desires.

atheism: The view that God does not exist as a being external to human thought.

axis mundi: A mythological axis of the world often represented by a pole, tree, or mountain connecting the earth with the sky and the underworld.

bodhisattva: A title for any person who has taken a vow to become enlightened (a buddha) and lives a life of compassion intent on gaining enlightenment for himself/herself and all others as well.

canon: Literally meaning "rule" or "standard" and is used as a general term for any authoritative set of sacred or secular writings.

civil religion: A set of beliefs and rituals that unite the diverse elements of a society into a unifying ideology.

cluster definition: A type of definition that lists a set of traits or characteristics of the idea being defined without claiming that any one trait or a finite set of traits is the essence (necessary and sufficient characteristics). *See* **functional definition** and **substantive definition.**

communitas: The social solidarity that develops during the liminal or transitional phase of a rite of passage.

comparison: A fair and balanced account of the similarities and differences among examples of phenomena.

cosmogonic myths: Sacred stories about the beginning of the universe.

cosmological: In relation to the functions of myths, this term refers to sacred narratives that render a picture of the universe.

cosmological myths: Sacred stories about the order and structure of the universe.

critical tolerance: An attitude that endorses freedom of religion but does not necessarily approve of every religious belief and practice.

Dao (Tao): This term is often translated as "the Way" and refers, in the Chinese religion of Daoism, to the ultimate truth, the source of all reality, and the Way of Nature.

deism: The belief that God created the universe but does not intervene in its operation.

demons: Superhuman beings midway between humans and gods, often described as evil and harmful, but also can be good and helpful.

description: Stating the facts of a case as objectively as possible by classifying some *x* under a category according to some property (*p*) of *x*.

dharma: In Hinduism, this refers to the sacred law which specifies caste duties. In Buddhism, it refers to the teachings of the Buddha.

Dreamtime: According to Australian Aborigines, a sacred time when everything that exists today was created.

duty ethics (deontological ethics): An ethical system based on the notions of duty, obligation, and obedience to rules.

ecstatic: Those experiences in which individuals enter altered states of consciousness when they may be overwhelmed by intense feelings of joy, raptures, and trance states.

eightfold path: The Buddhist middle way leading to nirvana, consisting of right understanding, right thought, right speech, right action, right occupation, right effort, right mindfulness, and right concentration.

emissary prophets: People who believe they have been given a divine message along with the assignment of getting others to believe that message. *See* **exemplary prophets.**

eschatological myths: Sacred stories about the end of history or the destruction of the world.

eschatology: Refers to ideas about "last things," or the end of time. This end may be thought of as otherworldly or this worldly and is often associated with judgment, punishment, and reward.

essence: That quality or qualities that make something what it is and not something else. These characteristics are both necessary and sufficient.

etiological myths: Sacred stories explaining why something came to be or got the way it is now.

evaluation: Second-order evaluation involves judgments about the value of some description, interpretation, or explanation. First-order evaluation refers to the formation of value judgments about religious claims and events.

exclusivism: The idea that one religion is true both in the sense of teaching the truth about ultimate reality and in the sense of providing the only valid way to salvation.

exemplary prophets: People who have significant religious experiences and see their mission as teaching others how to have those experiences for themselves. *See* **emissary prophets.**

explanation: There are different kinds: interpretations that deepen our understanding, a statement of cause that makes sense of the occurrence of some event or idea given some theory, an account of the structure/function of some phenomenon.

first-order activity: Engagement in some primary activity like practicing a religion or speaking a language. *See* **second-order activity.**

five dilemmas of institutionalization: A concept developed by the sociologist Thomas O'Dea that concerns the dilemmas religious organizations must face and try to solve as they become more complex. The five dilemmas are mixed motivation, symbolic, administrative order, delimitation, and power.

Five Pillars of Islam: The core of Muslim faith and practice consisting of witnessing that there is no God but Allah and that Muhammad is his Prophet, formal prayer (*salat*), giving to the poor, fasting during Ramadan, and pilgrimage to Mecca.

Four Noble Truths: The core of Buddhist teaching consisting of the claims that there is suffering, its cause is desire, there is release from suffering, and practicing the eightfold path will lead to release.

functional definition: A type of essential definition that focuses on what something does. *See* **substantive definition.**

functionalist theory, A theory about myth in particular and religion in general that claims their meaning is equivalent to their function or what they accomplish.

henotheism: The belief that many gods may exist, but people should worship only the one that shows special concern for them and their interests.

hermeneutics: A method for interpreting information, particularly textual information, that pays close attention to the context and structure of a text.

hierophanic: This term is derived from *hierophany*—literally a manifestation or revelation of the sacred.

history of religions: Developmental and comparative studies using historical and linguistic techniques to understand religions.

iconoclastic: Literally refers to "breaking images," but in religious studies usually refers to movements opposed to the use of images in worship.

ideological rituals: Rituals that seek social control by changing the mood, behavior, sentiments, motivations, and values of people.

ideology: Any set of doctrines or beliefs that form the basis of a political, economic, or religious system.

imam: A title for a prayer leader, a leader of the Islamic community, and, in Shia Islam, a title for the twelve great leaders of Islam the last of whom is in hiding or occultation, but will return at the end of history.

inclusivism: A position that does not deny the idea of truth in all religions, but still asserts the superiority of one religion as containing the most complete truth that includes or fulfills the truth found in other religions.

insider's viewpoint: The view of a religious participant who seeks understanding in order to increase faith. *See* **outsider's viewpoint.**

interpretation: An account of what something means involving seeing x as a sign of y.

jihad: This word means "struggle" in Arabic. It can refer to spiritual or inner struggle to conform our wills to God (Greater Jihad) or to armed struggle in the defense of Islam (Lesser Jihad).

karma: The word means "action" and often refers to the law of action—namely, that every action produces a result that ultimately determines a person's rebirth.

koan meditation: A technique used in the Rinzai school of Zen that involves a master giving a short paradoxical question to a student in order to shock the student out of dualistic modes of thought.

latent functions: In contrast to manifest functions, latent refers to the hidden and often unintended functions of a myth or ritual action. *See* **manifest functions.**

manifest functions: In contrast to latent, this term refers to the intended and obvious function of a sacred story or ritual. *See* **latent functions.**

mantra: Sacred sounds chanted for purposes of meditation and prayer.

Middle Way: This refers to the Buddhist eightfold path in particular and is sometimes used to refer to the Buddhist religion as a whole.

millenarianism: The term was first used to refer to the thousand-year reign of Christ mentioned in the Book of Revelation, but has been generalized by scholars to refer to any movement that expects a utopian age.

monism: The claim that reality is ultimately one, not two (dual) or many (plural).

monotheism: The belief that there is only one God.

morality: A set of norms or rules designed to regulate and govern the conduct of humans with one another, with other living creatures, and with their environment.

mysticism: This word is used in a wide variety of ways to refer to movements, religions, or ideas deriving from or centering on mystical experiences. There is no widespread agreement about how best to define mystical experiences, but descriptions range all the way from union with God to deep insight into the nature of reality.

myth: Sacred story.

myth and ritual theory: A school of scholarly interpretation that claims there is a necessary link between myth and ritual such that we cannot understand one without understanding the other.

nirvana: A Buddhist term meaning extinction of suffering and release from the cycle of rebirth. *See samsara.*

nomos: This Greek word translated as "law" is often used in a general sense to refer to anything that exhibits a meaningful order.

numinous: Derived from the Latin word for spirit, this word refers to experiences of awe, mystery, dread, and finiteness before a majestic overwhelming power that is wholly other and hence beyond human reason to comprehend.

ontological argument: A kind of argument for God's existence based on the claim that God, rightly defined as the most perfect being, must exist.

outsider's viewpoint: The academic study of religion that seeks understanding from an objective, nonsectarian viewpoint. *See* **insider's viewpoint.**

pantheism: The view that the essence of the universe is divine.

pantheon: A collection of gods and goddesses organized as a family tree.

phenomenological theory: When applied to myths, this theory opposes reductionistic explanations of sacred stories and advocates the comparative method for understanding myths.

phenomenology of religion: Sometimes used as equivalent to history of religions, but better thought of as a particular theory and comparative method that assumes religions to be manifestations of the sacred. It opposes all "reductionism" or causal explanations by social scientists on the grounds that religion is *sui generis* (literally, "of its own kind").

philosophy of religion: Part of the field of religious studies that uses rational, philosophical argument to formulate, understand, and answer fundamental questions about religious matters.

pluralism: There are at least two distinct meanings of this word in a religious context. One meaning is descriptive and refers to the fact that there exist different and what appear to be conflicting religious truth-claims. The other meaning is normative and refers to a philosophical or theological position that asserts there are many different genuine paths to salvation expressed in the many diverse religions of the world.

polytheism: The belief in and worship of many gods.

postmodernism: This concept is used in many different ways but often refers to a critique of the notion of truth as objective and free from political, religious, class, and other biases. It emphasizes that truth is a contested concept.

prophetic principle: A term used by Paul Tillich to refer to a religious tendency to sharply distinguish the sacred from any identification with material things and images. *See* **sacramental principle.**

Protestant ethic thesis: Max Weber's claim that the theology of Calvinistic Protestantism had a major impact on the rise of the spirit of capitalism.

prototype: An ideal exemplar of the type or category in question.

psychology of religion: The use of psychological methods and techniques to explore the relationship between human psychology and religious matters such as the impact of religion on moral development.

rationalistic theory: A theory that interprets myths in particular and religion in general as prescientific explanations of the world.

reductionism: Often used by phenomenologists in a pejorative sense to refer to what they see as inappropriate explanations of religious phenomena in terms of non-religious factors.

religio: Latin word for religion that means either taking care in practicing rites like sacrifice or being under an obligation to practice rites. Combining both meanings we get "the obligation to practice rites carefully."

religions of salvation: A class of religions that teach things are not as they should be and need to be transcended; often contrasted with religions of sanctification.

religions of sanctification: A class of religions that teach things are as they should be and the religious task is to maintain this situation.

religious experience: Any kind of experience, from visions and voices to intense feelings of love and devotion that the person having the experience believes to be religiously significant.

ren (*jen*): A key Confucian virtue translated in a variety of ways such as "human excellence," "love," "benevolence," "humaneness," and "kind-heartedness."

revitalization rituals: These movements, along with their complex ritual activity, seek to revitalize a culture or a religion seen as dying or in the process of being lost.

rites of passage: Rituals and ceremonies marking the passages or transitions of life such as birth, puberty, marriage, illness, and death.

ritual: This term refers to stylized, symbolic bodily gestures and actions, repeated in specified ways on occasions of significance and in special contexts usually involving what the participants take to be sacred presences.

ritualistic: In the context of the functions of myths, this term refers to sacred narratives that explain and justify ritual actions.

sacramental principle: A term used by Paul Tillich to refer to the tendency of religions to invest material things such as statues, images and locations with the quality of being sacred. *See* **prophetic principle.**

sacred: A term derived from Latin for that which is done "inside the temple" (sacrifice). It refers to that which set apart, extraordinary, and totally different from the profane (what is done outside the temple).

salvation rituals: Rituals designed to change a person's identity from a spiritually corrupt, polluted, sinful, or lost person to a spiritually saved state of freedom from sin, corruption, ignorance, and the like.

samsara: A world of suffering and rebirth in which people are trapped by ignorance and desire. *See* **nirvana.**

satori: Japanese Zen Buddhist term for enlightenment.

scapegoat: Some object, usually an animal like a sheep or a goat that is made to carry the guilt and sins of others.

second-order activity: The study of some first-order activity or practice. The academic study of religion is a second-order activity. *See* **first-order activity.**

secularization: For some people secularizatrion refers to the diminishing role of religion as a serious social influence in the modern and postmodern age. Others interpret it as a change in religion that emphasizes individual spirituality and choice along with the view that religion is primarily a private matter.

semiotics: The study of signs. The study is divided into three parts: pragmatics (the study of the way people, animals, or machines use signs), semantics (the study of the meaning of signs), and syntax (the study of the relations among signs).

shaman: This is the name for a religious figure usually found in tribal societies who engages, with the help of spirit guides, in healing, divining, and other functions important to the community through the means of ecstatic trances or visions.

Sharia: This term refers to Islamic law as a whole and derives from an Arabic word meaning "path" or "way to water."

Sitz im Leben: A German term meaning "situation" or "place in life." Technically the term refers to the establishment of the context of a text (where, when, by whom, to whom it was written, and its purpose or function) for purposes of interpretation.

sociology of religion: This area of religious studies applies standard sociological theories of human social behavior to religion in an attempt to uncover the way social factors influence religious beliefs and practices.

spirituality versus religion: The development of spirituality is the goal of many religions, but many believe it is not necessary to belong to a religious organization in order to pursue spiritual development.

structuralist theory: A theory of myth in particular and religion in general that claims there are underlying logical structures (often thought to be binary oppositions) that order myths and religion, much like there are underlying syntactical rules that order language.

stupa: A Buddhist shrine, usually shaped something like an inverted bell with a long handle. Stupas symbolically represent in architectural form key aspects of Buddhism and often contain scripture or serve as reliquaries.

substantive definition: A type of essential definition that focuses on the "what" or content (substance) of religion. *See* **functional definition.**

Sufism: The name for a mystical movement within Islam.

symbolic theory: A theory of myth in particular and religion in general that claims meaning is symbolic, hence hidden beneath the literal surface.

syncretistic: The adjectival form of syncretism, which refers to a blending of various religious elements. It is sometimes used in a pejorative way to name religions that seem incoherent. However, all religions are syncretistic to one degree or another.

taboo: A restriction or prohibition common to a religion or culture intended to protect the sacred and prevent pollution by the profane.

teaching of versus teaching about religion: The difference between sectarian (teaching of) and nonsectarian (teaching about) instruction pertaining to matters of religion.

technological rituals: Rituals that have as their goal producing or preventing a change of state in nature so that humans can benefit.

theocracy: A political theory that subordinates human rule to the rule of God. Its leaders claim to rule on behalf of the divine and by a system of laws they allege are revealed by the deity.

theodicy: In its theological sense, a theodicy is any proposed solution to the problem of evil that reconciles the existence of an all-good and all-powerful God with the evil that exists in the world that such a God created and guides. In its broad sense, theodicy refers to any proposed explanation of evil and other anomic events.

theology: Literally, theology means talk about God and hence the study of God. More broadly it refers to an activity of insiders who seek to articulate coherent and systematic accounts of ideas central to their religious tradition

therapeutic and antitherapeutic rituals: Rituals that seek to produce a change in the state of human health, either to heal the sick or bring sickness to the healthy.

Torah: A Hebrew word that has multiple meanings, including reference to the first five books of the Hebrew Bible, to a scroll containing divine law, to revelation in general, to teaching, to the essence of the divine law, and to the source of salvation.

totem: Most often a sacred animal or plant representing the power of a social group often thought of as the first ancestor.

Trinitarianism: The teaching that God's nature is a tri-unity rather than a simple unity.

typology: A classification system by types used for ordering diverse elements.

Unitarianism: The belief that God's nature is an absolute, simple unity.

virtue ethics: An ethic or system of morality centering on developing a virtuous person, that is, a person of moral excellence and good character.

YHWH: The name of God revealed to Moses by a voice in a burning bush that was probably pronounced "Yahweh," but is considered by Jews too holy to speak. It is usually translated as "I am who I am."

yoga: A Sanskrit word referring to different kinds of spiritual disciplines and paths, including the disciplines of meditation (*raja* yoga), devotion (*bhakti* yoga), action (*karma* yoga), and knowledge (*jnana* yoga).

zazen meditation: This Japanese word means "sitting meditation" and refers to a technique developed in Soto Zen designed to express the buddha-nature we all possess.

Credits

Index

Page numbers in *italics* indicate illustrations.

Apophis, 48
apostolic socialism, 247–248, 252, 259
appearances (phenomena) of the sacred, 35
Aquinas, Thomas, 27, 28, 174, 198, 284
Arabia, 138
archetypes, 149
architecture, 116–120
Aristotle, 198
Arjun, Guru, 279, 280
Arjuna, 45–46
Ark of the Covenant, 118
art, and religion, 115
asceticism, 134, 149, 204, 289
ascetic Protestantism, 290
Ashaglun, 182
Ashvaghosha, 135
Association of Shinto Shrines, 273
Atharva, 262
atheism, 54–55, 218
Athena, 48
Atman, 53, 310
Atman/Brahman, 178
atonement, 92
    Christian theories of, 286–287
    rites of, 84
    and sacrifice, 95
Auditors, 183
Augustine, St., 175, 226
Aurelius, Marcus, 52
Aurobindo, Ghose, 77
Auschwitz, 159
Australian Aborigines, 47, 104, 120
    Dreamtime, 108–110, 111, 113–114, 172
    gender roles, 109–110, 111
    religion of sanctification, 276
    religious practices and beliefs, 108–110
    theodicy of participation, 171–172
authority, types of, 259–260
autonomy, 150
Avalokiteshvara, 243, 244
Averroes, 76
axis mundi, 103–104
Azande, 161–162
Azzam, Abdallah, 213

Bab (gate), 318, 322
Babis, 318
Babism, 318, 321–322
Babylonian New Year (Akitu), 83–87
Babylonians, 61, 63, 70, 92, 214

bad karma, 170
Baha Allah, 318–319, 322
Baha'i, 317–323
    and Babism, 321–322
    beliefs and practices, 320–323
    dilemmas of institutionalization, 322
    history, 318
    Nineteen-Day Feast, 322
    organized in pyramid fashion, 319–320
    Palestine as Holy Land, 319
    ritual practices, 322
Baha'i Cycle (Cycle of Fulfillment), 320
Baha'i Guardianship, 320
Bahram, 183
Bakongo, 48
Bali, 49
ba (life force), 293
Bantu-speaking peoples, 107
baptism, 123–124
Barna, George, 230
Barnes, Nancy Schuster, 266
The Battle for the Family (LaHaye), 23
Bema, 183
Ben Maimon, Moses, "Thirteen Principles," 49
Berger, Peter, 162
Bhagavad Gita, 45–46
bhakti yoga, 147, 148, 279
bias, types of, 18–21
Bible, 76, 170, 262, 283
biblical revelation, 41
Big Bang theory, 75
Bill of Rights, 218, 225
bimah, 118
binary oppositions, 73
bin Laden, Osama, 211, 212–217, 222–223, 227, 229, 231
"black and white" fallacy, 214–215
Black Caribs, 267
Black Elk (Hehaka Sapa), 87–90, 91
Black Elk Speaks (Neihardt), 87
Black Hills, 114
"Black Hole" of Tehran, 318
Blind People and the Elephant, 315–316
blood, symbolism of, 91
bodhi, 136
bodhisattva, 135–137, 243
Bodhissattva of Compassion, 243
bodhi tree, 112, 135
bodily memory, 94

occultation, 164
"oceanic feelings," 148
O'Connor, Sandra Day, 220
O'Dea, Thomas, 257–259
offering thanks, 95
Ogden, Shubert, 177
Oglala Sioux, 48, 87, 88, 92
Ogun, 48
Ojibwa, 47
Oko, 48
Old Testament, 125, 262, 283, 306
Olympus, Mount, 104
Om, 120–121
om mani padme bum, 243
omnibenevolence, 174, 176
omnipotence, 174, 176, 177
omniscience, 174, 176
ontological argument, 42–43
openness, 4, 9
oral traditions, 70, 261
ordination, 124
Oregon Employment Division v. Smith, 220
original sin, 284
The Origin of Species (Darwin), 75
orisha deities, 48
Orthodox Church, 41, 115
Orthodox Judaism, women and, 265
Orthodox synagogues, 118
Osiris, 48, 293
otherworldly eschatological theodicy, 169, 173
otherworldly salvation, 292
Otto, Rudolf, 141–142
out-of-body journeys, 132
outsider's view of religion, 2, 3

pacifism, 226
Padmasambhava, 242
pagodas, 117
Palestinian/Israeli conflict, 301
Pan, 49
Pan-Indian culture, 87
pantheism, 52–53
pantheons, 48–49
"paradise of innocence," 150
parokhet, 118
Parshava, 204
Parsi, 2, 51
participant observation, 34
participation, theodicies of, 171–173, 294
Parvati, 56

Passover, 70, 98, 99, 103, 113
Patanjali, 146, 147
Patel, Daya J., 56
patriarchal religions, 265
Paul, Apostle, 127, 128, 265, 266, 285, 293
Paul III, Pope, 75
Peace of Westphalia, 301
penance, 124
Penitente Brotherhoods, 202–203
penitential rituals, 202
Peoples Temple Full Gospel Church, 225,
    246–252, 259
  preservation of order, 256
  preservation of sense of purpose, 256–257
  production of goods and services, 255–256
  recruitment and reproduction, 253
  socialist commune, 255
  socialization, 254–255
  viewed as cult, 246–247, 254
Perfect Truth Sect, 38
periodic ritual, 92
Persian notion of resurrection of body, 293
personal revelations, 131
perspective, 5
pesah, 98
peyote, 220
phenomena, 309
phenomenological theory of myth, 73
phenomenology of religion, 35
philosophy of religion, 27
pilgrimage, 117
Pinyin system, 39
pipal tree, 135
Pius IX, Pope, 319
Plantinga, Alvin, 305–306
Plato, 193
Pledge of Allegiance, 229
Plotinus, 53
pluralism, 308–310
pogroms, 180
polemics, 3
polygamy, 218–219
polytheism, 46, 47–48, 304
popular Shinto, 270, 272
possession, 132
postmodernism, 302
power
  as a basic religious category, 45
  dilemma of, 258–259
  profane, 45